Constituent Moments

Jason Frank

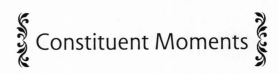 Constituent Moments

ENACTING THE PEOPLE IN POSTREVOLUTIONARY AMERICA

Duke University Press

Durham and London

2010

Duke University Press gratefully
acknowledges the support of the Hull
Memorial Publication Fund of Cornell
University, which provided funds towards the production of this book.

To my parents, for everything

There is no voice of the people.
There are scattered voices and polemics
which in each instance divide the identity that they stage.
—JACQUES RANCIÈRE,
Les scènes du peuple

"Origins" never stop repeating themselves.
—JACQUES RANCIÈRE,
Dis-agreement: Politics and Philosophy

DUKE

UNIVERSITY

PRESS · PUBLICITY

COMBINED ACADEMIC

PUBLISHERS

48 BALDSLOW ROAD

HASTINGS, EAST SUSSEX

TN34 2EY UNITED KINGDOM

tel/fax: 44 (0)1424 436533

CONSTITUENT MOMENTS

Enacting the People in Postrevolutionary America

Jason Frank

Price:

Paper   978-0-8223-4675-3   £ 16.99

Library cloth edition   978-0-8223-4663-0   £ 67.00

(Please note that unjacketed cloth editions are primarily for library use. Non-library reviewers should quote the paperback price.)

Publication Date: May 14, 2010

Please send two copies of the published review.

Contents

ACKNOWLEDGMENTS   ix

INTRODUCTION: Constituent Moments   1

1. Revolution and Reiteration: *Hannah Arendt's Critique of Constituent Power*   41

2. Crowds and Communication: *Representation and Voice in Postrevolutionary America*   67

3. Sympathy and Separation: *Benjamin Rush and the Contagious Public*   101

4. Spaces of Insurgent Citizenship: *Theorizing the Democratic-Republican Societies*   128

5. Hearing Voices: *Authority and Imagination in Wieland*   156

6. "Aesthetic Democracy": *Walt Whitman and the Poetry of the People*   182

7. Staging Dissensus: *Frederick Douglass and "We the People"*   209

CONCLUSION: Prospective Time   237

NOTES   255

BIBLIOGRAPHY   301

INDEX   331

Acknowledgments

This book traveled an itinerant path to publication, with different sections written in Baltimore, San Francisco, Los Angeles, Durham, Chicago, Ithaca, and New York City. Along the way I benefited from the suggestions and criticisms of many friends and colleagues, whom I gratefully acknowledge here.

In a distant but important sense, the project was first inspired in the undergraduate classrooms of two remarkable teachers at the University of California, Santa Cruz: Peter Euben and Jack Schaar. Their political theory courses were life-changing in the most elevated and pedestrian of senses. On the elevated side, Peter and Jack taught their students that critical reflection could be called by a commitment to democracy's unfulfilled promise. On the pedestrian side, they suggested something to do after graduation: political theory as vocation and avocation. Peter remains a close friend, and both of their examples are an inspiration.

The book took early shape as a doctoral dissertation at Johns Hopkins

University, where Bill Connolly, Dick Flathman, and Kirstie McClure created an exciting environment to study political theory. I am grateful for their ongoing advice and encouragement. I also thank Jane Bennett, Sharon Cameron, Matt Crenson, Jennifer Culbert, Suzette Hemberger, Anthony Pagden, Dorothy Ross, Giullia Sissa, Gabrielle Spiegel, and Larzer Ziff. As is often the case in graduate school, a lot of learning took place outside of the classroom. I was lucky to be surrounded by a wonderful cohort of aspiring theorists at Hopkins, many of whom remain friends and influences. I thank in particular Adam Lerner, Jeff Lomonaco, Davide Panagia, and Kam Shapiro.

Cornell's Government Department has been a terrific place to teach and research, thanks to the generosity of the institution and to the engaging smarts of my students and colleagues. I thank in particular my theory colleagues Susan Buck-Morss, Burke Hendrix, Isaac Kramnick, Diane Rubenstein, and Anna-Marie Smith. I am also grateful for the support—intellectual and otherwise—that I have received from Glenn Altschuler, Richard Bensel, Val Bunce, Gary Davis, Mary Katzenstein, Ron Herring, Peter Hohendahl, Jonathan Kirchner, Dominick LaCapra, Larry Moore, Ted Lowi, Hunter Rawlings, Ken Roberts, Harry Shaw, Sid Tarrow, and Nick Winter. The political theory students at Cornell have continually challenged my thinking and helped me navigate the imperatives of teaching and research. I thank the participants in my graduate seminars on democratic theory, language and politics, and American political thought, particularly Desmond Jagmohan, Shannon Mariotti, Alison McQueen, and Michelle-Renee Smith. I am also grateful for the friends at Cornell who have helped make Ithaca home: Becky Givan, Ellis Hanson, Cary Howie, Phillip Lorenz, Tracy McNulty, Judith Peraino, Masha Raskolnikov, Camille Robcis, Amy Villarejo, and Brad Zukovic.

In the broader academic world this project has benefited from the suggestions of more people than I can list or remember. Remembered thanks to Lawrie Balfour, Banu Bargu, Fonna Forman-Barzilai, Susan Bickford, Keith Breen, Tim Breen, Rom Coles, Emilios Christoloudidis, Kim Curtis, Joshua Dienstag, Lisa Disch, Tom Dumm, Stephen Engelman, Jim Farr, Sam Frost, Michael Gillespie, Ruth Grant, Jay Grossman, Michael Hardt, Vicky Hattam, Stanley Hauerwas, Don Herzog, Catherine Holland, Andreas Kalyvas, Nick Kompridis, Sharon Krause, John Larson, Jill Locke, Karuna Mantena, Lida Maxwell, John McCormick, Sarah Monoson, Michael Morrison, Andrew Norris, Paulina Ochoa-Espejo, Melissa Orlie, Paul Patton, Nicholas Phillipson, Mark Reinhardt, Andy Schaap, Mort Schoolman, Mike Shapiro, George Shulman, Tracy Strong, John Tambornino, Scott Veitch, Dana Villa, Hayden White, and Catherine Zuckert. A special thanks to three friends whose intelligence and generosity have made the political theory world a better place to live and work: Bonnie Honig, Patchen Markell, and Liz Wingrove.

Every one of these chapters was presented at a conference, workshop, or colloquium. I would like to thank my hosts and audiences at the American Bar Foundation, Cornell University, Duke University, the New School for Social Research, Northwestern University, Queen's University (Belfast), the University of California, San Diego, the University of California, Los Angeles, the University of Chicago, the University of Exeter, the University of Glasgow, the University of Illinois, Champaign-Urbana, the University of Melbourne, the University of Minnesota, Twin Cities, and the annual meetings of the American Political Science Association and the Western Political Science Association. For research support I thank the Ahmanson-Getty Fellowship at UCLA's Center for 17th- and 18th-Century Studies, the New Directions Postdoctoral Fellowship at Duke's Franklin Center for Interdisciplinary Research, the National Endowment for the Humanities, and Cornell University's Mellon Faculty Fellowship and Institute for the Social Sciences.

Courtney Berger gracefully guided this project through the publication process, and I am grateful for her patient support. Kate Washington's and Fred Kameny's copyediting helped me cut the manuscript down to size. The manuscript was also greatly improved by the keen editorial suggestions of two anonymous reviewers for Duke University Press. Versions of three chapters were previously published elsewhere, and appear here in revised form. I thank the editors and reviewers of these earlier essays. Chapter 3 appeared as "Sympathy and Separation: Benjamin Rush and the Contagious Public," *Modern Intellectual History* 6, no. 1 (2009); chapter 6 appeared as "Aesthetic Democracy: Walt Whitman and the Poetry of the People," *Review of Politics*, summer 2007; and a shortened version of chapter 7 appeared as "Staging Dissensus: Frederick Douglass and 'We the People,'" in *Agonistic Politics and the Law*, ed. Andrew Schaap (London: Ashgate, 2009). Portions of the revised chapters are reprinted here with the permission of these publishers.

Finally, I would like to thank my family in Salt Lake City for their love, good humor, curiosity, and support. My partner Jerry Johnson has endured my occasional bouts of writers' self-absorption, intellectual frustration, and political outrage, and he has done so for the most part with loving patience. I love him for that, and also for walking the dogs, learning to cook, and not letting me take myself too seriously.

Democracy inaugurates the experience of an ungraspable, uncontrollable society
in which the people will be said to be sovereign, of course, but whose identity will
constantly be open to question, whose identity will remain forever latent.
CLAUDE LEFORT, Democracy and Political Theory[1]

Introduction

Constituent Moments

Since the revolutionary period most Americans have agreed with John
Adams that "in theory . . . the only moral foundation of government
is the consent of the people." Subsequent political history has returned
time and again to the question that followed: "But to what extent shall
we carry out this principle?"[2] Adams asked this unsettling question in a
letter to James Sullivan on 26 May 1776, eleven days after the Continental Congress had decreed that new state governments should be established "on the authority of the people," and just over a month before independence was officially declared "in the name and by the authority of
the good people of these colonies." The question resonates over the long
span of postrevolutionary American politics to the present day.

Sullivan, a prominent lawyer in Boston and a member of the provincial
congress of Massachusetts, had suggested in an earlier letter to Adams

that the Continental Congress should consider altering existing property qualifications for voters, to better align them with the proclaimed principles of just or "actual" representation affirmed by the colonists in their decade-long struggle with Parliament and Crown.[3] Since all men live under law, Sullivan reasoned, all should be granted the right to vote. As the states prepared to replace their colonial charters and form new governments, Sullivan urged that they consider instituting universal male suffrage. At issue in Sullivan's letter was not simply how to more fully carry out the principle of consent—as in the progressive democratization of governing institutions celebrated in Whig histories of American political development from Lincoln to Rawls—nor how better to represent the various constituencies or their interests, but rather the logically prior and more painfully ambiguous question of who constitutes the authorizing and consenting people in the first place. While seeking "a more equal representation" based in "true republican principles," Sullivan also worried about the "levelling spirit" that accompanied these claims. Sullivan at once suggested and evaded this question in his letter, but in this he was far from alone. "How to decide who legitimately make up 'the people,'" Robert Dahl notes, "is a problem almost totally neglected by all the great political philosophers who write about democracy."[4] Yet the problem haunts all theories of democracy and continually vivifies democratic practice. Determining who constitutes the people is an inescapable yet democratically unanswerable dilemma; it is not a question the people can procedurally decide because the very question subverts the premises of its resolution.

In his response to Sullivan's suggestions, Adams prophesied the looming magnitude of this problem—the problem of the legitimacy of the people[5]—for postrevolutionary American politics: "Depend upon it, sir, it is dangerous to open so fruitful a Source of Controversy and Altercation . . . There would be no End of it. New Claims will arise. Women will demand a Vote. Lads from 12 to 21 will think their Rights not enough attended to, and every Man, who has not a farthing, will demand an Equal Voice with any other in all Acts of State. It tends to confound and destroy all Distinctions, and prostrate all Ranks, to one common Levell."[6] Adams's letter suggests that the people who are usually envisioned—in everyday political speech as well as in most democratic theory—as a prepolitical source of sovereign authority are actually the site of both extraordinary and everyday acts of political contestation. Subsequent American political history has borne out his suggestion. While Adams focused on challenges to the vertical boundaries around the people—the "levelling" of "distinction" and "rank"—later challenges would be directed at the horizontal boundary as well—from the pressures and claims of "alien" constituencies. "To follow the career of the term the People," Daniel T. Rodgers has noted, "is to watch men invest a word with extraordinary meaning and then, losing hold of it to other claimants, scuttle from the consequences."[7] Political theorists opposed to the more radical iterations of popular politics, from Plato to Filmer, from Madison to de Maistre, have tirelessly pointed out the inherent instability of the people, and they have been right to do so.[8]

Both democratic history and democratic theory demonstrate that the people are a political *claim*, an act of political subjectification, not a pre-given, unified, or naturally bounded empirical entity.[9] In the United States the power of claims to speak in the people's name derives in part from a constitutive surplus inherited from the revolutionary era, from the fact that since the Revolution the people have been at once enacted through representation—how could it be otherwise?[10]—and in excess of any particular representation. This dilemma illuminates the significance and theological resonance of popular voice: *vox populi, vox Dei.* The authority of vox populi derives from its continually reiterated but never fully realized reference to the sovereign people beyond representation, beyond the law, the spirit beyond the letter, the Word beyond the words—the mystical foundations of authority.[11] The postrevolutionary people are at once enacted through representational claims and forever escaping the political and legal boundaries inscribed by those claims. This book explores political and cultural dilemmas that attended these postrevolutionary dramas of popular self-authorization—dilemmas arising from the people's revolutionary enthronement as the unlocatable ground of public authority—and the orienting power of these historical examples for contemporary democratic theory.

I

The people reign over the American political world as God rules over
the universe. It is the cause and the end of all things; everything rises out of it and is
absorbed back into it.   ALEXIS DE TOCQUEVILLE, *Democracy in America*[12]

The people have been a remarkably potent symbol—and force—over
the course of United States political history, and remain so still (albeit in
a disconcertingly muted form). Many astute social and political thinkers
nonetheless bridle at the vague indeterminacy of the term, at the way
this "fiction" or "myth" is invoked in public discussion to obscure political realities or, even worse, as "a way of legitimating collective fantasy."[13]
Many have agreed with the Marquis de Mirabeau's declaration that
"the word people necessarily means too much or too little," that "it is a
word open to any use."[14] Others believe it too ambiguous or dangerously
populist to merit serious theoretical analysis.[15] Pierre Bourdieu, to take
one prominent example, argues that political recourse to "the people,"
even in the "scientific" guise of public opinion polling, captivates subject
populations through a "political metaphysics" that enthralls them to the
rulers claiming to speak in their name.[16] From a very different methodological perspective, the social choice theorist William Riker argues that
there is simply no knowable "voice of the people" aside from the often
"inaccurate or meaningless amalgamations" of voting. For Riker this unavoidable epistemological deficit mandates rejecting "populism," and its
"quasi mystical" claim to politically enact the people's voice, in favor of
a resigned "liberalism," with democracy little more than an occasional,
somewhat fumbling check on governmental power.[17] Political realists of
all sorts, left and right, class analysts and methodological individualists,
typically deride the supposed mystification attending political appeals
to the people.

If the notion of the people is a fiction or mystification, it is one with
a profound political efficacy, playing a complex but foundational role in
the interweaving traditions of American political thought and culture.
In the jeremiads of Puritan New England, the covenanted people were
figured as a new Israel given "speciall Commission" to establish "a City
upon a Hill" as a beacon of moral righteousness to the world.[18] The civic
republican currents of American political thought and culture figure the

people as both a particular social class—the common, the poor—and the collective *populus* jealously guarding their liberties against the central government's always encroaching, corrupting power.[19] American populists took this collective opposition to "interests" and "élites" and placed it in the hands of laboring people alone.[20] Traditions of popular constitutionalism similarly construed the people as the defenders of the constitution and, when the need arose, the direct enforcers of constitutional norms.[21] Natural law liberalism, as transformed by postrevolutionary American constitutionalism, cast the people as the *makers* of the constitution, a constituent power enabling the contractual emergence from a state of nature into a new constitutional order. "The people," as James Wilson stated in the Pennsylvania ratifying convention of 1787, "possess, over our constitutions, control in *act*, as well as right."[22] Finally, in what Rogers Smith has recently called the "ideologies of ascriptive Americanism," the people—substantively figured as the race or the nation—have served to justify a history of racial and ethnic discrimination and violence, from draft riots against free blacks and the destruction of indigenous peoples to lynch mobs and anti-immigrant violence.[23] Despite historians' efforts to isolate and analytically distinguish these traditions, they have been inextricably commingled in American political thought and culture. These traditions have a common authorizing appeal to the people that remains an ambiguous and contested inheritance.

Each of these interweaving traditions figures the people as the "legitimate fountain of power," as a sovereign authority, but they differently construe how, when, where, and by whom this power is to be exercised. Remarkably diverse movements and policies, reforms and reactions, have invoked the sovereign authority of the people. The people have been used to justify popular revolution against colonial authorities and to found a constitutional order premised on "excluding the people in their collective capacity"; to embolden the states and to empower the union; to authorize vigilantism and to affirm the rule of law; to create a broad populist front against Gilded Age economic exploitation and to perpetuate some of the nation's worst racial atrocities; to increase the power of the presidency and to return power to the grassroots.

This book claims that the potency of vox populi in American history derives in part from its persistent latency or virtuality, from the paradoxical political reality that the people are forever a people that is not . . . yet. Thus claims made in the name of the people always transcend the horizon of any given articulation, drawing their power from their own unrealized futurity. The legitimating vitality of the people, their "*coup de force*," derives from their constitutive surplus.[24] The inability of the people to speak in their own name does not simply mark a legitimation deficit for postrevolutionary democratic politics but also its ongoing condition of possibility.

The rhetorician Kenneth Burke recognized the virtual potency of "the people" in American political thought and culture in a speech, "Revolutionary Symbolism in America," that he delivered before the American Writers' Congress in 1935. Burke argued that the revolutionary left—the Congress was convened by the American Communist Party and Burke's audience was a who's who of *engagé* artists and intellectuals—should replace the divisive and limiting symbol of "the worker" or "the proletarian" with the universalizing ideal of "the people," which, Burke claimed, "rates highest in our hierarchy of symbols."[25] Importantly, and controversially for his audience, Burke saw neither "the people" nor "the worker" as a sociological entity but instead as a political or rhetorical construction. Burke based his strategic plea to lionize the people in socialist and communist propaganda in a general theory of symbolic action that emphasized how such symbols could capture the "subtle complex of emotions and attitudes" in a scheme of "polarizing social cooperation."[26] Echoing George Sorel (whom he had read) and Carl Schmitt (whom he had not), Burke argued that all political movements, whether conservative or revolutionary, are made of such polarizing "myths."

In a term that became central to his later thought on the relationship between political authority and tropes, Burke attributed to these myths the all-important power of "identification."[27] Because the idea of "the people" is a myth "closer to our [American] folkways" and draws on "spontaneous popular usage," Burke argued, it could tap the latent revolutionary potential of this "subtle complex of emotions and attitudes." "The people" could then be employed as a powerful tool of immanent critique, revealing how widely proclaimed commitments to a government of, by, and for the people are systematically undermined in practice. Moreover, as Burke insightfully noted, "since the symbol of 'the people' *contains connotations both of oppression and of unity*, it seems better than the exclusively proletarian one as a psychological bridge for linking the two conflicting aspects of a transitional revolutionary era, which is Janus-faced, looking both forwards and back." Burke invokes here the "double inscription" of the people in a postrevolutionary era, that is, the persistence of the people as at once a source of public authority and a source of resistance to public authority.[28] Burke's attentiveness to a "Janus-faced" people also captures the reiterative logic of reenacted dramas of popular authorization made over a history of democratic claims making.

The audience's vehemently negative response to Burke's speech also exemplified this double inscription. Even the title of Burke's speech— "Revolutionary *Symbolism* in *America*"—was sure to antagonize many in a Marxist audience of materialist-internationalists, and yet the audience rejected not only Burke's general theory of symbolic efficacy and political identity formation—"We are not interested in the myth. We are interested in revealing the reality," one participant declared[29]—but also Burke's claims about the revolutionary potential of "the people," in particular his claim that "the people" is charged with a powerful political indeterminacy, his claim that it could operate as what Ernesto Laclau calls an "empty signifier" and be seized upon for radical democratic ends.[30] "We have a traitor among us!," shouted the American Communist Party leader Joe Freeman. The proletarian novelist Mike Gold dismissed Burke's invocation of "the people" as nothing more than the reactionary "abstractions of the bourgeoisie." Allen Porter reminded the audience that right-wing populists like Father Coughlin regularly invoked "the people" to deny social antagonism; it was the principal conveyor of the delusional exceptionalist myth that America was a classless society. Friedrich Wolf likened Burke's "people" to Hitler's *das Volk*, and noted that such falsely unifying terms had "historically . . . been a ruse for the exploiting class" to obscure the brutal realities of class domination.[31]

The debate that Burke's speech and the audience's critical response provoked transcends its immediate context, capturing the troubled double inscription of the people in American political thought and culture. Both Burke *and* his critics were right: the people have been a force of democratic unsettlement and of consolidation, of popular empowerment and retrenchment, of resistance and entrapment. The people are the entity in whose name the state governs, *and* a higher power that can resist the authority of the state. For reasons historically rooted in the American Revolution, the people both menace and ground the political order; they are at once a constituent and a constituted power.[32]

The people have been the central authorizing fiction in postrevolutionary American political culture and the figure that reveals its underlying
contingency, its persistent exposure to transformative contestation and
change.

   This double inscription of the people enables what I call constituent
moments, when the underauthorized—imposters, radicals, self-created
entities—seize the mantle of authorization, changing the inherited rules
of authorization in the process. At such times political claims to speak in
the people's name are felicitous, even as they explicitly break from the
established procedures or rules for representing popular voice. I refer
to "felicity" to invoke J. L. Austin's theory of the performative utterance.
However, in contrast to Austin's reliance on authoritative "felicity conditions" which secure the "uptake" of the performative utterance—the
background contextual conditions that determine when the christening
"really" christens, when the vows "really" marry, etc.—constituent moments dwell in a space where there is enacted felicity that nonetheless
breaks from the conventions of authorized context—a felicitous infe-
licity. Constituent moments question the existence of such a unitary
background context wholly separate from the utterances and *claims* that
help constitute it.[33] In their enacted felicity, constituent claims effectively change the conditions and contexts through which they are heard
and recognized *as claims*. Constituent moments invent a new political
space and make apparent a people that are productively never at one
with themselves. Like the broader category of civil disobedience, which
can base resistance on appeal to any "higher" principle, constituent moments enact a political power that transcends the state's legal organization; unlike some instances of civil disobedience, however, constituent
moments enact their claims wholly on the democratic authority of the
people themselves: out of these enactments a new democratic subject
emerges.

   Constituent moments illuminate how in postrevolutionary contexts
the people enact and then transcend their own self-representations. The
remainder of this introduction outlines the emergence of this double
inscription of the people during the revolutionary and postrevolutionary
years, exploring how a widely recognized formal problem in contemporary democratic theory—sometimes called "the boundary problem," or
the "dilemma of constituency"[34]—emerged as a practical political prob-

lem within late-eighteenth-century American political discourse and practice. In United States political history this double inscription is a discursive and practical legacy of the American Revolution. If Tocqueville is right that "peoples always bear some marks of their origin,"[35] a revolutionarily self-enacted people also remains forever haunted by the immanent source of its own transcendence. The tracing of the people's revolutionary origin undoes the purity of this origin, revealing how the revolutionary enactment of the people does not ground and perpetuate a political identity so much as it spurs its continual revision and transformation over a history of democratic claims making.

II

The instant formal government is abolished, society begins to act; a general association takes place . . .   THOMAS PAINE, *The Rights of Man*[36]

"We have it in our power to begin the world over again," Thomas Paine wrote in *Common Sense* (1776), concluding with a stirring call to "unite in drawing a line, which, like an act of oblivion, shall bury in forgetfulness every former dissention."[37] Unifying acts of oblivion are endemic to revolutionary and founding moments — they mark an apparently consensual origin before the onslaught of postrevolutionary agonistic politics — but rarely are they so lucidly embraced or rhetorically ennobled as in Paine's text. Paine hoped that the political divisions among colonists in the decade-long march from resistance to revolution would be overcome by a common embrace of the self-creating power of the people themselves. "Independence," Paine wrote, "is the only *bond* that ties and keeps us together."[38] Paradoxically, what Paine calls *for* in *Common Sense*—the people's enacted independence—is also taken as its own binding precondition. Historians concur that the American people, far from being the unified subject behind the Revolution, were instead "an unexpected, impromptu, artificial, and therefore extremely fragile creation of the Revolution."[39] In a rhetorical move typical of the period's texts, and that Jacques Derrida illuminated in his well-known reading of Jefferson's *Declaration of Independence*, Paine's pamphlet both argued for the preexisting, natural independence of the American people and sought to elicit this politically enabled people from the unformed multitude of his reading public.[40] While Paine and Jefferson are both frequently presented as naïve advocates of democratic voice — celebrators of the unbounded authority of the people's will — their most famous texts enact an aspirational people never present with itself. These founding texts of the American Revolution make legible a sovereign people that both requires and resists representation. In openly addressing the authority of the people themselves (rather than petitioning the already constituted authority of Parliament or the Crown, as had earlier pamphleteers) they seek to elicit and enact the very people on whose authority their claims are made; their texts draw authority from the future anterior, from the political horizon of what will have been.[41] It is these revolutionary texts' underauthorization that oddly grants them a higher authorization, their ability to enact claims that can only be retrospectively vindicated.

Paine's revolutionary "we" tapped the discursive resources of pre-independence debates over representation and sovereignty and also aimed to transcend those debates' contentions. The "we" of Paine's "We have it in our power" — like that of Jefferson's "We hold these truths to be self evident" or the constitutional "We the people" — brings us to the heart of dilemmas surrounding popular sovereignty in the revolutionary and postrevolutionary years. It does so by showing that the people require representation in order to be enacted, yet this authorizing entity also — and by definition — resists the closure of representation. The voice of the people is a figure of impossible presence. Briefly sketching the emergence of this discourse and its accompanying political practices illuminates how the formal paradoxes and aporias of democratic theory surrounding "the legitimacy of the people" emerged from within the discursive praxis of revolutionary politics, while also anticipating these paradoxes' postrevolutionary political legacy as constituent moments.

It is widely accepted that the American Revolution profoundly changed the meaning and practice of popular sovereignty in the West, transforming the people from a source of power defensively appealed to in constitutional crises — as the people had been figured in the Anglophone world since the sixteenth century's religious wars — to an agent capable of ongoing, collective self-government and, when necessary, radical constitutional reform.[42] However, a government based in popular sovereignty was not the colonial rebels' initial goal. The colonists backed hesitantly into this revolutionary position, and postrevolutionary Americans have been struggling with the conflicted inheritance of this apotheosis of the people ever since.

From the beginning of the Imperial Crisis, such colonial resistance leaders as Samuel Adams, Richard Henry Lee, and James Otis invoked the people to authorize political claims against their colonial governors. The people they invoked, however, were the corporate entity that civic republican or "country" discourse identified as the repository of uncorrupted virtue and the last line of constitutional defense against the scheming machinations of a corrupted court élite.[43] Under the customary constitution, as interpreted in the colonies, it was ultimately the people who decided constitutional controversies. During the initial agitations over the Sugar Act in 1764, and to a greatly amplified degree in the popular mobilizations against the Stamp Act in the following year, these leaders appealed to the assembled people as a constitutionally authorized force of direct resistance to the government's purportedly unconstitutional policies.[44]

The first organizations that led the resistance to Parliament's tax policies—self-created organizations collectively referred to as the "Sons of Liberty"—claimed to represent the people's interests against both the constituted authority of their colonial governors and the unconstitutional policies of Parliament itself. The colonists understood the Sons of Liberty and the crowds they organized to resist the Stamp Act as legitimate emergency enactments of the people's defensive power. "Whenever government used the authority delegated to it by the people so as to threaten the safety of society," Edmund Morgan writes, "it was said the people had a right to resist and reduce it within its proper bounds."[45] At such moments the people were proclaimed as a power higher than the constituted authorities, yet still within the bounds of constitutional law. The people were enacted as a "quasi-legal" defense of the constitutional order, but not formally mandated or procedurally enacted from within that order. As a circular published in the Boston Gazette in 1765 put it: "while they are thus collected, [the people] act as a supreme, uncontrollable Power, from which there is [no] Appeal, where Trial, Sentence, and Execution succeed each other almost simultaneously."[46] The Sons of Liberty, as well as the committees, congresses, conventions, crowds, and non-importation societies that followed them in the late 1760s and 1770s, did not claim to break with the constitution, to revert to the contractual scenario of a natural state, but instead relied on the longstanding Whig discourse of popular resistance that figured the people as the ultimate defenders and enforcers of constitutional law. They were an American iteration of the tradition of popular constitutionalism, according to which, in the legal historian Larry Kramer's words, "constitutional limits [were] to be enforced through politics and by the people rather than in the courts."[47]

Just over twenty years later, during the debates over constitutional ratification in 1787–88, the people were quite differently figured, enthroned as the constitution's creators—what democratic theorists term a constituent power.[48] As James Wilson, a key theorist of this transformed conception of the people's sovereignty, said in his opening address to the Pennsylvania ratifying convention, the people must be understood as "a power paramount to every constitution, inalienable in its nature, and indefinite in its extent."[49] The people's discursive and practical transformation from a constitution-interpreting and constitution-enforcing power to a constituent power engaged in transformative acts of "higher lawmaking" unfolded gradually over two decades of political ferment.[50] Although the two traditions persisted side by side beyond the founding, Gordon Wood has described the conceptual transformation as "one of the most creative moments in the history of political thought."[51]

The revolutionary embrace of the people's constituent power, as already noted, was not the original principle animating colonial resistance but an unintended consequence of that resistance's discursive and practical negotiations. The sovereign people were not latently expressed in pre-independence struggles so much as they were enacted through these struggles—particularly those over political representation—and through the improvisational repertoires of resistance themselves. To say that popular sovereignty was implicit in these practices of resistance is to retrospectively posit an agent—the people—that is actually produced through them. The people of the American Revolution were not a unified identity awaiting expression but a virtual incipience awaiting enactment or dramatization. The people were enacted through the practical repertoires of the Revolution itself.

There is therefore a dynamic tension between what the rebelling colonists explicitly claimed and what they did, between the constitutionally defensive people they invoked to justify their resistance and the self-authorizing people whom this resistance enacted. It was only in the rebellion's final stages, as royal governments collapsed in 1774 and 1775 and authority was transferred from the king to the Continental Congress said to represent the people, that the revolutionaries began to fully understand the scope of this change and the postrevolutionary dilemmas it would pose. The story of this transformation is subtle and complicated, and has been admirably detailed by Willi Paul Adams, Pauline Maier, Edmund Morgan, Gordon Wood, and others; I briefly recount its basic outlines here, in somewhat stylized form, to better clarify its theoretical stakes. The transformation emerged, first, from a dialectical unfolding of the arguments over representation and sovereignty between the colonists and their colonial governors, Parliament, and Crown, and, second, from a retrospectively principled vindication of the self-created governing practices that emerged from within the improvised repertoires of political resistance.

Parliament's passage of the Stamp Act in 1765 provoked a massive wave of resistance in the North American colonies, animated by the belief that taxation by the unrepresentative authority of Parliament was illegitimate. The ensuing debates concerning political representation reflected divergent understandings of constitutional law and the political inheritance of the Glorious Revolution of 1688. Parliament's unquestioned claims to sovereignty soon emerged as a necessarily related issue. The Imperial Crisis thus began over questions of political representation and concluded with debates over the ultimate location of sovereignty. As Edmund Morgan demonstrates, these two theoretical problematics were always mutually implied.[52] This mutual implication might explain why Gordon Wood can claim in one text that "of all the conceptions of political theory underlying the momentous developments of the American revolutionary era, none was more important than that of representation," and in another that sovereignty "was the single most important abstraction of politics in the entire revolutionary era."[53]

The colonists' central argument regarding Parliament's tax policies was that representatives must be more directly accountable to their constituencies (that is, actual people from particular locations rather than the abstractions of fixed social orders). Parliament, conversely, defended itself through what George Grenville's secretary, Thomas Whately, described as a theory of "virtual representation," according to which Parliament represented not specific districts but a deliberative body through which all "the Commons of Great Britain are represented."[54] The doctrine of virtual representation allocated representatives to the "rotten boroughs," districts with few or no inhabitants (some literally under water), and denied representation to such growing districts as Manchester and Birmingham; it also had the practical virtue of blurring the precise outline of the represented constituencies. If Parliament represented the collective good of the realm, and this good was to be determined by what Edmund Burke later called "a deliberative assembly of one nation, with one interest, that of the whole,"[55] then nagging questions of direct correspondence to a given constituency need not arise. The people could remain a normative fiction shielded from inquiry into its precise constituents. The colonists' critique of virtual representation, and their embrace of "actual" representation, shifted authority, indirectly at first, from representatives to the represented, from governors to the governed. The colonists' theory of actual representation was a potent rhetorical tool against Parliament's claims, but as we shall see, it raised self-consuming questions about the nature of its authorizing subject.

As the colonists developed arguments concerning actual representation in the 1760s and 1770s they were compelled to articulate with more precision the nature of the constituency "actually" represented—the people. The more theoretical scrutiny was focused on this authorizing subject, the more the outline of that subject seemed to recede from clear view. The resulting "dilemma of constituency" ultimately laid bare to many postrevolutionary Americans the invariably political praxis of representation and the contestability of all representational claims, particularly those purporting to represent the ground of all public authority, those proclaimed in the people's name.[56] The revolutionary and postrevolutionary American context was charged with a heightened political awareness and suspicion of representational claims, but it was also a period marked by the proliferation of institutions making such claims. John Adams already remarked on this dynamic in his *Dissertation on the Canon and Feudal Law* (1765): "This dread of representation has had for a long time, in this province, effects very similar to what the physicians call hydrophobia, or dread of water. It has made us delirious; and we have rushed headlong into the water, till we are almost drowned, out of simple or phrensical fear of it."[57] Postrevolutionary American political culture was characterized by a perpetual crisis in representation.[58]

In addition to revealing the ambiguous contours of the people, colonial arguments about actual representation also indirectly endowed this ambiguous figure with increasing agency. Debates over representation and the precise role of representatives profoundly affected the understanding of the people so represented. These debates provide a case study in how a discursive contest around what is supposedly supplemental—in this instance the nature of political representation—comes to construct the object that it purportedly supplements: the people represented. In the decade before the Revolution the sovereign people emerged indirectly through debates over the nature of political representation, not the other way round. While colonists demanded political representation that more accurately reflected different constituencies' interests, tempers, and manners, their discourses actively constructed the constituencies' very sovereignty. These colonial debates, with their emphasis on direct accountability, set off one people from another—Americans from Britons—and also attributed growing agency to the represented people. The people went from a reserved, deferential, and passive body whose interests could be represented without their direct say to a demanding and "taking" people forever jealous of their governors' power.[59] In these prerevolutionary debates over political representation, the people became simultaneously more ambiguous and more powerful; the power attributed to the people expanded alongside their increasing unlocatability. This transformation established important conditions for post-revolutionary constituent moments.

If the colonists backed into their ultimately revolutionary position on popular sovereignty, they were also guided toward this position by the logic of British counterarguments concerning the location of sovereignty and by their improvisational practices of resistance themselves. Parliamentary sovereignty was taken as an essential component of the ancient constitution, theorized in Blackstone's *Commentaries on the Laws of England* and enacted by the Glorious Revolution. Many British defenders of Parliamentary sovereignty saw the colonists' initial appeal to the authority of the Crown above Parliament as dangerously reactionary and threatening to the rights secured in 1688. This seemingly reactionary appeal became dramatically radical, however, once the constitutional claim was no longer based in an appeal to the Crown but on the claimants' own authority. Drawing on influential arguments like those presented in Demophilus's *The Genuine Principles of the Ancient Saxon or*

English Constitution, during the 1760s Americans relied on increasingly divergent interpretations of the British Constitution that emphasized the enforcing and interpreting power of the people themselves as a continuing part of constitutional politics, rather than as something deployed solely at points of revolutionary rupture. The ubiquitous question "Who shall judge?" was unequivocally answered in these years by "the people," and the judgments were made regarding not only the application of law but also its content and constitutionality.[60]

The growing disparity between British and American readings of the ancient constitution around issues of representation repeatedly highlighted the need for a final court of appeal to adjudicate between these readings. For the colonists this disparity brought to the fore the question of sovereignty, which the British had emphasized since the beginning of the colonial dispute. The colonists' early reluctance to directly challenge Parliament's sovereign authority is reflected in both the nature of their claims and the deferential tone in which they made them. But as colonists attempted through nuanced and sometimes puzzling arguments to divide and disperse Parliament's centralized sovereign claims, they increasingly found themselves returning to the people's final authority. In other words, even as the logic of colonial arguments about actual representation was indirectly empowering the people, colonial invocations of the vox populi as the ultimate court of appeal for adjudicating constitutional conflicts were functioning similarly. The people petitioning Parliament in defense of the constitution slowly gave way to the people surpassing the Parliament's constitutional power altogether and proclaiming separate sovereignty. This radical position was first attributed to the colonists by British defenders of Parliamentary sovereignty, as they came to argue (rightly, as it turned out) that this treasonous position was the ultimate and inevitable consequence of the colonists' arguments and actions. The British subcabinet official William Knox stated the problem succinctly in 1769: "There is no alternative. Either the colonies are part of the community of Great Britain or they are in a state of nature with respect to her, and in no case can be subject to the jurisdiction of that legislative power which represents her community, which is the British Parliament."[61] As their debates over constitutional interpretation deadlocked, colonists repeatedly fell back on the ultimate authority of the separate American people.[62]

The colonial theory of actual representation and the discursive pressure to articulate a conceptually coherent position concerning the ultimate ground of public authority were not the only factors leading to the revolutionary enthronement of the sovereign people. This people had also been enacted in myriad improvisational institutions of political resistance that emerged in the decade before Revolution. Before Congress officially declared independence, and before the preceding enactment of smaller town-, county-, and state-level declarations of independence,[63] a dizzying array of self-created revolutionary institutions spoke for the people. "Beginning with the revolutionary movement," Gordon Wood summarizes, "(but with roots deep in American history) the American people came to rely more and more on their ability to organize themselves and to act 'out of doors,' whether as 'mobs,' as political clubs, or as conventions."[64] During the revolutionary and postrevolutionary years, "out of doors" came to signify not only "in the street" or "in the squares" but also collective action taken outside of established political channels. Committees, conventions, popular juries and crowds, however distinct their functions, however varied their political enactments, attempted to "gather power from outside the political system"; they were quasi-legal institutions that allowed the people to emerge and that made "possible a new actor collective in nature."[65]

The people acting through self-created institutions were initially invoked as defenders of constitutional liberties, and their "quasi-legal" forms of constitutional resistance had a long and constitutionally authorized pedigree. But in the decade before Revolution these emergency institutions slowly began to take over the duties of government itself. As James Morone summarizes, "they set the price of necessaries, boycotted colonial courts, formed alternative tribunals, examined the merchants' books, punished public offenders . . . regulated trade, intervened between debtors and creditors, issued licenses."[66] The transfer of power from Parliament to the people took place in practice before it was declared in principle. "Royal governors stood helpless as they watched para-governments grow up around them, a rapid piecing together from the bottom up of a hierarchy of committees and congresses that reached from the counties and towns through the provincial conventions to the Continental Congress."[67]

These self-created institutions claiming to act in the people's name gave a practical dimension to emerging claims about popular sovereignty (later emphasized by Tocqueville),[68] but their improvisational quality also posed dilemmas to later attempts to codify the norm in postrevolutionary constitutional orders. These self-enactments of the people did not simply disappear into the constitutional orders proclaimed on the authority of "We the people": they persisted as an outside (but never wholly independent) court of appeal for and challenge to those orders. It was through participation in such varied resistance organizations that colonists enacted their popular constituent power *avant la lettre*, and that some later populists claimed to enact theirs against the "duly constituted" republican regime.[69]

Here too the practices of resistance to colonial government outpaced the explicit intention of its leading agents. Through the practical organization of these improvised popular committees, they became "seedbeds not just for a revolution against England, but for a repudiation of traditional models of government and political behavior."[70] This radical outcome, and the expansive articulation of the people that emerged from it, certainly derived from longstanding Whig theories of popular resistance, but in practice they also transformed those theories. This transformation's complicated history is too often overlooked by political theorists who look only to the period's dramatic conceptual change to account for its shifting understanding of the people. In emphasizing the spectral role of the people as a constitution-making constituent power (about which more below), political theorists too often neglect the myriad ways in which this conceptualization grew out of practical interpellations of the people as a constitution-interpreting and constitution-enforcing power. The seemingly spectral invocation of the people's constituent power, sometimes criticized by radical democratic theorists,[71] emerges from the practical enactments of the "people out of doors." And despite the frequent claims of both defenders and critics of the constitution, the people's revolutionary emergence is not resolved by the constitutional founding but continually reiterated in democratic claims-making practices that follow and that cannot be easily subsumed into a progressive history of constitutional development. The dilemmas of authorization that mark these iterations are what I characterize as constituent moments.

III

Democracy was and is the only political ideal that condemns its own denial of equality and inclusion.   SHELDON WOLIN, "Transgression, Equality, Voice"[72]

The claims of revolutionary resistance organizations to speak in the people's name, as with claims made in the more official declarations of Congresses and conventions, were largely uncontested by patriots. So long as there was a unified "we" mobilized against a common British enemy, the "dilemma of constituency" did not emerge as an acute political problem. "The people as *event*," as Pierre Rosanvallon has put the point, "can seem to resolve, for a time, the constitutive aporia of representation."[73] The authenticity of the organizations' claims was ensured by their obvious superiority to the other contending institution: the British Parliament. In the wake of independence, however, this dilemma became live and salient, as diverse constituencies and purportedly representative institutions began making competing claims to speak in the people's name. "What do 'those who are continually declaiming about *the people, the people* . . . mean by the people?' it was asked in exasperation. No part of government, even their representatives, seemed capable of embodying them. By the 1780's the people had become simply the collective community standing outside the entire government—a final court of appeal to which every aggrieved group took its case."[74] In postrevolutionary contexts the people must be represented as the ground of public authority, yet cannot be represented with uncontroversial definitiveness. This impossible imperative need not be paralyzing, however, but can also be politically productive. It engendered the acute cultural pressures and dilemmas explored in the chapters that follow. Appeals to the people were no longer transcendent appeals to heaven that superseded politics—Paine's line of "oblivion"—but the motor of a distinct form of political contestation. The self-evident "we" of Jefferson and Paine became the subject of competing claims. Through this process of political contestation, the self-evidence of the revolutionary "we" was replaced by a growing awareness that this "we" is an important but always tentative achievement.[75]

Independence had clarified that the people were not Britons, but had left unresolved what representation of popular voice would become authoritative. Who makes up the people? What are its territorial boundaries? How is popular voice to be politically enacted or institutionally embodied? As Marc Harris has written, while "the revolution professedly made the collective people sovereign, . . . it did not settle how the public will should be institutionalized nor which representations of that will carried greatest weight."[76] The political struggles over this issue helped inaugurate a crisis in authority and representation that was a central preoccupation of postrevolutionary American culture and politics.

This crisis of representation and authority—and the political contests that ensued—is represented and dramatized in a remarkable copperplate engraving made in 1784 by the Polish artist Daniel Nicolas Chodowiecki (figure 1). Chodowiecki's depiction of the burning of British stamps by a crowd in Boston in August 1765 makes legible postrevolutionary dilemmas of the representation of the peoples' voice, while also suggestively marking the continuity between questions of political and aesthetic representation.[77] The engraving retrospectively projects a postrevolutionary dilemma of constituency into the originary moment of revolutionary enactment, insofar as the event depicted—the popular mobilization against the Stamp Act—was already considered the historical origin of the events that had led to the Revolution and independence, as well as of post-independence forms of popular contention.

Chodowiecki chose to represent this originary scene—the engraving was the first of twelve illustrations accompanying M. C. Sprengel's engaging narrative of the Revolution and the War of Independence—by synecdochically associating the crowd in Boston with the revolutionary liberation of the people themselves. The crowd stood for a larger entity than the empirically gathered people—the normative people—and for their future independence. As such, the image also dramatizes the important historical transition described by Charles Tilly and George Rudé from the direct-action crowd—whose target was entirely local (the prosperous merchant, the adulterer, the constable)—to the representative crowd, authorized by broader normative claims of the people or the rights of man.[78] The engraving, like the text it accompanies, clearly depicts the pageantry of the American Revolution while transforming this pageantry into a sign of larger historical significance akin to Immanuel Kant's later reflections on the prophetic significance of the French Revolution to enlightenment and emancipation. "Who could not be moved,"

Die Americaner widersetzen sich der Stempel-Acte, und verbrennen das aus England nach America gesandte Stempel-Papier zu Boston. im August 1764.

1. "Protest gegen die Stempelakte, 1764 [1765]." Copperplate engravings by Daniel Chodowiecki in "Allgemeines historisches Taschenbuch oder Abriß der merkwürdigsten neuen Welt-Begebenheit enthaltend für 1784 die Geschichte der Revolution von Nord-Amerika" ("General Historical Pocketbook or Outline of the Most Curious Occurrences in the New World containing for 1784 the History of the Revolution of North America"), by C. M. Sprengel, Berlin 1783. Courtesy of the Library of Congress.

as Sprengel writes, "to see how a people without long preparation and planning, reacting to a seemingly small and only remotely threatening danger, suddenly leaves its ploughs and starts fighting for something nobler than the reasons for which princes fight, not for glory, not for gain, but for the most holy rights of humanity."[79] Unlike the assuring spectatorial judgments of Kant's "wishful participants" in *The Conflict of the Faculties*, however, Chadowiecki's image suggests a complicated proximity to the events at hand, and a quite different dilemma from Kant's progressive unfolding of rights in history.[80] Chodowiecki's image dramatizes the indeterminate boundary around the people, and the enacted claims that this indeterminacy invites on multiple dimensions — vertical, horizontal, and temporal. The engraving conveys a powerful sense of the people's expansiveness and uncontainability: first, by dramatizing the boundary that translates the quantitative assemblage of individuals into the qualitative collective of a unified people; second, by dramatizing the boundary around who counts as a part of that authorizing entity; and third, by dramatizing an unfinished temporality that gestures to the horizon of what is yet to come, to a people that is not . . . yet. I will explore each point in turn.

Like the spectators filling the windows on the engraving's left side, their gazes fixed on the events unfolding in the square below, the viewer is a positioned observer of this unfolding crowd scene. However, unlike the distant spectators safely observing events from two or three stories above street level, the interpellated viewer is thrust at eye level into the action. At a remove of only a few feet, and propelled by the image's leaning figures toward its pictorial center — the four-cornered hat held in the patriot's outstretched arms — the viewer is an entering participant of the crowd action: one among many entering the pictorial plane from beyond the limits of its frame. While Chadowiecki gathers the assembled people within the walled perimeter of the public square, the assembly pointedly escapes the boundary's frame. Bodies are cut off on the left and right sides of the image; the crowd disappears behind the smoke from the burning stamps; the image enfolds the viewer and pushes past the image's foreground to the invisible space beyond.

Chadowiecki's composition suggests an inability to capture the assembled people definitively within a single representation; the mode of depiction attempts to represent the people's ultimate unrepresentability.[81] The image graphically suggests that the people, while requiring an observable representation to be, also exceed the confines of any given representation. Chadowiecki depicts the ambivalence around who is included and who is excluded by the always fungible boundary frames around the people.

The pictorially unrepresentable character of Chadowiecki's assembled people is also conveyed by his choice to prominently feature two qualified people, to count the uncounted—the young African man and the white woman, who together seem to be rushing to join the assembled crowd from beyond the frame of the image's lower right corner, to make their claims on inclusion in this assembled people. Chadowiecki's pointed inclusion of two persons excluded from the official political life of Massachusetts—though not from the unofficial politics of the people out of doors—suggests the uncontainable quality of the people that so worried Adams. However, Chadowiecki's image replaces Adams's prophetic warning with a prophetic embrace. Chadowiecki's wry postrevolutionary appreciation of the future enactments already contained *in potentia* within the originary event of colonial resistance suggests that the engraving's central (white, male) figures and actors do not see the far-reaching consequences of their own authorizing appeal to the people once these appeals are taken up by other claimants: the patriots quite literally do not see what is going on behind their backs.

Particularly illuminating in this regard are the young African's gestures and the trajectory of his gaze, both important elements of an engraving completed by an eighteenth-century master of manner and sensibility, one known for his detailed portrayals of the manners of eighteenth-century bourgeois Prussian life. The young African in the image seems to be observing and modeling his actions on the image's central figures, thereby dramatizing an inaugural mimesis to be reiterated in subsequent claims as future imitations reopen and transform public space. Rather than directly facing the burning pyre as are most of the image's characters, the African youth is looking *away* from the fire and toward the two men in the left foreground who seem to be discussing the paper that one of them holds, most likely a circular denouncing the Stamp Act and advertising the public meeting. As the African youth directs his attention to these figures, his body mimics the theatrical gestures of the central figure holding his hat in his outstretched arms. The right arm is similarly outstretched, and the right leg similarly lifted, as his body thrusts forward. Through this depiction of observation and modeling, Chadowiecki represents the educative and contagious environment that was (and still is) believed to attend crowd actions. He thereby dramatizes the period's popular trope of liberty's contagion. The movement of these figures depicts the unfinished temporality of the action, its gesture to an unfinished democracy, one still to come.

IV

All power indeed flows from the people; but the doctrine that the power, actually at all times, resides in the people, is subversive to all government and all law.
JUDGE ALEXANDER HANSON, *Maryland Journal*, 22 June 1787[82]

Two broad developments in postrevolutionary political thought responded to the dilemma of constituency resulting from the Revolution's enthronement of the people as the basis of public authority. The first was a continuation of the revolutionary tradition of popular constitutionalism, whereby the authorizing voice of the people was claimed by self-created associations—committees, conventions, popular juries, and crowds—alongside and sometimes against duly constituted—that is, republican—government. The second development, more widely discussed in the historical literature, is the eventual constitutionalization of the people in the form of conventions like the Massachusetts ratifying convention of 1780, and formal amendment procedures, like those elaborated in article V of the United States Constitution. Robert Cover has aptly described this as "the awesome [postrevolutionary] transition from revolutionaries to constitutionaries."[83] In the first tradition there is continued emphasis on direct action and figuring the people as an extra-governmental entity authorizing or regulating force; in the second there is a growing emphasis on constitutional organization and the necessarily formal mediation of popular voice. Benjamin Rush captured the latter sentiment, which became most pronounced in the debates over constitutional ratification, in an "Address to the People of the United States" (1787). "It is often said," Rush wrote, "that 'the sovereign and all other power is seated *in* the people.' This idea is unhappily expressed. It should be—'all power is derived *from* the people.' They possess it only on the days of their elections. After this, it is the property of their rulers, nor can they exercise or resume it, unless it is abused."[84] In contrast to theorists who claim that these traditions should be understood as mutually exclusive, I will argue that they are best understood as interrelated; together they give shape to a democratic tension that enables the postrevolutionary—and post-Founding—inheritance of constituent moments.

It is well known that postrevolutionary America saw the proliferation of groups claiming to speak in the people's name, but whereas in the prerevolutionary years these associations emerged against and alongside colonial governments, they now emerged alongside, and sometimes against, the constituted authorities of the postcolonial republican states. Vigilantes in North Carolina, the Green Mountain Boys in Vermont, "resistance networks" in Pennsylvania, and the followers of Daniel Shays in western Massachusetts are only some of the groups that made such claims in the 1770s and 1780s.[85] Despite the different grievances which motivated their actions—both repugnant and admirable—all were united in their claim to act on the authority of the people. As James Morone has summarized, "the reification [of the people] that launched the revolution now imperiled the regime."[86] The Revolution's proliferation of extra- or quasi-legal institutions to "empower the people directly" did not end with independence but would "become one of its major political legacies."[87]

Yet the appeal to order in the face of what many saw as the "excesses of democracy" or looming "mobocracy" was also carried out in the people's name, and it was accomplished in part through the innovations of postrevolutionary American constitutionalism. A frequently noted irony of the postrevolutionary years is that the popular politics of the 1780s were contained by further enhancing the legal authority, if not the actual power, of the people themselves.[88] This containment was achieved by deflating the people's legislative sovereignty and the continued legitimacy of an ongoing politics "out of doors," while simultaneously affirming the people as the makers of higher law. A near-consensus emerged among the postrevolutionary élite that the legitimate exercise of popular power must be a constitutional exercise of power. The struggle with Parliament had largely destroyed conceptions of legislative sovereignty in America and had entrenched a firm distinction between regular and fundamental law in the American political imagination. Ten states adopted new constitutions in the year after independence; in nine of these, the sitting, constituted government created the constitution. Although in 1776 there was already some awareness that only the constituent power of the people themselves could engage in constitution making, it was not until the proposed constitution of 1780 in Massachusetts that popular conventions were created as the chosen method of legitimate ratification.[89] Beginning with the ratification of the Massachusetts constitution, and culminating in the ratification of the United States Constitution in 1787, the people, acting through conventions, were figured as the ultimate creators of constitutional law and a power above their legislative representatives. During these years the people were embraced as a constituent power.

Scholarly discussions of popular constituent power in revolutionary and postrevolutionary America therefore often focus on the innovative role of constitutional conventions.[90] As the colonists fought against Parliament's proclaimed sovereignty, they insisted on the people's higher authority, and following the historical example of the Glorious Revolution, which for the colonists epitomized constitutional change through popular action, the constitutional convention was taken as this authority's premier institutional embodiment. The convention was not a constituted authority—like a state legislature or Parliament—and this extralegality was what gave it a superior authoritative claim. It provided the theological supplement of that which is "beyond" or "prior to" the law. In eighteenth-century Britain the conventions were understood as "irregular bodies" whose acts lacked the Parliamentary acts' legitimacy. The Americans seized on this irregularity to proclaim the convention's superior authority to acts of Parliament. Because they were legally deficient bodies outside the bounds of regularly constituted authority, they attained superior authority in times of constitutional crisis. As Gordon Wood summarizes, "the convention in American thinking eventually became something more than a legally deficient legislature, indeed became an extraordinary constitution-making body that was considered to be something very different and even superior to the ordinary legislature—all so rapidly and suddenly that it is difficult to capture its origins."[91]

As Wood suggests, this difficulty in capturing "origins" is related to the practical emergence of conventions as constitution-making bodies out of longstanding popular practices in which these irregular conventions were constitution-interpreting rather than constitution-making powers. James Burgh's writings on the customary constitutional understanding of conventions were influential in these developments. Burgh's *Disquisitions* were "the standard sourcebook for reform propagandists in the 1780's."[92] While Burgh could insist that "power in the people is like light in the sun, native, original, inherent, and unlimited by any thing human," he understood this power as primarily interpretive and restorative.[93] He was perhaps the preeminent exponent of the theory that the people may act collectively in defense of their constitutional rights. His *Disquisitions* assembled the thoughts of authors ancient and modern on efforts to reform and *restore* the constitution and save the state. The core of Burgh's concerns in the *Disquisitions*, and clearly the reason the work was so avidly read in the colonies, was representation—and its limits. Burgh's work is paradigmatic in arguing the revolution's principal point: that *no* governmental entity could ever fully embody the will of the people.

Federalists later appealed to this insight to legitimate their attempt to replace the Articles of Confederation and the states constituted under its authority with an entirely new federal constitution. James Wilson and James Madison argued for appealing to the people themselves, as the ultimate ground of political power, to authorize bypassing the states' constituted authority under the Articles of Confederation. They also figured this as a way to better stabilize the government's authority. They thereby recast a onetime principle of revolutionary unsettlement as a source of order and the consolidation of national power. As James Wilson wrote, the "revolution principle—that, the sovereign power residing in the people, they may change their constitution and government whenever they please—is not a principle of discord, rancor, or war: it is a principle of melioration, contentment, and peace."[94] Political theorists and historians have sometimes interpreted the Federalist refiguration of the people's role as a preeminent example of democratic rhetoric being invoked to overcome democratic practice. By appealing to the constituent power of the people, Federalists presented themselves as "champions of the people's superiority to their government," while the Anti-Federalist opposition that appealed to constituted public authority and the sovereignty of the individual states were seen as narrow, rule-bound proceduralists.[95] The Federalists appeared as inheritors of the revolutionary apotheosis of the people, and the Anti-Federalists appeared as conservative defenders of constituted authority under the Articles of Confederation. As Wood writes, the Federalists "appropriated and exploited the language that more rightfully belonged to their opponents."[96]

Historians and political theorists have often taken the affirmation of the people's constitutional authority as a singularly dramatic development in American political history, one with myriad consequences, both positive and negative, for the future development of democracy. What was dangerous to seventeenth-century conservatives was thereby transformed into the principal political tool through which late-eighteenth-century American conservatives established governmental control over the people. In this sense popular sovereignty merely worked to the same end as the monarchical ideologies that it replaced—to subordinate the many to the few. The constitutional appeal to the people limited the post-revolutionary politics of the people; one people was politically set against another. This abstracted conception of the people not only empowered an energized federal government, others lament, but also removed any social basis from the conceptualization of the people. Because of this abandonment of any idea of the people as a particular social class "institutional or governmental politics was . . . abstracted in a curious way from its former associations with the society."[97] As Kenneth Burke's audience recognized, this abstracted conception of the people contributed to Americans' subsequent inability to think in terms of social class; it impoverished and abstracted American political discourse and made it difficult to control the domination of politics by a wealthy élite.

Though the antidemocratic dimension of this appeal to the people's constituent power has been widely recognized by historians, democratic theorists have more typically embraced this constitutionalization of popular voice as one of the great and lasting achievements of the Revolution. This normative endorsement has taken many forms, some of which will be explored in the following chapters. Stephen Holmes has offered one of the more compelling versions, by arguing that Madison and other Federalists offered an updated liberal theory of positive constitutionalism. In this tradition, drawn importantly from Jean Bodin, the constitution is more than a negative check on the people's power: it is a way of organizing or constituting their power. Refusing the paradox that so often preoccupies constitutional scholarship—popular sovereignty and democracy as opposed to constitutionalism and rights—Holmes persuasively argues that Madison understood these seemingly competing principles as necessarily presupposed. Rather than reiterate these oppositions (or any of the analogous binaries), Holmes critiques the entire model of "negative constitutionalism" on which the oppositions are based. Holmes argues that to preserve the voluntariness of democratic will, voluntariness itself must be first restricted. It is through such self-binding mechanisms that the American founders navigated what Holmes calls the paradox of precommitment. Democratic will, to be capable of voluntary action, *cannot exist* outside its constitutional organization. Far from *limiting* the power of the people, it is only *through* constitutions that democratic power can be effectively organized in the first place. "It is not obvious that the people can have anything like a coherent will prior to and apart from all constitutional procedures."[98] "The idea that the people as a whole wield the *pouvoir constituent*, prior to all procedural restraints and outside the discipline of electoral law, may be a useful legal fiction. (It serves to deny that any single subgroup may rightfully seize extra-constitutional power.) But to say that 'the people' of a modern nation-state, while truly *legibus solutus*, or unbound by law, can spontaneously choose a new political order, is unrealistic."[99] In a statement that echoes Madison's claim in Federalist No. 40 that the people cannot act "spontaneously" and "universally" of their own accord, Holmes summarizes that "the people cannot act as an amorphous blob."[100]

Here Holmes updates a central tenet of legal positivism. As H. L. A. Hart writes in the *Concept of Law*, "the rules are *constitutive* of the sovereign . . . we cannot say that the rules specifying the procedures of the electorate represent the conditions under which the society as so many individuals obeys itself as an electorate; for 'itself as an electorate' is not a reference to a person apart from the rules."[101] Like Hart, Holmes has an extremely governmental understanding of democratic agency. Both theorists envision "the people" only as a rule-bound electorate. "If popular sovereignty can be expressed only on the basis of pre-existing legal rules for aggregating preferences, it becomes manifestly incoherent to locate the source of all legal regulations in the will of the people."[102] This is a very controversial "if," but rather than engage this controversy, Holmes associates theoretical attempts to articulate a democratic will outside of constitutional and legal organization with "democratic mysticism." However, the constituent power of the people is "mystical" or "mythological" only if we limit ourselves to conceptualizing the people as an empirically available "entity" or "social datum": a unified will that acts outside of claims made in its name. As I have already suggested, and will demonstrate in the chapters that follow, we need not assume that the people must have a prior coherent collective identity if they are to enact their constituent power (that would not be enactment, we might say, but expression). The constituent power of the people is not merely "mystical" if we turn away from assuming there must be a coherent "entity" or "will" to be found and look instead to its concrete enactments or effects in different forms of political subjectivization. Finally, Holmes's "solution" to dilemmas of self-authorization does not directly confront the paradox of who constitutes the people in the first place. I agree with Jeremy Waldron that Procrustes might be a better mythic figure than Ulysses to model these moments of democratic precommitment, insofar as they resemble not so much "the triumph of preemptive rationality" as "the artificially sustained ascendancy of one view in the polity over other views whilst the complex moral issues between them remain unresolved."[103] Political contention over these foundational issues persists beyond the founding.

If Holmes and many other liberal admirers of American constitutionalism understand the self-authorizing people of the Revolution as wholly realized within the constitutional order, Sheldon Wolin and other radical democratic critics of American constitutionalism sometimes view the revolutionary people as wholly betrayed by the constitutional order, and persisting as an outside force. "When democratic revolution leads to a constitution," Wolin writes, it "marks the beginning of its attenuation."[104] Wolin writes that "in the American political tradition, the people has had two 'bodies.'" In the first "body," inherited from the Revolution, the people would "not just participate in politics, but would join in actually creating a new political identity, to 'institute,' 'alter,' or 'abolish' governments, to lay a 'foundation' and organize power." In the second "body," for Wolin based in the constitutional founding, "the people" were an essentially passive, depoliticized entity invoked only to authorize the state's expanding power.[105] This opposition between the Revolution and the founding risks oversimplifying the story of the people's postrevolutionary double inscription, just as Holmes's identification of the two does. *Pace* Wolin, it is not the constitutional people *versus* the revolutionary people; *pace* Holmes, it is not the constitutional subsuming of popular will, but the relation of tension by which each sustains the other. Both theorists, otherwise opposed in so much of their thinking, neglect how in postrevolutionary American contexts the people are at once a constituted and a constituent power, whose enactments can never be wholly free of the resulting paradox. From the perspective of this book, neither position gives due attention to the remainder of the people, to the persistence of the people not as a purely outside force but as an internal surplus of the order founded in their name. The constitutional "We the People" is not wholly subsumed in the text that represents it. Of course radical democratic critics of American constitutionalism are right to emphasize the antidemocratic intent of the Founders, and a long line of historians, beginning dramatically with Charles Beard, has chronicled the extent to which, in Richard Hofstadter's words, the discussions at the Philadelphia Convention were pervaded with "a distrust of man that was first and foremost a distrust of the common man and democratic rule."[106] But the manner of overcoming the "excesses of democracy"—appealing to the constituent power of the people—also enabled a democratic history of unintended consequences. The attempt to overcome the people by appeal to the people enabled and authorized an ongoing history of constituent moments, of effective claims to speak in the people's name that nonetheless break from the rules established by their authority. What Anne Norton has called the transubstantiation of the people into their constitutional text produces an excess, one that occasionally reemerges from within the constitutional economy of representation as an "otherwise."[107] Despite the interdependent claims of the constitution's theoretical proponents (like Holmes) and antagonists (like Wolin), ratification did not finally resolve the "constituency dilemmas" of the people that emerged in the postrevolutionary years. While historians have often emphasized how quickly the United States Constitution inspired the "veneration" that the Federalists sought—Hannah Arendt memorably called it the "ability to look on yesterday with the eyes of centuries to come"[108]—its authorizing "We the people" continually elicited a voice that transcended the text's authoritative letter.[109]

The approach to the problem of constituency suggested here clearly resonates with Bruce Ackerman's groundbreaking work on "constitutional moments," and his elaborate attempt to recall for modern Americans "the revolutionary roots of their own Constitution."[110] Ackerman's "constitutional moments," moments of dramatic constitutional revision and "higher lawmaking" that follow the founding—Reconstruction, the New Deal, and civil rights—are essentially refoundings that tap the originary transformative power of the people unchecked by existing constitutional arrangements. Along with the work of other theorists of "the republican revival" in constitutional theory, Ackerman's can be understood, as Andrew Arato has put it, as "a revival of the doctrine of constituent power in the United States."[111] Ackerman, like Wolin, believes that the people have two bodies: one is the factional, interested body of ordinary politics (its presence as the will of all); the other is a higher deliberative body of higher law (general will).[112] On extraordinary occasions—constitutional moments of higher lawmaking—the latter body of the people transforms the constitutional order in the name of a common good. During periods of "constitutional" as opposed to "normal" politics, the people (generally with the mediating assistance of a strong president) break through the governing institutions which organize them and transform these institutions themselves. According to this view, formal procedures (most notably and controversially, article V of the United States Constitution) are merely imperfect ciphers of the people.

Constituent moments similarly return to these "revolutionary roots," though without the focus on constitutional law and formal political constitutions. Constituent moments break from authorizing rules in ritual practice other than formal law or legal procedure; illegality is not the necessary mark of constituent moments. In addition, returning to this founding moment of popular authorization, tapping its resources in the form of constituent moments, does not simply reveal a beacon of "higher lawmaking" in whose light formal illegality, mass energy, public spiritedness, and extraordinary rationality are united.[113] Instead it reveals the extent to which democratic politics—on an extraordinary as well as a much more quotidian level—is always characterized by the risk of *claims* made without fully authorized grounds, by self-authorized claims to speak in the people's name that can only be retrospectively vindicated. The mythology of founding and the appeal of our own great lawgivers may in fact keep us enthralled by the extraordinary moments of the appearance of the people's constituent power, enthralled by the drama of the exception.

This book therefore suggests that these dilemmas appear and reappear not simply in moments of constitutional crisis but in the fabric of every-day political speech and action. It posits a history not of epochal consti-tutional shifts but of micropolitical enactments across several rhetorical and political contexts. It explores dilemmas of authorization that spring from these moments in both the formal political settings of constitu-tional conventions and political associations and the informal political contexts of crowd actions, political oratory, and literature. Focusing only on the exceptional historical shifts of "constitutional moments" can ob-scure how the performative dynamics of popular claims exemplified in founding moments attend democratic claims made in seemingly ordi-nary political settings. This captivation threatens to blind us to the extent to which the extraordinary inhabits and sustains the democratic ordi-nary, to the way these capacities are continually elicited from within the midst of political life. Democratic theory would do well to attend to the nuances of these small dramas of self-authorization. The postrevolution-ary inheritance of constituent moments takes us beyond analogous con-cerns of constitutional law and into the different cultural and political locations where these dramas of authorization are enacted.

V

Thus the following chapters turn not primarily to how dilemmas of au-thorization inform postrevolutionary constitutional debate but to how these dilemmas are navigated and addressed in more improbable loca-tions—crowd actions, self-created societies, novels, poetry, and political oratory, with a focus also on responses to this unsettling enactment of the people on the level of feeling and sentiment. My goal is to clarify the persistent appearance of these paradoxical dynamics across diverse cul-tural and political locations and to illuminate the continuities between them. This focus suggests that the affirmation of political paradox that characterizes so much contemporary democratic theory, especially in its radically democratic guise, is at once historically insightful, and yet perhaps also too formal in its central preoccupations. Focusing attention on the postrevolutionary navigation of political paradox across multiple sites is meant at once to acknowledge the paradox's persistence and to di-minish its captivating hold on the contemporary theoretical imagination as a continually reiterated formal problem, to shift the emphasis from formal theoretical logics to the practical navigation of these dilemmas in exemplary instances of postrevolutionary writing and politics. The chapters that follow are exemplary not in the sense of being examples of a prior theoretical rule, problem, or paradox—the example as mere illustration. Instead they explore particular historical encounters with the dilemmas brought about by constituent moments as a way of suggesting the theoretically illuminating dimension of these historical singularities. Each chapter dwells in the specificity of its case, while also tracing the theoretical significance of the example beyond its particular instance. The navigations of these dilemmas therefore have what Hannah Arendt would call "exemplary" instead of "absolute" validity.

To elaborate the theoretical dilemmas surrounding postrevolutionary America's constituent moments—and to illuminate the productively dynamic interplay between history and theory—chapter 1 critically explores Hannah Arendt's use of historical storytelling to theorize politics in *On Revolution*, focusing on her central claim that revolutionary and postrevolutionary Americans did not wrestle with the dilemmas of authorization associated with constituent power. In posing a series of critical questions to Arendt's interpretation of American revolutionary and postrevolutionary experience, chapter 1 aims not simply to point out Arendt's historical inaccuracies but to contest the exemplary orientation that she draws from her narrative. Arendt's Tocquevillean contrast between the American Revolutionary experience of what she calls "mutual promising" and the French Revolutionary invocation of popular will ultimately veils the dilemmas of authorization and forms of political contention associated with constituent moments. In portraying the American revolutionaries as wholly liberated from the logics of sovereignty, and the "absolute" of constituent power, Arendt wrongly describes their experience and mischaracterizes that experience's orienting potential for contemporary democratic theory. There is an unexplored option written out of Arendt's dichotomous presentation of the American and French cases, found in the productive reiteration of popular constituent power in a federal American context. This reiteration took the form of a culture of popular constitutionalism in the postrevolutionary years and beyond, partly engendered by constitutive ambiguity surrounding the democratic people.

This argument is given historical elaboration in chapter 2, which focuses on the representative status of the revolutionary and postrevolutionary crowd. As noted above, debates over "virtual" and "correspondent," "mandated" and "delegated" forms of representation profoundly
shaped the political discourses of the period. Chapter 2 argues that these
debates at once signal and initiate a political crisis in representation.
Furthermore, this crisis is exemplified in the authoritative claims made
through crowd actions, as well as in the debates themselves and in the
theoretical difficulties of locating or communicating popular "voice."
The scholarly focus on disembodied and representational publics in late-
eighteenth-century Anglophone contexts (often influenced by the work
of Jürgen Habermas) obscures the extent to which crowd repertoires
enacted the paradoxes of democratic autonomy. Crowd actions claimed
both to instantiate the collective entity in whose name the democratically legitimated state was authorized and also to embody those who
fell outside the established parameters of political representation. This
tension is evident in the period's attempts to distinguish "constitutional
crowds" from "licentious mobs" and "the people" from "the multitude."
Building from this historical example, chapter 2 argues that constituent
moments enacted by the crowd emerged from the fact that "the people"
are, in the words of Jacques Rancière, "always more *and* less than the
people": that democratic representation is always in part a crisis in representation.[114]

Many writers in late-eighteenth-century America expressed anxiety
over the inherent volatility of crowds and large public assemblies. Chapter 3 considers these concerns with the enacted people in light of prevailing eighteenth-century theories of sympathy. The regularity of crowd
actions provoked by the events of the Revolution focused a good deal
of critical attention on the unreason attending gatherings of the people
out of doors, however quasi-legitimate these gatherings were taken to
be. For critics these embodied publics threatened to corrupt an orderly
representational public sphere, along with its implied subjects of reasoned deliberation. Critics feared that the unregulated communication
of affect between bodies gathered in public might unleash what Michael
Meranze has called "an anarchy of reciprocal imitations." It was in
eighteenth-century theories of sympathy that this theory of contagious
bodily mimesis was most rigorously developed and most widely dissemi-

nated. Chapter 3 turns to how the reformative concern with the political organization of sympathy in postrevolutionary America—in particular, reform through the spatial choreography of the citizenry—shaped one prominent response to the crisis of political authority that followed the War of Independence: that of Dr. Benjamin Rush. For Rush the spatial separation and coordination of citizens was an important precondition for producing the deliberative citizens—the "republican machines"—required by America's new republican forms of government.

The dilemmas of authorization posed by postrevolutionary enactments of the people were not definitively resolved by the founding. Chapter 4 explores how the Democratic-Republican Societies of the 1790s reenacted the dilemmas of popular authorization inherited from the Revolution and, in doing so, educated citizens in the agonistic practices of free citizenship. The chapter argues that the societies created a crucial space for post-founding self-enactment and political subjectivization. Derided by George Washington and other Federalist opponents as illegitimately "self-created societies," the Democratic Societies have been generally misunderstood by political scientists and political theorists studying the early republic. Employing the research frameworks of American institutional development on the one hand and of the Habermasian public sphere on the other, political scientists and political theorists have typically understood the Democratic Societies as either early progenitors of the party system or exemplary sites of political deliberation. Each of these interpretations misses what was most important—and theoretically most productive—about the Democratic Societies' brief flourishing. Taking their cue from the Jacobin clubs then emerging in England and France and from the extraparliamentary traditions of the American Revolution, the Democratic Societies established spaces of insurgent citizenship, sites of critical political education where (some) citizens could come together and "discover their own strength." Understanding the Democratic Societies' revision of prevailing practices of democratic citizenship critically illuminates the civilitarian norms governing some contemporary research on the democratic value of associations and, more importantly, directs attention to the paucity of such spaces of political subjectivization in contemporary political life.

Chapter 5 turns from political action and associations to early American literature to establish the breadth of the period's cultural preoccupation with problems of popular authorization described above. The literature of postrevolutionary America is centrally preoccupied with the question of political agency and the boundaries of human autonomy, both individual and collective. This chapter engages the paradoxes of self-rule through the lens of one of the period's best-known literary works: Charles Brockden Brown's Gothic novel *Wieland* (1798). Brown's novel reflects on the dilemmas of voice and ventriloquism that marked postrevolutionary American politics. It makes legible widespread cultural concerns over the ground of public authority and its proper representation by highlighting the irreplaceable role of the imagination in constituting public authority based in popular voice. Brown's novel takes the revolutionary formula *vox populi, vox Dei* as the starting point for an analysis of democracy and enthusiasm, which Brown understands in terms of their mutual appeal to the imagined authority of unmediated voice, of the spirit beyond the letter. While historians have frequently noted the "radical and fanatical tendency" linking democracy with enthusiasm during the Age of Revolutions,[115] Brown's novel reveals a deeper connection than mere temperament in their shared emphasis on the extra-textual authorization of voice and its supplemental elicitation of a public's imaginative projections, or of what I characterize as the novel's scenes of "transportive interpellation." *Wieland* explores the unavoidably spectral but nonetheless effective indeterminacy of the revolutionary slogan *vox populi, vox Dei*.

The final two chapters explore how the dilemmas of authorization associated with constituent moments are addressed in the work of two prominent democratic thinkers from the nineteenth century: Walt Whitman and Frederick Douglass. Chapter 6 turns to Whitman's poetic attempt to wrestle with the postrevolutionary legacy of constituent moments to illuminate the orienting power of this example for contemporary democratic theory. Whitman was a key theorist of American democratic self-enactment and citizenship, and this chapter argues for the significance to contemporary democratic theory of Whitman's "double inscription" of the people, thought through the frame of the democratic sublime. Whitman's account of "aesthetic democracy" emphasizes the affective dimensions of political life. For Whitman popular attachment to democracy required an aesthetic component, and he aimed to reconfigure popular sensibility through a poetic depiction of the people themselves as a sublimely poetic, world-making power. Whitman's vox populi at once required and exceeded poetic representation to have this transformative effect. Through his poetic translation of the postrevolutionary vox populi, Whitman hoped to inspire a robustly transformative and contentious democratic politics. Moreover, he found the resources for these acts of political regeneration in the poetics of everyday citizenship and the democratic resources of ordinary life.

The book's final chapter begins with a reading of one of the greatest works of American political oratory—Frederick Douglass's "What to the Slave Is Your Fourth of July"—as an example of what Jacques Rancière calls the "staging of dissensus." This chapter synthesizes the theoretical implications of the previous chapters into a reading of American history, suggested by Douglass, as a process of democratic self-enactment, forever promised yet forever unfulfilled. This interpretation, which builds on the foregoing discussions of the people's double inscription, contrasts sharply with prevailing academic and popular narratives. These governing narratives have frequently suggested that the universal principles "declared" in 1776, although imperfectly applied at the time of their articulation, have nonetheless been incrementally expanded over the (dialectical) course of American history. A contradiction, it is suggested, existed between the universality of the rights declared and the particularity of their historical application (to "white, propertied, Christian, North American male heads of household").[116] American history thus is seen to comprise, in Habermas's words, "a process of self-correcting attempts to tap the system of rights ever more fully." Lincoln paradigmatically offered this interpretation in his Gettysburg Address; John Rawls provides an influential contemporary version in *Political Liberalism*.[117] This powerful narrative offers a vision of constitutional revision and reform that is at once juridical and self-congratulatory. It is a narrative of political solace, as it invites its public to look back on an unjust past and console itself for this injustice by admiring our contemporary state of affairs. It does not encourage attentiveness to the newly emergent claims, but instead aims to perpetually reiterate the forces of reconciliation. As this chapter details, however, Frederick Douglass's emphasis on the vitality of enacted dissensus suggests an approach focused instead on "unsettlement," one that corresponds to the analysis of constituent moments offered here. Rather than describe juridical rights incompletely applied, Douglass emphasized the people incompletely enacted. Douglass shifted the narrative focus of American history from legal application or recognition to the democratic struggles that demand them. In the redemptive narratives of Douglass's biographies, and as conveyed in his many speeches, Douglass affirmed an account of the people that exceeds constitutional "rules of recognition," but that also cannot be reduced to an external self-organizing "multitude." Douglass offers a narrative of the American past that equates its full comprehension in ever-emergent forms of transformative democratic politics. Douglass appeals to a future people — a "third people," a people still to come — to authorize his claims, and aims through that appeal to transform his audience into the kind of people capable of hearing and acting on such claims as claims that have a claim on them. Douglass actively resisted acts of remembrance and commemoration that convert the past — even a revolutionary past — into a monument of nostalgic identification.

In that spirit, this book ends with a discussion of Douglass's speeches, and their more contemporary echoes in the work of James Baldwin and Ralph Ellison. More than an admiring analysis of their content and argument, it is an elaborated example of how they transformatively elicited the public imagination. In conclusion, I emphasize how democratic theory enlists the imagination to figure its audience's relationship to the political past, as well as engaging their understanding through rational argument and normative justification. How we imagine our relationship to a revolutionary past gives shape to who and how we are as a democratic people. In this, as elaborated in the next chapter, we can learn a great deal from the narrative theorizing of Hannah Arendt.

An act can only be called free if it is not affected or caused by anything proceeding it and yet, insofar as it immediately turns into a cause of whatever follows, it demands a justification which, if it is to be successful, will have to show the act as the continuation of a preceding series, that is, renege on the very experience of freedom and novelty. HANNAH ARENDT, *The Life of the Mind*[1]

Perhaps the political genius of the American people, or the great good fortune that smiled upon the American republic, consisted precisely in . . . blindness, or, to put it another way, consisted in the extraordinary capacity to look upon yesterday with the eyes of centuries to come. HANNAH ARENDT, *On Revolution*[2]

§ 1 §

Revolution and Reiteration

Hannah Arendt's Critique of Constituent Power

Like Frederick Douglass, Hannah Arendt had a deep appreciation of the redemptive power of historical narrative to shape individual and collective identity, to inspire political action, and to provide exemplary orientation for political judgment. In her historical "storytelling," Arendt sought a mode of political theorizing appropriate to a time when the authority of tradition had been irrevocably broken, and when political actors were required "to understand without preconceived categories and to judge without the set of customary rules which is morality."[3] In the wake of the revolutions of the modern age we have "lost the continuity of the past," Arendt writes, left with only a "fragmented past which has lost all certainty of evaluation."[4] Under these conditions the past is transmitted "without testament," and therefore open to contentious appropriations. Nowhere is this more evident than in the contested history of the revolutions themselves. For Arendt political theorists return to the past "not to resuscitate it" or to "contribute to the renewal of extinct ages," but to bring these "fragments" and "pearls" up to the surface as orienting guideposts to judgment, guideposts that provide "exemplary" though not "absolute" validity.[5] Arendt's remarkable interpretation of the American Revolution is an extended attempt at such exemplary recovery; as such, *On Revolution* is a landmark of historically situated democratic theory.[6] Because of this, and because of that text's overlapping theoretical preoccupations with the themes developed here, this chapter offers a critical assessment of Arendt's understanding of the American Revolution and the revolutionary politics of the people.

Arendt is often read as one of the twentieth century's principal theorists of ungrounded, self-enacted democratic politics. The political, she writes, brings the new into the world and perpetually returns us to "the problem of the beginning, of an unconnected, new event breaking into the continuous sequence of historical time" (205).[7] Because Arendt sees political freedom as being so inextricably bound to the "miracle" or "natality" of human action, some readers have suggested that she also sees established channels of political participation and governing norms of judgment as remaining always insufficient to action.[8] According to this view, while human *behavior* can be judged according to fixed moral or legal standards, that is not true of free political *action*, because "it is in its nature to break through the commonly accepted and reach into the extraordinary."[9] To Arendt the political must therefore be grasped as an "event," and in the modern age revolutions are "the only political events which confront us directly and inevitably with the problem of beginning" (21).

This said, Arendt was also one of the twentieth century's most nuanced critics of constituent power, the theoretical category most frequently invoked in contemporary democratic theory to account for this experience of historical rupture and the creation of a *novus ordo saeclorum*.[10] For reasons I will clarify below, I disagree with those who claim that Arendt was merely attempting to "tame" the theory of popular constituent power, or worse, that she dressed it up in an "abbot's frock."[11] In exploring and historically evaluating Arendt's reasons for rejecting a theory of popular constituent power in her comparative study of the American and French Revolutions, I will clarify my own understanding of postrevolutionary constituent moments.[12]

Arendt's discussion of constituent power in *On Revolution*—which Jeremy Waldron has rightly called her "most constitutionalist work"[13]— illuminates the theoretical and practical dilemmas that the concept poses to political modernity. She at once engages and resists the paradoxes of democratic legitimacy and collective political autonomy that I explored in the Introduction, paradoxes based in the inability of the people to give birth to themselves as a self-authorizing subject. Despite what some of her contemporary radical democratic admirers claim, Arendt did not affirm the productivity of democratic paradox in her account of beginnings and the natality of political action;[14] she is one of the sharpest critics of the "paradox of politics."[15] Arendt's critique of democratic paradox is moreover inseparable from her critique of constituent power. Both critiques are based in her attempt to provide a phenomenology of political freedom that is neither bound to the determinations of sovereignty and will—and the attending dangers of Schmittian decisionism—nor grounded in the rights-based foundationalism typically associated with neo-Kantian theories of political liberalism. To paraphrase Bonnie Honig's recent formulation, Arendt's approach to democratic paradox is neither decisionist in the radical democratic style of theorists like Ernesto Laclau and Chantal Mouffe, nor deliberationist in the style of neo-Kantian deliberative theorists like Seyla Benhabib and Jürgen Habermas.[16] There have been important attempts to position Arendt into one or another of these theoretical camps, to make her, in Albrecht Wellmer's words, "more amenable to contemporary democratic theory."[17] But in contrast to those preoccupied with paradox in contemporary democratic theory, Arendt aimed to free readers from the captivating grip of these theoretical *petitiones principiorum* and their attending obsession with foundation and ground, or what she called the misguided attempt to introduce an "absolute" into the political realm. Arendt's attempt to disenthrall readers from the spell of paradox and of the absolute is powerfully exemplified in her narrative celebration of the American Revolution and its sustained critique of constituent power.[18]

The problem with Arendt's account, as indicated above, is that dilemmas associated with constituent power *were* an important aspect of postrevolutionary American politics. In posing a series of critical questions to Arendt's historical interpretation of American revolutionary and postrevolutionary experience, I aim not merely to indicate historical inaccuracies in Arendt's narrative—her account has been described as "notably fabulist"[19]—but instead to argue that Arendt is inaccurate for theoretically interesting and productive reasons. In *On Revolution* Arendt delineates a Tocquevillean contrast between the American revolutionary experience of "mutual promising" and the French revolutionary invocation of unified national will. That contrast ultimately veils the dilemmas of popular authorization created by the American Revolution and its very different invocation of a dispersed and interpretive, as opposed to centralized and willful, understanding of constituent power. In revolutionary and postrevolutionary America the dilemmas of collective self-authorization associated with constituent power were politically navigated through a layered complexity of diverse political cultures and overlapping jurisdictions (Sheldon Wolin describes this political plurality as "labyrinthine")[20] and by a productive ambiguity over who speaks in the people's name. The ambiguity is politically productive in the sense that it elicited transformative forms of political contention over who is authorized to speak on the people's behalf. As detailed above, it is not that dilemmas of authorization failed ever to be raised in the American context—one of Arendt's central claims—but that they were dispersed across a porous terrain of public authority that did not terminate in the final instance of sovereign command. This is very different from Arendt's claim that "perhaps the greatest [American] innovation in politics as such was the consistent abolition of sovereignty within the body politic of the republic" (153). Despite Arendt's central claims in *On Revolution*, revolutionary and postrevolutionary American political culture was marked by a continuing contest over competing "sources of authority regarding the interpretation and application of law," over competing claims of popular authorization.[21] Arendt too quickly subsumes these forms of popular contention under a consensual practice of "mutual promising," and under the persistence of formal legality.

Arendt's failure to recognize constituent power's importance to American popular constitutionalism is surprising when viewed from the perspective of the history of American political thought. R. R. Palmer, for example, writes that constituent power was the American Revolution's "most distinctive contribution to the world's stock of political ideas."[22] Gordon Wood similarly claims that the eighteenth-century American idea of a sovereignty permanently located in the people at large marked "one of the most creative moments in the history of political thought."

Willi Paul Adams, dating the first English use of the term "constituent power" to the debates over Vermont statehood, claims that Americans invented not only the concept of constituent power "but also the name for it."[23] These are all contestable historical claims, but they effectively highlight constituent power's centrality to the American revolutionary and postrevolutionary experience. Moreover, rather than trace the intellectual origins of the concept of constituent power to theorists such as Thomas Hobbes, George Lawson, John Locke, and the radical Leveller tracts of the 1640s, these historians of American political thought have typically emphasized how the conceptual innovations associated with constituent power emerged gradually from two decades of practical innovations in the quasi-legal politics of the "people out of doors," in the revolutionary politics of committees, conventions, popular juries, and crowds. As I have argued above, in the colonists' political struggles with Parliament and Crown over fundamental questions of constitutional interpretation, they enshrined, first tacitly and then explicitly, the people as the ultimate locus of *interpretive* constitutional authority;[24] this was the discursive precondition for identifying the people as an agency of constitution-*making* power, a constituent power as generally understood.

In portraying the American revolutionaries as wholly liberated from the logics of sovereignty and the "absolute" of constituent power, Arendt wrongly describes both their experience and the exemplary potential of that experience for contemporary democratic theory. Arendt's dichotomous presentation of the American and French cases leaves out an unexplored option, found in the productive reiteration of popular constituent power in a federal American environment of overlapping jurisdictions and contested institutional improvisations. After the Revolution this reiteration took the form of a culture of popular constitutionalism partly engendered by the ambiguity of who counts as the people, and by the political contests over who is authorized to speak in their name. Postrevolutionary practices of popular constitutionalism enacted a participatory, expansive, and agonistic form of political subjectification differing significantly from the theory of constitutional augmentation that Arendt derives from her reading of the American Revolution. I will suggest in conclusion, however, that even if the practices of political subjectification associated with constituent power go underemphasized in *On*

Revolution, they resonate with other key moments in Arendt's work, in particular a set of provocative arguments in her late essay "Civil Disobedience."

I

The revolutions . . . occurred within a tradition which was partly founded on an event in which the 'word had become flesh.' . . . Authority as such had become unthinkable without some sort of religious sanction. HANNAH ARENDT, *On Revolution* (160)

Arendt's discussion of constituent power in *On Revolution* occurs in a chapter that wrestles with "the most troublesome of all problems in revolutionary government, the problem of an absolute" (158). Arendt saw the absolute as a temptation for revolutionaries who had irrevocably broken with the normative order of the ancien régime, yet found themselves struggling to legitimate their creation of a new normative order, no longer able to rely on the heteronomic supports of traditional authority or transcendental appeals to divine sanction. Arendt, like so many German intellectuals of her generation, regarded this as a problem of political theology, poetically captured in the revolutionary slogan *vox populi, vox Dei* (160). As the quotation above makes clear, the politico-theological demand for transcendental supports of worldly authority preoccupied even the revolutionaries most intent on creating a new political order based in popular self-determination itself. For Arendt this requirement was based in an illegitimate theological identification of law with command.

The best-known revolutionary theorist of this problem was the Abbé Sieyès, thanks to his attempt in "What Is the Third Estate?" to ground the legitimacy of the acts of the French National Assembly in the constituent power, as opposed to constituted power, of the people or nation. The paradoxical dilemma that Sieyès faced was not his alone. Rousseau had called it the "great problem of politics": how to make the people the origin of law, yet not place the people above the law.[25] Attempting to constitute a new popular government, but "having no authority to do what they set out to achieve," modern revolutionaries sought "an external source to bestow legality upon them and to transcend as a higher law the legislative act itself" (161). To justify their formally illegal acts revolutionaries sought refuge in the legally transcendent authority of an absolute.

Arendt therefore saw Sieyès's theory of *pouvoir constituent* as a way *out* of the dilemma posed by this paradox or vicious circle: "Sieyès, who in the field of theory, had no peer among the men of the French Revolution, broke the vicious circle . . . first by drawing his famous distinction between a *pouvoir constituent* and a *pouvoir constituè* and, second, by putting the *pouvoir constituent*, that is, the nation, into a perpetual 'state of nature' . . . Both power and law were anchored in the nation, or rather in the will of the nation, which itself remained outside and above all governments and all laws" (163). Arendt understood Sieyès's purported "solution" to the paradox of preconstitutional legitimacy as a disastrous mistake. Alongside Arendt's better-known claims about the "rise of the social" and its catastrophic role in the French Revolution is a corresponding critique of the Revolution's Rousseauian affirmation of unified sovereign will and its terroristic legacies in what she called the history of "revolutionary nationalism." The nation was, Arendt writes, "the cheapest and the most dangerous disguise the absolute ever obtained in the political realm" (195). Sieyès wrote that constituent power was the nation's "greatest and most important" power, and while carrying out this function, the nation must be "free from all constraints, from any form."[26]

The emphasis that Sieyès placed on the formless form-giving power of the nation is essential to most theories of constituent power that follow his, most influentially that of Carl Schmitt.[27] In *Constitutional Theory* Schmitt defines constituent power (*die verfassunggebenden Gewalt*) as "the political will whose power or authority is capable of adopting the concrete global decision on the mode and form of political existence."[28] Schmitt likens constituent power to an unstructured "Urgrund," or "formless formative capacity."[29] It is an "absolute beginning" that springs out of "normative nothingness and from concrete disorder." Schmitt believed that eighteenth-century revolutionary theories of constituent power, with their insistence on absolute beginning and willful self-creation, were living rebukes to Enlightenment rationalism. Their political rearticulation of a willful god capable of creating a world *ex nihilo* and establishing an order without being subject to it was the paradigmatic modern instance of the "state of exception." Like Arendt, Schmitt believed that the revolutionary slogan *vox populi, vox Dei* powerfully exemplified the willful political theology that underwrote the eighteenth-century revolutions, in which, in Schmitt's words, "the aftereffects of the Christian theological images of God's constituting powers, despite all clarification, were still strong and vital."[30] However, as Schmitt made clear in his critical genealogies of modern constitutionalism, this originary power was quickly disavowed by the same constitutional orders that these revolutions founded. This point was in fact a central component of Schmitt's critique of liberal constitutionalism, which he believed could not account for the legitimacy of the political will that created it and thereby could not recognize how this extraconstitutional and normatively unjustified will subtended or haunted existing constitutional arrangements. As William Scheuerman has written, for Schmitt "liberalism's failure to take constituent power seriously, to look into its own troubled (normatively unjustified) origins is . . . its Achilles heel."[31]

This Schmittian theological insistence on normatively unbound and unified will—the decision "in its absolute purity"—obscures for contemporary democratic theory how constituent power was practiced and conceptualized in eighteenth-century America, and may also have prevented Arendt from recognizing the central role that it played. Arendt's critical account of constituent power in *On Revolution* seems captivated by the concept's distinctly Schmittian articulation as a *potestas legibus soluta*. Her discussion of Sieyès's theory of constituent power corresponds very closely with Schmitt's in *Constitutional Theory*, and the same can be said of her contrast of the American and French cases around the legal question of constituent power. In his account of this contrast Schmitt argues that revolutionary Americans had not yet formulated the "new principle" of constituent power with "complete clarity," because "a new political formation arose and the act of constitution making converged with the political founding of a series of new *states*."[32] The combined American focus on founding states and constitutions—celebrated by Arendt as the American *constitutio libertatis*—was derided by Schmitt because it obscured the self-awareness of constituent power's "formless formative capacity." In Schmitt's view it was the revolutionary French who discovered the "fundamental novelty of such a process . . . [and] with complete awareness . . . took its destiny into its hands and reached a free decision on the type and form of political existence." It was the French who discovered the nation as the constituent subject. Whereas Schmitt thereby decried the failure of revolutionary Americans to experience the groundlessness of their act of collective self-determination, to experience a willful "absolute beginning," Arendt celebrated revolutionary Americans on this very basis. For revolutionary Americans, she writes, "there existed no gap, no hiatus, hardly a breathing spell between the war of liberation, the fight of independence which was the condition of freedom, and the constitution of the new state."[33] Arendt follows Schmitt's analysis in this distinction, but then comes to the very opposite evaluation. Schmitt celebrates the French discovery of national constituent power and then ridicules the American failure to directly confront it, while Arendt affirms what she considers that practical superiority of revolutionary Americans in not being captivated and paralyzed by a false politico-theological problem.

In a rare acknowledgment of Schmitt's work, Arendt described him as "the most able defender of the notion of sovereignty," one who clearly recognized that "the root of sovereignty is the will; Sovereign is who wills and commands."[34] The Schmittian dimension of Arendt's critical account of constituent power resonates with her insistence that Sieyès's invocation of the people is identical to an invocation of a unitary national will, and her emphasis on its purely exceptional status in relation to established law. "The constituent power in France was identified with the changing will of the mobilized multitude, on which no stable rule of law could be erected, culminating in a permanent political reservation and threat in the face of all constituted powers" (207). (Arendt distinguishes this "*mobilized* multitude" from the admirably "*organized* multitude" she finds in America.) Arendt saw the resulting foundation of law and power in popular will as inaugurating a familiar self-destructive dynamic — central to liberal interpretations of the French Revolution from Tocqueville to François Furet — that saw the Jacobins and then Napoleon making good on this "permanent political reservation and threat" and setting out to destroy the established constitutional government in the people's name.[35] "The will of the multitude," Arendt concludes, "is everchanging by definition. A structure built on it as its foundation is built upon quicksand" (163).

Although Arendt believed that this self-consuming dynamic of the French experience sharply contrasted with that of their revolutionary American counterparts, she recognized that it was nonetheless a contrast based in a surface commonality. The "conviction that the source and origin of power resides in the people" was "the one tenet that the men of the two eighteenth century revolutions held in common" (179). Arendt

believed that this shared tenet was enacted in two fundamentally different practical and legal contexts. *Le peuple* "were neither organized nor
constituted" but were instead a "natural force which in its very violence
had been released by the revolution and like a hurricane had swept away
all the institutions of the *ancien régime*" (181). Arendt's association of *le
peuple* with a natural force invokes her familiar antipolitical set of associations with the realm of necessity, the body, and the social. Indeed the
French invocation of le peuple was disastrous not only in positing a unified sovereign will outside the bounds of law but also in its intimate association with the poor and their pressing demands to alleviate the misery
of their physical condition. While in *Origins of Totalitarianism* Arendt still
had a positive appreciation for "the Revolutionary ideal of the people,"
noting for example the "fundamental error [during the Dreyfus affair]
of regarding the mob as identical with the people,"[36] by the time of *On
Revolution* she closely associated the French invocation of le peuple with
moblike immediacy and the collapse of the worldly relational spaces in
which political freedom could be enacted and appear. Because of this,
she writes, "it is by no means merely a matter of misguided theory that
the French concept of *le peuple* has carried, from its beginning, the con-
notation of a multiheaded monster, a mass that moves as one body and
acts as though possessed of one will" (94). In *On Revolution*, as Arendt's
critics have often recognized, the poor are always "streaming" and "teem-
ing," bringing the demands of the body and its needs out of the private
realm and into the public light.

While there are suggestive parallels between Schmitt's and Arendt's
understandings of the American and French Revolutions, Arendt also
followed Tocqueville's analysis in *Democracy in America*, believing not
only that colonial America lacked poverty, and therefore was not absorbed by "the social question," but also that there were two additional
reasons why revolutionary Americans avoided the paradox of popular
authorization attending the French Revolution and its appeal to the absolute of popular constituent power. The more important was the historical
background of American colonial experiments in self-government; the
second was that American revolutionaries did not overturn a political
absolutism but instead a constitutional monarchy with attending limits
on state power.[37] It was by this threefold "good fortune," according to
Arendt, that Americans were not thrown into a state of nature by their

revolutionary experience, and not captivated by the attending paradoxical dynamics of constituent power (165). The American Revolution
merely "liberated the power of covenant and constitution making as it
had shown itself in the earliest days of colonization" (168). The point
is made even more baldly—and less tenably—in Arendt's earlier essay
"What Is Authority?": "The framing of the Constitution, falling back on
existing charters and agreements, confirmed and legalized an already
existing body politic rather than made it anew. Thus the actors of the
American Revolution were spared the effort of 'initiating a new order
of things.'"[38] Arendt would qualify this view slightly in *On Revolution*,
in which she emphasized that while the American Revolution began as
an act of "restoration or renovation," the experience of public freedom
generated from their rebellion helped the revolutionaries to appreciate
their own powers of political initiation. Arendt suggests that the very
fact that "the concern with stability and the spirit of the new . . . have
become opposites in our political thought and terminology . . . must be
recognized to be among the symptoms of our loss" (223). Like the liberated French, revolutionary Americans encountered what Arendt called
"the abyss of freedom," but instead of being trapped in the metaphysical
coils of a posited absolute beginning, paralyzed by the paradox of founding, they admirably navigated these dilemmas *in medias res*.[39] While it
is "characteristic of human action . . . that it always begins something
new," she would later write, "this does not mean that it is ever permitted
to start *ab ovo*, to create *ex nihilo*."[40] Summarizing these qualifications,
Andreas Kalyvas has accurately described Arendt as a "theorist of relative
new beginnings."[41]

For all her emphasis on the unprecedented event and the groundless "abyss of freedom," Arendt's focus throughout her discussion of the
American Revolution is on practical or experiential continuity on the one
hand and theoretical misapprehension of that experience on the other.
Revolutionary Americans, in Arendt's account, never wrestled with the
dilemmas of collective self-authorization that pervade constituent moments and the competing claims of authorization that these dilemmas
bring about. As we have seen, however, the problem of the new and the
paradoxes of constituent power were a persistent problem for revolutionary and postrevolutionary Americans, one of the central theoretical
dilemmas that underwrote the period's political debates, right up to and

including the debates over constitutional ratification itself. To provide an orienting example of ungrounded political freedom that remains none-theless untouched by the violent arbitrariness of the exception, or by what Derrida has called the "mystical foundation of authority," Arendt cleansed the postrevolutionary years of their agonism by attributing to the revolutionaries a consensual avoidance of the dilemmas of constitu-ent power through an overly sharp and ultimately anachronistic distinc-tion between power and law.[42]

II

The very concept of Roman authority suggests that the act of foundation inevitably develops its own stability and permanence, and authority in this context is nothing more or less than a kind of necessary "augmentation" by virtue of which all innovations and changes remain tied back to the foundation which, at the same time, they augment and increase.   HANNAH ARENDT, *On Revolution* (202)

Although Arendt concedes that both American and French revolution-aries appealed to the sovereignty of the people, the Americans, in her account, made a sharp distinction between the people as the source of all power and the people as the source of law. The Americans, Arendt writes, were "an organized multitude" [again, as opposed to a "mobilized multitude"] "whose power was exerted in accordance to law and lim-ited by them" (166). Many historians, preeminent among them Pauline Maier, have also emphasized the extent to which Americans undertook resistance, rebellion, and revolution "under the rubric of legality."[43] Yet the doctrine of "always under law" did not erase tensions between popular power and popularly authorized law. Maier, for example, insists again and again on the centrality of "quasi-legal" institutions like con-ventions, committees, and crowds, and the ever-changing relationship between law and power during the era. Containing the actions of the revolutionaries within the limits of a pre-given law which need only be applied to changing political circumstances veils the performative and improvisational aspects of their political enactments. It also obscures the sharply agonistic politics that often attended these enactments, particu-larly in the postrevolutionary years and in the politically volatile decade following ratification.[44] As detailed in later chapters, Shays's Rebellion, Anti-Federalism, the "self-created" Democratic Republican Societies of the 1790s, and the Whiskey Rebellion all exemplify the contention that emerged around competing claims to speak in the people's name, and to do so under the rubric of *contested* legality.

In contrast to Arendt's historical account, the political-legal practices of revolutionary and postrevolutionary American popular constitutionalism regularly *obscured* the distinction between popular power and law. In these practices, the people were envisioned as the source of constitutional authority, but it was a source, as we have seen, that was itself the locus of ongoing political contest. Shannon Stimson has argued that what most clearly distinguished revolutionary American jurisprudence from England's was the blurring of the line between popular power and law in the institutions of popular juries. The ubiquitous question "who shall judge?" was unequivocally answered in these years by "the people," and their judgments applied not only to the application of law but to its content and constitutionality. Stimson writes, "The claim that 'the people' retain, and should know they retain in the final analysis, the supreme say regarding the rightful exercise of power delegated to the government was the central claim of the colonial pamphleteers . . . the very core of the colonials' 'revolution principle' as explicitly and repeatedly reiterated in election sermons, popular pamphlets, and newspapers was 'the people's' capacity . . . to challenge law."[45] The sharp contrast that Arendt draws between power and law leads her too quickly to dismiss this crucial aspect of American revolutionary experience, and to neglect its subsequent legacy. Her dismissive discussion of the inheritance of revolutionary "lawlessness" is uncharacteristically one-dimensional, and largely relegated to the footnotes of *On Revolution*. She simply declares its "anti-revolutionary" dimensions and states that in the "context" of *On Revolution* such "so-called revolutionary trends can be neglected" (320). The legal consensus emphasized in *On Revolution* masks the centrality of these contests to postrevolutionary political experience.

Arendt's claims concerning the abolition of popular constituent power and the forms of contention that emerged around it in revolutionary America[46] are clearly and compactly expressed in the following passage, which I quote in full since I will refer to it as the basis for further evaluating her central claims:

> The framers of the American constitution, although they knew they had to establish a new source of law and to devise a new system of power, were

never even tempted to derive law and power from the same origin. The seat of power to them was the people, but the source of law was to become the constitution, a written document, an endurable objective thing, which, to be sure, one could approach from many different angles and upon which one could impose many different interpretations, which one could change and amend in accord with circumstances, but which nevertheless was never a subjective state of mind, like the will. It has remained a tangible worldly entity of greater durability than elections or opinion polls. Even when, at a comparatively late date, and presumably under the influence of Continental constitutional theory, the supremacy of the constitution was argued 'on the ground solely of its rootage in popular will,' it was felt that, once the decision was taken, it remained binding for the body politic to which it gave birth; and even if there were people who reasoned that in a free government the people must retain the power [quoting Benjamin Hitchborn] 'at any time, for any cause or for no cause, but their own sovereign pleasure, to alter or annihilate both the mode and the essence of any former government and adopt a new one in its stead,' they remained rather lonely figures in the Assembly. In this, as in other cases, what appeared in France as a genuine political or even philosophical problem came to the fore during the American Revolution in such an unequivocally vulgar form that it was discredited before anybody bothered to make a theory out of it. (157)

Revolutionary Americans avoided the vicious circle of popular legal authorization not by appeal to constituent power as an extralegal absolute but, on the contrary, by never acknowledging it as a vicious circle in the first place. Two points seem of particular importance. The first is Arendt's claim that in America the source of law was to be in the written constitution rather than the people; the second is her claim that the appeal to constituent power came "late" in America and "presumably under the influence of Continental constitutional theory," and therefore never generated for American revolutionaries a "genuine political or even philosophical problem." I will take up each of these points in turn.

Arendt's affirmation of the written constitution rather than the people as the source of law leaves unanswered the question of the ultimate legality of constitutional law, or rather where the ultimate interpretive authority for determining that legality would be located (166). The traditions of American popular constitutionalism took the people themselves to be the ultimate authority on questions of legal interpretation, but there was no clear consensus on who made up that people or how their power could be represented or enacted. Americans, unlike the French for Arendt, "distinguished clearly and unequivocally between the origin of power, which springs from below . . . and the source of law, who [*sic*] seat is above, in some higher and transcendent region" (182). According to Arendt, this ultimate source of law was left productively vague in the American context and never seriously questioned or contested. It was the Americans' "good fortune," for example, that there was "never any serious questioning of the *pouvoir constituent* of those who framed the state constitutions and, eventually, the Constitution of the United States" (165). But even a passing familiarity with the ratification debates shows that the *pouvoir constituent* of those who met in Philadelphia was regularly questioned by their Anti-Federalist opponents.[47] Madison openly wrestled with this question in the *Federalist Papers*, most powerfully in no. 40.[48] Most remarkably, Arendt claims that "the political genius of the American people," or the "great good fortune which smiled upon the American republic," consisted in a certain "blindness" of the American people into these fraught and contested origins, in their "extraordinary capacity to look upon yesterday with the eyes of centuries to come" (198).

This provocative and relatively unexplored claim suggests that Arendt's neglect of the problem of constituent power in revolutionary and post-revolutionary America, and of the contentious politics surrounding it, may be an intentional emulation of this admirable American "blindness," a pragmatic consideration not to dig too deeply into the unavailable foundations of constitutional authority (and, relatedly, to define the people more precisely as the basis of constitutional authorship). Arendt's praise of a certain "blindness" to probing too deeply into the unanswerable question of the absolute of the *vox populi* should be read alongside other attempts in her work to free readers from the ultimately nihilistic grip of such paralyzing pursuits, as in her account of the French Revolution's all-consuming drive to unmask hypocrisy, or her discussion in *The Human Condition* of how the Cartesian quest for certainty and the Archimedean point culminates in modern world alienation. All these accounts derive from a broadly Nietzschean understanding of how the quest for the transcendental or the absolute beyond appearances ironically culminates in a consuming nihilism.[49] Translated into the terms of constitutional authority in *On Revolution*, this avoidance of self-consuming quests for absolute foundation seems to entail a not fully justified reverence for a constitutional tradition. Arendt approvingly quotes John Adams's claim that "a constitution is a standard, a pillar, and a bond when it is understood, approved and beloved. But without this intelligence and attachment, it might as well be a kite or a balloon, flying in the air" (146). In contrast to most contemporary democratic and constitutional theory, this attachment comes from "remembrance," not from philosophical justification: "The authority of the republic will be safe and intact as long as the act itself, the beginning as such, is remembered whenever constitutional questions in the narrower sense of the word come into play" (165). It was through remembrance of this purportedly consensual act — of the people deliberately founding a new body politic — that the constitution was shrouded in "an atmosphere of reverent awe which has shielded both event and document against the onslaught of time and changed circumstances" (204). These imagined stories of remembrance — which Arendt compares while not wholly identifying with founding myths — help constitute the authority of the constitutional order and exemplify how the "human mind" has attempted to navigate the dilemmas associated with beginning (205). I will return to this theme again in the Conclusion.

There is another important aspect of Arendt's argument that supports this emphasis on practical continuity and imaginative attachment as the basis of constitutional authority. Arendt frankly admires American constitution worship, which for her revolved around the authority of the act of foundation and the constitutional reiteration of this act, through what Arendt describes as the process of "augmentation." The reiteration of revolution, Arendt suggests, comes in periodic acts of constitutional augmentation similar to the Roman return to founding principles. Arendt develops her theory of augmentation most thoroughly in "What Is Authority?" In this exploration of the republican theory of civic foundation, Arendt notes that *auctoritas* itself is derived from the Latin *augere*, to augment.[50] But where Arendt believes that the Roman trinity of authority, tradition, and religion has been irretrievably severed in the modern age, she also seems to "recognize the unique possibilities of another kind of authority" in American constitutionalism.[51] "The very authority of the American constitution resides in its inherent capacity to be amended and augmented" (202). But by Arendt's account this historical process of amendment and augmentation is not itself the object of political struggle and debate. How this process of augmentation is to occur, and according to what preconstituted procedures and rules, is an important and unresolved political question in the period,[52] and a question that quickly returns to the neglected dilemmas of self-authorization associated with popular constituent power. Arendt's distinction between the French and the American approaches to the people as the source of power and the source of law is ultimately based on a rather narrow conception of constitutionalism—one surprisingly governmental in its focus for a theorist who so clearly values, in at least some of her work, the democratic resources of extra-institutional politics.[53] One important issue at stake here is Arendt's largely unqualified embrace in *On Revolution* of the doctrine of judicial supremacy and her understanding of the Supreme Court as "the true seat of authority in the American republic," or as she approvingly (mis)quotes Woodrow Wilson, "a kind of Constitutional Assembly in continuous session" (200). While not a legal positivist, in *On Revolution* Arendt nonetheless subsumes constituent power within the formal institutions of the judiciary and embraces a practical correspondence— she calls it a "working reality"—between the people and the law that organizes them.[54]

This formal correspondence of the people and the law is related to how Arendt envisions the significance of the constitution's writtenness. The emphasis placed on writing constitutional charters in the 1770s and 1780s indicated an important postrevolutionary American innovation in modern constitutionalism. To Arendt this emphasis made the constitutions "objective endurable things," and in contrast to the volatile immediacy of will or voice, postrevolutionary American written constitutions created a durable space of mediation in and through which political freedom could appear. (Arendt does, however, criticize the United States Constitution in the concluding chapter of *On Revolution* for not literally instituting spaces of political freedom—Jefferson's ward government.) The textuality of the constitutions also solved another important problem for postrevolutionary Americans, one related to their preoccupations with constituent power. Michael Warner has persuasively argued that the textualization of popular voice in the form of written constitutions provided a much-needed mediating stability to a postrevolutionary political culture characterized by other more immediate enactments of popular voice (in the form of conventions, committees, popular juries, and crowds).[55] Far from being self-sufficient or self-authorizing documents, the postrevolutionary constitutions frequently point to an authority beyond themselves for their authority, most obviously exemplified in the Preamble's invocation of "We the People." The writtenness of the early American constitutions has been frequently discussed, but less often noted is that this writtenness frequently referred beyond itself to an external voice to authorize its statements. These are texts, in other words, that generate legal authority by referring to their own incompleteness. Like many liberal constitutional scholars, Arendt, at least in *On Revolution*, invokes the people as a reservoir of lawmaking power that is enacted and organized solely through the constitutional amendment process. Eighteenth-century Americans, in contrast, saw the people as an interpreting and enforcing power as well, one exercised in many ways, not only through formal amendment procedures. Larry Kramer's recent comments directed at contemporary constitutional theorists seem to apply equally to Arendt: "Contemporary commentators tend to assume not only that someone must have final authority over constitutional questions, but that this someone must be a particular government agency."[56]

Another of Arendt's central arguments about the avoidance of the dilemmas of constituent power in revolutionary and postrevolutionary America centers on her claim that the experience of political freedom and "public happiness" engendered by the American Revolution has been lost to historical memory because it was never given an institutional location and an attending theoretical vocabulary. Revolutionary Americans could not account for the novelty of their experience because they remained tied to "the narrow and tradition-bound framework of their general concepts," mystified by inherited and obsolete theoretical vocabularies, especially those of sovereignty and contract (195). This claim disorients contemporary historical sensibilities conditioned by three decades of historiography since the linguistic turn. Arendt's repeated emphasis on the category of "experience" and her celebration of the "sound realism" and "common sense" of revolutionary Americans may seem to place her among other celebrants of American exceptionalism and the "genius" of American political pragmatism who wrote in the 1950s. Yet this simple equation is misleading. Arendt explicitly dismissed the analysis of liberal consensus writers like Daniel Boorstin, who insisted that the "genius" of American politics lay in its purported avoidance of theory or ideology. Although Arendt did not share Boorstin's epistemologically naïve reification of immediate "experience," she does emphasize that the novelty of the revolutionaries' practical experience dramatically exceeded their relatively meager innovations in thought (219, 195).[57] There remains in much of Arendt's work a troubling distinction between theory and practice, which becomes acute in her critical discussion of constituent power in *On Revolution*: "It was experience . . . rather than theory or learning, that taught the men of the Revolution the real meaning of the Roman's *potestas in populo*, that power resides in the people" (178). The "real meaning" of *potestas in populo*, as opposed to its theoretical mystification in the concept of constituent power, derived from what Arendt describes as the early American encounter with the "grammar" of human action related to "mutual pledging" or "promising." In her account of the revolutionary American experiment in "mutual promising," Arendt offers an exemplary alternative to what she considers the mystifying rubric of popular sovereignty and the paradoxical dynamics that inhabit it.

As with her return in *The Human Condition* to ancient Greek politics instead of ancient Greek political philosophy, in *On Revolution* Arendt sought to recover an authenticity of political experience among American revolutionaries before it was distorted by traditional theoretical vocabularies. Through this act of theoretical recovery, Arendt hoped to offer an orienting historical exemplar. Had Americans succumbed entirely to obsolete theoretical frameworks and remained tied to the "bondage of tradition," she writes, they too would have "crumbled under the onslaught of modernity" (196). I take Arendt to be referring to the perpetual crisis of political authority triggered by a corrosive search for foundations that simply are not there. In the American revolutionary compacts it is "events rather than theories or traditions that we are confronted with" (172). Arendt's invocation of the "elementary grammar of political action" indicates the phenomenological dimension of these "events" for her:

> Nothing but the simple and obvious insight into the elementary structure of joint enterprises as such, the need "for the better encouragement of ourselves and others that shall joyne with us in this action," caused these

[early American] men to become obsessed with the notion of compact and prompted them again and again "to promise and bind" themselves to one another. No theory, theological or political or philosophical, but their own decision to leave the Old World behind and venture forth into an enterprise entirely of their own led into a sequence of acts and occurrences in which they would have perished had they not turned their minds to the matter long and intensely enough to discover, almost by inadvertence, the elementary grammar of political action and its more complicated syntax, whose rules determine the rise and fall of human power. (173)

By grammar of action Arendt means that "action is the only human faculty that demands a plurality of men"; by syntax she means that "power is the only human attribute which applies solely to the in-between space by which men are mutually related" (175). The grammar and syntax combine in the act of foundation by virtue of the making and the keeping of promises, which in the realm of politics "may well be the highest human faculty" (175). Arendt's account of mutual promising or pledging in revolutionary America therefore replaces the inherited and purportedly misleading theoretical abstractions of sovereignty and consent and the paradoxes associated with them.

Arendt's controversial attempt on the one hand to categorically separate law from power, and on the other to isolate American political experience from its misleading reliance on inherited vocabularies of popular sovereignty, is an elaboration of her broader attempt to provide a theory of political freedom irreducible to sovereignty or will. "Under human conditions, which are determined by the fact that not man but men live on the earth, freedom and sovereignty are so little identical that they cannot even exist simultaneously. Where men wish to be sovereign, as individuals or as organized groups, they must submit to the oppression of the will, be this the individual will with which I force myself, or the 'general will.'"[58] Rather than try to contain sovereignty in a rights-based normativity or formal proceduralism, however, Arendt hoped through her retelling of the practical actions of the revolutionaries to disenthrall readers from the dynamics and paradoxes of sovereignty in the first place, perhaps most especially those paradoxes that lead the theoretical imagination to become enamored with the misleading rubrics of norm and exception. "If men wish to be free, it is precisely sovereignty they must renounce."[59] Yet the revolutionary Americans whom Arendt admired did not renounce sovereignty, but neither did they simply embrace it. Instead they appealed to the people's constituent power as an abiding resource of political contention and popular revitalization, inaugurating claims that could not be justified in advance of the contentious practice of claiming them.

III

It is so difficult to find the *beginning*. Or, better: it is difficult to begin at the beginning. And not try to go further back.   LUDWIG WITTGENSTEIN, *On Certainty*[60]

While emphasizing practical and experiential continuity, Arendt does acknowledge the heteronomy of beginnings in *On Revolution*. "It is in the very nature of a beginning to carry within itself a measure of complete arbitrariness. Not only is [the beginning] not bound into a reliable chain of cause and effect, the beginning has, as it were, nothing whatsoever to hold on to" (206). Yet Arendt goes to great lengths to counter what she calls "the age-old [yet] still current notions of the dictating violence of all beginnings" (213). In fact the overarching theme of *On Revolution* is announced in its opening pages: how to break with the biblical injunction that "whatever brotherhood human beings may be capable of has grown out of fratricide, whatever political organization men may have achieved has its origin in crime" (20). In Arendt's view the American revolutionaries were ultimately saved from this introduction of the arbitrary and the violence of the absolute by the introduction of a different kind of absolute, one that must be distinguished from constituent power and that she regards as a "principle" immanent to the action of founding itself. "The absolute from which the beginning is to derive its own validity and which must save it, as it were, from its inherent arbitrariness, is the principle which, together with it, makes its appearance in the world . . . The principle which came to light during those fateful years when the foundations were laid—not by the strength of one architect but by the combined power of the many—was the interconnected principle of mutual promise and common deliberation" (212). According to Arendt, it is this principle, rather than an "Immortal Legislator" or "self-evident truth," or any other "transcendent, transmundane source" (204), that becomes the ultimate source of authority for the American founders.

Deliberative democratic theorists have sometimes cited the passage just quoted as proof that Arendt was a proponent (or at least a proto-theorist) of a normative proceduralism; in some instances they have even tried to equate this invocation of principle to the praxis-immanent principles of universal pragmatics or communicative rationality.[61] The passage would seem, for example, to approximate Seyla Benhabib's account of a hermeneutic circle in which we "presuppose the recognition of one another's moral rights" to inaugurate the process of discursive legitimation, yet in which these rights themselves are also "specified as a result of the discursive situation."[62] David Ingram has offered something like this interpretation of the passage.[63] Andrew Arato has taken up a slightly different interpretation, arguing that Arendt's invocation of political principle as the basis of democratic legitimacy was one of her central insights. "The advantage of focusing on principles is that it allows us when choosing or evaluating an approach today to focus not on the choice of a model or a concrete type of organization but rather the plurality of principles plausibly used to legitimate the results produced by a variety of historical experiences."[64] This is because "a principle, unlike a rule or legal model, is not generally derived from preexisting legal norms . . . Thus [principles] have the advantage of being able to draw on moral resources that have not been formalized and that are available when appeal to legal resources would inevitably turn circular at moments of foundation."[65] In this reading the invocation of principle is a kind of guideline to aid in navigating the dilemmas of self-authorization that characterize constituent moments.

These interpretations pose a larger set of normative and philosophical difficulties that it is not my purpose to explore here. I want only to suggest that certain idiosyncrasies in Arendt's understanding of principle may not be accounted for in these interpretations, and may help to further illuminate the contours of her critique of constituent power. Principle is a much less foundational term for Arendt than it is for contemporary proponents of public reason. It is closer to ethos, style, or disposition than principal thought in the Kantian or neo-Kantian mode. In *The Life of the Mind* Arendt calls this immanent principle an "art of foundation" that enables actors to "navigate the perplexities intrinsic to every beginning."[66] She likens principle again and again to the virtuosity of a performing artist (in contrast to that of a master architect), and to Machiavelli's highly particular and aesthetic understanding of *virtú*.[67] Similarly, in "What Is Freedom?" Arendt distinguishes principle from a command or law that might order freedom and action. Drawing on the work of Montesquieu, Arendt sees principle as not dictated by a reason-giving intellect, or by the will, as it is in Kant, but claims instead that it "becomes manifest only in the performing act itself."[68] "Principle" involves what "inspirits" the concrete actions within the polity.[69] Arendt explicitly contrasts this to mere lawfulness, "which can only set limitations to action, and never inspires them" (64). The examples that she gives are honor and glory, love of equality (virtue), and distinction or excellence. This discussion of principle is directly connected to her account of the inspiring "spirit" of the Revolution, "public happiness," and the "revolutionary treasure." If this invocation of principle falls short of offering the kind of context-transcendent validity claims sought by neo-Kantian theorists of democratic deliberation, its emphasis on "inspiration" also seems more attentive to the motivation deficits that typically challenge these theories.[70]

Arendt's attempt to derive authority from a principle immanent to the act of founding itself, when read alongside her legalistic account of the Revolution and founding, also poses difficulties for those who read Arendt as a theorist of agonistic democracy. Bonnie Honig, in a well-known essay comparing Arendt's and Derrida's accounts of foundation, argues that Arendt's theory of augmentation works to generate authority through perpetual acts of "deauthorization."[71] I would argue that Arendt's attempt to escape the arbitrariness of these beginnings by appeal to immanent principle requires, in her account of the American Revolution, a unitary and consensual moment of mutual promising that is clearly at odds with this agonistic emphasis—agonism, as I have argued above, is largely written out of Arendt's account of postrevolutionary politics.[72] As demonstrated in the chapters that follow, there are different exemplary resources in the history of revolutionary and postrevolutionary American politics for agonistic democratic theorists than those Arendt provides in *On Revolution*. Arendt's theory of augmentation and mutual promising, built from her idiosyncratic historical account of the American Revolution and founding, replaces a focus on the captivating dilemmas posed by the problem of constituent power. Rather than posit a unitary people and nation that stands outside of law and is the fount of law, a notion of which Arendt was rightly critical, constituent power as enacted in post-revolutionary America was marked by productive ambiguity around the authorizing figure of the people. It was this constitutive ambiguity that in part prevented the people from becoming the kind of political absolute that Arendt so rightly feared, but that also sustained a much more agonistic democratic politics that her account of mutual promising in *On Revolution* allows.

What Arendt is surprisingly unable to see in her contrast between the unified French popular will and the American people's "manyness" is that for revolutionary Americans, invocations of the people came to signify *at one and the same time* the authority underlying the existing constituted order, and the power of those who were marginalized or somehow excluded in the name of that order. As I argue in the Introduction, in postrevolutionary America the *voice* of people was at once enacted through representation and thought to exceed the claims of any particular representation or institutional embodiment. This "double inscription" of the people establishes the conditions for the practice of democratic claims-making that are only ever authorized and vindicated after the fact of their proclamation or enactment. Arendt misses this dynamic, for example, when she describes the American appeal to the people as neither an absolute nor a fiction, but a "working reality of the organized multitude whose power was exerted in accordance with laws and limited by them" (166). True, the people weren't invoked as a unified nation above all legal authority, but "working reality" is invoked to do more theoretical work that it can bear. It veils the fraught and inherently contestable nature of democratic claims to speak in the name of a people that is not . . . yet.

He who takes the law into his own hands will render a service to justice only if he is willing to transform the situation in such a way that the law can again operate and his act can, at least posthumously, be validated.   HANNAH ARENDT, *Eichmann in Jerusalem*[73]

Arendt's neo-Roman theory of augmentation fails to fully account for the fraught and only retrospectively authorized dimensions of democratic claims-making associated with constituent moments. This is not true of

all of Arendt's work. At the conclusion of her long essay on civil disobedience, written in response to the American civil rights movement of the
1950s and to what she feared was the ideological perversion of the student and antiwar movements of the 1960s, Arendt clearly distinguishes
the collective activity of civil disobedience from the individualist and
Thoreauvian activity of the conscientious objector. She describes civil
disobedience as "nothing but the latest form of voluntary association
. . . quite in tune with the traditions of the country."[74] Arendt understood the multiform actions of civil disobedience—lunch counter sit-
ins, bus boycotts, street demonstrations, and more—as a continuation
of the practices of self-enacted mutual promising that she admired in the
Revolution. The difference, of course, is that these were illegal activities
directed against the unjust laws of the Jim Crow state. Arendt concedes
that although "civil disobedience is compatible with the *spirit* of American laws, the difficulties of incorporating it into the American legal system and justifying it on purely legal grounds seem prohibitive."[75] These
difficulties, she writes, "follow from the nature of law in general": the
law cannot justify the violation of law. Arendt asks in this essay whether
it would be possible to find a recognized "niche for civil disobedience in
our institutions of government." In reply to her own hypothetical question, Arendt turns to the Supreme Court's refusal to hear cases in which
the government's "illegal and unconstitutional acts" during the Vietnam
War were contested by the state of Massachusetts. Invoking the "political question doctrine," the Court decided that certain acts of the two
other "political branches of government" were not subject to judicial review. Arendt likened this dangerously extralegal invocation of the sovereign decision (quoting Graham Hughes) to "a smoldering volcano" that
threatened to erupt into "flaming controversy." Arendt sees this "loop-
hole through which the sovereignty principle and reason of state doctrine are able to filter back in" as illuminating the real limitations and
the "failure" of judicial review, an idiosyncrasy of American constitutionalism much admired in *On Revolution*. "The establishment of civil disobedience among our political institutions," Arendt suggestively writes,
"might be the best possible remedy for this ultimate failure."[76] That is, a
turn to civil disobedience appears here as a remedy for the limitations of
judicial review. It might be time to return to a serious consideration of
the consequences of this argument.

Here Arendt looks to the future possibility of a popular constitutionalism that actually had its roots in America's revolutionary past. Arendt
thought that the political "emergency" of the 1960s might provoke
Americans to find this "niche" for civil disobedience in democratic life,
but an earlier emergency had already found it: the Revolution itself.
Civil disobedience in this view is not, as Jeremy Waldron has recently
claimed, but a "despairing echo of constitutional politics," a "strange and
sad" symptom of its "lamentable decline,"[77] but a concrete instantiation
of political freedom. In seeking to return this political question of the
legality of law to a form of popular politics, Arendt in this late essay
allows a form of constituent power to reenter her theory through a considered reevaluation of the limits of judicial supremacy. The question to
ask in conclusion is whether the boundary that Arendt insists on maintaining between popular power and law could be maintained with such
categorical distinction once such constitutional questions were returned
"to the people themselves." Arendt's work suggests that the resources of
popular constitutionalism in American political history remain an ambiguous legacy. In several of her works Arendt approvingly quoted the
poet and French resistance fighter René Char: "our inheritance was left
to us by no testament." As for Char, so with us: we may not yet know
what it is we have inherited.[78]

Thy constitution, Chaos, is restor'd;
Law sinks before thy uncreating word;
Thy hand unbars th' unfathom'd gulf of fate,
And deep in darkness 'whelms the new-born state.
The Anarchiad (1787)[1]

Crowds and Communication

Representation and Voice in Postrevolutionary America

When Joel Barlow and the other "Connecticut Wits"—Lemuel Hopkins, David Humphreys, and John Trumbull—composed *The Anarchiad* in twelve installments between October 1786 and September 1787, America had been shaken by more than two decades of intensified political activity—much of it enacted outside formal channels of political participation. From the Stamp Act crisis of 1765 to Shays's Rebellion, begun in August 1786, widely participatory politics regularly drew people into the streets of America's cities and towns, and active political associations were forged even on the edges of the frontier. By the 1780s this explosion of revolutionary spirit was being widely condemned for the "chaos" that it threatened to unleash on public order and the possibilities of governance. Onetime proponents of extralegal political mobilization now worried, in Samuel Adams's words, that "self Created Conventions or Societies of men," while they had "served an excellent Purpose" in mobilizing the people against British rule, threatened to consume the "constitutional and regular governments" established in their wake.[2] Of particular concern was the "self created" authority of postrevolutionary crowds. In his *Circular to State Governments* (1783) George Washington prayed that God would "incline the hearts of the citizens to cultivate a spirit of subordination and obedience to government."[3] Barlow and his co-writers were not alone in fearing that "mobs in myriads" posed a real danger to the "Clerks, Lawyers, and Sheriffs" who secured the fragile institutions of "the new-born state."

The task of mobilizing the citizenry against popular insurgency was a difficult one. As Kimberly Smith has argued, "the suppression of popular rioting and the establishment of the value of rational argument were long-term projects that extended well into the nineteenth century."[4] Not only did large and diverse constituencies — men and women, black and white — participate at one time or another in these gatherings of the "people-out-of-doors," but these actions were justified in the political discourses of the American Revolution. "Eighteenth-century Americans," Pauline Maier writes, "accepted riots with remarkable ease," and they did so because these actions had acquired a "quasi-legal" status.[5] In this chapter I explore how ambivalence over the legitimacy of postrevolutionary crowds interacted with the ratio-critical communicative imperatives of the republican public sphere on the one hand, and attempts to establish representative governments on the other. As contested enactments of the *vox populi*, postrevolutionary crowds illuminate dilemmas of popular authorization at the heart of theories of democratic legitimacy; they are early iterations of the contested politics that emerge around constituent moments.

As such, the "democratic excess" of the crowd poses a challenge — theoretical and historical — to the Habermasian model of the public sphere applied to late-eighteenth-century America in recent years. First, the direct embodiment of crowd action — and the proclaimed authority of popular *voice* — challenged the formation of a disembodied and socially unmarked public based on rational argumentation, and enacted a different basis of authorization, albeit one still marked by contestation over the authority of its claims. Second, the deeply conflicted language of sympathy and affect, often associated with crowd gatherings, and later developed in nineteenth-century theories of crowd psychology, troubled attempts to consolidate a sociopolitical order based on a uniform politics of representation. The postrevolutionary American crowd was not simply what Charles Tilly characterizes as a "direct-action crowd"— directed against local targets (e.g. the local merchant) and motivated by limited goals (e.g. lowering the price of bread)—but a "representational crowd" based in the authority of a larger symbolic and normative entity: the voice of the people themselves.[6] Although the postrevolutionary crowd challenged emerging logics of political representation, it did not oppose to them the articulated immediacy or presence of sovereign voice. Instead it revealed the impossibility of definitively closing the gap between the established institutions of representative government and the people they claimed to represent.

Postrevolutionary crowds therefore enacted constituent moments in that their *claim* to embody popular voice broke from established procedures for popular representation. Yet in making this claim they also opened a space of political contention over what authoritatively constitutes such a representation in the first place. The key phrase "thy uncreating word," which recurs throughout *The Anarchiad* (an adaption of Pope's *Dunciad*), points not to the disorienting proliferation of printed texts during the period (as emphasized by scholars of the public sphere) but to the interruptions of a communicative economy based on representation, and to the emergence of an unruly democratic sensibility not codified into any given language or script; it points to that which formally and physically exceeded the consolidation of both institutionalized politics of representation and an orderly public sphere. What the voice of the postrevolutionary crowd ultimately communicates is the incompleteness of any governing schema of representation and the unsettling but also never fully present enactments of the vox populi.

I

Laws passed under the "pressure of the street" could hardly be understood any longer as embodying the reasonable consensus of publicly deliberating private persons.   JÜRGEN HABERMAS, *Structural Transformation of the Bourgeois Public Sphere*[7]

In the immediate postrevolutionary period there was a near-consensus among patriot writers (who would later be riven by intransigent political conflicts) that an open public sphere was necessary to the survival of the republic. We see this view powerfully articulated in John Adams's well-known essay arguing against the canon and feudal laws. In that essay Adams narrated early American history as a history of progressive enlightenment and liberty and of consensual affirmation of the rule of law. American settlers, he wrote, "formed their plan, both of ecclesiastical and civil government, in direct opposition to the *canon* and *feudal* systems" because the settlers recognized that these systems were the means through which the tyranny of the few was most effectively established over the many.[8] For these tyrannical systems to be opposed, it was crucial that the free circulation of knowledge be not only permitted throughout the colonies but actively fostered. "The fact is certain," Adams wrote, that "wherever a general knowledge and sensibility have prevailed among the people, arbitrary government and every kind of oppression have lessened and disappeared in direct proportion."[9]

According to Adams, the authority of oppressive systems of law was ultimately based in the ignorance of the people and the "dark ribaldry" of their rulers; even though men have been endowed by God with understanding, and so have an inalienable right to knowledge, this right has been typically denied them by their rulers. Adams's project in his essay was to outline the epistemological basis of legitimate government and political rule, to delineate before his reader "the true map of man" on which a just polity could be established and through which political mystification could be finally eliminated. This "map of man" as a knowing and at least potentially independent being leads Adams to conclude his essay with a series of directives urging his fellow citizens to be intrepid in their pursuit of knowledge and their participation in the emerging public sphere: "Let us tenderly and kindly cherish therefore the means of knowledge. Let us dare to read, think, speak and write. Let every order and degree among the people rouse their attention and animate their resolution."[10]

Adams was soon to see these hopes fulfilled, perhaps dangerously surpassed. After the Stamp Act crisis America saw an explosion of politically oriented printed works: newspapers, magazines, pamphlets, and broadsides proliferated throughout the colonies.[11] Bernard Bailyn, tracing the ideological background of these developments, has written that this explosion of print materially facilitated "the most creative period in the history of American political thought."[12] Adams was certainly not alone among his contemporaries in recognizing this facilitation and in actively encouraging it. Metaphors suggesting the spread of light and illumination through the dark shadows of custom and superstition dominated the writing of the period.[13] Jefferson, a more radical advocate than Adams for the intellectual and political autonomy of the citizenry, wrote that the people must be given "full information of their affairs thro' the channel of public papers" and that "those papers should penetrate the whole mass of the people."[14] The high estimation of public debate and deliberation on issues of common concern was not limited to the educated republican élite. A democratic laborer like William Manning—a man whose writings are valued as rare articulations of postrevolutionary America's largely inarticulate lower classes—had a fundamental faith in the capacity for widely distributed knowledge to secure the liberty and independence of the people, even believing that it would ultimately prevent extralegal crowd actions like Shays's Rebellion.[15] The distribution of knowledge was thought by all three of these men to be an important limitation on the unchecked arousal of popular passions.

It might seem in retrospect that Adams's early enthusiasm for a free press was overzealous, or at least inconsistent coming from a man who, as the second president of the United States, would authorize the Alien and Sedition Acts (1798), the early Republic's primary example of governmental censorship. But we should not see Adams's seemingly contradictory positions on public participation as hypocritical, nor necessarily as a sign of his increasing conservatism. Like his friend Benjamin Rush, who will be discussed in detail in chapter 3, Adams understood that the circulation of knowledge could not only be crucial to preserving liberty but could also serve as an important means of social control and regulation: in Rush's words, it was a necessary precondition for converting "men into republican machines."[16] A closer inquiry into the form of public sphere that Adams, Rush, and other revolutionary leaders advocated, as opposed to that which actually took shape during these years, will reveal fewer tensions between these positions than are at first apparent.

Freedom of the press was the most crucial aspect of this emerging conception of the public sphere in America (though plans for public education and the reliability of the post were also important components of these debates). When Adams wrote, "let every sluice of knowledge be opened," it was in the context of celebrating the capacity of the free press to bring public scrutiny to bear on matters previously hidden from public view.[17] And "none of the means of information are more sacred," he wrote, "or have been cherished with more tenderness and care by the settlers of America, than the press."[18] In passages such as these Adams provided a classic American articulation of what Carl Schmitt later called the "general liberal principle": the belief that a unitary and generally accepted truth could emerge "from an unrestrained clash of opinion and that competition [could] produce harmony."[19] The inherent tension of this position, one later forced upon Adams by the polarized politics of the 1790s, was that to publicly advance the true and the good, one needed also to permit the false and the bad.

That this tension had to be accepted was a commonplace of radical Whig, "Country" political discourse. In *Cato's Letters* John Trenchard and Thomas Gordon underscored that only through exposure to public view could the false and pernicious be definitively eradicated: "Guilt only dreads liberty of speech, which drags it out of its lurking holes, and exposes its deformity and horror to daylight."[20] Whether this demand for transparency arises from nascent liberalism of the late eighteenth century and the early nineteenth or an older civic republican political discourse need not concern us here. These two "paradigms" of political thought are poorly understood as incommensurable worldviews.[21] What is important is that this widespread demand for social transparency illuminates the formation of a communicative imperative in the eighteenth-century American public sphere, one also directed against forms of popular political action that seemed to interrupt the disembodied communicative economy of the public sphere and its terminus in formal representative institutions.[22]

Discussing revolutionary pamphleteers in America, Bailyn argues that "they sought to convince opponents, not . . . to annihilate them."[23] With the widely accepted emphasis on transparency and self-reflective communities of discourse, on government by public opinion, it is perhaps not surprising that some historians of early America should have embraced the Habermasian model of the bourgeois public sphere to make sense of the period's volatile political culture. Habermas's emphasis on discursively generated procedures of political legitimacy seems applicable in a political context where both traditional and divinely sanctioned bases of authority were under increasing pressure and where heteronomy was giving way to emerging conceptions of democratic autonomy. Where his earlier studies of the public sphere provided a historical normativity, Habermas's "linguistic turn" sought to reveal the implicit "context transcendent validity claims" attending the communicative functions of languages in all "postconventional" societies. As Maeve Cooke writes, "from *Transformation of the Public Sphere* to *Faktizität und Geltung*, Habermas has kept the vision of a self-regulating, deliberative political and public realm as central to the very project of a critical social theory."[24] Habermas's discourse ethics can therefore be understood as a theoretical codification of the emancipatory kernel of free and open communication already emphasized in his historical account of the bourgeois public sphere. A brief outline of Habermas's theory of the eighteenth-century public sphere will clarify the difficulties that this framework has in accounting for the politics of the postrevolutionary crowd.

According to Habermas, during the eighteenth century "a political consciousness developed in the public sphere of civil society which, in opposition to absolute sovereignty, articulated the concept of and demand for general and abstract laws and which ultimately came to assert itself (i.e. public opinion) as the only legitimate source of this law."[25] This development marks an important shift, a "structural transformation," from a feudal conception of publicity to the *critical* publicity of the bourgeois public sphere. Under feudalism publicity and public representation were performances of authority on the part of the monarch and nobility: it was representation not *for* but rather *before* the people.[26] According to Habermas, feudal authority's multiple public performances—coronation ceremonies, military parades, public feasts and celebrations—depended on the consumption of the performances by an essentially passive *publicum*. Changes within the feudal system, however—particularly the rapid expansion of the market from the fourteenth century on—reconfigured this relationship of domination. As the market developed and expanded, private (bourgeois) individuals developed a coherent and shared interest in trade against feudal estates and the political regulation of the state. The locus of power shifted, or fractured, and the diversity of private interests assumed a public relevance.

It is from this newly public significance of the private that a critical public sphere emerges, according to Habermas, in the proliferation of newspapers, coffeehouses, literary journals, and salons. "The *publicum* developed into a public, the *subjectum* into the reasoning subject, the receiver of regulations from above into the ruling authorities' adversary."[27]

A new ground of political legitimacy arose from this conception of a critical public. No longer was legitimate authority related to the social position of a particular speaker, but instead emerged from the rational strength of argument itself: from a process of discursive legitimation that aimed to rationalize politics in the name of morality.[28] To eliminate the threat of arbitrary rule, or on the basis of an unjustifiable claim, an argument's power was to have nothing to do with an unreflective reliance on *who* the speaker was, or on the rhetorical power of language; the authority of reasoned persuasion was to replace the authority of influence. Ultimately ideas rather than individuals would compete in the public sphere, distancing the ideas under debate from the bodies of their proponents. The disembodiment of reason was essential to faith in the rational outcome of public debate, as seemingly universal subjects, freed from the limitations of social and historical determination, could communicate on an ideational level, pursuing together and apart the elusive goal of a just consensus. In more recent work Habermas describes the dispersion of overly "concrete" articulations of popular voice and the emergence of a fully "desubstantialized" understanding of popular sovereignty: he celebrates the historical disappearance of the people into "those subjectless forms of communication that regulate the flow of discursive opinion- and will-formation that have the presumption of practical reason on their side."[29] In Habermas's democratic theory the people as a (contested) collective subject is replaced by a diffuse deliberating public; direct (but again, contested) democratic agency is replaced by a "siege" of influence on governing institutions. Applied to postrevolutionary American politics, this framework — from the enacted people to the disembodied public — does not so much describe a historical development as retrospectively invest with authority the élite side of a contentious public debate.

II

The public voice, pronounced by the representatives of the people, will be more consonant to the public good than if pronounced by the people themselves.
FEDERALIST NO. 10[30]

Habermas addresses the philosophical arguments that underlie this emerging understanding of the public sphere, but as many of his critics

have noted, his early work does not fully engage the material underpin-
nings of its practice, particularly the materiality of print, focusing instead on the ideological content of these theoretical public-sphere debates. Michael Warner, on the other hand, while borrowing much from
Habermas's account, has gone further in arguing for the centrality of
print technology in creating the necessary conditions for the emergence
of the public sphere, particularly in postrevolutionary America. The very
medium of print, according to Warner's account, was necessary to the
disembodied sense of self upon which Habermas's discursive legitimacy
depends. "The impersonality of public discourse," Warner writes, was
"seen both as a trait of its medium and as a norm for its subjects."[31] While
avoiding technological determinism and emphasizing the irreducible
role of cultural mediation, Warner has influentially shown that in late-
eighteenth-century America the proliferation of print coincided with,
and reinforced, the republican faith in the emancipatory potential of
freely circulating knowledge. Together, print and the content of republican ideology about the circulation of knowledge established a broad-
based cultural understanding of a representational public, and of public
authority constituted by the mediating effects of such representation (a
mediated authority that Warner, as discussed in chapter 1, believes was
also exemplified by American innovations in *written* constitutionalism).
The public of print discourse that secured this discursively generated
conception of legitimacy was, Warner writes, "an abstract public never
localizable in any relation between persons."[32] It was this abstracted gen-
erality of public opinion rather than the embodied (but contested) singularity of voice, according to Warner, that provided the key to republican
writing and its authoritative claims in the public sphere.[33]

While Warner, along with many others, explores the normative limitations of Habermas's model—for example, the way its abstraction privileges the socially "unmarked" category of the white propertied male—he
also overstates its historical applicability to eighteenth-century America.[34]
Jay Fliegelman, Sandra Gustafson, and Christopher Looby have emphasized the continued significance of voice, sincerity, and embodiment to
the rhetorical generation of authority during the period.[35] The disavowed
authority of voice haunts the deliberations of the postrevolutionary public sphere, which emphasizes reasoned deliberation, formal procedures,
and the representational mediation of public authority. The contested
authority of the postrevolutionary crowd signaled the persistence of the

authority of popular voice in the period. Looby writes that in revolutionary and postrevolutionary America "the widespread cultural investment of authority in vocal forms like political oration and sermons [and, I would add, crowd assembly] created a counterpoint of anxiety about the sufficiency of textuality as a ground of authority, and inspired a widespread enchantment with vocal forms as necessary supplements to if not alternative grounds for authority."[36] Enacted voice, in contrast to the abstraction of print publics and public opinion, allowed for compelling performances of personal sincerity and authenticity, and the revolutionary and postrevolutionary crowd embodied that authority. Dynamic speakers like Patrick Henry moved political audiences not by the strength of their arguments alone but through a charismatic singularity attached to physical presentation. Jefferson's description of Henry's infamous speaking abilities captures both this ambivalence and the "sublime" authority adhering to these performances: "His eloquence was peculiar, if indeed it should be called eloquence; for it was impressive and sublime, beyond what can be imagined. Although it was difficult when he had spoken to tell what he had said, yet, while he was speaking, it always seemed directly to the point. When he had spoken in opposition to my opinion, had produced a great effect, and I myself had been highly delighted and moved, I have asked myself when he ceased: 'what the devil has he said?' I could never answer the inquiry."[37] The spoken word's power in Henry's case comes less from *what* is being communicated—the force of his arguments, say, or the information he conveys—than from something inexpressible in his delivery, a mysterious but necessary supplement to his communication that Jefferson cannot precisely articulate. It seems, in fact, to be "beyond what can be imagined." The undeniable power of public performances during the period troubled revolutionary leaders, who feared their potential for demagogic abuse and their ability to foster the unmediated release of public passions and popular enthusiasm, a charged term in American political discourse after the public turbulence of the Great Awakening.[38] Nancy Ruttenburg argues that the "aggressive uncontainability" of itinerant speech during the Great Awakening was crucial to the formation of an expansive "democratic personality" in eighteenth-century American political culture.[39]

While revisionist accounts of the late-eighteenth-century American public sphere have helpfully demonstrated how different forms of public and different bases of public authority competed in revolutionary and postrevolutionary America (and drawn attention to the politics attending these different forms), they sometimes risk overly dichotomizing this difference in the terms of orality and print, setting the supposedly authentic immediacy of voice against the artifice and mediation of representation.[40] Popular voice and popular representation are not mutually exclusive but interdependent. As we will see, the claim of the crowd was not free of the vicissitudes of political representation. Instead the postrevolutionary crowd enacted the authority both of the embodied, empirical participants and of a larger representative and normative entity: the people. Attempting to validate the democratic populism and authenticity of oral publics, some scholars have relied on a kind of phenomenological essentialism to support their argument.[41] Thus Harry Stout, while looking beyond the content of historical documentation to the projected significance of different communicative forms, writes that "unlike print, which is essentially passive, reflective, and learned, sound is active, immediate, and spontaneously compelling in its demand for a response."[42] Others have seen an intrinsically subversive element in these oral, face-to-face publics, and argued that in postrevolutionary America voice was simply identified with disorder and formlessness in both literary texts and political discourse.[43] Voice, in this account, was not the primary ground of authorization but a continual, dangerously charismatic force of deauthorization.

There are elements of truth to both positions because of a pronounced ambivalence toward the "sublime" authority of voice, but it is an ambivalence that goes well beyond the seemingly ahistorical essence of an oral culture. Truer to the arguments about language and communication at the time, and closer to the ineffable supplement that Jefferson invokes in his account of Henry's speech, is the problem of affect and affectation. Affect not only is an irreducible element of both written *and* oral communication but adheres to nonrepresentational modes of communication as well—to the images, gestures, music, and sympathetic transferences of feeling that many writers in the period thought both crucial and threatening to the maintenance of social order (an issue explored further in chapter 3). It was affect that was at stake when Barlow stated in *The Anarchiad*, "it did not matter so much who had the power of making laws, as who had that of making songs for the people."[44]

In a contemporary theoretical idiom, affect can be described as an emotive intensity distinct from, though bound up with, the representational information communicated in speech or act.[45] It is the element of communication that resonates with clusters of sub-representational and pre-cognitive forces in the body, though not with "natural" or "instinctive" forces somehow untouched by historicity or cultural organization. Affect resists being territorialized into a particular cultural form or reduced to the emotions of a particular subject. Affect exceeds the economy of communication of which it is a part, or as Brian Massumi writes, "formed, qualified, situated perceptions and cognitions fulfilling functions of actual connection or blockage, are the *capture* and closure of affect."[46] Although affect has aspects of ineffability — it enables articulation while being itself inarticulate — it also plays a crucial though often neglected role in our understanding of the political culture of a given time or place. The affective dimension of the revolutionary and postrevolutionary American public, and its emphasis on the authority of popular voice, may be at least as important as its conceptual dimension, the dimension so thoroughly explored in recent years by historians influenced by the linguistic turn.[47] To trace the contours of the affective, and its relation to the dilemmas of authorization that marked the postrevolutionary period and its constituent moments, we should first investigate how it was understood to operate in the texts — spoken, written, acted — of late-eighteenth-century America. Doing so suggests a way of understanding how the political discourses of the period continually returned to what seemed a necessary but also inarticulate element of discursive and representational form: the affective supplement that at once sustained the authority of voice and threatened to undermine it.

During the North American colonies' greatest prerevolutionary debate over the politics of language and crowds — which occurred during the Great Awakening of the 1740s — affective speech and its relation to public authority was of central concern. "Old Lights" ministers feared the radical enthusiasm and antinomian leanings of itinerant preachers like George Whitefield. The large crowds that gathered to hear these "New Light" sermons — the largest public gatherings in North American colonial history to that point — were drawn together, opponents feared, by collective passions elicited by charismatic voice rather than a disciplined love of the gospel or a learned grasp of theological truth. Even a sympathizer like Jonathan Edwards, a man who wrote extensively on the limitations of reason and worldly communication and on the irreducible immediacy of divine grace, worried that the itinerants were confusing the still-mediated Word behind the words with the immediate communication of grace. While Edwards praised the ability of men like Whitefield to "revive the mysterious, spiritual, despised and exploded doctrines of the gospel," and to do so "full of a spirit of zeal for the promotion of a real vital piety," he also worried that the itinerants threatened to communicate "heat without light," religious affectation without knowledge.[48]

Edwards knew that communication entailed degrees of both, or that there was always a supplement in communication to the written or aural representation of ideas, to the mere epistemological transmission of information. As the "more vigorous and sensible exercises of the inclination and will of the soul," affections in Edward's account were an irreducible part of human action, even or especially in the realm of faith.[49] While Edwards believed that the faculty of understanding was crucial to knowing the world, it could never be a substitute for the faculty of "inclination," or sufficient for acting in the world. "We see the world of mankind to be exceedingly busy and active; and the affections of men are the springs of the motion: take away all love and hatred, all hope and fear, all anger and zeal and affectionate desire, and the world would be, in great measure, motionless and dead; there would be no such thing as activity amongst mankind, or any earnest pursuit whatsoever."[50] Edwards believed that a semiotic theory of linguistic communication was insufficient because it could not adequately account for how the affections were moved through language — how communication required a supplement beyond reason to convert an audience. Of course for the Calvinist Edwards the sublime ineffability of grace was the ultimate source of truthful communication. When Edwards wrote that "by all that we see and experience, the *moral* world and the *conversible* world are the same thing," he did not direct his readers to the morality inherent in rational argumentation, but to the divinity that is a precondition for both morality *and* language in the "conversible world."[51] Authority, for Edwards, ultimately resided in our "apprehension" of things, which requires the affective element of inclination communicated by God, rather than the "mere cogitation" of Lockean epistemology.

Hugh Blair, the most widely read theorist of rhetoric in North America during the period, elaborated a similar but more distinctly secular distinction with reference to the language of public address. Although the "new Scottish school" of rhetoric (of which Blair was a key representative) did not share the Ciceronian emphasis on public speech, focusing instead on the gentility of letters circulated among élites, Blair still elaborated an intricate theory of the relationship between different forms of speech and public life. This theory was built upon the key distinction between the cognitive and the passionate crucial to so much eighteenth-century thought. Blair writes: "Convincing and persuading, though sometimes confounded, are of very different import. Conviction affects the understanding only; persuasion the will and the practice. It is the business of a philosopher to convince us of truth; it is that of the orator to persuade us to act comfortably to it by engaging our affections in its favor . . . the orator must not be satisfied with convincing; he must address himself to the passions; he must paint to the fancy, and touch the heart."[52] Blair argued that this art of eloquence was particularly pronounced in democratic Athens, where it first emerged, but that it was also present in a more regular and codified form during the Roman Republic. Relying on a familiar narrative of linguistic development, Blair argued that since that time this art had declined, as a more analytic form of language emerged, one better suited to "that accurate turn of thinking" that marks the modern world and the "phlegm and natural coldness of its disposition."[53] This more analytic and cognitive language—cleansed of unnecessary metaphor and the supplements of physical gesture and tonal variation—is, according to Blair, crucial to science but wholly unsuited to the politics of popular assembly. Rousseau makes a similar albeit more philosophically elaborate argument in his *Essay on the Origin of Language*. It is not only passionate speech that binds people together, but gesture and movement itself. "Passion is easily excited in a great assembly, where the movements are communicated by mutual sympathy between the orator and the audience."[54] Both Blair and Rousseau emphasize another dimension of the affective in much eighteenth-century political thought, the forms of nonrepresentational communication discussed during the period in the terms of human sentiment and sympathy.

For many eighteenth-century American writers it was not knowledge or reason alone that ultimately undergirded the sociopolitical order, but the ongoing communication of sentiments and passions. Although reason could regulate and tame the pre-cognitive communication of passions, it could not be their substitute. For America's founding figures "natural sentiments like sympathy played an active role in the dispensation and preservation of law and order."[55] Philosophically this understanding of sympathy's centrality was influenced by the work of Francis Hutcheson, David Hume, Thomas Reid, and Adam Smith. In his *Treatise on Human Nature* Hume defined sympathy as "that principle, which takes us so far out of ourselves, as to give us the same pleasure or uneasiness in the characters of others, as if they had a tendency to our own advantage or loss."[56] This communication of sentiment and its attending displacement of self, while clearly carried on through the medium of the senses, is not conceptually processed, instead experienced as corporeally irresistible or compulsive. Two bodies may communicate sentiments to one another without the intention of either subject being involved; a mimetic-corporeal mode of communication is resistant to explicit articulation or representation. This is not to deny that sympathy could be altered or actively cultivated (as I will explore further in chapter 3, some prominent postrevolutionary reformers were preoccupied with precisely this issue), or that a form of sympathy could occur through textual mediation (novels during the period were often preoccupied with "the power of sympathy"), but rather to emphasize that sympathy could not be fully mastered or brought under the government of reason or of community sense. The dilemmas of authorization associated with constituent moments were navigated, if never fully resolved, by an assemblage of sympathetic communication and sentimental exchange that could not be determined in advance and that established collective ties but also contained the power to unsettle them. Thus alongside the affective authority of voice, the unruly volatility and contagiousness of sympathy and the sentiments were widely discussed in the political discourses of postrevolutionary America. While sympathy formed the foundation of sociopolitical order, it could also disrupt or subvert this order. Similarly, while the sincerity and embodiment of voice were an irreplaceable component of public authority, they also seemed to resist or subvert the stability of authority based in representation (or the authority of a written text like a constitution).

A better understanding of the political volatility of voice in revolutionary and postrevolutionary America, and its troubled relation to representational authority, requires a closer look at the practices that were thought to enact it: especially those of the revolutionary and postrevolutionary crowd. The postrevolutionary crowd may be productively conceptualized as a claim rather than a sociological entity, as a contested form of political action rather than the popular expression of a moral economy. Arguments over the legitimacy of postrevolutionary crowds were struggles "over the nature of the political, the spaces in which politics would happen, and the character of the people who would participate."[57] These struggles reveal the indeterminacy that haunts the authority of the people's voice, and the competing claims to speak on its behalf.

III

Government was in the Hands of the Mob, both in Form and Substance.
PETER OLIVER, *Origin and Progress of the American Revolution* (1781)[58]

Emphasis on the affective authority of voice and the contagious communication of the passions brings into focus a different view of the crowd from that traditionally offered by historians of political thought and social historians. While much has been written on how the "quasi-legitimacy" of revolutionary and postrevolutionary crowds was based in Whig political theory and constitutionalism, and also on how the crowd functioned as an enforcer of communal social norms, the emergent authority of the postrevolutionary crowd also sprang from its (contested) claim to represent the sovereign authority of the people. How the crowd came to assume this representative status is difficult to trace. "The representative character of the mob," Kimberly Smith writes, "was part of the background of meanings and practices that informed revolutionary rhetoric." "Eighteenth-century discourse about mobs contains little in the way of argument about their representativeness."[59] The singularity of the postrevolutionary crowd's claim to embody popular voice is not fully captured by either the inherited appeals of the crowd's defense of constitutional principles (emphasized by historians of legal and political thought) or the crowd's enforcement of a moral economy (emphasized by the social historians). The postrevolutionary crowd represented the fraught authority of embodied voice, understood both as a challenge to the authority of representation and also as not wholly free from its vicis-

situdes. Postrevolutionary crowd publics did not seek to refine and rationalize public will on the model of the public sphere so much as to make
a claim to realize that will through "direct local action."[60]

The repertoires of the Anglo-American crowd can be traced back to the
political turmoil of seventeenth-century England, and beyond that to the
fairs, charivari, and "rough-music" of the early modern world, to what
Mikhail Bakhtin called the carnivalesque and "unofficial" element of
early modern popular European culture.[61] In eighteenth-century America
crowd repertoires were both remarkably widespread and remarkably diverse; they included not only annual Pope Day parades in Boston and
the intermittent political petitions of the "people out of doors" but anti-
impressment riots, anti-inoculation riots, attacks on sexual deviants and
religious minorities, house sackings, and court seizings.[62] Eighteenth-
century crowds were not the product of outbursts of irrational enthusiasm described by earlier historians working under the influence of Gustave Le Bon's social psychology.[63] Marxist historians like E. J. Hobsbawm,
George Rudé, and E. P. Thompson effectively discredited many of the assumptions underlying these accounts by exposing the earlier historians'
unreflective use of reactionary categories to describe eighteenth-century
crowds, their lack of attention to the motivations behind crowd action,
and their neglect of historical documents providing different perspectives on crowds and their goals and repertoires. These Marxist historians typically understood eighteenth-century crowd activity as a rational
enforcement of traditional social mores. Crowds were, in Hobsbawm's
words, forms of "primitive rebellion." In a classic formulation of what has
come to be known as the "moral-economy argument," E. P. Thompson
wrote: "It is possible to detect in almost every eighteenth-century crowd
action some legitimizing notion. By the notion of legitimation I mean
that the men and women in the crowd were informed by the belief that
they were defending traditional rights and customs; and, in general, that
they were supported by the wider consensus of the community."[64]

The social historians' emphasis on the interests and the motivations
of eighteenth-century crowds has provided a detailed portrait of the social context of crowd action, and of the normative orientation of crowd
actors, their reliance on "legitimizing notions." But this approach has
also tended to neglect the way that crowds interacted with and challenged the authority of formal political institutions, how crowds came to

be seen during the "Age of Revolutions" not merely as defenders of communal norms but as vehicles of constituent agency. Social historians, partly because of their materialist emphasis, have typically not focused on the manner in which crowd publics effected formal political and symbolic aspects of late-eighteenth-century American political culture, particularly around the questions of representation and voice. These latter aspects are important to emphasize because it was over the course of the postrevolutionary years that the crowd came to be understood not only as "an idea-laden entity" motivated by "legitimizing notions" but as an enacted representation of the people. Remnants of the "direct-action crowd" persisted in revolutionary and postrevolutionary America, but to view these crowd actions only through the lens of moral economy arguments is to miss its relation to the dilemmas of authorization associated with constituent moments.

Charles Tilly has shown how British "repertoires of contentious gatherings" dramatically changed between the late eighteenth century and the early nineteenth, and his typology illuminates some of the important changes in crowd activity in early America. In America as in Britain, the 1760s and 1780s were the "period of invention" for these newly emergent forms of popular contention. Whereas older crowd repertoires were, to adopt Tilly's schema, parochial in their goals, particular and responsive in their claims, and bifurcated in the objects of their claims, the emergent repertoires were cosmopolitan in their goals, autonomous in their claims, and consistent in using similar contentious repertoires across a range of conflicts. The crowd went from being a localized collective seeking immediate redress of grievances—the "direct-action crowd" acting only on the authority of those gathered and seeking redress from those immediately present—to a representative crowd often seeking indirect redress of grievances and proclaiming to act on the behalf of a larger symbolic entity: the people. Rudé puts the distinction this way: for the typical direct-action crowd (epitomized by the food riot), "The sole target was the farmer or prosperous peasant, the grain merchant, miller or baker. . . . There was no question of overthrowing the government or established order, of putting forward new solutions, or even of seeking redress of grievances by political action."[65]

The postrevolutionary crowd often mixes elements of both the direct-action and representational crowds, but I want to emphasize its representative status. The postrevolutionary crowd too made a *claim* to represent the people; it was not, as we will see, a self-evident instantiation of the people (how could it be?). Instead, the postrevolutionary crowd illuminated the indeterminacy of any such authoritative claim. The changing discourses of legitimation that surrounded revolutionary and postrevolutionary crowd activity reveal how it did so. In eighteenth-century America the crowd was widely understood "as a quasi-legitimate part of the standing social and political order."[66] Crowd actions in eighteenth-century America were "quasi-legitimate," because they were often understood as a just and constitutionally sanctioned response to the despotism of government. Thus John Adams could write that "it is a general, if not universal truth, that the aptitude of the people to mutinies, seditions, and tumults and insurrections, is in direct proportion to the despotism of the government."[67] In revolutionary America this perceived governmental "despotism" was often linked to the problems of political misrepresentation, and thus crowds emerged as a marker of political representation's failure. Gordon Wood has noted that "of all the conceptions of political theory underlying the momentous developments of the American Revolutionary era, none was more important than that of representation," and none was more hotly contested.[68] Throughout the 1760s and early 1770s colonists decried the misrepresentation of the British Parliament, feared the misrepresentation of their interests by royal agents, and argued vociferously for political institutions of closer representative accountability. The revolutionary crowd responded to the proclaimed failure of virtual representation, while also foreshadowing the difficulties that postrevolutionary Americans would face with the more directly accountable or "actual" forms of political representation they would institute to take its place.

The conflict over different forms of political representation reinforced a wariness in revolutionary and postrevolutionary America of nearly all forms of representation. In 1765 John Adams was already writing that his contemporaries' common "dread of representation has had for a long time in this province effects very similar to what the physicians call *hydrophobia* or dread of water—It has made us delirious—and we have rushed headlong into the water, till we are almost drowned, out of simple or phrensical fear of it."[69] The fear of misrepresentation engendered a flurry of experiments in representational politics, and an attending wariness of authoritative claims to definitively represent the people.

Some historians have argued that the familiar crisis of political representation emerging during the period was therefore accompanied by a broader cultural crisis in representation, as, in David Waldstreicher's words, "political language, personal identity, and paper currency all seemed to [lose] their secure foundations in reality."[70] Postrevolutionary crowds should be understood in relation to this broader sense of representational crisis, in that the crowd questioned the authoritative correspondence between the people and their political representatives, even under postrevolutionary republican constitutions. Political recourse to gatherings of the "people-out-of-doors" when representative politics seemed in the midst of irreparable breakdown took on a particularly radical meaning in the years following the Revolution. Whereas through most of the seventeenth and eighteenth centuries in the Anglo-American world riots "took place within the existing structure of authority and tended to reinforce that structure even as they defied it,"[71] during the revolutionary years crowd gatherings became potential sites of self-generating political authority, a locus of constituent power. Crowds appeared not only as symptoms of the constitutional order's breakdown — in other words, as agents of constitutional or moral defense — but as agents of constitutional transformation and change. While crowds existed outside institutionalized channels of political representation — therefore the emphasis that historians often place on their "*quasi*-legality" or "*quasi*-legitimacy" — in the years leading up to independence they enacted a form of collective agency that not only was critical of existing political forms but sought to overtake or partly replace them. As John Phillip Reid has argued, revolutionary crowds "combined elements of constitutional defense and legal initiative."[72] In this way the people, in part through the enacted agency of revolutionary crowds, moved from being a defensive, interpretive power to a self-constituting, constituent power. Gouverneur Morris captured both the emerging self-authorizing agency of the crowd and the fear it provoked among the patriot élite in a well-known letter to Thomas Penn in 1774: "These sheep [the people], simple as they are, cannot be gulled as heretofore. In short, there is no ruling them; and now . . . the heads of the mobility grow dangerous to the gentry, and how to keep them down is the question. While they correspond with the other colonies, call and dismiss popular assemblies, make resolves to bind the consciences of the rest of mankind, bully poor printers, and exert with full force all their other tribunitial powers, it is impossible to curb them . . . The mob begin to think and to reason. Poor reptiles! it is with them a vernal morning, they are struggling to cast off their winter's slough, they bask in the sunshine, and ere noon they will bite, depend upon it. The gentry begin to fear this."[73] Morris's invocation of the thinking and reasoning mob — and of its "tribunitial powers" — provides an exemplary instance of how representation and voice were interrelated in postrevolutionary politics. The crowd could be understood at once as beyond or outside representation — a direct embodiment of popular will — and as an institution claiming to represent popular voice. The familiar narrative of an increasingly representational public sphere in eighteenth-century America, outlined above, neglects the simultaneous authority of voice and representation in the politics of the postrevolutionary crowd.[74] Because of this neglect the common narrative cannot fully account for the dilemmas of authorization that this form of political action posed to attempts to establish the authority of a new representational political order, a representational authority based at once in the institutions of representative government and the deliberations of the public sphere.

While most patriot writers went to great lengths to distinguish the legitimate crowd from the irrational and enthusiastic mob, it was difficult to define their differences through uncontroversial criteria — formal and legal or more informally political. "Complaints and justifications of mob action permeate colonial [and, I would add, postrevolutionary] politics," Kimberly Smith writes, "constituting a central axis of pre-Revolution discourse about citizenship and political action."[75] John Adams was acutely aware of the importance — and the difficulty — of distinguishing illegitimate mobs from popularly authorized crowds.[76] Like many of his contemporaries, Adams recognized an important quasi-legal role for the crowd in resisting despotic government. Adams likened popular tumults to a kind of natural occurrence responding reflexively to unjust domination, and in this he was not alone. William Pitt, speaking before the House of Lords in 1770, described the "tumults" occurring in America as "ebullitions of liberty": "they are only some breaking out in the skin of the body politic, which if rudely restrained and unproperly checked, may strike inwardly, and endanger the vitals of the constitution."[77] In Adams's view such insurrections were almost always legitimate in absolute monarchies, where they are a natural and therefore justified reaction to despotic power. But as government becomes subject to the rule of law and to representative institutions of popular accountability, such justifications for insurrection increasingly disappear: "in complete republics," Adams writes, they are justified "least of all."[78] This view was not only held by the relatively conservative Adams. Thomas Paine made a similar point when he wrote in his "Dissertation on Government" that "the republican form and principle leaves no room for insurrection, because it provides and establishes a rightful means in its stead."[79] A growing mistrust and fear of crowd politics and a sense of their illegitimacy under republican government pervades the postrevolutionary writings of Adams and many other "friends of government"; even late in his life, however, when he was widely criticized by democratic republicans as an antirevolutionary conservative, Adams never rejected crowd actions as illegitimate in and of themselves. Instead Adams attempted to elaborate a set of principles that could clearly distinguish between the illegitimate mob and the representative crowd, principles that could provide both political and legal criteria. The most important of these principles was that the actions of the crowd must not be motivated by merely factional or "private" concerns, and that the crowd must instead represent the people "as a whole" rather than one social constituency or another. Adams's representative crowd was construed as an embodiment of popular will. He elaborated principles that could, in other words, condemn a riot while affirming the possible legitimacy of a democratic revolution. The practical difficulty in applying these principles resided in disagreements over what constituted a truly "public" concern and a legitimate representation of the people "as a whole."

Adams first attempted to establish these principles in his controversial defense of the British troops charged with the Boston Massacre in 1770. In his address to the jury Adams was at pains to show that the crowd that gathered to taunt and harass the British soldiers — thus precipitating the killing of five civilians — did not legitimately represent the people lionized by patriot leaders but instead merely a degraded fraction of the population; Adams denigrated those killed by the British troops as "the most obscure and inconsiderable that could have been found on the continent."[80] While his contemporaries had explored "a great variety of phrases to avoid calling this sort of a people a mob," Adams argued that a mob was indeed the proper name, "unless that name is too respectable for them." For Adams the people, properly understood, were incompatible with what he described as "a motley rabble of saucy boys, negroes and mulattoes, Irish Teagues, and outlandish jacktars."[81] Instead the people, properly understood, were synonymous with respectability. Approvingly citing Pufendorf in his *Novanglus* essays, Adams writes, "we do not mean by the word *people*, the vile populace or rabble of a country, nor the cabal of a small number of fractious persons, but the greater and more judicious part of the subjects of all ranks."[82] Adams was outraged that the Boston Massacre mob in King Street, led according to Adams by the "mulatto" Crispus Attucks and the Irish immigrant Patrick Carr, had many persons ascribing "their doings to the good people of the town!"[83] These men were not deserving of the name "rebel" because they were mere criminals, beyond the pale of the judiciously constituted people.

In his later reflections on these events in his *Autobiography* Adams again emphasized the illegitimacy of the Boston Massacre crowd—its limited, private aims and lowly participants—as a way of both justifying his defense of the British troops and securing his own revolutionary credentials (about which he was notoriously sensitive). It would have been better, he claimed, "for the whole People to rise in their Majesty, and insist on the removal of the Army, and take upon themselves the consequences, than to excite such Passions between the People and the Soldiers as would . . . keep the town boiling in a continual fermentation."[84] A riot aimed at the army itself rather than particular soldiers, that sought the complete overthrow of British rule rather than assaulting its colonial representatives, was therefore legitimate. "If popular Commotions can be justifyed," he wrote in 1774, "it can be only when Fundamentals are invaded, nor then unless for absolute Necessity and with great Caution. But these Tarrings and Featherings, these breaking open Houses by rule and insolent Rabbles, in Resentment for private wrongs . . . must be discountenanced."[85]

These criteria for distinguishing the illegitimate mob from the representative crowd seem clear enough, but in the postrevolutionary context it was far from self-evident what constituted a grievance based on "private wrongs" as opposed to one of violated "Fundamentals." Was Shays's Rebellion, to take one prominent example, undertaken by what Abigail Adams called "ignorant, restless desperadoes without conscience or principle," by "mobbish insurgents" bent on "sapping the foundation, and destroying the whole fabrick at once?"[86] Or was it an instance of rightful public "regulation," as Daniel Shays and his followers argued? Adams's criteria, while nuanced in their application, do not definitively *resolve* the issue or elevate it from legitimate political disagreement. Adams's criteria, we could say, form the relevant questions, but in no way determine the answers: Who properly represents popular voice, and how? Who are the people represented? What is a "public" concern over fundamentals versus a factious private interest? His criteria do not resolve the dilemmas of authorization associated with crowd enactment of these constituent moments, but instead suggest a way of navigating them.

When Adams searched for signs of a crowd's legitimacy he sometimes invoked additional aesthetic criteria to explain them. Consider his evaluations of the Stamp Act crowds and of the Boston Tea Party. In the first instance Adams contrasted the "honorable and glorious action" that pulled down the Stamp Act offices of Andrew Oliver in Boston on 14 August 1765 and what he considered the petty and ugly attacks on Governor Thomas Hutchinson's home later that month. Both acts could be said to have been animated by the same goals and principles—they were engaged by equally representative crowds motivated by the unrepresentative tax policies of Parliament—but the glory of the one contrasted with the ugliness of the other. The people properly enacted will appear glorious and majestic, Adams suggests, and this appearance of glory may be taken as a sign of legitimacy. "The people should never rise without doing something to be remembered—something notable. And striking." This is what Adams admired in the Boston Tea Party, which he described "as the most Magnificent movement of all." Adams found a "Dignity, a Majesty, a Sublimity" in this event that led him to judge it "an Epoch in History" before that history had in fact been written as epic.[87]

IV

By the 1780s the people had become simply the collective community standing outside the entire government–a final court of appeal to which every aggrieved group took its case.   GORDON S. WOOD, *The Creation of the American Republic*[88]

The lack of uncontroversial criteria for distinguishing the legitimate crowd from the illegitimate mob became particularly vexed in post-revolutionary America as patriot unanimity dissolved into an increasingly factional politics. After independence the continuation of crowd activity, now directed against the patriot rather than the colonial élite, challenged the ubiquitous assumptions of popular unity in revolutionary political discourse. The crowd's vigilance in the face of the new republican authorities assumed darker, occasionally satanic, overtones once the contested authorities were no longer the British but American patriots and once the communicative imperatives of the emerging public sphere seemed increasingly threatened by the oblique proximity of crowd action. The postrevolutionary crowd did not enact the unitary nature of an independent people but staged a people internally divided. Two examples of postrevolutionary crowd activity usefully illustrate how the postrevolutionary crowd was thought to embody popular voice while also exposing its internal division.

The crowd attack on James Wilson's house in Philadelphia in 1779 is in many ways exemplary, and can be understood as an important turning point in both the activity and the élite perception of the American crowd. After this event Henry Laurens, the former president of the Continental Congress, wrote: "we are at this moment on a precipice, and what I have long dreaded . . . seems to be breaking forth—a convulsion among the people."[89] This enactment of the "people-out-of-doors" illuminated the deep political divisions haunting post-independence America and the growing conflict over what counted as a legitimate form of popular politics. It also reveals how crowds in the period had aspects of both the direct action and representational crowds. On 4 October 1779, after months of conflict over the popular regulation of prices in Philadelphia, members of the Philadelphia militia protested what they saw as local merchants' continuous price gouging as militiamen were off fighting the Revolutionary War. As Captain Ephraim Faulkner, the Militia leader put it: "The labouring part of the City had become desperate from the high price of the necessities of life."[90] Many though by no means all postrevolutionary crowd actions were provoked by such economic concerns, but as the event at "Ft. Wilson" indicated, these forms of economic hardship were not easily distinguishable from political disempowerment. The militia members that protested in the streets on 4 October had sought price regulations for much of the previous summer—through the formal political channels of the town meetings and indirectly by intimidating merchants. James Wilson was an obvious target of these interconnected complaints. As a prominent member of the conservative Republican Society (formed in opposition to the radical Pennsylvania Constitution of 1776) and of the Patriot élite, he had continually opposed attempts at popular price regulations in the Supreme Executive Council and the Assembly. The gathering of two hundred militiamen who paraded through town on 4 October, and eventually confronted Wilson and other "gentlemen" at his house, was motivated by direct economic incentive as well as the forced political inefficacy of the "lower" part of the population. One historian concludes that "those who marched on 4 October were poor militia men who had good reason to do so. Their grievances were longstanding and long unredressed. Most probably did not go to Wilson's house to attack it; but most, if not all, were mentally and physically prepared to fight, as they would not have been in 1775. Four years of military and political activity had laid the basis for the militia's self-activity on 4 October."[91]

It was not simply economic motivation that led to the events at Ft. Wilson but also the increasing frequency and political legitimacy of collective "self-activity," what Benjamin Rush called the Revolution's troubling political legacy of a popular tendency towards "extempore conduct."[92] Crowds were not only justified in the revolutionary discourses of the day: they were also political repertoires participated in by all kinds of citizens and also noncitizens, by those granted and denied juridical recognition. During the decade leading up to the Revolution, many Americans were habituated into the self-created forms of popular politics exemplified by the crowd. The justificatory framework of an accompanying theory did not wholly account for these repertoires. Those who focus solely on the history of ideas insufficiently address the embodiment of political culture evidenced by the repertoires of crowd activity and the multiplication of festivals and parades in the revolutionary and postrevolutionary years. For a fearful Patriot élite, events like the one at Ft. Wilson seemed to indicate that the attempts to establish a communicative economy based on authorized representation could not secure the social and political order against those whose grievances could not be heard or recognized within the existing set of representative institutions. The enactment of the postrevolutionary crowd seemed to imply broader egalitarian claims beyond their immediately articulated goals, or the normative frameworks appealed to in order to justify them. Postrevolutionary crowd actions "revealed a submerged strain of popular egalitarianism and radicalism that aimed at undermining the dominant ideology of social hierarchy."[93]

Eight years after Ft. Wilson another crowd action took place in Pennsylvania, this time targeting the recent ratification of the U.S. Constitution by the Pennsylvania state ratifying convention.[94] On 26 December 1787 a group of Federalist supporters of the constitution gathered in the "public streets of Carlisle" to celebrate ratification, and had their celebration "violently prevented" by a large group of opposing Antifederalists. Here is how one eyewitness described the "riot": "The armed party [of Antifederalists] having accomplished their premeditated designs of preventing the public rejoicing proceeded to spike the cannon, and having made a large fire, committed to the flames the cannon and its carriage . . . They then sent for an almanac, containing the Federal Constitution, which was formally burned. Loud Huzzas were repeated, with damnation to the 46 members [who supported ratification], and long live the virtuous 23 [who had opposed it]."[95] The following day the "Friends of Government" again gathered to perform their interrupted ritual celebration of the Pennsylvania ratification, and with what one supporter described as "good order and coolness and determined spirit" they completed their toasts and a ritual reading of the constitution, and then, with "every appearance of harmony and good humor . . . returned without any disturbance to their homes." After the Federalist ritual of authorization, however, yet another Antifederalist crowd gathered: "Immediately after, a drum beat—the mob gathered—collected barrels and proceeded with noise and tumult to the courthouse."[96] The Antifederalist crowd gathered this time not to interrupt Federalist ceremonies of celebration but to enact its own counterrituals of deauthorization.

In the Carlisle riots both sides seemed to see these rituals of authorization and deauthorization as a kind of informal extension of the ratification procedure. For the Federalists the celebration aimed to "attract the eyes of praise and approbation" to the ratifying majority, while casting "censure and contempt" on its opponents. The Antifederalists, by contrast, aimed to deflate the authority of the formally ratified constitution, and to refuse its legality. As the Carlisle Antifederalist "One of the People" wrote, "The government which [the Federalists] are so enthusiastically fond of is as yet an ideal phantom, a chimera, a mere theory detested and execrated by every true friend to government."[97] In the hopes of sustaining the Constitution's reality as a mere fiction, the Antifederalist crowd burned effigies of Chief Justice Thomas McKean and (again) James Wilson, two of the Constitution's most prominent supporters in the state ratifying convention. "They formed in order, had the effigies carried in front, preceded only by a noted captain of the militia, who declared he was inspired from Heaven, paraded the streets, and with shouts and the most dreadful execrations committed them to the flames."[98]

These events occasioned a flurry of essays in local newspapers, soon after reprinted throughout the country, to set forth "true representations" of the significance of the riots. The pseudonymous writers "An Old Man," "One of the People," "Another of the People," and "The Scourge" competed to offer authoritative accounts of the events, and to prophesy their significance for the country's future. "Proceedings of this kind are really alarming," concluded the Federalist "An Old Man," and "directly tend to the dissolution of all government." To highlight the crowd's lack of authority, Federalists typically emphasized the social invisibility of its members, casting suspicion on their claim to speak on the people's behalf. "It is remarkable that some of the most active people in the riot of Wednesday evening, and the mob of Thursday," "An Old Man" continued, "have come to this country within these two years—men perfectly unknown, and whose characters were too obscure to attract the notice of the inhabitants of this place."[99] Another Federalist wrote these were "men equally void of credit, character, and understanding."[100] Rather than act on behalf of the public good, as the Antifederalists claimed, the rioters were fueled, Federalists declared, by merely private motives. The rabble was composed of "needy obscure and starving adventurers, whose precarious freedom depends on the nod of their numerous creditors."[101] While the crowd professed to be acting on behalf of the people, "Another of the People," wrote (his very choice of pseudonym underscoring the stakes of his claim), the "rabble" was actually falsely led by narrow and vengeful interests. The "riot" was initiated, he wrote, by a disgruntled worker who had not been paid for the work he did in setting up the Federalist celebration.

While the Federalists claimed that they celebrated the people's work, as represented in the state ratifying convention, the Antifederalists of Carlisle claimed the Federalists were instead *refuting* the people's authority. They appealed, in other words, to another people. Responding to "An

Old Man," the Antifederalist "One of the People" argued that it was the "intended rejoicers," and not those who broke up their celebration, "who were an unhallowed riotous mob."[102] It was the Federalist celebration that stood for dangerously self-created authority, as no "town meeting" was ever called to "consult the people, whether they approved of [the celebration] or not." Because three-fourths of the local citizenry were opposed to the proposed constitution, "One of the People" reasoned, the Antifederalist crowd was actually a better representation of the (local) people's will.[103] On this logic, the rejoicers act on the authority of the state convention, representing the people of the state, while the rioters acted on behalf of the local people (who have not, however, formally designated them as representatives). Elaborating the consequences of this line of argument, and responding directly to the warning from "An Old Man" about the threatened "dissolution of government," "One of the People" ultimately targeted the legitimacy of the Philadelphia Convention and its production of a new constitutional text proclaimed on the authority of "We the People": "Now of all others, the new Federalists ought to be silent about the dissolution of governments, for they professedly avow the dissolution of all governments and is [sic] endeavoring to establish an unheard of monster on their ruins."[104] "They are the determined enemies to the government of Pennsylvania, to the Confederation of the United States, and to every government that ever existed in the world."[105]

The dilemmas of authorization attending the events at Carlisle continued into its legal aftermath. After the events warrants were issued for the arrest of twenty-one rioters, and on 25 February the accused appeared before the Court of Common Pleas. Most of the accused accepted parole at the hearing, but the judge ordered the seven who refused parole to jail until trial. These seven, who also refused to accept the bail offered by supporters, questioned the legitimacy of the ratifying convention's authority. On hearing news of their imprisonment, a large group of supporting militiamen from the surrounding countryside mobilized to release their fellow "anticonstitutionalists" from jail. After a series of negotiations under the threat or "pressure from the streets," these efforts were finally successful in having the prisoners released the following month. Legal authority in this instance cannot be easily isolated from a broader assemblage of popular authority, and the controversies that sustain it.

What do we learn from these events about the persistent quasi-legitimacy of crowd action in the postrevolutionary years? Postrevolutionary crowds not only threatened the self-evidence of American unity and threw into question the newly established institutions of political representation symbolizing that unity. In the postrevolutionary context, crowd action seemed to point to problems intrinsic to popular representation itself, rather than to correct the gaps of misrepresentation and "virtual representation," as they had during the revolutionary years. Not only was it impossible, in John Adams's words, for the terror of crowd activity to "be described by words or painted on canvasses,"[106] but crowds also comprised many who had been denied the dignity of official political representation. The common dismissal of—again in Adams's words—"a motley rabble of saucy boys, negroes and mulattoes, Irish Teagues, and outlandish jacktars" participating in crowd activity highlighted their increasing illegitimacy in the eyes of the patriot élite during the 1780s.

Within the civic republican political discourse that shaped the conceptual horizons of many revolutionary and postrevolutionary Americans, the crowd remained a figure that provoked great ambivalence. On the one hand, civic republican discourse often treated crowds as the embodiment of citizen vigilance and the popular "jealousy" of power crucial to keeping a republic free. Jefferson provided the best-known example of the former stance when, defending Shays's Rebellion in a letter to Abigail Adams, he wrote: "the Spirit of resistance to government is so valuable on certain occasions, that I wish it to be always kept alive. It will often be exercised when wrong, but better so than not exercised at all. I like a little rebellion now and then. It is like a storm in the atmosphere."[107] On the other hand, crowd phenomena could, when read through the common lens of Polybian history, signify the breakdown of the virtuous republic into faction, democratic anarchy, and then tyranny. Here again the irresolvable question was whether the crowd stood for the people or merely for an interested faction. Jefferson's defense of crowd vigilance, while by no means anomalous, was by the late 1780s not as common among the patriot élite as the growing condemnation of crowd anarchy. This latter position may be found in the numerous postrevolutionary condemnations of "democracy";[108] as Gary Nash has shown, crowd action was inextricable from the language of democracy during the period.[109] For most of the colonial and postcolonial élite "democracy" was "the worst of all political evils." [110] John Adams, recognizing this nongovernmental aspect of democratic politics, wrote that "the word democracy signifies nothing more or less than a nation of people without any government at all." [111]

Postrevolutionary élites carried further this association of democracy with a kind of anarchy by attaching democracy to a politics opposed to representation and mediation. But the widespread fear and suspicion of democracy in the period's political theory has veiled the popularity and frequency of democratic practices emerging in the political culture of the time. For while political theorists used democracy rhetorically to signify the dangers of institutional instability and the multivalent crisis in representation that it inaugurated, democracy should also be understood as a "cultural condition" that existed "before it was proclaimed as a political principle," as a political impulse and disposition that existed "in the absence of a theoretical vocabulary." [112] Looking to the postrevolutionary crowd is one important way of pursuing such an understanding. Political élites increasingly emphasized representation to take legitimacy and justification away from this cultural condition manifest in the democratic politics of the "people-out-of-doors." For the founders, mobbing was the most direct manifestation of the democracy that the representative principle was meant to blunt. [113] Had the voice of "the people" that was embodied in crowd activity during the revolutionary and postrevolutionary years articulated a sovereign voice all along, one now providing the authoritative ground for a new representative government? Or was the crowd's "voice" always less than univocal, less than present, shot through with all the antagonisms of the political, and thus incapable of providing such a ground? The postrevolutionary crowd communicated the failure of any attempt to definitively represent the people, or to make their voice fully present and articulate; it communicated the proclaimed inarticulacy of popular voice.

Critics of the postrevolutionary crowd, who usually preferred the term "mob," frequently emphasized the mute violence or the meaninglessness of its claims: "the people shouting, huzzaing, and making 'mob-whistle,' as they call it, which, when a boy makes it in the street is not formidable thing, but when made by a multitude, is a most hideous shriek, almost as terrible as an Indian yell." [114] For all its frequently proclaimed inarticulacy, the postrevolutionary crowd communicated the persistence of con-

tention over authorized forms of political representation, and the possibility of popular claims beyond the institutions that based their authority
in popular voice. These crowds did not communicate the immanence of
sovereign voice but the authority of a people always enacted through
representation and in surplus of any given representation. *Vox populi, vox
Dei*—a phrase taken directly from the English Civil War—was indeed
the call of the revolutionary crowd during the Stamp Act riots of 1765
and throughout the revolutionary and postrevolutionary period. But this
voice was not the pre-articulate or virtual voice of *a* people. In his work
on the "rituals of the American Revolution," Peter Shaw provides a provocative account of a latent crowd unconscious, arguing that the crowd
rituals of the American Revolution "served to convey those cultural imperatives of the colonists that could not gain explicit expression until
the nation had been declared."[115] In the years before *Common Sense*—in
which Paine boldly called for nothing short of American independence,
leveling his accusations directly at the sovereignty of George III rather
than at Parliament—American unrest had been largely directed against
a nonrepresentative Parliament and royal ministers who misrepresented
the colonists' interests. Americans did not directly question the king's
sovereign authority over the colonies until the very year of independence
and Revolution. According to Shaw, however, this popular appropriation
of the king's sovereignty, while only articulated in 1776, remained latent
in the crowd "rituals of the Revolution": "The great outburst of 1776 has
been aptly termed a 'killing of the king'—an orgy of symbolic destruction
necessary to the establishment of popular sovereignty. So it was. And it
can be added that this killing completed the killings of effigial substitutes
for the king. Once again, as in the case of the Stamp Act opposition, an
unconscious process took a ritual form, expressing enmity toward the
king which earlier symbolizations had succeeded in containing."[116] In
this quasi-psychoanalytic account, the conscious opposition to the king
in 1776 finally *expressed* the sovereignty of the American people—of the
American nation—that had been implicit but repressed in the "rituals
of revolution" for more than a decade. This explanation assumes a common voice of a people prior to the various acts of enactment, thereby
missing the performative dimensions of these ritual enactments of the
vox populi. I would argue by contrast that the constituent power of the
people was not immanent to these acts—a collective voice awaiting ex-

pression—but only enacted and reiterated through them, through the series of contested constituent claims made on the people's behalf. This understanding of the vicissitudes of voice provides a different context for understanding how crowd actions operated in the political culture of postrevolutionary America; it suggests a way to account for the extra-legal authority of the people without appeal to the sovereign presence of a people's voice.

In his recent work on the "eclipse of politics" in the contemporary West, Jacques Rancière elaborates a provocative theory of democracy that resonates strongly with the postrevolutionary American case as I have described it. Rancière writes that democracy is not fully compat-ible with any given set of institutional structures or constitutional forms. For Rancière the democratic appearance of the political is tenuously self-sustaining, built on a certain spontaneity of public sentiment, and is best understood as what Wolin calls a "fugitive experience."[117] Argu-ing against the modern equation of democracy and popular sovereignty, Rancière turns to an articulation of the people that resists being reduced to either the collective articulation of an underlying commonality or con-sensus (like a Rousseauian "general will," or deliberative democracy) or the majority sum of its differentiated parts (contemporary liberal inter-est group and opinion poll politics, aggregative theories of democracy). Democratic politics, in this rendering, does not entail the synecdochic, state-like relation between the part and the whole, but is rather found in the relation between the non-part and the whole, between those who are not recognized within an established field of political representation and the entirety of that field. Rancière writes that "politics exists when the natural order of domination is interrupted by the institution of a part of those who have no part. This institution is the whole of politics as a specific form of connection. It defines the common of the community as a political community, in other words, as divided, as based on a wrong that escapes reparation. Beyond this set-up there is no politics. There is only the order of domination and the order of revolt."[118]

In place of the sharp dichotomy of these two orders, Rancière sug-gests the interrelationship between the order of the police and the order of politics. This latter relationship entails an alternate political subjec-tivization, one by which citizenship is conceived of as a political prac-tice rather than a juridical category, by which political actors need not perfectly correspond with juridical subjects and may productively exist in an ambiguous state of "quasi-legality." This mode of political subjectivization, Rancière elaborates, entails "a disidentification, a removal from the naturalness of a place, the opening up of a subject space where anyone can be counted since it is the space where those of no account are counted, where a connection is made between having a part and having no part."[119] In this theoretical description we can hear the trace of the etymological trajectory of "the mob" in "the mobility," a tenuously nomadic political collectivity that does not fit within the bounds of institutional form, a political communication (for Rancière a *political* reason) that does not provide the stable assurance either of mutual transparency or of situated and particularized voice.

Rancière's democratic invocation returns us to the epigraph with which this chapter began. "Thy uncreating word" of the *Anarchiad* crowd is not a word that founds or institutes, nor one that communicates without remainder to the listener; it works to trouble the sender-receiver model of communication. "Thy uncreating word" has a double meaning within *The Anarchiad*. Barlow and the other Connecticut Wits took the phrase (and much else in their poem) from Pope's *Dunciad*. But the context of its use, both within the textual economy of the American poem and within the poem's context in American political culture, differs from Pope's. While the Wits take from Pope an emphasis on the ordering power of language and its capacity to establish a sense of reality, their concerns are with the *political* power of language and representation to institutionalize a sense of the real, and the danger posed to this institutionalization by the "Mobs in Myriads" that "blacken all the way." Unlike the "creating" or founding words of America's written constitutions, or of the rational discussion of the bourgeois public sphere, the "uncreating word" of the postrevolutionary American crowd forever resists final representation or articulation. The postrevolutionary crowd marks a democracy of the *in*articulate insofar as it was perceived as a shadowy, virtual, inchoate identity without the crystallizing or articulating voice of a "leader" to give it form, to give it sovereign voice. The voice of the postrevolutionary crowd communicates the failure of any attempt to definitively represent the people, to make its will fully present and articulate. The crowd communicates the proclaimed inarticulacy of popular voice. It is a way of keeping the people present in their absence.

It is often said that "the sovereign and all other power is seated *in* the people." This idea is unhappily expressed. It should be—"all power is derived *from* the people." They possess it only on the days of their elections. After this, it is the property of their rulers, nor can they exercise or resume it, unless it is abused.   BENJAMIN RUSH, "Address to the People of the United States"[1]

The subjects must be kept apart. That is the first maxim of modern politics.
JEAN-JACQUES ROUSSEAU, *Essay on the Origin of Languages*[2]

Sympathy and Separation

Benjamin Rush and the Contagious Public

On 4 July 1788 the citizens of Philadelphia participated in a grand "Foederal Procession" honoring the ratification of a new federal government under the United States Constitution. While Philadelphians had celebrated Independence Day before and were familiar with the politics of processions, parades, and less organized gatherings of the people out of doors, many participants believed this procession carried a greater, almost epochal significance. It certainly appeared this way to Dr. Benjamin Rush—a signatory of the Declaration of Independence and an important early American reformer—who articulated this amplified resonance in a letter published in several newspapers throughout the states. Rush did not simply report the event; he sought to illuminate its "philosophical" significance. His letter offers insight into early American reformers' emphasis on regulating the aesthetic-affective dimensions of political life, and doing so in part through the spatial choreography of the American citizenry.[3]

Rush begins his account by comparing the procession favorably with the "splendid processions of coronations in Europe," signaling at the outset an unexpected continuity between what American Patriots usually derided as the manipulative mummery of monarchy—its slavish attention to fashion, personal distinction, and court rituals—and the power of spectacle still attending republican political forms.[4] The dual burden of Rush's letter was to reveal the continued significance of the aesthetic-affective domain to postrevolutionary political "innovations" while also emphasizing the differences between "the effects of a republican and a monarchical government on the minds and bodies of men." While these regimes relied equally on regulating affect to attain their citizens' (or subjects') assent and loyalty, Rush saw important differences in their strategies. Broadly, where monarchical political aesthetics enacted rule through strategies of rank and by invoking mystery, republican aesthetics relied on unification and strategies of transparency and public consensus. This latter reliance, Rush suggests, was nowhere more powerfully evident, nor more obviously required, than in the Philadelphia procession of 1788.

No city in postrevolutionary America was more intransigently divided by partisan politics than Philadelphia. Political divisions over constitutional ratification, articulated in both the press and the streets, deepened the controversy provoked by the radically democratic Pennsylvania Constitution of 1776. Throughout the late 1770s and the 1780s disputes between Anti-Constitutionalists and Constitutionalists dramatized the growing differences between the city's civic leaders and its "lower orders," occasionally through acts of startling collective violence. For Rush, an outspoken critic of the Pennsylvania Constitution, the city's 1788 Fourth of July Procession revealed that the political consensus that had hitherto eluded postrevolutionary Philadelphians, and by extension all American post-colonials, might be at last achieved, and achieved *legitimately*, through the dynamics and "soft compulsions" of aesthetic experience.[5] The procession, Rush asserts, had been "the happy means of uniting all our citizens in the government." The coordinated spectacle of the federal procession achieved a sympathetic identification where particular arguments had failed to bring about a deliberative consensus: "The order of the procession was regular, and begat corresponding order in all classes of spectators. A solemn silence reigned both in the streets and at the windows of the houses. This must be ascribed to the sublimity of the sight, and the pleasure it excited in every mind; for sublime objects and intense pleasure never fail at producing silence!"[6] Rush's emphasis on "the order of the procession" contrasts sharply with the disorder attending many of postrevolutionary Philadelphia's public gatherings; in place of the clamor of popular voice there was assent signified by silence. The spatial coordination of affective exchange is captured here in the crucial phrase "begat corresponding order in all classes of spectators."[7] Precisely how, we might ask, was this order "begotten"? The mimetic exchange that Rush identifies between the "order of the procession" and the "order of all classes of spectators," as we will see, typifies his medico-political understanding of sympathy. Here this mimetic symmetry is sustained by a sense of the sublime, which, since its original theorization in the works of Longinus, had entailed the sublime object's ability to "transport" subjects without obtaining their rational consent. Rush relies here on the pleasure and awe of sublime spectacle — what Edmund Burke memorably called its intermingling of "terror" and "delight" — to achieve political assent.[8] "Tis done!," Rush exclaims. "We have become a nation."[9]

This chapter explores how Rush employed the medico-political understanding of sympathy that he acquired as a medical student in Edinburgh to evaluate the behavior of a licentious citizenry, and how this understanding shaped his efforts to reform citizens through acts of spatial choreography. Like many writers in late-eighteenth-century America, Rush was troubled by large and volatile public assemblies. The frequency of crowd actions during the Revolution focused critical attention on the unreason attending gatherings of the people out of doors, however quasi-legitimate they were taken to be. For critics like Rush, these resolutely embodied publics, far from sustaining spaces of reasoned deliberation, corrupted emerging visions of an orderly, emancipatory public sphere. The affective communication between bodies gathered in public threatened to unleash what Michael Meranze has called an "anarchy of reciprocal imitations."[10]

It was in eighteenth-century theories of sympathy that this theory of bodily mimesis was most rigorously developed and most widely disseminated. As many cultural and literary historians have recently argued, sympathy was understood as both the "cement" that cohered the social order and a perpetually destabilizing threat to that order.[11] In John Mullan's words, eighteenth-century "attempts to detect the fundamental expressions of solidarity were liable to have to deal with expressions of solidarity which were disruptive of social cohesion."[12] Building on these arguments, but applying them primarily to physical rather than metaphorical public spaces, I argue that in Rush's writings on sympathy we glimpse the importance of spatial and environmental reform as a part of the broader moral and political reform in the postrevolutionary years. In particular, I argue that the institutional tactics of separation and spatial coordination pursued by Rush aimed to control and regulate — in Michel Foucault's word, "canalize"[13] — the potentially disruptive communication of sympathetic affect among the newly nationalized citizenry. This regulation of affective exchange sought to limit the new republic's continued reliance on the politics of the people out of doors, as well as to reform the constitutional practices of citizenship and the sentimental structure of the citizenry. In Rush's work we see an effort to habituate postrevolutionary citizens to self-government through an intricate spatial choreography. Rush's art of sympathy was also an art of separation, entailing the navigation of social proximity and distance capable of producing the self-governing "republican machines" he thought necessary for the new republic regime.[14] It was in part through this spatial choreography of citizenship that Rush pursued his paradoxical project of training the citizenry for moral and political independence.[15]

I

GREAT GOD! of what materials hast thou compounded the hearts of thy creatures! admire, O my friend! the operation of NATURE—and the power of SYMPATHY!
WILLIAM HILL BROWN, *The Power of Sympathy*[16]

In his *Travels through Life* Rush wrote that he considered his two years studying medicine in Edinburgh from 1766 to 1768 as "the most important in their influence upon my character and conduct of any period of my life."[17] Aside from the medical education, and in particular the powerful influence of his teacher William Cullen, Rush saw these years as politically formative. "For the first moment in my life I now exercised my reason upon the subject of government," Rush wrote, concluding that "no form of government can be rational but that which is derived from the Suffrages of the people, who are the subjects of it." No longer did Rush consider kings "as essential to political order as the Sun is to the order of our Solar System."[18] While Rush had in 1765 supported colonial protests against Parliament's Stamp Act—denouncing colonial governors' attempts to "suppress the spirit of liberty"—it was not until he moved to Edinburgh that the "great and active truth" of republican principles provoked him to "try the foundation of my opinions on many other subjects."[19] Through his encounters in London and Edinburgh with such political and intellectual luminaries as James Burgh, Adam Ferguson, David Hume, Samuel Johnson, Catherine Macaulay, and John Wilkes, his participation in Edinburgh's Whiggish Revolution Club, and his studies at Europe's most distinguished medical school, Rush experienced an intellectual transformation that deepened his principled commitment to the American colonists' cause. In theory, though he claims not yet in practice, Rush had become a republican.

Rush's medical and political education in Edinburgh framed his understanding and evaluation of unfolding political developments once he returned to Philadelphia in July 1769; it indelibly shaped the sentimental republicanism he tirelessly advocated in the 1770s and 1780s.[20] While Rush's participation in the American Revolution and the War for Independence contributed to the further "evolution of [his] republican principles," and would ultimately lead to a "disorganization" of the "principles of medicine" that he learned from Cullen, the broad outline of these principles remained with him throughout his life. Of particular importance to Rush's medico-political interventions in the 1770s and 1780s was the conception of sympathy he acquired in Edinburgh, understood as a central category of both sociopolitical and physiological analysis. As Evelyn Forget has argued, the theorization of sympathy in late-eighteenth-century Scotland blurred the "distinction between medicine and what became social theory" and established a "logical continuity between physiological and sociological investigation."[21] No late-eighteenth-century American figure employed this "logical continuity" more rigorously than Rush. His medico-political understanding of sympathy shaped many of his proposed reforms of the human and social body once he returned to revolutionary Philadelphia. Through the con-

ceptual lens of sympathy, Rush argued persistently for the interrelationship of physical and moral or political health; he invariably tied disorder
in the polity to derangement in the mind and body. Because I will focus
on Rush's understanding of sympathy's contagiousness and irresistibility,
broader eighteenth-century preoccupations with contagious sympathy
are key to understanding Rush's institutional approach to sympathy as
an art of separation.

   Sympathy was of course a key moral category of Anglophone thought
during the long eighteenth century, figuring centrally in the moral
sentimentalism of Anthony Ashley Cooper (the Third Earl of Shaftesbury) and Francis Hutcheson, the essays of Joseph Addison and Richard
Steele, and the treatises of Scottish Enlightenment thinkers like David
Hume and Adam Smith. It was also an essential category of the vitalist medical discourse of the Edinburgh school of Joseph Black, William
Cullen, Alexander Munro *secundus*, and Robert Whytt.[22] The widespread
moral appeal to sympathy in the eighteenth century was part of a larger
response to moral theories — especially those of Thomas Hobbes and
Bernard Mandeville — premised upon individual self-interest. In place
of contractual and interest-based accounts of social and political life,
which were grounded in mechanistic egoism and the presumed independence of their choosing subjects, eighteenth-century theorists of sympathy asserted constitutive relationality and the self-evidence of human
sociability. Despite important differences between these theorists, each
envisioned the self as inherently capable of feeling the sentiments and
passions of others through recognizably mimetic mechanisms; in all
their work there is evidence of what Walter Benjamin described as the
"mimetic faculty" of human beings.[23]

   Describing the sympathetic process of natural imitation early in the
century, Francis Hutcheson wrote that all passions and emotions are
"naturally contagious." Individuals "not only sorrow with the distressed,
and rejoice with the prosperous, but admiration or surprise . . . raises a
correspondent commotion of mind in all who behold him. Fear observed
raises fear in the observer before he knows the cause, laughter moves to
laughter."[24] Elaborating on the mimetic dimension of sympathy, but also
emphasizing the role played by physical proximity, Shaftesbury theorized sympathy through its relation to another key term of eighteenth-
century moral and political discourse — "enthusiasm."[25] In his influential

"Letter concerning Enthusiasm," Shaftesbury invoked the contagious dimension of sympathy when situated within the context of the gathered multitude: "One may with good reason call every passion 'panic' which is raised in a multitude and conveyed by . . . contact or sympathy . . . in this state their very looks are infectious. The fury flies from face to face, and the disease is no sooner seen than caught. Such force has society in ill as well as in good passions, and so much stronger any affection is for being social and communicative."[26] Shaftesbury's influential account of sympathy emphasizes contagiousness, with the multitude agitated to such an extent that looks themselves—the external sign of an internal state—become "infectious." The imitation of "looks themselves" is not a consequence of prior understanding, according to Shaftesbury's account, but a physical mimesis that generates an internal passionate state. The physical environment here determines its constituents' affective and internal disposition. The contagious dimension of sympathetic exchange was such a commonplace by the end of the century that the *Encyclopaedia Britannica* in 1797 bluntly described sympathy as "an imitative faculty, sometimes involuntary, frequently without consciousness."[27]

Shaftesbury, Hutcheson, and other moral sentimentalists asserted a relatively reassuring conception of human nature through their affirmation of a natural "moral sense," but to their moral rationalist critics this affirmation raised dilemmas regarding human autonomy and the moral role of reasoned reflection and choice. At the risk of oversimplifying the well-developed rationalist critique, it was argued that if the sympathetic communication of sentiment and "fellow feeling" occurred irresistibly, if human passions were "naturally contagious," then the question of choice threatened to depart the moral sphere.[28] Although irresistible sympathy offered a compelling response to moral egoism, it also threatened to undermine the independence of human agency and emerging conceptions of moral autonomy—an issue, as we will see, that also haunted Rush's efforts to reform citizens into independent "republican machines." Moreover, sympathy could engender factional associations that undermined social and political stability. "Popular sedition, party zeal, a devoted obedience to factious leaders," Hume wrote, were "some of the most visible, though less laudable effects of . . . social sympathy in human nature."[29] Because sympathy was understood as both salutary "fellow feeling" and a threat to autonomy, society's "cement" and a basis for its potential undoing, moral sentimentalists came to argue that sympathy should be subject to deliberate cultivation and discipline. It was only through the "constant and strenuous art of guiding, informing, and deliberately exercising the sympathetic imagination," John Radner argues, that the "man of feeling" could retain the necessary independence of judgment.[30] Eighteenth-century moral sentimentalists thus emphasized both sympathetic communication and sympathetic cultivation, redirection, and reform: the art of sympathy. Rush also held this view, writing that while the "moral faculty" is "innate" it may nonetheless be "suspended, or directed improperly." He believed that a "regimen" might "improve, or alter the diseased state of the moral faculty."[31] The broad influence of moral sentimentalism on Rush and his contemporaries led many of them to affirm, in Rush's words, that "sensibility is the sentinel of the moral faculty. It decides upon the quality of actions before they reach the divine principle of the soul."[32] Because the moral faculty "is quick in its operations, and like the sensitive plant, acts without reflection," it was essential to give proper form to its perceptions. Rush gloried in the fact that "the intimations of duty and the road to happiness are not left to the slow operations or doubtful inductions of duty, nor to the precarious decisions of taste," but worried that the reliability of the moral faculty could be corrupted.[33] Like duty and taste, sympathy had to be properly regulated.

As with many of his other frequently used terms — "mixing," "combining," "circulating," "associating" — sympathy for Rush connoted both political and physiological reform.[34] Sympathy provides the conceptual lens for understanding the analogical relationship between the physical and the social body in Rush's thought, and his vision of their mutual regulation and reform. Just as Scottish Enlightenment thinkers like Hume and Smith envisioned the coherence of the social and moral world through the sympathetic "movement of the passions,"[35] for influential figures of Scottish medicine sympathy described the communicative organization of the body. By the mid-eighteenth century Edinburgh medicine had departed significantly from the Leiden school's mechanistic approach. Under Robert Whytt's intellectual leadership, it had developed an alternative theory of bodily integration based on a vitalist redescription of the human nervous system. Although Whytt died the year Rush arrived in Edinburgh, Rush's influential teacher William Cullen had adopted Whytt's system's basic outlines. According to Christopher Lawrence, Whytt was the first to give to the term "sympathy" "a clearly defined structural and functional significance" in physiology, and Cullen retained "all of the characteristics of Whytt's sentinel principle — purposeful action, coordinated ability, and, most importantly, unconscious feeling."[36] In the work of Whytt and Cullen, sympathy referred broadly to what Rush later described as "a certain connection of feeling in the nerves" that allowed the parts of the (healthy) body to resonate in harmonious communication.[37] It also established "a still more wonderful sympathy," as Whytt wrote, "between the nervous systems of different persons, whence various . . . morbid symptoms are often transferred . . . without any corporeal contact of infection."[38] Peter Hans Reill notes that this physiological concept of sympathy "enabled late Enlightenment life scientists to account for action at a distance and simultaneous reaction in widely dispersed parts of the organized body," and to break definitively with earlier mechanistic paradigms.[39] Just as sympathy, in the work of the moral sentimentalists, explained the circulation of binding affections in the social body, physiological sympathy, in the theories of Whytt and Cullen, was conceived as the working currency of a corporeal communicative economy.[40]

According to this theory the discrete parts of the body not only communicate with directly neighboring organs and nerves (what Rush called a "sympathy of continuity") but must also be brought into accord based on the organism's overall functioning (regulated by the mind, and described by Rush as the "sympathy of contiguity"). "From this view of the subject, we perceive that the different parts of the body not only perform their more immediate offices, but also such as are of a general nature and tendency. Just so it is with the wheels of a clock: they turn round as their more immediate function, but by their connection with and action upon each other, they produce the general effect of keeping time."[41] Keeping the differently disposed gears arranged so as to achieve their "general nature and tendency" was an important aspect of Rush's reforms; the use of the same term for the integrative power of the physical and social body was a key foundation of Rush's "medical jurisprudence."[42]

Rush believed that knowing the regular and irregular contiguities of the body allowed the physician to intervene efficiently. By knowing that the stomach, for example, sympathizes more closely with the trachea than with the lungs, Rush would counsel his students that they "could more certainly cure cynache trachealis than pneumony by means of a puke."[43] But because Rush cautiously departed from Whytt's and Cullen's influential writings[44] and understood sympathy to also occur outside the strict materialism and natural vitalism of the nerves, he also formulated a dynamic account of mind-body relations (and salvaged a spiritual element missing from strict Edinburgh materialism) that characterized his medico-political reforms. Because sympathy operated beyond the capacity for strict empirical observation, Whytt called it a *facultas incognita*. For the Edinburgh theorists, sympathy, as Forget notes, "was not observable, either in its social aspects or in its bodily operation. It was visible only in its presumed effects."[45] While this quasi-theological attribution of invisible causes to visible effects troubled the strict materialism of Whytt and Cullen, the devout Rush embraced it as proof of the presence of divine will in the workings of nature. Rush rejected his teachers' immanent materialism, later arguing that "Self-existence belongs only to God."[46]

Rush's lifelong faith in a transcendent god and in the truth of revelation was acquired at a very early age. Rush was raised in the Great Awakening context of his mother's strong evangelical, millenarian beliefs. Before attending the College of New Jersey (Princeton), Rush was educated at Gilbert Tennent's strongly New Light West Nottingham Academy, and he was a lifelong admirer of George Whitefield. Although Rush became one of early America's preeminent men of science, he never believed that science posed any challenge to his Christian faith; he always mistrusted the cold secularism of his more Deistic colleagues.[47] Moreover, Rush not only believed in the ultimate compatibility of Christianity and republicanism, he came to see them as necessarily entailed by one another. "A Christian . . . cannot fail of being a republican," he wrote, "for every precept of the Gospel inculcates those degrees of humility, self-denial, and brotherly kindness, which are directly opposed to the pride of monarchy and the pageantry of a court."[48] To sustain this doctrine of political and religious interdependence, Rush ultimately rejected his early Calvinism in favor of what Donald D'Elia has called the "loving heresy of universal salvation."[49] In Edinburgh Rush's religious faith led him to disapprove of Cullen's dismissal of the authority of revelation and to condemn Hume's religious skepticism, but while Rush's "sense of sin" may have abated in Edinburgh, it is not true that his discovery of Republican ideals there led to a decline in his "thirsting after God."[50] As we will see, Rush's post-revolutionary reform efforts were animated by his millennial desire to prepare the way for the "regeneration of our world," and by his commitment to what Robert Abzug describes as the "resacrilization of everyday life."[51] For Rush the sympathetic connections that bound together the social and physical world were a revelatory sign of divine intelligence.

As "the viceregent of divine benevolence in our world," sympathy secured the complicated interdependence of different orders—it structured the great chain of being—and authorized Rush's remarkable reliance on analogical reasoning. To better understand the particularities—and peculiarities—of Rush's "medical jurisprudence" we must first turn to his analogical understanding of the relationship between the human and social body. As Rush remarked in a letter to Thomas Jefferson in 1797, he was often "struck by the analogy of things in the natural, moral, and political world,"[52] and his writings are often organized around such central analogies as that between the physical body and the body politic. This is of course one of the founding analogies of western political thought, but for Rush the analogy was quite literal and physical. In a time and place known for its regular use of corporeal analogies in social and political life, Rush's contemporaries singled him out as a particularly obsessive analogist. Samuel Cooper, Rush's colleague at Pennsylvania Hospital, wrote to his friend William Bache that in his controversial theory of disease, Rush "infers all from many circumstances & elucidates the Whole by analogical reasoning for which you know he is remarkably famous."[53] Indeed one does not read far in Rush's essays, lectures, letters, and notes before finding government described in terms of human psychology, human psychology in terms of government, and disorder in the state's constitution state analogized to disorder of the corporeal constitution. At the outset of his lectures on medicine at the University of Pennsylvania, Rush oriented his audience by declaring that "the human mind may be compared to the British Government," and then proceeded to a detailed elaboration of the analogy.[54] He would later take the United States Constitution as his model of analogical well-being, believing that its various branches and departments copied "the wisdom discovered in the structure of the human mind of an individual."[55]

It is misleading to consider Rush's analogical method as a merely heuristic device, or as being in contradiction to his commitment to empirical

investigation. To Rush, who remained committed to the truth of revelation, it was in the divinely secured association between realms that true,
scientific meaning was disclosed and the grounds of reformative intervention secured. The mutual derangements of body, mind, and polity
demonstrated this truth, and the reform of one realm could never succeed without corresponding reform of the others. Consequently, Rush's
diagnosis of pathology in one often pointed to causes arising from another. It was this background reliance on analogical interconnectedness
that led Rush to assert an "indissoluble union between moral, political,
and physical happiness."[56] Of central import to these investigations was
the interdependence of the spiritual and physical dimensions of individual and collective existence. "How wonderful," Rush exclaimed, "is
the action of the soul upon the body! — Of the body upon the soul!"[57] To
reform the soul, it became clear to Rush, one had to first take hold of the
body.[58] The physical reform of the moral and political life of his fellow
citizens distinguished Rush's efforts once he returned from Edinburgh to
an America rushing headlong into revolution.

II

Two learned and famous physicians, Sydenham and Rush, have taught us that
the plague and the yellow fever, and all other epidemical diseases, when they prevail
in a city, convert all other disorders into plague. I cannot help thinking that Democracy
is a distemper of this kind . . .   JOHN ADAMS TO BENJAMIN RUSH,
6 February 1805[59]

Soon after Rush returned to Philadelphia in July 1769 he accepted an
academic post as professor of chemistry at the College of Philadelphia,
and from this position he began to promote his newly acquired medical
theories in pamphlets and newspapers. He was soon "held up to public
notice" and "familiar to the public ear" as both a physician and a social
reformer.[60] The sentimental republicanism that Rush had acquired in
Edinburgh was practically developed by the "part [he] took in the American Revolution," which "led [him] to try [his] opinions upon many other
subjects as well as that of government."[61] While Rush actively participated in the period's political debates — writing a number of revolutionary articles under the pseudonym "Hamden," encouraging and titling

the publication of Thomas Paine's *Common Sense*, and fiercely opposing the Pennsylvania Constitution of 1776 — he directed his energy primarily toward social rather than governmental reform. In the 1770s and 1780s he publicly advocated for temperance, free public schooling, the abolition of slavery, penal reform, better sanitation, and the reform of public festivals and assemblies. The breadth and depth of his moral, medical, and political reforms are clearly indicated in a letter to Richard Price in 1786 about the unfinished state of the American Revolution: "We have changed our forms of government, but it still remains yet to effect a revolution in our principles, opinions, and manners so as to accommodate them to the forms of government we have adopted. This is the most difficult part of the business of the patriots and legislators of our country."[62] Rush dedicated himself to that business for two decades before growing disillusioned in the 1790s with public life and the possibilities of social reform.[63]

Rush believed that the physician was uniquely positioned to address the physical, moral, and political health of the new nation because he could best understand the physical and physiological dimensions of virtue and vice. "They entertain very limited views of medicine," Rush wrote, "who suppose its objects and duties are confined exclusively to the knowledge and cure of disease."[64] Although biographers have sometimes likened Rush to his friend Paine, noting their equally "uncompromising revolutionary spirit," Rush was more interested in the business of governance than Paine and, like many other members of the patriot élite, he worried deeply about the "excesses of democracy" unleashed by the Revolution.[65] Because he believed that republican citizens had to be habituated into a capacity for virtuous self-government, Rush called for an integrated set of institutions to encourage moral and physical improvement throughout civil society, in the belief that republicanism was more than a form of government, and closer to what Franco Venturi calls a "form of life."[66] Republicanism implied a capacity for self-government in many areas of human endeavor.[67] Rush repeatedly contrasts a healthy capacity for self-government with the loss of individual and collective self-control. "Certain states of society . . . and forms of government have considerable influence in predisposing to derangement." Monarchy and aristocracy, for example, "corrupt all the powers of the mind."[68] Well-organized republican governments, on the contrary, "stimulate the passions, which afterwards act upon the understanding, and impart to it a force, which prevents it from relapsing into the repose of public apathy."[69] "Those governments are best accommodated to the nature of man, in which the same kind of powers are exercised over him, which were given to him for the government of himself." By this Rush meant "properly balanced and well administered" government.[70] If not properly balanced and administered, republican governments too could degenerate into a state of popular licentiousness. In Rush's view the corrupting power of popular government was typified by the revolutionary politics of the people out of doors, which by the 1780s seemed to Rush and many others to threaten post-independence political institutions. Because of the "political insanity" of insurgents like Daniel Shays, Rush feared that postrevolutionary Americans were entering a "wilderness of anarchy and vice."[71]

Thus Rush's commitment to popular government was tempered by warnings about the people's unhealthy, immoral tendencies to vice. "Is not history as full of the vices of the people, as it is of the crimes of kings? . . . The people are as much disposed to vice as their rulers, and . . . nothing but a vigorous and efficient government can prevent their degenerating into savages."[72] "In our opposition to monarchy," Rush wrote, "we forgot that the temple of tyranny has two doors. We bolted one of them by proper restraints; but we left the other open, by neglecting to guard against the effects of our own ignorance and licentiousness."[73] Rush believed that the weakness of postrevolutionary governments, along with the popular "passion for liberty," had bred an unhealthy political culture, exemplified and encouraged by the radical Pennsylvania Constitution of 1776, which Rush believed had resulted from revolutionary enthusiasm and established the institutional environment for perpetuating it. "Our people (intoxicated with the *must* or first flowings of liberty) have formed a government that is absurd in its principles."[74] Borrowing the pseudonym "Ludlow" from a prominent radical of the English civil war, Rush published a series of essays attacking the constitution of 1776 for its incautious neglect of "the ancient habits and customs of the people of Pennsylvania" and its dangerous exposure of "laws and government to frequent and unnecessary innovation."[75] His critique was focused on the constitution's radically democratic elements: its creation of an annually elected unicameral legislature, the septennial election of a "Council of Censors" empowered to nullify legislation, the abolition of property requirements for adult male suffrage, the open publication of proposed laws before legislative votes, and the popular election of magistrates and militia officers. Rush was so closely associated with the constitution's conservative critics that the painter Charles Wilson Peale depicted him in 1783 metaphorically opposing the constitution as an "earthquake" that threatened society's foundations.

Underwriting these dangerous innovations, Rush believed, was an "excess of the passion for liberty" as well as a misconceived understanding of popular sovereignty. Making an argument on which he would elaborate ten years later in the debates over constitutional ratification, he urged his fellow citizens in 1777 not to confuse the idea that "all power is *derived* from the people" with the revolutionary idea that "all power is *seated* in the people." "Government supposes and requires a delegation of power," Rush wrote. "The idea of making the people at large judges of the qualifications necessary for magistrates, or judges of laws, or checks for Assemblies proceeds upon the supposition that mankind are all alike wise, and just, and have equal leisure."[76] Rush worried that self-created popular authority would rob citizens of the capacity for deliberative political judgment and subject them to the sway of popular passions. A government that relies on the regular elicitation of the public passions prevents the establishment of the independent, virtuous character that Rush associated with republican citizenship. Since physicians have "frequent opportunities of witnessing the destructive effects of the passions upon the human body," they must "advocate those governments only which filter laws most completely from the passions of legislators, judges, and the people."[77]

Rush regarded the crowd's attack on James Wilson's house in Philadelphia in 1779, discussed in chapter 2, as evidence that the Pennsylvania Constitution provoked the popular derangement he associated with the behavior of the people out of doors. As a prominent member of the conservative Republican Society (formed in opposition to the constitution of 1776), Wilson had continually opposed attempts by radicals in the supreme executive council and the assembly to regulate prices.[78] The gathering of two hundred militiamen who paraded through Philadelphia on 4 October and eventually confronted Wilson and other "gentlemen" at his house (and were then fired upon by men inside, killing six and wounding many) was motivated by both direct economic incentive and the perceived political inefficacy of the "lower" part of the population. In a letter written shortly after the incident, Rush blamed it on the government's creation of a public environment that favored or elicited mob politics: "Poor Pennsylvania! has become the most miserable spot on the surface of the globe. Our streets have been stained already with fraternal blood—a sad prelude we fear of the future mischiefs our Constitution will bring upon us. They call it a democracy—a mobocracy in my opinion would be more proper. All our laws breathe the spirit of town meetings and porter shops."[79]

Inspired by events like the "Ft. Wilson riot," Rush eventually developed a quasi-physiological theory of the popular politics that tied political disorder to the derangement of mind and body. In "An Account of the Influences of the Military and Political Events of the American Revolution upon the Human Body" (1789) he traced the unique impact of the "novelties" of the Revolution not simply upon the "understandings, passions, and morals of the citizens of the United States" but "upon the human body, through the medium of the mind."[80] As a Revolutionary War doctor, Rush was well placed to observe the effects of war on the body of the soldiery. There were the obvious effects of "thirst" and "pulmonary consumption," as well as a fortitude excited by the "sense of danger," and the "Nostalgia" or "*homesickness*" that seemed to be a particular threat "among the soldiers of the New-England states."[81] The political life of the Revolution also produced a frenzied energy in the body politic; it "deposed the moral faculty, and filled the imagination in many people, with airy and impracticable schemes of wealth and grandeur."[82] The Revolution made people prone to "a peculiar species of extempore conduct." Rush diagnosed this irregular conduct as a disease brought on by "the dissolution of civil government," which continued after the peace of 1783, when Americans found themselves "wholly unprepared for their new situation." "The excess of the passion for liberty, inflamed by the successful issue of the war, produced, in many people, opinions and conduct, which could not be removed by reason nor restrained by government."[83] The same passions that had engendered and sustained the Revolution and War of Independence, Rush feared, would undo their capacity to exercise independent judgment necessary for republican citizenship. Rush characterized this disease of participatory excess and this rage for liberty as a "species of insanity" named "*anarchia*."

Rush's myriad projects of moral, medical, and political reform must be understood against the backdrop of his concerns with postrevolutionary "mobocracy," "anarchia," and "democratic excess." Although the people were to be granted rights and would form the basis of legitimate public authority, they also had to be disciplined into this capacity for delegated self-government. "The business of education has acquired a new complexion by the independence of our country," insofar as it had to train citizens capable of the responsibilities of citizenship.[84] Education broadly conceived had to "convert men into republican machines, if we expect them to perform their parts properly, in the great machine of the government of the state."[85] Donald D'Elia has argued that "Rush's positive conception of government as the molder of men through institutions was the key principle of his social thought."[86] Although postrevolutionary thinkers often disagreed about which virtues should be cultivated or which institutions best suited a republican citizenry, they widely presupposed a "formative" conception of politics.[87] Rush's medico-political emphasis on the role of environmental considerations and physical regimen distinguishes his reform efforts, but it also illuminates his understanding of the necessity of combining social and political reforms to produce the "republican machines" required by a well-regulated popular government. These social and political reforms, moreover, would help prepare the way for "the approaching regeneration of our world," which Rush and many of his contemporaries believed the Revolution had heralded.[88] "It is possible we may not live to witness the approaching regeneration of our world, but the more active we are in bringing it about, the more fitted we shall be for the world where justice and benevolence eternally prevail."[89]

III

In America, everything is new and yielding. Here, genius and benevolence may have full scope. Here the benefactor of mankind may realize all his schemes.
BENJAMIN RUSH TO WILLIAM PETERKIN, 27 November 1784[90]

Environmentalisms of various kinds were central to the thought of many canonical eighteenth-century social and political theorists.[91] Montesquieu's reflections on climate in the *Spirit of the Laws* and the "four stage theory" of Scottish Enlightenment thinkers like Ferguson and Smith are just two well-known examples of how environment was believed to structure social and political practices, and to organize subjectivity itself. In eighteenth-century America it was perhaps J. Hector St. John de Crèvecoeur who most eloquently expressed the environmentalist ideal in his *Letters from an American Farmer*. In it Crèvecoeur announced the birth of a "new man," likening his fellow Americans to "machines fashioned by every circumstance around us."[92] Rush similarly believed that in America "everything is in a plastic state." "Human nature," he wrote, "here (unsubdued by the tyranny of European habits and customs) yields to reason, justice, and common sense."[93] The *tabula rasa* empiricism of Locke's *Essay on Human Understanding* provided the philosophical foundations for these explorations of the environmental formation of subjectivity, but Rush drew less immediately on Locke's work than on that of his more pious popularizer David Hartley.[94] From Hartley's theory of medullary vibrations and ideational associations Rush learned how transformation in the physical environment could structure bodily practices and channel sympathy, giving form to the proper mental association of ideas and leading to the development of character appropriate to a free republic.[95]

Rush bridled at the realization that in America "hitherto the cultivation of the moral faculty [had] been the business of parents, schoolmasters and divines," and insisted that in an enlightened republic such formative obligations would "be equally the business of the legislator, the natural philosopher, and the physician."[96] "God has committed our moral conduct to more than a single legislative power."[97] This moral cultivation would target not only the citizenry's corrupted principles but, more importantly for Rush, their corporeal habits and dispositions; "it was as useless to attack the 'vices' or diseases of the mind with lectures on morality, as it was to berate a person sick with fever."[98] Rush thought there was no moral cost to this appeal to "purely mechanical" habituation over rational principle. "If the habits of virtue, contracted by means of this apprenticeship to labor, are purely mechanical, their effects are, nevertheless, the same upon the happiness of society, as if they flowed from principle."[99] "A physical regimen should as necessarily accompany a moral precept, as directions with respect to air—exercise—and diet, generally accompany prescriptions for the consumption and the gout."[100] What is needed "is the proper direction of those great principles of human conduct: sensibility, habit, imitation, and association."[101]

Rush's "Inquiry into the Influences of Physical Causes upon Morals" detailed his medical understanding of the mutual conditioning of mind and body and the resulting impact of the physical environment on moral development, thus outlining a biopolitical program in which "the American physician should no longer be confined to the knowledge and treatment of disease but extended to include every aspect of health and virtue in the new republic."[102] His work as a physician and as a political reformer was unified through his conception of "medical jurisprudence" and his distinctive medico-political conceptualization of sympathy.[103] "I am fully persuaded, that from the combined action of causes, which operate at once upon reason, the moral faculty, the passions, the senses, the brain, the nerves, the blood and the heart, it is possible to produce such a change in the moral character of man, as shall raise him to a resemblance of angels—nay more, to the likeness of GOD himself."[104] The startling perfectionism of such passages is more reminiscent of Enlightenment radicals like Helvétius and Condorcet than of the moderate and cautious reformism of the moral sentimentalists who had influenced Rush. The millennialist enthusiasm that animated his postrevolutionary reforms committed Rush to a formative politics that belies familiar portrayals of late-eighteenth-century America as simply an "age of realism."[105] Rush recognized that some of his contemporaries would criticize his reliance on the environmental formation of virtuous character for its embrace of human malleability and for dangerously neglecting the consent of reformed citizens. After all, his beliefs meant that the principles of virtuous republican citizenship could be produced aside from the striving or reasoned reflection of citizens. The question was whether "copying the features and external manners" of the virtuous could itself create virtue.

Rush's answer to this question was an enthusiastic and largely unqualified yes. Through imitation, habit, and association, citizens could be made to adopt the comportment constitutive of virtuous citizenship. Rush believed that habits and associations inculcated according to Enlightened and scientific specifications would save postrevolutionary Americans from their democratic licentiousness. Indeed, he so hated prevailing American customs that he once proposed having "schools established, in the United States, for teaching *the art of forgetting*."[106] Rush believed, in other words, that a corrupt citizenry must paradoxically be forced into the human capabilities supporting free citizenship.

Rush set out to form his "republican machines" through a variety of institutional reforms. His invocation of the integrated machinery of government, in which the "wills of the people . . . must be fitted to each other by means of education before they can be made to produce unison and regularity in government," is sometimes taken as proof that he sought a distinctly non-Madisonian empire of uniformity in the New Republic.[107] The metaphor, however, actually suggests more similarity than difference between Rush and Madison.[108] Rush did seek "regularity and unison in government," but uniformity was to arise from the operation of multiple and distinct "parts." "The wills" of the people remain plural even if they must be "fitted to each other." In this and similar passages Rush seemed to demand a very positive and differential practice of political self-government: all have parts to perform in the government, and activity on multiple levels of state and civil society is to be elicited rather than passivity enforced. Rush's emphasis on properly manifested "vitality" and "excitation" is also relevant. Rush was wary of imposing one vision of the good on a republic composed of vital differences. To exploit rather than diminish difference, and to activate rather than immobilize the machine's different parts—one thinks here again of the "sympathy of contiguity" and the resonant workings of Rush's body-clock—these parts would have to be harmonized in accordance with scientific principles. In both the human and the social body this was a matter of understanding the sympathetic communication between parts, arranging the parts to produce a harmony within the whole. The resulting mode of governance was not primarily about imposing restrictive laws but rather aiming toward the proper disposition of things.[109] Rather than restrict human behavior, Rush's reforming institutions would enhance and foster. Rush believed that promoting virtue—"the living principle of the republic"—could not be achieved by "laws for the suppression of vice and immorality" but only by "disseminating the seeds of virtue and knowledge through every part of the state."[110]

Rush's reform proposals were often preoccupied with regulating and encouraging the circulation of meanings throughout the body politic, and they entailed creating large-scale networks of public education— perhaps Rush's single greatest concern—as well as containing much detail about controlling public significations. He counseled the nation's newspaper editors, for example, to avoid the spread of intrigue, lest it "destroy the delicacy of mind, which is the safeguard of a young country," and to instead "let the [socially useful] advancement of agriculture— manufactures—and commerce" be their principal objects.[111] Similarly, when he proposed governmental departments he included mottoes elaborately declaring (one might say belaboring) their purpose.[112]

Of particular concern for Rush was the postrevolutionary persistence of unregulated public spaces. In an address in 1789 to "the ministers of the Gospel of every denomination in the United States," he was at pains to point out "a few of those practices, which prevail in America, which exert a pernicious influence upon morals." Of the eight principal sources of "public vice" that Rush listed, six involved poorly regulated gatherings: "the meeting of citizens for militia exercises"; the "Pandora's box" of public fairs; popular attendance at trials; the "vulgar sports" of horseracing and cockfighting; "clubs . . . where the only business of the company is feeding"; and public amusements on the Sabbath.[113] Rush feared that such invitations to public debauchery, alongside the extra- institutional politics of the people out of doors, posed a threat to the mil- lennial future that he and many contemporaries envisioned for America. Rush saw American "mobocracy" as a pernicious side effect of the Revo- lution, and he hoped that the "citizens of the United States" might "dis- cover as much wisdom in adopting a vigorous federal government to *pre- serve* their liberties as they did zeal and fortitude in *defending* them."[114]

That said, Rush believed that properly orchestrated public spectacles were of value to republican governments for their educative power and their ability to elicit the political attachments of the citizenry. In a letter in 1782 that prefigures many of the themes elaborated in his "philosophi- cal" account of the grand "Foederal Procession" of 1788, Rush described the French *fête* for the dauphin's birthday as "truly republican," even though it celebrated the "birth of a prince."[115] Rush detailed the dynam- ics that prevented this public gathering from degenerating into "a riot or some troublesome proceedings." The French minister who planned the fête "was not unmindful of this crowd of spectators" ("amounting, probably, to ten thousand people," Rush notes). To provide a pedagogi- cal spectacle for the "curious and idle . . . who were not invited to the entertainment," the minister had "pulled down a board fence" to "gratify them with a sight of the company." It is this exemplary display in which Rush seems most interested: how a truly mixed company of guests—

"a world in miniature. All the ranks, parties and professions in the city, and all the officers of government were fully represented"—could nonetheless orchestrate a social harmony that was "truly republican." "The company was mixed, it is true, but the mixture formed the harmony of the evening," he writes: "A decent and respectful silence pervaded the whole company. Intemperance did not show its head; levity composed its countenance . . . and the simple jest, no less than the loud laugh, were unheard at any of the tables. So great and universal was the decorum . . . that several gentlemen remarked that the company looked and behaved more as if they were worshipping than eating."

A delicate social navigation of gratification and self-denial characterized the worshipful proceedings. The entertainment was "delightful" but also "rational." Just as the "Foederal Procession" in 1788 begat "corresponding order" between its participants and spectators, so did Rush suggest a similarly sympathetic order would arise between "idle" observers and participants in the fête for the dauphin. Rush makes it clear that public gatherings could be crucial for securing as well as disrupting order; they could provide either patriotic environments inspiring sympathetic loyalty to the state or unregulated spaces that undermine loyalty. The Revolution's "unruly rites of rebellion," as David Waldstreicher has put it, had to be transformed into "ruling rites of assent."[116] Questions of proximity and distance, mutuality and solitude, manifest themselves repeatedly in Rush's work, most famously in his influential account of juridical judgment and penal reform.

Rush was at the forefront of Philadelphia's penal reform movement in the 1780s and 1790s, and was also the preeminent theorist of this reform. According to Rush, assemblies for public punishments threatened to corrupt individuals' natural sympathy for each other, and to undermine legal authority. Punishments presented a socially corrosive rather than edifying public spectacle and encouraged a disordered sympathetic communication. In an address that became the basis of his subsequently successful efforts at penal reform, delivered at the home of Benjamin Franklin to the Society for Promoting Political Inquiries, Rush wrote that "by an immutable law of nature distress of all kinds, when *seen*, produces sympathy, and a disposition to relieve it."[117] "*Active* sympathy," which is connected with agency, "can be fully excited only through the avenues of the eyes and the ears."[118] Public punishments provided a spectacle of sympathetic identification that could not be gratified—the convict could not be assisted—resulting in what Rush called "abortive sympathy." When crowds gathered to witness state executions, their sympathetic identification with the criminal went unfulfilled, and the sentiment withered over time like an unused muscle. Rush had earlier argued that slavery had a similar hardening effect on the capacity to sympathize.[119] The sympathetic identification between crowd and criminal also threatened to undermine the authority of the juridical power behind the punishment. Moreover, the spectacle of punishment threatened to contaminate the assembled public with the sympathetic presence of the convict's body. When viewers sympathize with the criminal, they "secretly condemn the law which inflicts the punishments—hence arises a want of respect for laws in general, and a more feeble union of the great ties of government."[120] Sympathy "secretly" threatens both the integrity of the social order and the inviolability of the self. It must be at once practiced and selectively resisted.[121] Removing the body of the convict from the stage of "active sympathy," Rush hoped, could work to advantageously "suspend the action of sympathy altogether" where it was not socially beneficial.[122]

Michael Meranze has argued that the fear of sympathetic communication with the criminal in public spaces provided an important justification for establishing penitentiaries in the early Republic. "Mimetic corruption" endangered the communicative economy of an increasingly representational public. The penal reformers of postrevolutionary Philadelphia, following the associative account of sentiment sketched above, understood the body as a social character of excessive signification. As a result of this excess, Meranze writes, "critics of public labor reimagined the city itself as a hall of mirrors where vice and criminality spread through mimicry and contagion."[123] Robert Sullivan similarly argues that late-eighteenth-century American debates over public punishment were concerned with enforcing new forms of political subjectivity. In contrast to the public shaming practices of civic republican penal practices such as the pillory, the increasing emphasis on penal isolation, which Sullivan associates with a nascent liberalism, aimed to produce "an isolated being who is anything but the embedded, fettered, citizen of classical early modern republicanism."[124] In Sullivan's view the penal practices of seclusion and imprisonment, of which Rush was a prominent advocate, seem directed to produce the very subject that liberal political philosophy demands: independent, deliberative, and removed from the anarchic and affective reciprocations of bodies gathered in public.

Rush believed that solitude had a profound reformative power. In a letter to the clergyman Enos Hitchcock in 1789, Rush wrote: "too much cannot be said in favor of SOLITUDE as a means of reformation, which should be the only end of all punishment . . . A wheelbarrow, a whipping post, nay even a gibbet, are all light punishment compared with letting a man's conscience loose upon him in solitude . . . For this reason, a bad man should be left for some time without anything to employ his hands in his confinement. Every *thought* should recoil wholly upon *himself*."[125] Since "the powers of the human mind appear to be arranged in a certain order like the strata of the earth," Rush wrote in his commonplace book, "they recover these powers when they assume their natural place, in isolation from others."[126] While Rush recommended solitary confinement to "persons who are irreclaimable by rational or moral remedies,"[127] his larger concern was with a navigation of proximity and distance that can be best likened to a spatial choreography. Isolation allows for a recalibration of the sympathetic economy, but so too do company, conversation, and polite interaction. On these points Rush's views are connected to broader eighteenth-century movements to reform the social and physical environment, and to corresponding worries over the corrupting power of excessive proximity, including familiar concerns that animated debates over constitutional ratification and reform.[128]

It has been argued that at the close of the Anglophone eighteenth century the "center of moral life becomes the constant and strenuous art of guiding, informing, and deliberately exercising the sympathetic imagination."[129] The ameliorative imperative of physical separation and co-ordination should be understood as one important aspect of this art: for Rush and some of his contemporaries the art of sympathy was also an art of separation. Concerns with cultivating subjectivities appropriate to republican citizenship were questions not simply of self-fashioning but of institutional production, and spatial distribution was one important tactic for organizing an environment capable of producing the citizenry sought by early architects of American social and political institutions, including the citizenry sought by proponents of the constitutional state itself. While Rush's work does not easily fit familiar descriptions of early American political thought as fundamentally "realist," or that emphasize its eminently "practical, unsentimental appreciation of the givenness of human beings,"[130] his work does cast an illuminating light on the period's well-known preoccupation with the advantages of American space to sustaining a viable modern republic and engendering new forms of republican citizenship. Rush's work reveals how sympathy played an important but usually neglected role in these discussions.

The vast expanse of American space was of course often considered the key to understanding America's exceptionalism and to providing the necessary environmental conditions of free and independent citizenship. The focus was generally on the availability of western land, and its importance to sustaining a yeoman republic. However, the discussions of the spatial distribution of citizens sometimes also broached the dangers of contagious passion and sympathy in a small republic or in large public assemblies. In his *Defense of the Constitutions of Government of the United States*, John Adams wrote that because Americans "are sprinkled over large tracts of land, they are not subject to those panics and transports, those contagions of madness and folly, which are seen in countries where large numbers live in small places."[131] This concern with contagious proximity and its corruption of judgment also helped shape the political thought of the "Father of the Constitution," James Madison.

Madison made this argument apparent in his *Vices of the Political System of the United States*, written in April 1787 as he was preparing for the Philadelphia Convention. "The conduct of every popular assembly acting on oath . . . proves that individuals join without remorse in acts, against which their consciences would revolt if proposed to them under the like sanction, separately in their closets." The judgment-distorting force of passions is, Madison continued, invariably "increased by the sympathy of a multitude." Elaborating on the consequences of this insight for the extended republic of the United States, and in terms that seem to echo Adams, Madison wrote: "it may be inferred that the inconveniences of popular States contrary to the prevailing Theory, are in proportion not to the extent, but to the narrowness of their limits."[132] Popular governments were not threatened by the dispersion of an "extended sphere," as suggested by "the prevailing Theory" of small republics, but by too much proximity.

During the "great national discussion" of 1787–88 Madison elaborated on these arguments. He wrote that the "schema of representation" established by the proposed federal constitution would serve as a necessary "substitute for a meeting of the citizens in person," but that it would nonetheless preserve a representative body bound by "an intimate sympathy with the people" represented.[133] Sympathy and separation could be institutionally coordinated, Madison argued, to achieve positive collective ends. Madison's well-known appeal to a "schema of representation" alongside the development of his arguments for "extending the sphere" of government were proclaimed significant improvements over ancient political examples—both democratic and republican—and are often seen as distinctive, if not defining, features of the "new science of politics" pursued in *The Federalist* as a whole.

Expressing a concern with excessive proximity in public assemblies as well as in the territory of the republic, Madison argued that political deliberations within large public assemblies—even were these assemblies composed entirely of philosophers—would inevitably lose their reasoned character: "In all very numerous assemblies, of whatever characters composed, passion never fails to wrest the scepter from reason," Madison wrote. "Had every Athenian citizen been a Socrates; every Athenian assembly would still have been a mob."[134] When Madison proclaimed the inherent irrationality of "all very numerous assemblies," their inevitable descent into a nondeliberative "mob," he was invoking a familiar image of the crowd as a contagious carrier of untempered passion and potential violence. As far back as *The Republic*, Socrates had warned young men of philosophical inclination to avoid the irresistible compulsions of the mob. When a student finds himself among the multitude, Socrates counsels, "he gets carried away and soon finds himself behaving like the crowd and becoming one of them."[135] Similar invocations of the irrational contagion of large popular assemblies are found in the histories of Polybius, Tacitus, Livy, and more.[136] While images of contagious publics certainly circulated widely in the political discourses of the period, the conception of contagious sympathy, and the mechanisms of its spatial coordination, show that there was also a powerful contemporary *argument* behind Madison's striking assertion.[137]

Deep and abiding tensions haunted these discussions about the spatial coordination of public sympathy and the communication of popular passions. Such arguments suggested that the passions that sustained the Revolution might rob the newly independent citizenry of its capacity for self-government, and that the spatial choreography of citizenship responding to this danger might subsequently diminish the citizenry's capacity for collective action. While Rush was a firm proponent of the United States Constitution, he also worried that the "extent of territory" governed by it was the "one path that can lead the United States to destruction"; he worried that a "scattered" citizenry would have "no means of acting in concert with each other" to defend its liberties.[138] Rush feared sovereignty seated in the people, but also feared their inability to act collectively on their own behalf. It is an illuminating ambivalence that sprang from Rush's attempt to navigate the political tensions between sympathy and separation, between a productive and a self-destructive proximity of the people to themselves.

Aristocracy will . . . preach up the excellency of our Constitution . . . Let not this, however, lull us into a fatal security . . . Let us keep in mind that supineness with regard to public concerns is the direct road to slavery, while vigilance and jealousy are the safeguards of Liberty.   DEMOCRATIC SOCIETY OF PENNSYLVANIA, 9 October 1794[1]

We hear frequent mention of the "PEOPLE," the *majesty of the* PEOPLE." &C. &C. These are terms which are played off by certain *Jacobin* demagogues among us to serve their own ambitious purposes . . . but the vague and senseless manner in which these terms are so frequently used will have no influence with the enlightened citizens of America. . . .   "ORDER," *Columbia Centinel*, 3 September 1794[2]

{ 4 }

Spaces of Insurgent Citizenship

Theorizing the Democratic-Republican Societies

Shortly after ordering thirteen thousand federal troops to quell the Whiskey Rebellion of 1794, George Washington delivered his sixth annual address to the United States Congress. Washington blamed the recent tax uprising in western Pennsylvania on the volatile and divisive political climate that had taken hold in the early Republic. In particular, he assailed "certain self-created societies" that had "assumed a tone of condemnation" against government officials and encouraged "crimes which reach the very existence of social order."[3] In personal correspondence from the period, Washington called the insurrection "the first *ripe fruit*" of these societies.[4]

The object of Washington's attack were the Democratic-Republican Societies — voluntary political associations that organized in 1793 against the policies of Washington's Federalist administration. The accusation of political "self-creation" did not originate with Washington's address—it betrayed, as we will see, widespread postrevolutionary anxieties about the dilemmas of collective self-authorization—but the address did spark a rich and resonant debate over the legitimacy of "self-created societies" in a republican government.[5] Although constitutional ratification in 1789 had seemingly settled questions of constitutional order, many fundamental questions about that order and the legitimate parameters of public life were left unresolved: Did citizens have the right to organize themselves politically outside the channels of constituted governmental authority? How was the constituent power of the people to be legitimately represented or institutionally embodied? Who would hold ultimate interpretive authority over the constitution's meaning and extent? What were the boundaries of legitimate political dissent in a republic? The debates over the legitimacy of "self-created" societies in a republic touched on each of these fundamental questions.

Worrying about the consequences for political liberty in the new republic of Washington's accusations against the "self-created societies," Jefferson wrote that the "denunciation of the democratic societies is one of the extraordinary acts of boldness we have seen so many of from the fraction of monocrats."[6] Madison, for his part, referred to Washington's accusation as "perhaps the greatest error of his political life."[7] The passionate debates that ensued in Congress and in the press, when understood alongside the practices and aims of the societies, illuminate not only a peculiar chapter in the history of American political voluntarism, and an exemplary early navigation of the dilemmas of popular self-authorization associated with constituent moments, but also suggest some limitations attending the preoccupations of contemporary democratic theory.

In this chapter I begin by tracing the emergence of the Democratic-Republican societies and the political questions that most directly animated them, with particular attention to elaborating how the Federalist accusation of illegitimate "self-creation" reiterates the dilemmas of self-authorization associated with constituent moments. As we have seen, while there was a broad consensus in the period that popular sovereignty was "the fount of all political power," there was deep controversy over how the people were to be represented or institutionally embodied. This chapter shows that this irresolution persisted after the constitutional settlement. The inability to democratically determine the location of popular voice worked to further generate a democratizing politics, enabling the creation of new political associations claiming to act in the people's name. The example of the societies illuminates how dilemmas of constituency encouraged experimentation in contentious democratic practice in the early Republic's first decade.

I then turn to the practices of the societies, and to how these practices worked to cultivate and sustain the "spirit of liberty" that society members associated with their (threatened) revolutionary inheritance. By creating spaces that elicited political "attention and exertion," the societies aimed not only to create non-electoral mechanisms of élite accountability (although they importantly did that as well), but, simultaneously, spaces of political education through theatrical contention. Like Benjamin Rush, a member of the Democratic Society of Pennsylvania, the societies sought to reform the immanent voice of the empowered people. However, in contrast to Rush's emphasis on the choreography of disciplined "republican machines," the societies aimed to create spaces where the citizenry would be habituated into the vigilant and jealous political sensibility required for preserving their political liberty. They opposed the jealousy of power to the confidence in government demanded by their Federalist opponents.

The action that the societies inspired among their members and from the larger polity was at once politically instrumental and oddly self-directed. While the societies have been sometimes understood as important institutional precursors to the first party system,[8] a closer inspection of their institutional background, their goals, and the heated controversy that emerged around them after the Whiskey Rebellion in 1794 reveals a different impact on early American political development. The democratic societies exemplified a revolutionary tradition of popular constitutionalism and collective resistance that fell into steady decline in the following century. Nevertheless, their enactment of populist republican politics and a confrontational public sphere, along with their assertion of the legitimacy of voluntary political associations within republican government, prefigured the forms of mass democratic politics that emerged in the early nineteenth century. Assessing the democratic societies' political legacy requires grappling with their double valence as both fading remnants of a revolutionary past and harbingers of a partisan democratic future. The societies seemed to take the persistence of their own political enactments — their ongoing politics of "self-creation" — as their overriding goal. In establishing spaces of insurgent citizenship[9] — spaces of political declamation as well as political deliberation — the societies helped to create an assertive and oppositional public culture. This oppositional public culture was fostered by the dissemination of political knowledge and the transformation of public sentiments. Through the enacted educative drama of political self-creation, the societies contested inherited practices of deferential politics in the first decade of the Republic, and in doing so fostered a more popular and populist republicanism.[10]

To conclude this chapter, I turn briefly to debates in contemporary democratic theory concerning the role of voluntary associations and spaces of democratic deliberation in securing a stable and legitimate democratic polity. The example of the societies suggests that neo-Tocquevillian and deliberative democrats, while helpfully drawing attention to the importance of "member skills" acquired only through direct cooperational practice, focus myopically on the skills of socialization and trust on the one hand and ratio-critical argumentation on the other. Focusing only on spaces of conflict *resolution*, these reigning civilitarian positions neglect almost entirely the key democratic importance of spaces of conflict *articulation*. Assuming the existence of political conflict, wrongs, and claims-making practices — or what John Rawls called the "*facts* of pluralism"[11] — these dominant approaches in contemporary democratic theory neglect how wrongs are politically enabled or facilitated in the first place, how they are enabled to cross the threshold of political viability. Michel Foucault called this dynamic "problematization."[12] The example of the Democratic-Republican societies of the 1790s alerts contemporary democratic theorists to the neglect of this dynamic, signaling a better comprehension of the need for experimental spaces of democratic claims making — spaces of insurgent citizenship — to the goal of further democratization.

I

A democracy is a volcano, which conceals the fiery material of its own destruction.
FISHER AMES, Massachusetts Ratifying Convention, January 1788[13]

Revolutions, may they never cease until the whole world be regenerated.
PUBLIC TOAST, TAMMANY SOCIETY, 26 November 1794[14]

More than forty Democratic-Republican societies emerged in the United States between 1793 and 1795. Although concentrated in the mid-Atlantic region, the societies spread from Maine to Georgia, from Eastern seaboard cities to Kentucky's frontier.[15] Their membership was drawn from a broad social stratum that included wealthy urban merchants, small and medium-sized frontier landowners, and also many middle-class artisans and mechanics. Most society members were "self-made men" of one sort or another, and they reveled in this fact. Noting the participation of this recently politicized demographic, the acerbic arch-Federalist William Cobbett likened the societies to an assembly of "butchers, tinkers, broken hucksters, and trans-Atlantic traitors."[16] Despite their diverse social constituencies, all the societies were united in their glorification of the French Revolution — which they understood as a principled continuation of the American Revolution's struggle for liberty against tyranny — and in their opposition to what they understood as the Washington administration's betrayal of revolutionary principles. Society members believed that a host of Federalist policies — both domestic and foreign — typified this betrayal.

Domestically the societies were enraged by the perceived monarchical tendencies of Washington's administration, especially Alexander Hamilton's proposed funding program — the creation of a national bank, the federal assumption of war debt, the excise tax — but also in less formal arenas, such as the reverential celebration of Washington's birthday or mandated robes for the judiciary. The societies lionized Jefferson and demonized his Federalist opponents. As with their revolutionary forebears' attacks on acts of Parliament in the decade preceding independence, society members understood Federalist policies as a part of a conspiracy of the aristocratic few against the hard-won liberties of the people — a quasi-monarchical attempt to roll back the revolutionary advances begun in America and now taking hold in the "Old World." Society members described the Federalist administration and its supporters as aristocratic Anglophiles pursuing a policy of global "Liberticide."[17] They therefore participated in and perpetuated the broader political culture of conspiracy that was, as writers like Bernard Bailyn and Gordon Wood have amply demonstrated, an important part of their revolutionary inheritance.[18]

Internationally the societies railed against the administration's turn away from the revolutionary Franco-American alliance and its realignment with Britain, signaled by the Proclamation of Neutrality (1793) and Jay's Treaty (1794). The infamous visit to America in April 1793 of the French ambassador Edmond Charles Genêt ("Citizen Genêt"), who unsuccessfully attempted to persuade the reluctant Washington administration to support the French Revolution, promoted the creation of popular societies throughout the country (although he was not solely responsible for this proliferation, as many Federalists claimed). Genêt appealed directly to the people for support, looking beyond the representative and duly constituted authority of Washington's Federalist administration. As the Federalist "Columbus" wrote, Genêt "APPEALED FROM THE CONSTITUTED AUTHORITY TO THE PEOPLE OF AMERICA [and] from that moment all the printing presses in America [were] burdened with incendiary publications . . . the people [were] addressed in every possible form, to sustain this absurd and extravagant appeal."[19] Genêt's appeal to the people's constituent power led to the frequent Federalist caricature of society members as foreign agents loyal to the French. Genêt also suggested using the word "democratic" to describe the societies' overarching purpose, as a way of marking the international dimension of their struggle (as opposed to what he considered the more parochially American "Sons of Liberty").[20]

While the societies' grievances were obviously local, they consciously participated in a transatlantic revolutionary context. Society members, great admirers of Thomas Paine and his Rights of Man, regarded themselves as "citizens of the world." The societies should therefore be understood within the broader context of late-eighteenth-century transatlantic radicalism, as an important "part of a cycle of revolutionary influence moving around the north Atlantic" during this period.[21] The societies were acutely aware of participating in this broader revolutionary context.

They addressed one another as fellow citizens in an international revolutionary drama and believed that they faced a similarly international threat, noting for example that "the most extraordinary fact in the annals of the age" was "that *patriotic societies were the objects of denunciation in the same year in Great Britain, France, and the United States of America!*"[22]

The English historian Eugene Black has accurately characterized the eighteenth century as an "age of associations," and the Democratic-Republican societies had several precedents and associational repertoires on which to draw.[23] The societies' institutional inspiration was also both domestic and international. The most immediate precedent, and that most frequently mentioned by Federalist critics, were the Jacobin Club and the *sociétés populaires* of revolutionary France.[24] However, the societies also modeled themselves on radical British organizations such as the London Corresponding Society, the Sheffield Society of Constitutional Information, and the societies that emerged in the 1770s in support of "Wilkes and Liberty." Yet the most important precedent was not European but indigenous: the extraparliamentary traditions and associational repertoires of the American Revolution itself. The societies made this primary influence abundantly clear in their letters, minutes, toasts, and in some instances even their names, such as the Committee on Correspondence and the Sons of Liberty. The societies understood themselves as continuing a colonial and revolutionary tradition of extra-legal voluntary association and direct resistance by constituents claiming to speak in the people's name.

From a broader historical perspective, the societies continued the British Commonwealth tradition of having county conventions act as voluntary representations of the people's voice. They were late-eighteenth-century manifestations of the popular constitutionalist "anti-parliament," an association defined largely by its claim to embody popular voice against the false claims of representatives — duly constituted authorities — in state institutions. "In the extra-parliamentary association," T. M. Parssinen writes, "Irish, American, and British radicals found a means of channeling discontent, disseminating propaganda, petitioning parliament, and, as a last resort, organizing a revolution."[25] Through the associational repertoires of the anti-parliaments, radicals also found a space through which a more radicalized and "self-created" practice of citizenship could be enacted and cultivated. The idea of the anti-parliament gained popular appeal through both the practical experience of the Revolution and the radical tracts of such writers as Obadiah Hulme and James Burgh.[26] At its most radical, the anti-parliament was a claim for the inevitable failure of political representation and the need for the supplemental immediacy of popular voice. Here is how Burgh put the point in his *Political Disquisitions*: "But I assert, that, saving the laws of prudence, and of morality, the People's more absolute, sovereign will and pleasure, is a sufficient reason for their making any alteration in their form of government. The truth is, therefore, that the learned judge has placed sovereignty wrong, viz. in the government, whereas it should have been in the people, next, and immediately under God."[27] The central ideas animating the tradition of anti-parliamentary association were a belief in the sovereignty of the people, endorsement of a popular representative organization outside the organized institutions of the state, and the will to revolt against the perceived illegitimacy of existing institutions. Historians have often noted that associational life in the United States took off in the 1790s, and the democratic societies were the most politically visible of these entities. Although the societies undoubtedly played an important early role in the history of American voluntary association—famously celebrated by Tocqueville—because of this anti-parliamentary background they are poorly understood as merely another association in an emerging civil society. A closer look at their aims and at the debates surrounding their formation reveals why.

The societies asserted that "combinations of the sovereignty of the people, are the only security for general liberty and happiness," the only way to fix "the Rights of Man upon an immovable basis."[28] Their central claim was that government institutions only imperfectly represented the people and that claims could always be made against these constituted powers by appeal to the authority of the people themselves. The societies were what John L. Brooke has accurately portrayed as the "institutional embodiment of the radical enlightenment," the "final florescence" of a colonial and revolutionary tradition of extralegal voluntary association composed of "self-created" constituents claiming to speak in the voice of the people.[29] Though not as final a florescence as Brooke suggests, the societies extended this tradition of extralegal voluntary association in its radical enlightenment form while also revealing how these newer developments were closely aligned with the anti-parliamentary movement in

Britain of the 1770s, and a continuation of the British Commonwealth tradition. Drawing from these associational repertoires of popular will formation, the societies claimed to speak in the name of the people, thereby reiterating what we have seen to be a central and unavoidable point of political contention during the revolutionary and postrevolutionary years. Their claim to embody popular voice against the false claims of constitutional government reinvigorated in the 1790s a debate over popular sovereignty and representation that had animated American political debate and practice since at least the mid-1760s. James Kloppenburg, Forrest McDonald, Robert R. Palmer, J. G. A. Pocock, J. R. Pole, and Gordon Wood have all identified the doctrine of popular sovereignty as the "decisive achievement of the American political imagination."[30] According to Kloppenburg's interpretation, it was popular sovereignty, based in the practice and political self-understandings of colonial Americans, that united in political practice the conflicting idioms of American political discourse: Christianity, civic republicanism, and liberalism. Popular sovereignty, Kloppenburg writes, "seemed to represent at once the fulfillment of the Puritan concept of the covenant, the republican idea of a public-spirited citizenry, and the liberal idea of responsibly self-interested individuals exercising their right to self-government."[31] Although these conflicting political idioms may have been "fulfilled" in the abstraction of popular sovereignty, this abstraction secured nothing like a consensual resolution of the meaning of this abstraction in political practice.

Although there was broad consensus during this period in American history that political legitimacy was based in popular will, there was also deep controversy over how that will was to be represented or institutionally articulated. The example of the societies shows how this irresolution continued beyond the constitutional founding.[32] In part this controversy was a consequence of the period's persistent ambiguity between the people's constitution-making powers and their electoral power (an understandable ambiguity among people fresh from revolutionary and constitution-making experiences).[33] From another perspective, the controversy arose from the well-known American tension between regional and national political representation, and the conflicting claims of citizenship that this tension entailed.[34] But it was also the consequence, as we have seen, of a paradox that might be said to adhere to

the very conception of collective self-rule. "The people" is an entity produced only through representation—a productive "fiction"[35]—yet the
claim of popular sovereignty is that legitimate political representation
is grounded on the entity that is produced by it. The effect is taken for
cause. The inability to secure or locate once and for all the "voice of the
people" gave rise to democratizing politics and enabled the societies'
claims of "self-created" popular authorization, their frequent recurrence
to "the majesty of the people." The failure of final capture or authoritative representation of popular voice created open spaces for articulating
political wrongs and the repertoires of claiming that supported them. It
is this failure of capture that is at stake in the debates between Democratic Republicans and Federalists over the disputed legitimacy of political "self-creation" in a republican, constitutional government.

While the conflict between society members and Federalists was remarkably vehement, it is misleading to describe this conflict as partisan:
abiding by prevailing norms of civic republican political thought, both
sides agreed that partisanship or factionalism signified political corruption and was thus illegitimate. Each side of this political conflict claimed
to represent the good of the *whole* society; in the 1790s there was not yet
a sense of a "loyal opposition" in American politics. The refusal of legitimate partisan contention in fact contributed to the vehemence of the
period's political debate, with Federalists demonizing society members
as traitorous insurgents, loyal to the French, and society members similarly demonizing Federalists as aristocratic loyalists conspiring with the
British monarchy to rob the people of their revolutionary birthright.[36]
Some historians have argued that the conflict between supporters and
critics of the Federalist administrations of the 1790s brought the country
to the brink of civil war.[37]

Although there are variations within the debates between Federalists and Democratic Republicans over the question of self-creation, two
broadly distinct positions can be identified. For Federalists like Washington what seemed "most absurd, most arrogant, most pernicious to the
peace of Society" was that the societies formed themselves into "permanent censors," believing that they had the authority to judge "acts of Congress which have undergone the most deliberate and solemn discussion
by the Representatives of the people . . . endeavoring as far as the nature
of the thing will admit, to form *that will* into Laws."[38] For many Federal

ists parliamentary deliberation over political questions made subsequent public engagement in these questions unnecessary at best, subversive at worst. While each side accused the other of betrayal or treason, the societies embraced the legitimacy of political dissent within a republic to a much greater degree than their Federalist opponents (as the Alien and Sedition Acts would later demonstrate conclusively). The societies hoped to foster spaces of political dissent free from government interference; they were powerful advocates of the people's civil liberties who affirmed the people's right to challenge their governors' policies. The Federalists, conversely, sought a public sphere where associations within civil society worked *in concert* with the government, where political disputes were settled by duly elected officials and accepted by their constituents. Their model association was the élite Society of the Cincinnati. The Democratic-Republican societies were figured by their Federalist opponents as little more than self-appointed or self-elected political representatives.[39] Who were they to claim popular authorization in the face of duly constituted representatives? As one Federalist, himself writing as "THE PEOPLE," put the point: "Private clubs are unknown in the Constitution; they are self-created; they hold secret councils; they attempt to influence measures of government which respect the property of their fellow citizens, without suffering those fellow citizens to be represented in those clubs."[40] Or as another put it: "By 'The People'" is meant THE WHOLE PEOPLE . . . it is the *res publica* or common-weal, which no man, or no body of men, except such as be constitutionally appointed . . . can have a right exclusively to consult, act upon, or direct."[41]

Fisher Ames, a representative from Massachusetts and one of the most outspoken and articulate of the Federalist opponents to the societies, is perhaps also the best theorist of the Federalist position.[42] Sometimes considered a minor American Burke, Ames took on directly the notion that representation is but a "mere copy of the original, the people." Instead, he asserted, "representation is something *more* than the people."[43] Representation was not simply a copy of an originary will for Ames and other Federalists, but a refinement and rational improvement of that will. In Ames's account the people become sovereign only when they "delegate that power, which they cannot use themselves." In an early address before the Massachusetts ratification convention, Ames likened democracy to a "volcano."[44] The people, while the fount of power, are also the fount of an unusable, undisciplined, and undirected power: a non-sovereign power.[45] In a republican government, when that power of the people is properly organized and represented, there is no need for extraparliamentary politics. For Federalists, "self-created societies" were needed only during a time of what Noah Webster called "total renovation."[46] Under an established republican government they could only challenge the government's monopoly on that representative claim, and thereby subvert the government's duly constituted authority. According to Ames in a speech before Congress in 1794, the societies "arrogantly pretended sometime to be the people, and sometimes the guardians, the champions of the people. They affect to feel more zeal for popular Government, and to enforce more respect for republican principles, that the real Representatives are admitted to entertain."[47] Of course what constituted "real" representation was just the question. The Federalists feared the creation of parallel political institutions that would draw popular support away from the new government's fragile institutions just as American revolutionary institutions had usurped their colonial governors' authority. "If the clubs prevail," Ames wrote, "they will *be* the Government, and the more secure for having become so by victory over the existing authorities."[48]

The societies typically responded to these accusations by asserting that they were not challenging the constitution so much as defending its central principles. The societies couched their claims against the government in a constitutionalist idiom, and in doing so further extended the tradition of popular constitutionalism beyond the constitutional founding.[49] The people remained the authority behind the new constitutional arrangements, but their voice was not to be wholly subsumed within the constitutional text. For society members it was only by creating spaces where popular sentiments could be expressed and popular will enacted that the government could be kept within its constitutional bounds. As Madison, a supporter of the societies, asked in the title of an article written for Phillip Freneau's *National Gazette*, "'Who are the best keepers of the people's liberties?' 'The people themselves.'"[50] For society members, "combinations of the sovereignty of the people [were] the only security for general liberty and happiness."[51] This invocation of the people's self-authorizing constituent power expressed a marked suspicion of officially constituted political power as well as the need for extragovernmental articulations of demotic power to control the people's governors. If not by themselves, one Republican asked, "by whom, then, ought we to have been constituted?" "Are not all private associations established upon the foundation of their own authority sanctioned by the first principles of social life?"[52] Society members certainly did not believe they had to be authorized by the government, which the societies defined as a power inherently threatening to the liberties of the citizenry. As the German Republican Society of Philadelphia stated in an address to "the Free and Independent Citizens of the United States":

> All governments are more or less combinations against the people; they are states of violence against individual liberty, originating from man's imperfection and vice, and as rulers have no more virtue than the ruled, the equilibrium between them can only be preserved by proper attention and association; for the power of government can only be kept within its constitutional limits by the display of power equal to itself, the collected sentiments of the people. Solitary opinions have little weight with men whose views are unfair; but the voice of the many strikes them with awe. To obtain connected voice associations of some sort are necessary, no matter by what name they are designated. The checks and balances of government are inventions to keep the people in subordination, a reaction of some sort is necessary, therefore, to keep up the equipoise between the people and the government.[53]

What Publius described as the "auxiliary precautions" of institutional design and the separation of powers appeared as mere "parchment barriers" to society members, for whom the "substance" of the government's power could only be balanced by popularly organized power of the citizens it governed.[54]

The societies' claims to defend the principles of the constitution by opposing government were understood as mere subterfuge by many of their Federalist opponents. For some, notably Hamilton, the very meaning of the constitution seemed to be at stake. "It is not easy to understand," Hamilton wrote in a letter to Washington, "what is meant by the terms 'constitutional resistance.' The theory of every constitution pre-supposes as a *first principle* that the *Laws are to be obeyed*. There can therefore be no such thing as a 'constitutional resistance' to Laws constitutionally enacted."[55] He continued: "The operation, or what is the same thing, the execution of a law, cannot be obstructed, after it has been constitutionally enacted without illegality and crime."[56] Writing as "Tully" to mobilize militia support against the Whiskey Rebels, Hamilton similarly wrote that "sacred respect for the constitutional law is the vital and sustaining energy of a free government."[57] Hamilton was at pains to show that in contrast to the governing assumptions of the societies, *republican* government should not be understood as an external power requiring the "jealousy" and "vigilance" of its citizens, but instead their open "confidence." "The government," he wrote, "is YOUR OWN work"; "YOU are called upon not to support THEIR power, BUT YOUR OWN POWER."[58] Through such arguments Hamilton, Ames, and other Federalists attempted to "recast extraconstitutional political activity as the subversion of the Constitution."[59]

What was crucially at stake in these debates was the Revolution's tradition of popular constitutionalism and the dilemmas that emerged from this tradition regarding who could legitimately claim to speak in the people's name. For the societies the Constitution's "We the People" was ultimately still embodied in "the people at large," rather than in the constitutional text. In their replies to the Federalist accusation of illegitimate "self-creation," society members frequently invoked the "self-created" status of many public authorities, in particular—and perhaps most unnervingly for their Federalist opponents—the "self-created" constitutional authority of the Philadelphia Convention. When compared to the Philadelphia Convention, one anonymous Democrat wrote, these societies were "a mere shadow of self-creation." These arguments established a troubling continuity between the dilemmas of popular authorization that defined the debates over the authority of the Philadelphia Convention, the questioning of the convention's legitimacy by Anti-Federalists, and those that persisted after successful constitutional ratification.

While the societies claimed to speak the voice of the people, and the Federalists countered that voice was only present in the institutions of constitutional governance, the overall *effect* of this dispute was to reveal the provisional nature of *any* claim to popular articulation. "The people," Gordon Wood summarizes, "had become simply the collective community standing outside the entire government—a final court of appeal to which every aggrieved group took its case."[60] The effect of these competing claims was to reveal "the people" not as the firm ground on which republican politics was based but as a political invention or a form of claim. The ultimate ambiguity of the people, often noted in the debates around the societies, was an engine of democratic contestability; competing claims over the determination of that subject generated an oppositional democratic practice.

This interpretation makes some sense of the societies' common claim to be actively perpetuating the "spirit of '76," a spirit they realized could not be perpetuated without creating institutions similar to those that had instantiated the spirit in the first place. The societies seemed to have quite a sophisticated understanding of the interconnection between the "spirit" they admired and its dependence on continued "attention and exertion" sustained by institutions. As one Democrat put it in the pages of the *Independent Gazetteer*: "Whatever the United States might have been previous to the American Revolution, it is pretty evident that since their emancipation from British Rapacity, they are a great self-created society . . . had the British succeeded in impressing our minds with a firm belief in the infamy of self creation, we should never have been free and independent to all eternity."[61] The societies were mobilized to impress the opposite sentiment upon the minds and bodies of the American citizenry. In creating spaces of democratic contention they created a celebratory spectacle of self-creation to oppose the Federalists' opposing spectacle of deferential subordination, likened by one Democrat to the "mystical solemnity of forms imposed upon the people with a kind of awe" and by Jefferson to a sight "perfectly dazzled by the glittering of crowns and coronets."[62] The societies countered Federalist public culture by creating spaces that fostered what Thomas Pynchon describes in *Mason & Dixon* as the period's prevailing sense of the "unmediated newness of History a-transpiring."[63]

II

But in Kentucky you have a Democratic Society—that horrible sink of treason,
—that hateful synagogue of anarchy,—that odious conclave of tumult,—that frightful cathedral of discord,—that poisonous garden of conspiracy,—that hellish school of rebellion and opposition to all regular and well-balanced authority.
"XANTIPPE," *Virginia Chronicle*, 17 July 1794[64]

Sinks, synagogues, conclaves, cathedrals, gardens, and schools: "Xantippe" reveals a few of the many figurations that opponents of spaces of insurgent citizenship have relied upon to describe them. Forrest Mc-Donald has written that the Democratic-Republican societies played a key role in the "politicization of American life" during the 1790s, and historians have generally agreed that the period was distinguished by the passion of its political conflicts and by a marked extension of political sensibilities into everyday life.[65] More attention should be paid, however, to the techniques through which the Democratic-Republican Societies achieved this politicization. I now turn to what the societies actually did, what activities and events preoccupied them in the spaces they created for enacting a more broadly conceived and practiced citizenship. The societies envisioned citizenship as clearly exceeding established or formal channels of political participation — largely electoral — as well as the formal bounds of legal recognition. For society members, citizenship was a practice more than a juridical category. They addressed a public made up of their members and those who were not members as active participants in a political world, even if not fully enfranchised within the juridical order. Their activities enacted a citizenship meant to perpetually resist capture by formal institutions; they enacted a citizenship that was self-created and self-authorized.

As a corollary of the idea that people were "the best keepers of their liberty," republican thinkers of the period commonly expressed the belief that the people needed a political education to prepare them for the responsibilities of citizenship. Voluntary associations in the 1790s — from the secretive Freemasons and the élite Society of the Cincinnati to Benjamin Franklin's Junto and the democratic societies — justified themselves by emphasizing their educative or formative dimensions. The societies were neither political parties nor merely pressure groups. Instead they sought what John L. Brooke has described as "the self-conscious construction of a public culture," a widely disseminated public education for a free, independent citizenry.[66] To this end they disseminated political information and provided forums for popular mobilization against the government's purported violations of liberty. The societies believed that creating and perpetuating an informed, vigilant citizenry was essential to defending the people's liberties against the tyrannical conspiracies of the few; they believed the government could never be trusted to check itself. In place of the Federalist emphasis on order, national power, and deference, the societies hoped to foster widespread enthusiasm for politics, citizen mobilization, and vigilance. This educative or formative dimension of politics was generally articulated in the civic republican idiom of the virtues, and it was widely held that without popular virtue no institutional mechanisms alone could sustain popular liberties. As Madison said before the Virginia Ratifying Convention: "Is there no virtue among us? If there be not, we are in a wretched situation. No theoretical checks—no form of government can render us secure. To suppose that any form of government will secure liberty or happiness without any virtue in the people, is a chimerical idea. If there be sufficient virtue and intelligence in the community, it will be exercised in the selection of these men. So we do not depend on their virtue, or put confidence in our rulers, but in the People who are to choose them."[67] If "the existence and perpetuity of freedom depends on the people themselves," the society member Tunis Wortman said in an address to the Tammany Society of New York in 1796, increasing attention must be paid to "the influences of social institutions upon human morals and happiness."[68] In that each citizen was a "creature of education and a child of habitude," the institutional environment was understood, as we have already seen in the above discussion of Rush, as productive of a certain kind of subject or citizen.

Different associations envisioned public culture in sharply divergent ways. The period's passionate debates between Federalists and Democratic Republicans were concerned not simply with the pursuit of electoral power but with creating a cultural environment that would produce very different kinds of politics and citizens. Following Locke's influential educational writings, which Jay Fliegelman has called "the most significant text of the Anglo-American Enlightenment," members of these associations believed that political education should occur on different levels of human experience.[69] "It is the great work of the governor," Locke writes, "to fashion the carriage and inform the mind."[70] Through their activities, the Democratic Republican Societies pursued an education and a habituation into the practices of free citizenship.

The most apparent component of this civic education, and the component still most frequently commented on by contemporary historians, was the dissemination of political information and the creation of an informed citizenry. The Reverend Ebenezer Bradford was not alone in considering the Democratic Republican societies "Schools for Political Knowledge."[71] Their founding documents frequently emphasized the dissemination of political knowledge and the importance of identifying with an international revolutionary movement, as well as invoking the centrality of cultivating certain "tempers, sentiments, and manners" for the production of a free citizenry. The preamble from the Republican Society of Lancaster's constitution is representative: "Being convinced, that not freedom, either political or religious, can dwell except in a virtuous, enlightened, and well-instructed people; we the subscribers have, therefore, unanimously entered into an association under the name of the Republican Society of Lancaster, for promoting useful knowledge and political information, and for disseminating liberal and republican sentiments."[72] The repeated coupling of knowledge and sentiments is formulaic in the societies' documents, but underemphasized by most commentators. Considering the sentimental or affective dimension of the societies' activities illuminates their oddly self-referential and theatrical aspect and diminishes the state-directed narratives that have too often been ascribed to them. They were not institutions of electoral mobilization so much as spaces of democratic subjectification.

Burgh's *Political Disquisitions* emphasizes the central importance of shaping tempers, sentiments, and manners, and expresses worry that too much emphasis was placed by his contemporaries on narrowly juridical concerns: "If you be wise [Burgh counsels], you will lay infinitely more stress on *manners* than on *laws*. We for our poor part, act on the direct contrary principle. We have more law than needed for all the nations of the sixteen worlds of the solar system. And as to the arts, by which *character* and *manners* of a people are formed, we set them at a distance."[73] Many of the societies' memorials, resolutions, toasts, and addresses to the people pleaded explicitly for cultivating alternative and more contentious political tempers. Just as often, however, these political tempers were asserted as self-evident and *felt* components of the societies' revolutionary inheritance. As members of the German Republican Society of Philadelphia wrote in a correspondence with another of the Pennsylvania societies, "To recur to argument to substantiate a principle so evident is to suppose it doubtful; it is sufficient to say that this society is sensible of the benefits which result from political associations, and that it feels the right—a right purchased with the treasure and blood of our country."[74] The "benefits that result from political association" were élite accountability on the one hand—the censorial role of the societies—and the self-directed education entailed by enacting that accountability on the other. They were "benefits" at once politically instrumental and directly self-referential. Political contention had republican benefits that could be reduced not to the policy goals toward which it was directed, but in the kind of citizens—vigilant, assertive—that it shaped in the process.

The formative dimensions of this oppositional political action are clearly articulated in the opening salvo of the Democratic-Republican societies, the first published circular of Philadelphia's German Republican Society. This circular is emblematic of broader concerns with how acts of political self-creation could provide a political education for sustaining the people's liberties. The letter begins:

> Friends and Fellow Citizens,
>
> In a republican government it is a duty incumbent on every citizen to afford his assistance, either by taking a part in its immediate administration, or by his advice and watchfulness, that its principles may remain incorrupt; for this spirit of liberty, like every virtue of the mind, is to be kept alive only by constant action—It unfortunately happens that objects of general concern seldom meet with the individual attention which they merit, and that individual exertion seldom produces a general effect; it is therefore of essential moment that political societies should be established in a free government, that a joint operation be produced, which shall give that attention and exertion so necessary to the preservation of civil liberty.[75]

As this circular makes clear, the characteristic call to political action among the societies was not oriented by an Aristotelian or classical humanist vision of man as a political animal or as realizing his humanity only through participation in public life.[76] Political action secured the preservation of liberties, the often-invoked Rights of Man. It is important to also emphasize, however, the extent to which the societies thought that rights and liberties could be protected *only* through constant political engagement. The discourse of the societies provides numerous examples of such mixing and combining of the supposedly distinct paradigms of liberalism and civic republicanism, and supports contemporary arguments about the mutual imbrications of these traditions of political thought during the postrevolutionary era.[77] The societies envisioned rights not as trumps to democracy but as catalysts of its continuation.[78]

The German Republican Society's circular, like many others, begins with the essential point that for a free government to remain free, the people must sustain a "spirit of liberty." In warning their public not to be lulled into a "fatal security" or diverted "from the great object of our duty," the societies argued that "supineness with regard to public concerns is the direct road to slavery, while vigilance and jealousy are the safeguards of Liberty."[79] These terms—"vigilance" and "watchfulness"—are the two most representative descriptors of this spirit in the societies' writings. The German Republican Society of Philadelphia's announcement particularly urges that this spirit be applied to public things, what the author calls "objects of general concern." The author's demand for the animating persistence of "constant action" qualifies the opening paragraph's emphasis on the "virtue of the mind" and what we might call the cognitive aspect of attentiveness. The preservation of civil liberty requires "attention," the author writes, and also "exertion." The "constant action" that the societies urged was not just politically instrumental but an enactment of the liberties they were most concerned to defend and sustain. Continually reiterated in their letters, minutes, toasts, and public declarations are demands for what Hannah Arendt and Claude Lefort have both called the "right to have rights": the right to be a political being, to make claims not through appeal to an existing juridical authority but through the popular enactment and protection of rights themselves.[80] Democratic politics, envisioned in this way, was the very end of their politics. Oddly self-referential, the Democratic-Republican societies of the 1790s at times seemed to take their own existence as their overriding goal.

The societies were therefore established to create spaces through which this constant action was not only enabled but encouraged. They envisioned vigilance and the jealousy of power not simply as a state of the mind but as states of the body to be cultivated through an ongoing repertoire of contentious political practice, only a few of which actually involved engagement with state institutions or the official channels of political participation. Both opponents and supporters of the societies occasionally recognized this physical habituation of insurgent citizenship. Gouverneur Morris, for example, lamented that "there is a moral tendency and in some cases even a physical disposition among the people of the country to overthrow government,"[81] and Benjamin Rush, as we have seen, wrote that a zeal for liberty had engendered a "peculiar species of extempore conduct" among postrevolutionary Americans.

A graphic depiction of the societies from the period provides further

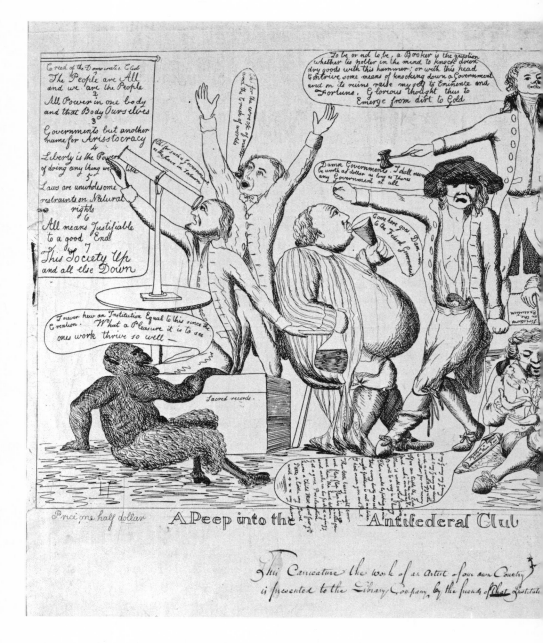

2. Graphic parody of the Democratic Society of Pennsylvania, 1793.
Courtesy of the Library Company of Philadelphia.

Creed of the Antifederal Club (upper left corner):

1. The people are All and we are the People.

2. All power in one body and that body ourselves

3. Government but another name for aristocracy

4. Liberty is the power of doing anything we like

5. Laws are unwholesome restraints on natural rights

6. All means justifiable to a good end

7. This society up and all else down

Figure in lower left corner: "Never been an institution equal to this since the creation.

What a pleasure it is to see one's work thrive so well."

Figure at telescope: "Oh for such a government as they have in heaven."

Figure with arms raised: "Oh for the wreck of matter and the crush of worlds!"

Figure drinking: "Damnation to the federal government."

Figure raising right arm: "Damn governments. I shall never be worth a dollar as long as there's any government at all."

Figure with gavel: "To be or not to be a Broker is the question. Whether tis nobler in the mind to knock down dry goods with this hammer; or with this head contrive some means of knocking down government and on its ruins raise myself to Eminence and Fortune. Glorious thought thus to emerge from Dirt to Gold."

Figure with dark hat and beard: "Ça Ira"

Fifth figure from right: "Will you subscribe to this and faithfully follow all the articles of our creed?"

Fourth figure from right: "Yes Damme he'll subscribe to anything, he has nothing to lose."

Third figure from right: "Well citizen Mungo, what think you of this?"

Figure in upper right corner: "Tink! Fine ting broder bokrah Our time nex."

Figure sitting with doll: "Oh my ganny my ganny and oh my ganny my diary such a sweet as this is neither for nor neary If we can tickle the lads and make em engage in the war then it would see our frontiers burnt to a rag in a hurry There would be frisking . . ."

Book: "Strictures on the executive."

Scroll: "Politics is a better trade than Law."

evidence of their central activities. "A Peep into the Antifederal Club" is a Federalist parody—from its description of the clubs as "antifederal" to the appearance of a devil and a Frenchman—that ridicules the Democratic Society of Pennsylvania, which William Cobbett described as the "mother" of American Jacobin clubs.[82] The image represents several activities that characterized the meetings of the societies: the declaration of principles found in the upper left corner of the image, the reading of correspondence, the keeping of minutes, the celebration of the French Revolution, the singing of revolutionary songs, the general toasting and speechifying that James Epstein argues was crucial to transatlantic cultures of "radical conviviality," and finally, in what was perhaps intended as most damning by the artist, the opening of speculations on the incomplete state of liberty in late-eighteenth-century America, on its circumscribed and racialized articulation of the self-authorizing people.[83]

This last point is made by the racially charged invocation of "Citizen Mungo" and his express pleasure in the proceedings before him, as he responds to his interlocutor's question—"Well Citizen Mungo, what think you of this?"—in a phrase that was surely meant to provoke fear and foreboding in the viewer: "our time nex." The mere presence of a "citizen" of African descent in the image, a presence not representative of the societies, invoked widely publicized events of the recent past, in particular the slave rebellion in the colony of Saint-Domingue in 1791 (the Haitian Revolution), which Federalists often figured as the logical consequence and extension of the French Revolution.[84] The image illustrates the Federalist fear that postrevolutionary appeals to the people, taken to their fullest consequence, could not be legitimately contained within the bounds of white, propertied men. As John Adams had prophesied two decades earlier: "new claims will arise." "A Peep into the Antifederal club" dramatizes a concern about the contingent lines of demarcation around the people during the "Age of Revolutions," and the unfinished state of revolutionary self-creation, here linking such enactments with the pervasive fear of slave rebellion. As with the engraving by Chadowiecki examined in the Introduction, but without the celebratory intent, this Federalist parody of the democratic societies focuses directly on the racial reiteration of revolutionary self-creation.

The general thematic of self-creation is also depicted in many of the image's central components: the second creed, "All power in one body and that Body Ourselves"; the devil's statement that "there is no institution equal to this since the creation"; the presiding president's claim for the transforming power from ruin to eminence, from dirt to gold; the scroll at the bottom of the page that reads simply, "Politics is a better trade than law." In addition to these particular statements, perhaps most important is the image's overall composition and tone, its emphasis on outstretched arms, declamatory gestures, and the language of public address. It is expressly theatrical, and while the theatricality is presented as parody, it also represents something very important to the activities of the societies: their ritualized theatrics of political opposition, declamation, and contest. The societies' regular practices of political declamation enabled and fostered the articulation of political wrongs that helped to cultivate the sensibilities of vigilance, watchfulness, and jealousy. The fostering of contentious claims was recognized by Federalist defenders of political order like Fisher Ames, who feared that the societies would *produce* more grievances than were actually *felt*, that they would invent or enact ever new claims: "If people have grievances, are they to be brought to a knowledge of them only by clubs? Clubs may find out more complaints against the laws than the sufferers themselves had dreamed of. The number of those which a man will learn from his own and his neighbors experience will be quite sufficient to every salutary purpose of reform in the laws or of relief to the citizen."[85]

Although the societies were at times concerned with sending remonstrances to their governors or debating elections, they were sites of political deliberation and political declamation, and the practices of declamation were self-justifying. In other words, the act of declamation was often taken to be as important as the particular political issue being declaimed against. The theatrical self-referentiality of the societies' position is expressed through their emphasis on publicity, an emphasis that belies the frequent Federalist charges of cabal and secrecy. Not only were their circulars, toasts, and remonstrances intended to provoke public discussion—sometimes in the press, sometimes in the streets, as when the Democratic Republican Society of Pennsylvania drew around five thousand people into a city square in Philadelphia to announce and discuss the revelation of Jay's Treaty with Britain—but the societies also helped to inspire what the historian David Waldstreicher calls the period's "politics of celebration."[86]

As Waldstreicher emphasizes, the societies designed counter-rituals to oppose the Federalists' forms of political theater. In the first year of

Washington's administration, even as he and other Federalists filled executive posts in the federal government, they also turned their attention to "the self conscious creation of a ritual and aesthetic environment that would visually and socially reinforce the new government's authority and legitimacy."[87] While the documents of the societies frequently assailed the monarchical spectacles meant to induce awe in the people, they did not forgo political aesthetics altogether. They conceived what can be characterized as an aesthetics of counterrule. While no longer "dazzled with adventitious splendor, or awed by antiquated usurpation," as one democratic republican put it, they still sought to erect new "temples": "Temples of LIBERTY on the ruins of Palaces and Thrones."[88] Simon Schama has nicely captured the persistence of republican political aesthetics: "Republics . . . if born in austerity . . . invariably flourish amidst pomp . . . an aldermanic rather than regal display, consistent with the public adjuring the rites of monarchy. It may have little in common with court mystique in which the aura of the god prince is veiled . . . republican pomp is no less grandiose. It is public rather than secluded, bombastic rather than magical, didactic rather than illusionist . . . It offers participation and loyal huzzahs rather than bowed heads and awed prostration."[89]

Instituting the celebration of Washington's birthday was one important way that the Federalists hoped to effect this civic reverence; mandating robes for the judiciary was another. Letters and other records show that Washington and key members of his administration deliberated intensely on what he called "the style proper for the Chief Magistrate."[90] In response, the societies mobilized a political counter-aesthetic most obviously present through their planning and organization of public festivals. As Federalists co-opted the celebration of Washington's birthday, the societies co-opted the symbolism of both the American and the French Revolutions: effigies, liberty caps, and liberty poles were crucial parts of these revolutionary repertoires.[91] They planned Fourth of July celebrations, commemorations of the Franco-American alliance, commemorations of French military victories and even of constitutional reforms in France. One contemporary noted, "never has a group of citizens given themselves up to [such] extraordinary series of celebrations in honor of the achievements of another country."[92]

Through these celebrations the societies also opened practices of citizenship beyond their own membership to the formally unenfranchised, in particular to women and people of African descent. They did not do so through their official membership so much as through the larger public spectacles that they created. They created spaces where, in Michael Warner's words, constituencies could be interpellated into a political world without being interpellated into a juridical order.[93] The societies aimed to educate their members and, by consequence more than intent, the public at large into a *sense* of their own opposition, their own "self-created" collective authority—to retain a lively sense, post-founding, of their constituent capacities.

The audacity of the societies' theatrical declamations helped deflate the staid, deferential republicanism of the Federalists into a more assertive and populist politics. As Sean Wilentz writes, the societies were aware that "overthrowing the Federalists' aristocracy required erasing that sense of embarrassment and inferiority."[94] From the perspective of the societies, "the splendid frippery, the pompous sophistry, with which the bands of slavery have been tinseled over, are now found like a species of rotten wood."[95] Debates around deferential politics and their relation to the political ideologies of the period are sometimes confused because deference cannot simply be reduced to an ideology or to explicit statements defending its practice. Deference is as much about comportment, manner, and habit as it is about principle or argument, and the societies very clearly recognized this in their policies to change their manners of address and comportment ("humble servants" were replaced by "fellow citizens"). Their "efficacy" can be measured, in other words, not simply in the electoral contests they may have helped mobilize and win for Republicans, but in the democratic and oppositional sentiments that they brought about.

Democracy means participation, but participation is not primarily about "taking part," as in elections or officeholding. It means originating or initiating action with others. SHELDON WOLIN, "Contract and Birthright"[96]

Participation is the invention of that unpredictable subject which momentarily occupies the street, the invention of a movement born of nothing but democracy itself. The guarantee of permanent democracy . . . is the continual renewal of the actors and the forms of their actions, the ever-open possibility of the fresh emergence of this fleeting subject. JACQUES RANCIÈRE, *On the Shores of Politics*[97]

In *Democracy in America* Tocqueville described the sovereignty of the people as "the creative principle" that clearly distinguished the American political experience from Europe's. While Tocqueville believed that this principle was generally to be found "at the bottom of almost all human institutions, usually it remains buried there." In America alone, he wrote, was popular sovereignty a principle "neither hidden nor sterile," but one based in the everyday practices, mores, and laws of the citizenry. In America "the sovereignty of the people has been adopted in practice in every way the imagination could suggest. It has been detached from all fictions in which it has elsewhere been carefully wrapped." For Tocqueville popular sovereignty in antebellum America had a lived and everyday reality.[98]

Contemporary Tocquevillians have translated Tocqueville's concern with the everyday aspects of collective self-rule into a concern with civil society. They have emphasized the importance of voluntary associations—from bird-watching groups to bowling leagues—to the cultivation of reciprocity and social trust. Hamilton might have simply called it confidence and contrasted it with vigilance or jealousy. The troubled location of public authority has dropped out entirely from most of these studies. Invoking the language of contemporary economics to explain Tocqueville's importance for contemporary democratic theorists and social scientists, Robert Putnam has written that "social capital lowers transaction costs and eases dilemmas of collective action." For Putnam and other associationist democrats, trust, social capital, and the ability to navigate the coordination pressures of complex societies are almost the sole basis of what associations contribute to make democracy "work."[99]

In more explicitly normative democratic theory, deliberation has become for many the high standard by which democracy is to be judged. As Lynn Sanders writes, "that increasing deliberation enhances democracy has become, in some theoretical circles, a truism." Sanders rightly points out that this truism has democratic costs insofar as it often overlooks how the imperatives of deliberation have been used historically— including in the period investigated here—to explore a way of ruling unruly democracy and silencing the most powerless members of the polity. "Taking deliberation as a signal of democratic practice," Sanders summarizes, "paradoxically works undemocratically, discrediting on seemingly democratic grounds the views of those who are less likely to present their arguments in ways that we recognize as characteristically deliberative."[100] Although deliberationists occasionally recognize the importance of noise, theater, declamation, testimony, and protest to "gain attention," their tendency to reduce insurgent politics to noncooperative assertions of political interest is insufficiently alert to the importance of spaces of political insurgency to the articulation of wrongs in a democratic polity.[101] It is most unfortunate that "dissent has fallen through the cracks of much mainstream democratic theory."[102]

The insurgent citizenship exemplified by the Democratic Republican societies addresses this absence. The societies reveal the importance of theoretical investigation into spaces of conflict resolution, and into spaces of conflict articulation. For deliberationists and associationist democrats political wrongs and political conflicts are a given; they are, one might say, exogenous to their democratic theories. The primary goal of that theory is to explore norms and procedures to justly and peaceably adjudicate and resolve these conflicts. In contrast, an emphasis on spaces of conflict articulation reveals the extent to which spaces of politicization are needed for political wrongs to be felt and articulated in the first place. From this perspective democratic theory should focus attention on how the claims-making practices of democratic politics are to be cultivated and fostered and lead to what Sheldon Wolin has recently called the "nurturing of discordant democracy."[103] A robust democratic ecology requires both kinds of spaces to enact the promises of further democratization. Historically situated studies of different spaces of insurgent citizenship may help to further this larger theoretical task. While the lack of investigation into such spaces may be a problem for contemporary democratic theory, the paucity of such spaces in contemporary political life is a much more serious problem for contemporary democratic politics.

The sovereignty of the people is a much more complicated, one might say more fictional, fiction than the divine right of kings. A king, however dubious his divinity might seem, did not have to be imagined. He was a visible presence, wearing his crown and carrying his scepter. The people, on the other hand, are never visible as such . . .
EDMUND S. MORGAN, *Inventing the People*[1]

[Carwin] dealt chiefly in general representations. Men, he said, believed in the existence and energy of invisible powers, and in the duty of discovering and conforming to their will. . . . A voice coming from a quarter where no attendant could be seen would, in most cases, be ascribed a supernatural agency, and a command imposed on them, in this manner would be obeyed with religious scrupulousness. Thus men might be imperiously directed in the disposal of their industry, their property, and even of their lives.
CHARLES BROCKDEN BROWN, *Memoirs of Carwin the Biloquist*[2]

{ 5 }

Hearing Voices

Authority and Imagination in Wieland

Voice is a troublesome and much contested category in contemporary democratic theory. When contemporary democratic theorists invoke voice they often do so in opposition to a politics of (mere) representation. Voice marks the presence or participation of an agent in political life, with this presence usually figured as more or less direct, immediate, unqualified, authentic. The presence of agents with shared "perceptions, concerns, and needs," it is sometimes claimed, is necessary for any truly inclusive democratic pluralism.[3] In response to these theoretical affirmations of political presence, and to the standpoint epistemologies that generally accompany them, democratic theories influenced by deconstruction have often invoked voice as the paradigmatic instance of a misplaced faith in "full and present speech," a faith underwritten by what Derrida calls the "metaphysics of presence."[4] Deconstructive democratic theory has been wary of claims to expressive self-sufficiency.[5]

While these familiar debates over voice and the representation of political identity have taken more and less nuanced forms, some democratic theorists have reserved the figure of voice for the invocation of popular will itself, for the democratic presence of the people. Sheldon Wolin's work has been exemplary in this regard. In his work on the inherently "fugitive" aspects of democratic politics, Wolin invokes voice to "call attention to . . . discursive traditions that emphasized, as the core of democracy, its demotic and participatory elements."[6] For Wolin democratic action posits the voice of the demos as "an autonomous agent" that "gathers its power from outside the system": "[Democratic action] begins with the demos constructing/collecting itself from scattered experiences and fusing these into a self-consciousness about common powerlessness and its causes . . . The demos becomes political, not simply when it seeks to make a system of governance more responsive to its needs, but when it attempts to shape the political system in order to enable itself to emerge, to make possible a new actor, collective in nature."[7] The ambivalence in Wolin's prose around these practices of self-created and self-authorizing popular voice is telling. The democratic agent that he posits is both the cause and the effect of action, a collective action forever in search of a collective subject. "Voice," Wolin writes, as captured by the revolutionary formula vox populi, vox Dei, "implied a citizenry that expressed itself corporatively." The physical presence of a people capable of framing its own understanding of its needs and its own evaluation of political circumstances, Wolin argues, is effaced by the technologies of political representation most commonly associated with democratic politics. Our reality, he writes, is "a democracy without the demos as actor. The voice is that of a ventriloquious democracy."[8]

Perhaps no single American text of the 1790s better dramatizes the democratic dilemmas of voice and representation than Charles Brockden Brown's antidemocratic novel Wieland; or The Transformation: An American Tale (1798). In this chapter I explore how Brown's novel — often considered the most significant literary text of the early Republic — understands and negotiates the paradoxes of popular authority and its representation, of voice and ventriloquism. As we have seen in chapter 4, in the years following constitutional ratification the postrevolutionary contests over where to locate the voice of the people remained precariously unresolved. While there was a general consensus in the 1790s that sovereignty was properly lodged in the vox populi, there was very little agreement on how that voice was to be represented, articulated, or institutionally embodied. This mobility of popular voice was cause for great concern among the early Republic's leading Federalists, and it is in some of their writing that we find the most lucid identifications of the theoretical problems involved. Wolin has written that "the idea of democracy comes to us . . . primarily through hostile interpreters," and this is no less true of late-eighteenth-century America than of fifth-century Athens.[9]

Brown's gothic novel is a literary reflection on the dilemmas of voice and ventriloquism that so profoundly marked postrevolutionary American politics. The novel makes legible widespread cultural concerns in the period over the ground of public authority and its proper representation by highlighting the irreplaceable role of the imagination in constituting public authority based in voice. Written at the end of the revolutionary decade following 1789 and set in the decade leading up to 1776, *Wieland* is "a book about the consequences of revolution" and a "plea for the restoration of civic authority in a postrevolutionary age."[10] I will argue that Brown's novel takes the revolutionary formula *vox populi, vox Dei* as the starting point for a fictional analysis of the historical and theoretical proximity of democracy and religious enthusiasm, keywords that Brown understands in terms of their mutual appeal to the imagined authority of unmediated voice, or the animating spirit beyond the letter of the law. While historians have frequently noted the "radical and fanatical tendency" linking democracy with enthusiasm during the Age of Revolutions,[11] Brown's novel suggests a deeper connection between them in their shared emphasis on the extratextual authorization of voice and its supplemental elicitation of a public's imaginative projections, in what I characterize as the novel's scenes of transportive interpellation.[12] Brown's novel explores the unavoidably spectral but nonetheless effective indeterminacy of the revolutionary slogan *vox populi, vox Dei*.

I

Isn't it the truth of voice to be hallucinated?
ROLAND BARTHES, *The Grain of the Voice*[13]

Brown's "American Tale" unfolds in the turbulent decade between the conclusion of the French and Indian War (1763) and the initial events of the American Revolution (1775). Set largely in the rural setting of the Wieland family estate in Mettingen, on the banks of the Schuylkill river, the novel is narrated as a series of letters from Clara Wieland to unnamed acquaintances who have requested that she explain the terrible sequence of events that have befallen her family, events that have resulted ultimately in the brutal murder of her sister-in-law, Catherine, and Catherine's children at the hands of Clara's brother, Theodor. A short summary of the events will help to orient the unfamiliar reader.

Clara and Theodor Wieland were orphaned at an early age, after their father, a religious enthusiast who had come to America to convert Indians, was killed in a fire of apparently supernatural origin. After their father's death (and, shortly after, their mother's), the children were raised by an aunt in accordance with enlightened principles. While the children's "education had been modeled by no religious standards," and they were left largely "to the guidance of their own understanding, and the casual impressions which society might make upon them," Theodor nonetheless inherited his father's melancholic disposition, an inheritance that suggests one of the novel's central themes: the haunting persistence of a disavowed past (24). In *Wieland* the Calvinist past insinuates itself unrecognized into the heart of the Enlightenment present. After Theodor and Catherine Pleyal marry, Catherine's brother Henry comes to live with them. The four initiate a kind of daily salon, spending their days discussing music, literature, and the mysteries of moral psychology. In the discussions between Henry and Theodor, Brown dramatizes the two great intellectual influences of the day: "moral necessity and Calvinistic inspiration were the props on which [Theodor] thought proper to repose," whereas Henry was "a champion of intellectual liberty, [and] rejected all guidance but that of reason" (28). *Wieland* ultimately shows this to be a false opposition—both faith and reason are rooted in the pathologies of the enthusiastic imagination—and in the character of Clara he offers a third option in the disciplined aesthete.[14]

Trouble soon interrupts this Enlightenment idyll. Shifting from a "serene and blissful" tableau to one "corroded by anxiety," the family is abruptly "visited by dread of unknown dangers" (79). The involuntary trust that once held the small community together through "bonds of love and sentiment" begins to fray as disembodied voices are heard sowing seeds of mistrust, faction, and discord. It is at this time that the inscrutable Carwin appears in the rural hamlet of Mettingen and is hesitantly welcomed into its society. An old acquaintance of Henry's, Carwin has a mysterious and duplicitous presence about him and is haunted by an even more mysterious past. After his arrival the situation in the Wieland household quickly degenerates. Having mastered the art of "biloquism"—the ability to "mimic exactly the voice of another, and to modify the sound so that it shall appear to come from [another] quarter"—Carwin uses this art to impersonate disparate voices and, the reader suspects but never knows for certain, the voice of God himself. In the novel's most dramatic scene Theodor Wieland is commanded by prophetic voice to sacrifice his family as a sign of his devotion. The Abrahamic injunction is carried out without divine intervention as he brutally murders his wife and children.[15]

In Brown's story the tranquil linearity of the Wieland family's former life is punctually ruptured by Carwin's vocal performances and their surprising and terrifying consequences. As Christopher Looby has written, in *Wieland* "everything happens because of voices and the words and noises carried by voices, and therefore everything that happens seems uncaused and unexpected."[16] The narrative moves in lurching accord with "magical transitions and [the] mysterious energy of voice" (250), suggesting a democratic temporality that contrasts sharply with the steady accumulation of inheritance and birthright (about which more below). In the aftermath of the murders Clara is left to cry that the only thing left of their formerly tranquil existence "was to linger out in agonies a short existence; and leave to the world a monument of blasted hopes and changeable fortune" (172). *Wieland* is itself that monument, a monument and prophetic warning to Brown's contemporaries about the unforeseen consequences of their dangerous reliance on the precarious (and sublime) authority of popular voice.

In treating voice as a disruptive and deceptive force and as a force of seductive compulsion, the novel at once illuminates and offers immanent critique of the authoritative importance of voice in postrevolutionary American political culture. It depicts voice as commanding an authority over its audience that exceeds conviction and that compels submission; the authority of voice is based in its ability to transport its audience beyond themselves, beyond rational consent. When Clara begins her account of Carwin's appearance at Mettingen—after first overcoming the temporary "palsy" that his recalled image induces in her—she emphasizes first his captivating physical appearance and then elaborates at length on the physical qualities of his voice. After lingering for a time on the riverbanks outside her house, Carwin appears at Clara's door and asks her servant, "Pry'thee, good girl, canst thou supply a thirsty man with a glass of buttermilk?" (58). The question is seemingly uncomplicated, but its vocal utterance conveys to Clara far more than its simple semantic content: "I listened to this dialogue in silence. The words uttered by the person without, affected me as somewhat singular, but what chiefly rendered them remarkable, was the tone that accompanied them. It was wholly new . . . I cannot pretend to communicate the impression that was made upon me by these accents, or to depict the degree in which force and sweetness were blended in them . . . It imparted to me an emotion altogether involuntary and uncontrollable. When he uttered the words, 'for charity's sweet sake,' I dropped the cloth that I held in my hand, my heart overflowed with sympathy, and my eyes with unbidden tears" (59). Clara's loss of control in the face of the novel "tones" and "accents" of Carwin's voice arises from what Brown marks throughout the novel as a supplemental surplus of meaning that is carried by vocal performance and that escapes textual mediation. Clara's repeated protests in her letters that such accounts seem "trifling or incredible" attempt to persuade the reader that the *reading* of her account cannot adequately convey the power of voice over her imagination. The descriptions of Carwin's voice in the novel dwell upon what Roland Barthes called the "grain" of the voice, the material supplement forming "a signifying play that [has] nothing to do with communication" or "representation."[17] It is this grain—described alternately in the novel as "mellifluent and clear," "terrible," and "impassioned"—that so captivates Carwin's audience, that imparts an overwhelming emotion "altogether involuntary and incontroulable." It is also in the utter singularity of the voice's grain that its paradoxical ground of public authority is based, an authority, Brown's novel suggests, enacted through the transportive interpellation of its audience.[18]

The expressive theory of meaning espoused by eighteenth-century writers such as Rousseau (especially in the *Essay on the Origin of Languages*) did not treat language as primarily concerned with communicating information and ideas, but rather emphasized the primacy of voice in actively shaping the perceptions of its audience.[19] This emphasis was popularized in late-eighteenth-century American pamphlets on neo-

Ciceronian oratory and eloquence. *Wieland* invokes the transportive aspects of voice to paint a comparatively dark picture of the purported independence of human judgment under "the guidance of reason alone," and to expose the terrible authority of eloquence in democratic politics.

Brown invokes this literature in the novel by noting its influence over the enlightened but melancholic Theodor. The "chief object" of Theodor Wieland's veneration "was Cicero": "He never tired of conning and rehearsing his productions. To understand them was not sufficient. He was anxious to discover the gestures and cadences with which they ought to be delivered. He was very scrupulous in selecting the true scheme of pronunciation for the Latin tongue, and in adapting it to the words of his darling writer. His favorite occupation consisted in embellishing his rhetoric with all the proprieties of gesticulation and utterance" (27). Jay Fliegelman has documented the widespread influence of the "elocutionary revolution" in late-eighteenth-century America, as well as its influence on Brown. Of particular importance to educated late-eighteenth-century Americans was James Burgh's *Art of Speaking* (1767), which was written as an instruction manual to correct perceived deficiencies of manner in public speakers (such as "monstrous improprieties as to the management of the eyes"). The "art" of speaking for Burgh is focused almost entirely on gesture, bearing, comportment, and voice, as they convey the passions central to a speaker's meaning. "What we mean," Burgh writes, "does not so much depend on the words we speak, as our manner of speaking them."[20] The authority of voice derives from its ability to "transport" its audience, and this act of transporting is directly tied to aesthetic experience: "True eloquence does not wait for cool approbation. Like irresistible beauty, it transports, it ravishes, it commands the admiration of all, who are within its reach. If it allows time to criticize, it is not genuine. It ought to hurry us out of ourselves, to swallow up our whole attention; to drive everything out of our minds, besides the subject it would hold forth, and the point it wants to carry. The hearer finds himself as unable to resist as to blow out the conflagration with the breath of his mouth, or to stop the stream of a river with his hand. His passions are no longer his own. The orator has taken possession of them, and with superior power works them to whatever he pleases."[21] While this passage may read like a preface to a coming attack on democratic demagoguery, Burgh understands the audience's involuntary absorption, its transportive interpellation, as a sign and requirement of the speaker's legitimate authority. The capacity of voice to bring forth an immediate response plays an important role in the constitution of public authority in postrevolutionary American political culture. As we saw in chapter 2, interpretations of the eighteenth-century American public sphere influenced by Habermas—most notably Michael Warner's—have emphasized the importance of print culture and the circulation of printed texts to enacting a republican theory of deliberative public authority, an authority that relied upon disembodiment and the force of the better argument for its legitimacy. Fliegelman and others have deflated this emphasis on disembodied authority and focused instead on the period's simultaneous reliance on the authority of voice. As Fliegelman has summarized, "eloquence was the new currency of cultural power in postrevolutionary American society."[22] There was an animating tension in postrevolutionary American political culture between the authority of written texts (like constitutions) and the authority of spoken voice. Sandra Gustafson has put the tension this way: "Claims to authenticity and relations of power were given form and meaning, through the reliance on or freedom from text in oral performance. Preachers and political orators signified unmediated access to truth in extemporaneous speeches, or they dramatized the stability of their spiritual or political intent by reading from a manuscript or referring to foundational documents."[23]

In *Wieland* Brown acknowledges the cultural authority of voice in the postrevolutionary context even while exposing its underlying instabilities and its ultimate inseparability from the paradoxes of representation that it hoped to replace. The seemingly more authentic ground of voice was appealing in a political culture aware of the figuration and contestability attending any representational relationship. From the debates over the misrepresentation of colonial interests by colonial governors and arguments with the British over "virtual" and "actual" representation in the 1760s to the contests over appropriate forms of political representation during the ratification debates, Americans were acutely aware of the extent to which any representation—between representative and voter, word and deed, even "signifier and signified"—was marked by distortion.[24] The authoritative claim of voice was to be "beyond" these misguided representations, textual or otherwise. Through the novel's device of ventriloquism, Brown rejected this fantasy of vocal authenticity, or rather revealed its persistent but disavowed reliance *on* fantasy. In a footnoted excursus on "Biloquium, or ventriloquism," Brown writes that "the power is difficult to explain but the fact is undeniable. Experience shews that the human voice can imitate the voice of all men and all inferior animals" (226). *Wieland* shows voice to be caught up in the very paradoxes of representation that it aspires to overcome. It can be read as a kind of literalization of "hearing voices" as the paradigmatic sign of phantasmatic instability. But for Brown those transported by voice — the public — were not passive but actively enrolled in this transportation through the projective power of the imagination. The involuntary transformative power of the imagination may be seen as the novel's central theme, and the unrecognized impact of imagination on the authority of voice its central political consequence. The novel examines the imagination's "power to transform shadows into monsters" (120) and reveals how this power works to shape the sublime enactments of voice into mystical foundations of authority.

Brown's novel dwells upon the constitutive power of the imagination in both exceptional and everyday circumstances. This point is made most clearly in Clara's several accounts of her own experience of hearing voices. Shortly after her initial encounter with Carwin, Clara finds herself unable to control the "airy speculations" that this encounter induces in her. Images of Carwin seem to dance in her head and provoke her to involuntary acts of mimesis: "This face, seen for a moment, continued for hours to occupy my fancy, to the exclusion of almost every other image. I had purposed to spend the evening with my brother, but I could not resist the inclination of forming a sketch upon paper of this memorable visage. Whether my hand was aided by any peculiar inspiration, or I was deceived by my own fond conceptions this portrait, though hastily executed, appeared unexceptionable to my own taste" (61). As Edward Cahill has written, the theory of the imagination that Brown invokes in *Wieland* is "the site of fanatical delusion and deceptive error . . . but also correct judgment, rational speculation, and transformative sublimity."[25] Brown focuses repeatedly on the dangerous possibilities of self-captivation (most poignantly *democratic* self-captivation, the phantasmatic identification with what is taken to be collective voice). The involuntarily activated imagination frequently leaves Clara and others in the novel "tormented by phantoms of [their] own creation" (95). Products of their imagination, but outside their control, these phantoms rob the novel's characters of their perceived autonomy: "My mind," Clara writes, "was thronged by vivid, but confused images, and no effort that I made was sufficient to drive them away" (63). "Images so terrific and forcible disabled me, for a time, from distinguishing between sleep and wakefulness, and withheld from me knowledge of my actual condition" (72). While "chimeras" and "hydras" are opposed to "facts" even in *Wieland*, Brown does not invoke or rely upon a more deliberative public free of imagination, but rather a more disciplined imagination.[26] Some characters seem more prone to such flights of fancy than others, in particular the melancholia that plagues Theodor; all, however, are ultimately unhinged by them.

It is Clara's reputation for "judicious discipline" that makes her the initial target of Carwin's deceit. In the "tales of apparitions and enchantments" Clara saw nothing but "ignorance and folly" (52). Clara presents a model of instructed virtue, and Pleyal, knowing that "mankind are more easily enticed to virtue by example than by precept," takes to recording all of Clara's behaviors in a journal of virtue: "Even the colour of a shoe, the knot of ribbon, or your attitude in plucking a rose, were of moment to be recorded. Even the arrangement of your breakfast-table and your toilet have been amply displayed" (140). It is voice that shakes Clara from her disciplined aesthetic of self. "The immediate effects" of Carwin's voice, Clara writes, "served only to undermine the foundations of my judgment and precipitate my resolutions" (169). Carwin expressly chooses Clara as a limit case to demonstrate the "power" of ventriloquism to inspire its audience's imagination, its power to "fill the mind with faith in shadows and confidence in dreams" (241). Carwin succeeds in seducing the imaginations of Theodor's melancholic Calvinism and Pleyal's Enlightenment rationalism, relatively easy targets of enthusiastic intoxication, as well as the seemingly unparalleled and moderate instructed vision of Clara.

Wieland advertises itself as a "series of performances" aiming at "the illustration of some important branches in the moral constitution of man" (1). The novel undermines the epistemic confidence of a seemingly disenchanted empiricism, stated so clearly in the novel's optimistic opening as follows: "The will is the tool of the understanding, which must fashion its conclusions on the notices of sense. If the sense be depraved, it is impossible to calculate the evils that may flow from the consequent deductions of the understanding" (39). The novel's focus on the projective imagination and its tendency, in Clara's words, to "take from me my self command" (220), shakes this confident moral psychology. Theodor's transformation most clearly indicates the loss of autonomy attributed to the constitutive imagination. Contemplating the horror of her brother's transformation, Clara is forced to reflect on the fragility of her own self-control: "Now was I stupefied with ten-fold wonder in contemplating myself. Was I not likewise transformed from rational and human into a creature of nameless and fearful attributes? Was I not transported to the brink of the same abyss?" (205).

As for how one might be preserved from such a fate, Brown's novel proposes and repudiates several possibilities: natural sentiment, realism, scriptural faith. "I was not qualified," Clara admits, "by education and experience to encounter perils like these; or, perhaps, I was powerless because I was again assaulted by surprise" (171). The novel's ultimate claim seems to be that no education or experience can guide one in an assured anticipation of the surprising articulations of voice. If popular voice is the ground of public authority, Brown seems to insist, we must understand the role of the imagination in constituting that authority, in constituting all authority. Brown's goal in *Wieland* is not to demystify the persistence of the imagination in constituting public authority in the early Republic, but to establish it on firmer, less chaotic ground. As I will elaborate, Brown hoped to replace the volatile sublimity of popular voice with a more reliable and disciplined sublimity of tradition. Without this stabilizing influence, the experience of time appears disjointed and irregular, an experience of time captured, as Clara writes, in the very narrative of that history offered by the novel. "My narrative," she writes, "may be invaded by inaccuracy and confusion . . . What but ambiguities, abruptnesses, and dark transitions, can be expected from the historian who is, at the same time, the sufferer of those disasters?" (167).

The projective role of the imagination in conferring authority on voice is at once more evident and of greater consequence when that voice appears publicly through the ventriloquism of a nonapparent entity that claims to be the ultimate ground of public authority. Such of course is the case with both sides of the revolutionary slogan *vox populi, vox Dei*. *Wieland* reveals the unnoticed theoretical and historical interdependence of religious enthusiasm and democracy haunting this revolutionary slogan. As the spirit exceeded the letter for the enthusiast, so did the democrats of the 1790s appeal to a living voice of the people outside the mediation of the representative institutions of government. The constitution, Madison said in a speech he delivered as a congressman from Virginia before the House of Representatives in April 1796, "was nothing more than a draft of a plan, nothing but a dead letter, until life and validity were breathed into it by the voice of the people."[27] Or, as the Reverend Samuel Miller insisted, public authority rests "not in the words and letters of the *Constitution*; but in the temper, the habits, and the practices of the people."[28] Brown's novel suggests that the confidence in democratic presence and popular voice was based on a strained and dangerous disavowal of the persistence of an enthusiastic past.

II

Where there is no revelation, the people perish.   PROVERBS 29:18[29]

Early commentaries on *Wieland* sometimes read the novel as an Enlightenment critique of religious enthusiasm, as "a sermon against credulity and religious fanaticism" and in favor of "all the advanced social and political opinions fathered by the French Revolution."[30] As already indicated, the novel's relationship to Enlightenment and enthusiasm is actually much more complicated. *Wieland* is centrally concerned with the problem of enthusiasm, but it takes these problems—associated with the extratextual authority of voice and the confusion of imagination with revelation—to be part of a much broader cultural phenomenon than these earlier readings of the novel suggest. Brown's novel is a critique of both fanaticism and the optimistic moral psychology associated by these critics with "Enlightenment," emphasizing their underlying similarities rather than their differences.[31] As Larzer Ziff notes, the novel "penetrates beneath the principles of the optimistic psychology of his day, and recognizes the claims that Calvinism makes on the American character."[32] Brown's novel establishes continuities between the dangers of enthusiastic voice and the dangers attending democratic appeals to the voice of the people. In the novel the disavowed specter of religious enthusiasm haunts the optimistic self-confidence of the democratic present. The

Jeffersonian dictum that "the earth belongs in usufruct to the living," and that "the dead have neither powers nor rights over it," is, Brown suggests, profoundly deluded.[33] His novel wars with what Judith Shklar calls Jefferson's "politics of perpetual newness," and what Catherine Holland calls the broader eighteenth-century American "fantasy of pastlessness, of political and historical unfetteredness."[34] Clara's opening account of her family history establishes the haunting power of the dead over the living, and shows it to be an inheritance and patrimony of violence.

Clara's narrative of her family history begins with her grandfather, whom she describes as "the founder of the German theater," and whose life was "spent in the composition of sonatas and dramatic pieces" (7). The grandfather's artistic sensibility and cultivated imagination earn him fame, but he is unable to directly pass this inheritance on to his son. As with all paternal relations in *Wieland*, that between Clara's father and grandfather is interrupted by unexpected and early death. While Clara's father is orphaned at an early age, he nonetheless inherits his own father's aesthetic sensibilities, though of a more melancholic sort. He is prone to a "habit of morose and gloomy reflection." While not a bookish man, it is a book that marks the great shift in his life, a book of the enthusiastic heresy of the free spirit.[35] Clara reports that at an early age her father came across a book written by "one of the teachers of the Albigenses, or French Protestants." The fateful passage that catches his eye — "Seek and ye shall find" — inaugurates her father's quest of spiritual discovery that draws him first into an intensive study of scripture and then beyond written scripture to the arresting call of divine voice.

The French Prophets, or Camisards ("short shirts"), the elder Wieland's particular route into enthusiasm, were a group of radical Huguenots who through acts of guerilla warfare militarily resisted the religious tyranny of Louis XIV. When a small number of them arrived in London in 1706 they became renowned for their trances, quakings, and glossolalic speech.[36] The most influential antienthusiastic tract of the eighteenth century, Shaftesbury's "Letter concerning Enthusiasm," was written in response to the Prophets. The particularities of the sect are not as important for the arc of Brown's narrative as what they stand in for, and what both the elder and Theodor Wieland represent is enthusiasm. While an excursus on the complexities of eighteenth-century understandings of enthusiasm is inappropriate here, some provisional orientation will be helpful for the analysis to follow. In the words of Charles Chauncey's "Enthusiasm Described and Cautioned against," a work sometimes thought to have influenced Brown in the writing of *Wieland*, the enthusiast "mistakes the working of his own passions for divine communication, and fancies himself immediately inspired by the SPIRIT of GOD, while all the while, he is under no other influence than an overheated imagination."[37]

Through Clara's narration of the events, Brown suggests that while the elder Wieland was moved by this work into enthusiasm, it was already potentially there in his predispositions. In reading the work of the French Prophets her father's gloomy disposition finds, Clara writes, its "object," and he is soon fully immersed in their teachings. At this early stage in the elder Wieland's conversion, authority resides strictly in scripture. All "conclusions were deduced from the sacred text," Clara tells us. "This was the fountain, beyond which it was unnecessary to trace the stream of religious truth" (9). This, however, was only a stopover at the site of textual authority. "The stream of religious truth" soon draws the elder Wieland beyond scripture to the invocation of the Word behind the words, the spirit beyond the letter. As the doctrine of the Camisards spiritually seduced the elder Wieland, it drew him beyond the authority of the scriptural mediation of authority. His pursuit of "seek and ye shall find" leads him into an idiosyncratic and wholly singular faith. His "system," which was ultimately an antinomianism, he believed had finally been "expressly prescribed to him alone" (13). "He allied himself with no sect, because he perfectly agreed with none. Social worship is that which by they are all distinguished; but that article found no place in his creed. He rigidly interpreted that precept which enjoins us, when we worship, to retire into solitude, and shut out every species of society" (12). Throughout the novel Brown associates enthusiasm with unsocial, unworldly fanaticism, depicting departures from worldly sociability as a precondition to the appearance of enthusiasm. (It is worth noting that social isolation was also associated in eighteenth-century thought with the aesthetics of the sublime, and sociality with the beautiful.)[38] Brown occasionally suggests (in a manner akin to Shaftesbury) that sociability could become a cure for the tendency toward enthusiasm. The elder Wieland excludes this possibility in his actions and submits wholly to this new authority. The further his questions take him into his solitary pursuit of the "streams of religious truth," the more "the empire of religious duty extended itself to his looks, gestures, and phrases" (10). The authority of divine voice is marked in the novel in his comportment and disposition as well as his speech; the living voice comes to reside in the flesh.

The elder Wieland's quest for *vox Dei* terminates in a prefiguring scene of violence. While praying to God in the solitary "temple" he built atop a dramatic rocky outpost near the family home, the elder Wieland is swallowed by flames in an apparent act of spontaneous combustion. As with the other dramatically violent episode in the novel—Theodor Wieland's later murder of his wife and children—Brown leaves the ultimate cause indeterminate: "Is it fresh proof," Clara asks, "that the Divine Ruler interfered in human affairs, meditates an end, selects, and commissions his agents, and enforces by unequivocal sanctions the submission to his will? Or, was it merely the irregular expansion of the fluid that imparts warmth to our heart, and our blood?" (22). Spiritualism or materialism?

The disaster that the novel is written to explain is also occasioned by enthusiasm. As with his father, Theodor Wieland's disposition led him at a young age into "sublimer views" (25). While the "images that visited" Clara and the rest were "blithesome and gay," those with which Theodor was most familiar "were of the opposite hue" (25). "All his actions and practical sentiments are linked with the long and abstruse deductions from the system of divine government and the laws of our intellectual constitution. He is, in some respects, an enthusiast, but is fortified in his belief by innumerable arguments and subtleties" (40). Theodor inherits the father's obstinate pursuit of spiritual truth, but the father's quest for spiritual truth becomes a radical and rationalist self-questioning in the son (which, as we will see, Brown associated with the work of William Godwin). "He deemed it indispensable to examine the ground of his belief, to settle the relation between motives and actions, the criterion of merit, and the kinds and properties of evidence." While the mind of the son was "enriched by science, and embellished with literature," he nonetheless inherited, despite himself, his father's enthusiastic temper (40).

This enthusiasm leads Theodor, like his father, first to a meticulous observation of textual authority and then to an appeal to an authority beyond words. Brown thus dramatizes these competing forms of postrevolutionary authorization. Clara indicates this in her abovementioned discussion of Theodor's fascination with Cicero and his diligent attempt to embellish his "rhetoric with all the proprieties of gesticulation and utterance": "Not contented with this he was diligent in settling and restoring the purity of the text. For this end, he collected all the editions and commentaries that could be procured, and employed months of severe study in exploring and comparing them. He never betrayed more satisfaction than when he made a discovery of this kind" (27). Soon after Carwin's appearance Theodor abandons this pious obedience to textual authority. Brown signals this transformation by introducing a telling new object of Theodor Wieland's fascination and research. Clara writes that soon after hearing the disembodied voices of Carwin, Theodor began "collecting and investigating the facts which relate to that mysterious personage, the Daemon of Socrates." Brown invokes Socrates's Daimon as a way of presaging the heteronomic voice to come, the entanglement of imagination and reason, and the imbrication of enthusiasm and philosophy.

As with the real murder by James Yates of his family in December of 1781, the event on which Brown's novel is based, Theodor Wieland is called upon by divine voice to destroy his idols.[39] Theodor attributes his deed to his search for God and his unending rationalist self-criticism of the grounds of judgment. It is the very quest for final authority or legitimacy that Brown seems to pathologize in the novel. There is no epistemic certainty at the end of Theodor's quest, but only a revelation which might be delusional and in any case escapes his attempts to know or represent it. Representation fails the arresting call of voice that urges Theodor to murder his family: "How should I describe the luster, which, at that moment, burst upon my vision! . . . I opened my eyes and found all about me luminous and glowing. It was the element of heaven that flowed around. Nothing but a fiery stream was at first visible, but, anon, a shrill voice from behind called upon me to attend. I turned: It is forbidden to describe what I saw; Words, indeed, would be wanting to the task. The lineaments of that being, whose veil now lifted, and whose visage beamed upon my sight, no hues of pencil or of language can portray" (201). Theodor, confronted with the murder of his family, makes an enthusiastic appeal to a power above human law that cannot be publicly conveyed and is known with certainty only by him: "Thou, Omnipotent and holy! Thou knowest that my actions were conformable to thy will. I know not what is crime; what actions are evil in their ultimate and comprehensive tendency or what are good. Thy knowledge, as thy power, is unlimited. I have taken thee for my guide and cannot err" (201).

At one point in the novel, while discussing a literary work, Pleyal as-

serts that to "make the picture of a single family a model from which to
sketch the condition of the nation, was absurd" (34). But of course that
was precisely what Brown had set out to do in *Wieland*. The destruction
of the Wieland family at the hands of an enthusiast enthralled to the
imagined authority of divine voice was Brown's allegorical representation of the looming destruction of America at the hands of radical democrats or "Jacobins" claiming to speak for the majesty of the people, enthralled by the imaginary omnipotence of their own impossible voice.

III

Democracy is Lovelace; the People are Clarissa.
JOHN ADAMS, letter to William Cunningham, March 1804[40]

Soon after the publication of *Wieland*, Brown sent a copy to Vice President Thomas Jefferson, an incident that Brown scholars often use as an
occasion to reflect on the political implications of literary production in
the early Republic. Why had Brown thought it important to send Jefferson a novel with no explicit political import, one whose setting seems to
avoid direct engagement with a broader political context? Brown's story
is a reflection of many things — epistemological uncertainty and the un-
reliability of the senses, the dangers of seduction, and the dissolution of
patriarchal authority — all of which could be considered to some degree
"political." However, the overriding theme of the novel is the dangers
attending an overactive or overenthusiastic imagination, and consequen-
tially the dangers that it poses for democratic politics. *Wieland* was meant
as a warning to Jefferson and his democratic followers that the imagination, once untethered from common sense and tradition, and based
instead on the unlocatable and volatile authority of popular voice, could
produce nightmares in which only madness reigned: fathers murdering
their wives and children, and the authorial voice (of God, of the People)
merely the ventriloquism of an evil (and in Carwin's case, foreign) genius.
The ultimate invisibility of the vox populi, like the invisibility of vox Dei,
elicited the overinvested imaginations of a democratic citizenry, Brown's
novel suggests, leaving that citizenry vulnerable to demagogic manipulation and deceit. Brown's novel at once invoked the dangers of aesthetics
for politics and worked to redress these dangers aesthetically.[41]

As such, Brown's novel is thematically similar to many others written in early America. The "force of the imagination" genre examined how the imagination came to overwhelm subjects, rob them of their reason, and leave them vulnerable to manipulation, seduction, and worse. The power of the imagination over not only the mind but the human body was brought home to readers with myriad stories printed and reprinted in magazines, newspapers, novels, and plays describing very real deaths through very imaginary ills and, conversely, remarkable cures through imaginative therapies. Isaac Disraeli's *Curiosities of Literature* described how patients delusional with fever might be healed by swimming in imaginary lakes.[42] Brown and many of his contemporaries understood fiction in such therapeutic terms. While it was almost obligatory for novels of the period to directly confront the dangers associated with novel reading—their tendency to fill the head of readers with dangerous flights of fancy—novelists were also at pains to show how literature and other artistic works could reform the distempered imagination.[43] Brown was not alone in claiming that novels and literature could in fact be *more* effective than political essays or "disquisitions" in such aesthetic and educative projects, insofar as they moved and persuaded readers beyond "cold and unattractive" reasoning. "The narration of public events," Brown wrote, "with a certain license for invention, is the most efficacious of moral instruments."[44]

On these points Brown would have found a sympathetic reader in Jefferson, who equally affirmed the ability of literary and artistic works to broaden the imagination and cultivate the moral sentiments.[45] "We are wisely framed to be as warmly interested for a fictitious as a real personage. The field of the imagination is thus laid open to our use and lessons may be formed to illustrate and carry home to the heart every moral rule of life."[46] Making the point even more bluntly in a letter to Peter Carr in 1787, Jefferson wrote that "the writings of [Laurence] Sterne form the best course in morality that was ever written."[47] Both Brown and Jefferson expressed a common understanding that the cultivation of civic virtues necessary for maintaining republican liberties demanded a cultivation of the imagination, the careful pursuit of an "instructed vision."[48]

But Brown was more deeply troubled than Jefferson by the unhinging of the imagination caused by the American Revolution and its aftermath.[49] Jefferson felt little of Brown's "postrevolutionary nostalgia."[50] For Brown and many of his less optimistic contemporaries, the Revolution magnified a more general and worrisome tendency of the imaginative faculty: its ability to be captivated and misled by its own imaginary productions (as we have seen, a worrisome tendency generally associated with religious enthusiasm). Frances Ferguson has suggested that eighteenth-century aesthetics itself was born as a separate sphere of study as interest intensified in this instability of the mental image, with the difficulties of "assimilating the imagination to epistemology and ontology on the one hand and ethics on the other."[51] Many Americans associated this instability of the imagination with the events of the Revolution, which they feared had, in the words of Benjamin Rush, "unhinged the judgment, deposed the moral faculty, and filled the imagination in many people, with airy and impracticable schemes of wealth and grandeur."[52] Responding to this overheated imagination, literature in the period often sought to reform the imagination and the sentiments it facilitated — in Brown's words, to "enchain the attention" — evincing a careful attunement to political aesthetics.

The letter that Brown sent to Jefferson along with the novel was clearly an appeal to win Jefferson's favor and enhance Brown's own reputation, but the letter's contents also sharply contrast with the usual condemnations of imagination found in many of the Federalist writers with whom Brown shared a political affiliation. Brown wrote: "I am conscious . . . that this form of composition may be regarded by you with indifference or contempt, that social and intellectual theories, that the history of facts in the processes of nature and the operations of government may appear to you the only laudable pursuits; that fictitious narrative in their own nature or in the manner that they have been hitherto conducted may be thought not to deserve notice, and that, consequently, whatever may be the merit of my book as a fiction, yet it is to be condemned because it is a fiction."[53] Brown's comparative invocation of fiction alongside "social and intellectual theories" and "the history of facts in the processes of nature and the operations of government" indicates his political motivations in writing the novel. Like Godwin's *Caleb Williams*, to which *Wieland* may be productively read as a response, Brown's *Wieland* is a *roman à thèse*.[54] It was, as Jane Tompkins has written, a "plea to restore civil authority."[55] As enthusiasts had challenged ecclesiastical authority, so did the democratic appeal to the voice of the people unsettle the civil authority in the postrevolutionary years, particularly in the fraught decade following constitutional ratification. As the elusive voice of the people appears an ever-receding (sublime) ground of public authority, the authoritative elicitation of the imagination takes on a new form; the ventriloquism is no longer that of the distempered enthusiast, but of extralegal participants in popular politics claiming to speak in the people's name.

The success of the Federalists over their Anti-Federalist opponents during the ratification debates can be attributed to some extent to their invocation of a new ground of public authority, to the "democratic" arguments they made to support a relatively aristocratic system of government. Rather than lodge power in the governmental institutions that represented the people—the legislatures of the various states under the Articles of Confederation or the state constitutions—the Federalists claimed to base public authority in the people themselves. In Gordon Wood's words, "those who criticized the revolutionary proceedings of the Philadelphia Convention soon found themselves in the embarrassing position of seeming to deny the voice of the people."[56] As noted in the Introduction, the Federalists' claim to be in fact more democratic than their Anti-Federalist opponents was most compellingly made by James Wilson, first in a widely circulated speech delivered in Philadelphia shortly after the close of the convention, and then again in the opening address to the Pennsylvania Ratifying Convention. While arguing for the system of political representation established under the new federal constitution, Wilson insisted that "reflected rays of delegated power" could not compare to the "luminary from which they proceed."[57] The constitutional text is but an emanation from the popular voice that in Madison's words "breathes life into a lifeless document." Wilson asks, "Were we to ask some politicians who have taken faint and inaccurate view of our establishments, where does the supreme power reside in the United States? They would probably answer, in their Constitutions. This however, tho' a step nearer to the fact, is not a just opinion; for, in truth, it remains and flourishes with the people."[58] Figuring the people as the "one great and noble source of power" had advantages in the course of the ratification debates, but, as explored earlier in the discussion of the Democratic-Republican societies, doing so had serious (and largely unforeseen) consequences for Federalist appeals to order in the decade following ratification. The immediate context behind the crisis of authority in which Brown wrote *Wieland* was the split between Federalists and Democratic Republicans in the years following the French Revolution. The 1790s saw the flourishing of Jacobin clubs, popular politics, the Whiskey Rebellion, and Federalist responses in legislation such as Alien and Sedition Acts. As Larry Kramer has summarized, "after the adoption of the Constitution, most Federalists had expected to amicably govern a quiescent population content to follow their wise leadership. Instead, they were shocked to find themselves wrestling with an unruly, rambunctious democracy-in-the-making."[59]

Brown dramatizes this crisis of authority and what he understands as the attending undisciplined arousal of the public imagination through the figure of Carwin. Like the members of the Democratic-Republican societies, members frequently figured as foreign agitators by their Federalist critics, Carwin enters the novel *disguised* as one of the people. "His gait," Brown writes, "was rustic and awkward. His form was ungainly and disproportioned. Shoulders broad and square, breast sunken, his head drooping, his body of uniform breadth, supported by long and lank legs, were the ingredients of his frame. His garb was not ill adapted to such a figure. A slouched hat tarnished by the weather, a coat of thick grey cloth, cut and wrought, as it seemed by a country tailor, blue worsted stockings, and shoes fastened by thongs, and deeply discoloured by dust, which brush had never disturbed, constituted his dress" (57). He had the look of one, Clara summarizes, "frequently to be met with on the road and in the harvest field." Carwin *appeared* to be a man of the people. But this appearance too is deceptive. Indeed, the very ambiguity of his popular appearance triggers a fit of reflection on Clara's part: "contemplating the image of this wanderer, and drawing, from outward appearances, those inferences with respect to the intellectual history of this person" (58).

While Carwin appears at first to be one of the people, we soon find his past is veiled in obscurity and mystery, we find out in fact that he had always entertained a "passion for mystery." "He afforded us," Clara laments shortly after his appearance, "no ground on which to build even a plausible conjecture" (82). The enigma of Carwin's appearance, his lack of a knowable past, a knowable identity, seemed to prompt unceasing speculation, but to also leave acquaintances with a pervasive sense of uncertainty and doubt. "The inscrutableness of his character, and the uncertainty whether his fellowship tended to good or to evil, were seldom absent from our minds," Clara writes (87). "Nothing could be discerned through the impenetrable veil of his duplicity" (107). Clara tried in vain "to discover the true inferences deducible from his deportment and words with regard to his former adventures and actual views" (109). In the figure of Carwin, Brown suggests that the greatest deception of all, the greatest and most dangerous act of postrevolutionary ventriloquism, is that carried out by men of suspect provenance claiming to speak in the people's voice, to ventriloquize that voice as the voice of God. The seductive voice of this schemer (like that of the notorious Stephen Burroughs of New Hampshire) invades the imaginations of even the most disciplined aesthete (Clara), not to mention suggesting to readers a false opposition between the enthusiast and the enlightenment rationalist.

While never fully clarifying Carwin's background in the novel (though this background is sketched in the unfinished sequel *Memoirs of Carwin, the Biloquist*), Brown offers hints of Carwin's provenance, all of which indicate that he is to be understood as a member of that collection of men recently chronicled by Michael Durey as "transatlantic radicals."[60] Pleyal, who had met Carwin initially while traveling in Europe, provides most of the clues. When the two met in Spain, Carwin, who had been born in western Pennsylvania (the site of the Whiskey Rebellion), appeared wholly Spanish. His "*transformation* into a Spaniard," we learn, "made him indistinguishable from a native" (79). This transformation included an adoption of "Romish faith," which Clara darkly hints was perhaps "counterfeited for political purposes" (78). Toward the novel's end we learn, when Clara chances upon a newspaper article, that "Francis Carwin was wanted for having escaped from Newgate prison in Dublin" (147).

As an "alien and an infidel," the inscrutable figure of Carwin expresses Federalist anxieties that the democratic movements of the 1790s were actually products of foreign conspirators; that they were claims by those who had no part of the people, as nationally defined.[61] These anxieties culminated in the Alien and Sedition Acts of 1798 (the same year the novel was published). The expressions of popular voice, and the horror and insurrection that Brown associated with them, led to another, more distinctly American or popular sublime (also, as we will see in chapter 6, positively invoked by Walt Whitman). The volatile political *mise-en-scène* of the 1790s evoked another sublime than the gothic repertoire of haunted castles, ancient monasteries, and titled nobility of the old world.[62] Brown has Clara indicate this change of scene when she writes, "the dreams of superstition are worthy of contempt. Witchcraft, its instruments and miracles, the compact ratified by a bloody signature, the apparatus of sulpherous smells and thundering explosions, are monstrous and chimerical. These have no part in the scene over which the genius of Carwin presides" (206). Carwin's "scene" is still very much a scene of the sublime, but Brown hopes to present in his "American Tale" a distinctly American sublime, one "growing out of the conditions of our country."[63] Brown's novel suggests that the enthusiastic inheritance of the new world left Americans susceptible to the claims of popular voice. For Brown as for Burke, the sublime was a necessary component of public authority, and was consolidated by the obscurity of its ever-receding ground. Habitual reverence and deference to venerable government whose authority resides in the mist of time was, as we have seen, being challenged in this decade to an unprecedented extent, and Brown's novel offers an aesthetic response to the disintegration.[64]

If Carwin represents revolutionaries of the old world coming to the new, *Wieland* in the end aspires for resettling the new world in the old. In the novel's conclusion Clara abandons the democratic sublime of the new world for another scene: the traditional sublime of the monuments of past ages. Clara's final letter is written from Montpellier in southern France. As her house is (literally) burned down at the novel's close, Clara joins Pleyal in a quest for restored tranquility—the restored tranquility of an instructed vision offered by the "shore of the ancient world." Entranced there by the "spectacle of living manners and the monuments of past ages," Clara is transported once again to her lost tranquility, a tranquility that the reader knows will be soon disrupted by the French Revolution. In the place of the volatile sublimity of popular voice, Clara is restored in the disciplined sublime of tradition.[65] It is through this engagement with the refinement of European tradition that Clara's heart is at last "reinstated in the possession of its ancient tranquility" (271). At the conclusion of *Wieland* Brown is trading in his earlier Godwinian radicalism for something like the political aesthetics of Edmund Burke. Like Burke, and unlike many of his Federalist compatriots, Brown did not believe that the role of the imagination in constituting public authority could be expunged once and for all. *Wieland* employs the device of the ventriloquism of voice not to demystify these ventriloquous acts so much as to remind readers of their inevitability.

The problem of organizing and making sense out of the cacophony of voices is a problem for the polity and a problem for the political scientist. The polity cannot run well unless some order can be given to the voice of the people.
SIDNEY VERBA, "The Voice of the People"[66]

Brown's novel ends with Carwin disappearing into some "remote district of Pennsylvania," suggesting the western frontier region that would later produce the Whiskey Rebellion. Clara Wieland takes refuge in the disciplined imagination and "instructed vision" offered by the authoritative traditions of the old world, which Brown at once contrasts with the volatility of authority based in popular voice and indicates will soon be transformed by the French Revolution's own appeal to *vox populi, vox Dei*. But the lessons that the novel has to offer to contemporary democratic theorists are not confined to Brown's own Burkean response to his earlier Godwinian radicalism. Brown's novel is a clear rebuttal of the Godwinian aspiration to "detect the imposture that would persuade us there is a mystery in government which uninitiated mortals must not presume to penetrate."[67] As a prolonged literary reflection on the "mystical foundations of authority," however, *Wieland* has the advantage of recalling attention to the role that the active eliciting of the imagination plays in constituting authority and how authority works through this imagination to achieve its effects. As already suggested, for Brown the key for understanding this relationship is in the aesthetic category of the sublime, in the sublimity of popular voice.

In addition to the novel's many "inscrutable" scenes of "terror and dread," Brown never resolves the central question that provokes Clara's reflections; he never provides the definitive "explanation" of events promised in Clara's opening letter. As in the female gothic genres explored in Bonnie Honig's recent work, the agent in *Wieland* is never made apparent; authority never emerges to speak in its own name.[68] While Clara is driven by "the inexpressible importance of unveiling the designs and character of Carwin," these designs are in fact never fully revealed. "Whether Wieland was a maniac, a faithful servant of his God, the victim of hellish illusions, or the dupe of human imposture, was by no means certain" (214). Carwin's own lengthy explanation of events near the novel's conclusion is itself doubtful. His admission of having a "passion for mystery" and a "habitual attachment to mystery" is only one of the elements taking away from the veracity of his account (236). (His habit of deception in practice is obviously another.) "Let that man who shall purpose to assign motives to the actions of another blush at his folly and forbear. Not more presumptuous would it be to attempt the classification of all nature, and the scanning of supreme intelligence" (166). In the end Clara seems intent to abandon her quest, and to acknowledge a kind of pathology in the drive to discover motives, first causes, and the ultimate grounds of authority: "I care not from what source these disasters have flowed; it suffices that they have swallowed up our hope and existence" (266). The ultimate grounds of authority, Brown suggests, do not bear looking into, and the quest itself can become a destructive and self-consuming obsession.

Like the dream that Clara has toward the novel's close, *Wieland* casts a flashing light on the sublimity of authority, its "mystical foundations." Figuring the scene of the novel as "a theatre of uproar and confusion," the novel nonetheless shines "gleams of light . . . into the dark abyss," enabling its readers "to discover, for a moment, its enormous depth and the hideous precipices" before them. As in Clara's dream, Brown hoped to transport readers "to some ridge of Aetna," making them terrified spectators "of its fiery torrents and its pillars of smoke" (269).

If Brown had initially followed Godwin's dictum, "I will follow truth wherever she leads," he abandoned this search in his literary work, and came to ultimately pathologize the quest, fearing its political consequences. In *Wieland* Brown presents a critique of any conception of political authority that would disregard its aesthetic components or that would rob it once and for all of its "mystery." It is through imagination, Brown suggests, that power inspires activities of obligation and through which it works its magic. In stark contrast with the seduction novels to which *Wieland* is most proximate, Brown importantly does not have Carwin act *directly* on so much as *through* his victims. The sublime inscrutability of this "agent" is what lends it its transportive power; it is the very absence or invisibility which elicits the imagination and the actions of its victim-subjects. Calling attention to this summary insight, Clara darkly concludes: "it will not escape your notice, that the evils of which Carwin and Maxwell were the authors, owed their existence to the errors of the sufferers" (278). "It was not his secret poniard that I dreaded. It was only the success of his efforts to make you a confederate in your own destruction, to make your will the instrument by which he might bereave you of liberty and honor" (151).

The issue that Brown ultimately poses to the democrats of his time — and our own — is to beware of the collective capacity to be seduced by the utterance of popular voice, to beware of captivating fantasies of collective self-presence. As Juliet MacCannell has written, "perhaps we require, after so much freedom to prescribe our own laws, a reminder by means of written law's alien or 'dead letter' of the horrific character of its object — that all law must ultimately come to seem to us as if from an Other. When that Other becomes too close to us, appearing as our own voice from within, we risk the worst."[69] Brown's novel reveals our irreducibly uncanny relationship to law and the impossibility of full democratic autonomy;[70] it suggests that since we are at once the agents and the sufferers of our own rule, fantasies of agency and fantasies of submission are a single part of the interpellative scene. Brown warns against the fantasy of overcoming this division with consummate finality, of conflating the voice of the people with a living present: with the voice of God. In the radical democratic claim of the people's ability to speak for themselves, free of institutional mediation or representation, Brown saw the disavowed presence of the enthusiast, the dangerous embrace of the spirit of the law beyond its dead letter. In recalling readers to these phantasmatic aspects of democratic life, Brown's novel ultimately seeks solace in the more instructed fantasy of the traditional sublime. Without affirming Brown's postrevolutionary nostalgia, but attending his wariness of democratic self-sufficiency, we might instead inquire further into those most fantastic acts of democratic ventriloquism — when, in Jacques Rancière's words, a part that has no part claims to speak in the name of the whole, to speak in the name of the very whole that secures the silence and invisibility of the uncounted. The early Republic's robust drama of ventriloquism and voice, dramatized in *Wieland*, suggests not that democracy be understood in direct opposition to representation — the fantasy of direct democrats, advocates of the living presence of popular voice — but that *democratic* representation be understood as also always a *crisis* in representation.

We have frequently printed the word democracy. Yet I cannot too often repeat that it is a word the real gist of which still sleeps . . . notwithstanding the resonance and the many angry tempests out of which its syllables have come from pen or tongue. It is a great word, whose history . . . remains unwritten, because that history has yet to be enacted.   WALT WHITMAN, *Democratic Vistas*[1]

"Aesthetic Democracy"

Walt Whitman and the Poetry of the People

Walt Whitman also associated popular voice with the sublime, but unlike Brown he enthusiastically affirmed this sublimity as an aesthetic resource of democratic regeneration. F. O. Matthiessen called Whitman "the central figure of our literature affirming the democratic faith"; more recently George Kateb described Whitman as "perhaps the greatest philosopher of the culture of democracy."[2] Both assessments seem warranted, and to them I would add another: Whitman is one of America's greatest theorists of the relationship between aesthetics and democratic politics. In texts like *Leaves of Grass* (1855) and *Democratic Vistas* (1871) Whitman unites these spheres in a conception of "aesthetic democracy." For Whitman the popular commitment to democracy requires an aesthetic evaluation, and he aims to enact the required reconfiguration of popular sensibility through the poetic depiction of the people as a sublimely poetic, world-making power. Whitman's invocation of the people's constituent power is in this sense sublimely autopoetic rather than autonomic; the people are at once the inexhaustible inspiration and the effect of poetic mediation. Through his poetry Whitman claimed to sing the multitudinous diversity of the vox populi back to the people, thereby enhancing their latent poetic capacity and aesthetically enabling a radical democratic politics of collective revision.[3] Whitman's conception of aesthetic democracy illuminates three regions of inquiry usually neglected in contemporary democratic theory: the relationship between aesthetics and politics, the invariably poetic construction of the people, and the people envisioned as a poetic, world-making power.

This chapter pursues these topics by exploring Whitman's reflections on aesthetic democracy and his experimental poetic invocation of the people's voice. The vox populi of Whitman's people, and of the democracy they enact, resides in their constitutive futurity, in their remaining forever a people that is not . . . yet.[4] Whitman's poetry figures the people as inexhaustibly sublime, in that they can be neither captured by representation nor finally embodied by political institutions.[5] For Whitman, in effect, "the people are always more and less than the people."[6] The democratic attachments that Whitman hoped to forge through his poetry revolve around the vivifying sublimity of this paradox of the people never at one with itself. While in certain respects Whitman's democratic faith resembles the "democratic aestheticism" celebrated in Kateb's influential work on Whitman, I argue that Whitman's is ultimately a more radically democratic vision than Kateb's Emersonian interpretation allows. Whitman's aesthetic democracy does not simply call for "receptivity or responsiveness to as much of the world as possible," but for an embrace of a world always in the process of becoming other than it is.[7] Whitman offers to contemporary democratic theorists a distinct understanding of the transformative poetics of citizenship, according to which the quotidian and embodied dimensions of democratic life, its aesthetic organization, are essential to democracy's "real gist" and meaning, its enactment beyond "pen or tongue." The most theoretically provocative and potentially productive dimensions of Whitman's work are found in his departures from the inherited ideological divisions of nineteenth-century American politics, and from the attachments of American political institutions. Whitman was preoccupied with the fraught inheritance of the Revolution, but for him that inheritance was best captured in the yet-to-be-enacted history of a democratic people.

I

Whitman's changing attitude toward American politics and political institutions has provoked much scholarly debate. There is no doubt that Whitman evinced a lifelong reverence for the members of the founding generation, particularly for that "beacon in history," the "matchless WASHINGTON."[8] In this Whitman was like many other followers of the "Young America" movement of the 1830s and 1840s, writers who, in newspapers like John L. Sullivan's *Democratic Review* (in which Whitman published frequently), advocated a strongly nationalistic response to European cultural dominance.[9] Mythologizing the Founders was an assertion of cultural independence; men like Jefferson and Washington stood as powerful unifying symbols in a period when "union" was considered a fragile and vulnerable achievement.

Beyond this widely shared cultural nationalism, Whitman's early political commitments also owed much to the founding generation's republican legacies. Jefferson's distinctly American civic republicanism was particularly influential in Whitman's early political education; the material requirements of independent citizenship, the importance of available land, and the turn away from the authority of the past all appear in Whitman's writing, early and late. Indeed the transformation of Jeffersonian ideology during the presidency of Andrew Jackson—in particular its urbanization—profoundly marked the political climate of Whitman's childhood. As his biographers emphasize, Whitman was born into a family of working-class Jacksonian Democrats, and his father was an ardent admirer of Jefferson and Paine.[10] Whitman's early political involvements and his newspaper editorials of the 1830s and 1840s rarely deviated from this Jeffersonian-Jacksonian ideological framework.[11]

Yet reading Whitman's later work solely through the lens of these earlier political commitments does not explain his idiosyncratic use of key terms like "democracy" and "the people" in the writing for which he is best known: that beginning with *Leaves of Grass* (1855). Unlike Noah Webster, who warned readers against using these words precisely because their advocates "have never defined what they mean by the *people,* or what they mean by *democracy*," Whitman used their polyvocality to his poetic and political advantage.[12] Whitman's distinctive contribution to American political thought is obscured when the "politics" of his writings are reduced to his early political affiliations and party activism.

The publication of *Leaves* came during a period of widely perceived social and political crisis that coincided with an extraordinary flowering of American literature: *The Scarlet Letter, Representative Men, Moby-Dick, Pierre, Uncle Tom's Cabin, Walden, The House of the Seven Gables,* and *Leaves of Grass* were all published between 1850 and 1855. David Reynolds has convincingly argued that this literary flowering should be understood as a response to the period's social and political turbulence. Whitman's literary response to the political events unfolding around him was twofold: on the one hand, and following other political romantics, he invoked a broadened understanding of literature and poetry for political ends; on the other, he turned away from institutions to an unmediated understanding of the people as the only reliable source of democratic regeneration. Whitman's vision of "aesthetic democracy" emerged from the interconnectedness of this twofold response. The social and political crisis of the 1850s was marked by widespread political corruption, a widening gap between rich and poor, rising immigration and corresponding anti-immigrant feeling, high urban death rates, and a fragmented political system in the wake of the death of the old party system.[13] Overwhelming all these factors, of course, was the expanding power of southern race slavery. The year 1850 saw the congressional passage of a more forceful Fugitive Slave Law, which sent southern slave-hunters into northern cities and made those harboring slaves in the North subject to federal prosecution. In 1854 the Kansas-Nebraska Act repealed the Missouri Compromise of 1820, opening the West to the expansion of America's "peculiar institution" and creating border wars between Missouri slaveholders and abolitionist or free-soil forces within "Bloody Kansas."

Whitman's reaction to the slow descent of the United States into civil war was notoriously uncertain. On the issue of slavery Whitman was a committed "antiextensionist." In the years before the Civil War he did not believe in the abolition of slavery (which he thought would bring about the dissolution of union) but rather opposed its further extension into the Western Territories (Lincoln held a similar view). Whitman's enthusiastic participation in the Free-Soil movement's early stages suggests that his antislavery activism was motivated primarily by his Jeffersonian concern that the West must remain open to independent white farmers, rather than a principled opposition to racial inequality. Moreover, in his editorials from the period Whitman strongly condemned what he considered the fanaticism of both northern abolitionists (particularly the constitution-burning Garrisonians) and southern proponents of slavery or secession. As the crisis grew, Whitman's faith in American political and legal institutions withered, and he sought to instead articulate latent common "intuitions" and poetically "celebrate the inherent" dispositions and sensibilities of the people (w, 145).

The text that best signals Whitman's apprehension in the face of growing political crisis is his vitriolic attack on the administration of Franklin Pierce in "The Eighteenth Presidency!" (1856). In a passage that resonates stylistically as a negative counterpart to his celebratory, open-ended democratic lists in *Leaves*, Whitman describes the period's party politicians as "Office-holders, office-seekers, robbers, pimps, exclusives, malignants, conspirators, murderers, fancy-men, post-masters, custom-house clerks, contractors, kept-editors, spaniels well-trained to carry and fetch . . . pimpled men, scarred inside with the vile disorder, gaudy outside with gold chains made from people's money and harlot's money twisted together; crawling, serpentine men, the lousy combings and born freedom sellers of the earth" (e, 1337–38). In passages like this—and this text has many—Whitman expressed the period's common suspicion of institutional politics and institutions of all kinds. He also exemplified the tone and temper of much of the writing circulating in mid-nineteenth century America. Departing from the purported ratio-critical norms of the public sphere, political debate in the period was marked by passionate invective, sentimental appeal, defamation, and the widespread recognition of the political uses of vehemence, disdain, and contempt.[14]

Much of this literature was written in the name of "reform" of one kind or another. The reform movements that characterized the political culture of antebellum America had by the 1850s been radicalized at the hands of their evangelical and deeply antiauthoritarian constituencies. "Ultraism" was a term in common use to designate this radicalized brand of reform politics and to distinguish it from its reasoned, deliberative, largely Unitarian variant.[15] Ultraists believed that individuals could be sanctified while on earth and used this moral perfectionism to argue against the complicity of compromise, institutional mediation, and political deliberation. The resulting animus against mediating institutions was compounded by a fiery renewal of antinomian thought and sensibility. The mediation of language was suspect for some of the age's more enthusiastic radical lights, as in John Brown's insistence on "action! action!" But even less revolutionary, more intellectual writers appreciated the impulse. Thoreau, for example, had publicly noted and celebrated precisely this aspect of Brown. "He was not a rhetorician," Thoreau wrote shortly after Brown's thwarted raid on Harper's Ferry, but "the greatest of preachers." "He did not set up even a political graven image between him and his God."[16] Emerson too noted the "fertile forms of antinomianism" that thrived in antebellum America, allowing for a "keener scrutiny of institutions and domestic life."[17]

Whitman was accused of participating in this antinomian reaction to what both he and Emerson characterized as the "fossilism" of inherited institutions. As he wrote in the first edition of Leaves (1855), "Unscrew the locks from the doors! / Unscrew the doors themselves from their jambs!" (LG, 50). In the "Calamus" section of the third edition of Leaves (1860) Whitman responded to those who criticized this anti-institutionalist or antinomian aspect of the first volume, evident in both its content and in its abandonment of inherited poetic forms (about which more below):

> I HEAR it was charged against me that I sought to destroy institutions,
> But really I am neither for nor against institutions,
> (What indeed have I in common with them? or what with the destruction
>   of them?) (LG, 281)

Whitman's indifference to institutions led at times to a reiteration of the period's common invocation of the force and power of immediacy: "We want no *reforms*," Whitman wrote, "no *institutions*, no *parties*—We want a living principle as nature has, under which nothing can go wrong" (W, 62). Like Emerson, Whitman would be "ashamed to think how easily we capitulate to badges and names, to large societies and dead institutions."[18] For Whitman, however, overcoming these inherited institutions' weight came not only from a spiritualized invocation of "nature," or the self-reliant individual (however removed from individual*ism* or sovereign mastery the Emersonian individual, properly understood, might be), but from a direct turn to the people in whose name these putatively democratic institutions ruled. In the crisis of social and political institutions in the 1850s Whitman glimpsed new possibilities for fulfilling their hindered democratic prospects, a promise of democratic regeneration through the aesthetic transformation of everyday life.

The crisis of the 1850s was understood by many of the era's writers as a crisis of both politics and meaning—a crisis in representation broadly understood. Responding to unfolding events in "Bloody Kansas," for example, Emerson wrote that "language has lost its meaning in the universal cant. *Representative government* is really misrepresentative . . . *Manifest Destiny, Democracy, Freedom,* fine names for an ugly thing. . . . They call it chivalry and freedom; I call it the stealing of all the earnings of a poor man and his little girl and boy."[19] Whitman wrote *Leaves* to address both levels of this representational crisis, but in doing so he did not aim to turn away from the corruption and complicity of politics altogether (as some have argued Thoreau did at Walden Pond). Instead, he looked to the latent resources of democratic life, particularly as manifest in America's growing cities, to restore the poetic vitality of both politics and language. While on the surface America's political institutions seemed compromised and diminishing of individuality (a point frequently reiterated in the writing of Emerson and Thoreau), Whitman believed that political engagement and encounter carried a deeper significance, one "descending below laws . . . [and] social routines" (W, 145), and overlooked by widespread ultraist condemnations of politics.

Admitting the "vile" and "incompetent" people sometimes put forward in a democracy, Whitman nevertheless wrote that "shams, etc. will always be the show, like ocean's scum; enough, if waters deep and clear make up the rest. Enough that while the piled embroidery shoddy gaud and fraud spreads to the superficial eye, the hidden warp and weft are genuine and will wear forever" (DV, 978). Like Thoreau and Emerson, Whitman recognized the "threatening evils" of political democracy— all three were particularly troubled by democracy's averaging forces and "statistical" propensities—but Whitman also found resources to combat these evils, not only in fathomless, spiritualized "nature" but in the very "roar of cities and the broil of politics" that Emerson's essay "Nature" posits as a dangerous or distracting artifice.[20] "To attack the turbulence and destructiveness of the Democratic spirit is an old story. . . . But with the noble Democratic spirit—even accompanied by its freaks and its excesses—no people can ever become enslaved."[21]

Whitman believed that spaces of political contest—in his words, the "arenas" or "gymnasiums" of freedom—were the necessary forums for creating the assertively independent citizens required for a regenerative democracy of everyday life, for the transformative poetics of everyday citizenship, understood as a lived practice rather than a juridical category. Political contest was not simply subject to overarching moral purpose for Whitman. He figured the political not as an instrumentalized realm serving competing ends, nor as a debased or diminishing distraction from the stylized cultivation of the self. His high evaluation of political engagement and contention—his estimation of its "restorative" capacities—clearly distinguishes Whitman from both his Emersonian and his ultraist contemporaries. It also gives passages like the following their resounding non-instrumentalist resonance: "A brave delight, fit for freedom's athletes, fills these arenas, and fully satisfies, out of the action in them, irrespective of success" (DV, 976). The action that Whitman believes these forums for democratic citizenship engender is explicitly agonistic: "I think agitation is the most important factor of all, the most deeply important. To stir, to question, to suspect, to examine, to denounce!" (C, IV, 30). "Vive, the attack—the perennial assault!" (DV, 976). Leaves at once speaks for and elicits a self capable of flourishing amid the democratic agonism called for in several of Whitman's texts. As he writes in "By Blue Ontario's Shore," for example: "he only suits these States whose manners favor the audacity and sublime turbulence of the States" (LG, 481). Democratic contest and agonism were for Whitman productive of the kind of self-reliant individuality that Thoreau and Emerson thought prior to politics, and also undercut or diminished by politics. Whitman's independent, democratic self is an effect of a milling space of political discord and democratic contest. Kateb has shown how Whitman envisioned a democratic culture capable of sustaining and enabling a robust and stylized "aesthetic individuality," but he mischaracterizes the relationship between them. The tension that Kateb identifies between a highly individualistic antinomianism and collective civic-mindedness is indeed present throughout Whitman's work, but Whitman's embrace of a radical democratic politics works to suspend the opposition between them. Take a passage from *Democratic Vistas* that Kateb also quotes, in part: "Bibles may convey, and priests expound, but it is exclusively for the noiseless operation of the isolated Self, to enter the pure ether of veneration, reach the divine levels, and commune with the unutterable" (DV, 989). The antinomianism of this passage — "commune with the unutterable" — is clearly reminiscent of Emerson's early essays and even carries with it the trace of theological controversy. But then the very next line — "To practically enter into politics is an important part of American personalism" (DV, 989) — reasserts Whitman's embrace of political action as constitutive of the self he sings and celebrates.

The practical and affective organization of democratic life below the level of institutions and laws was Whitman's primary concern after 1855 and is essential to his vision of aesthetic democracy and to the poetics of citizenship that it enacts. While this position was elaborated in the preface to the first edition of *Leaves*, *Democratic Vistas* stated it best: "For not only is it not enough that the new blood, new frame of democracy shall be vivified and held together merely by political means, superficial suffrage, legislation, etc., but it is clear to me that unless it goes deeper, gets at least as firm and warm a hold in men's hearts, emotions and belief, as, in their days, feudalism or ecclesiasticism, and inaugurates its own perennial sources, welling from the center forever, its strengths will be defective, its growth doubtful, and its main charm wanting" (DV, 959). According to Whitman, American democracy's crisis of the 1850s could not be resolved by reorganizing political institutions but only by addressing what Kateb has termed a particular "stylization of life," "a distinctive set of appearances, habits, rituals, dress, ceremonies, folk traditions and historical memories." However, while Kateb sees this concern as "secondary at best," and fears its nationalistic or collectivist tendencies, it was here that the promise of aesthetic interventions into democratic life became most evident to Whitman; it is also on this explicitly aesthetic terrain that contemporary democratic theorists may have the most to learn from him.[22]

II

As a newspaper editor for the *Brooklyn Eagle* and the *Aurora*, Whitman already appreciated the political power of words to shape political action and educate citizens. He was a committed participant in what the historian Richard Brown has characterized as America's evolving "discourse of the informed citizen," which identified education and the free circulation of information in an open public sphere as the primary basis for securing independent citizenship and the stability of free government.[23] Whitman participated in this discourse, but he also critiqued it, particularly in his literary contributions, which came to be valued as an extension of his editorial and journalistic efforts. As Betsy Erkkila has written, "the publication of *Leaves of Grass* in 1855 was not an escape from politics but a continuation of politics by other means."[24] It was a continuation, however, that also marked a transformation in Whitman's conceptualization of politics. Whitman's work was no longer engaged principally in contending over particular issues or clarifying ideological positions; instead Whitman addressed the overall condition of the polity as what he called a "passionate body," elaborating the "electric" or "resonant" interconnections between the utter singularity of the self and the multitudinous and contending voices of democratic politics.[25]

Art intended, Whitman wrote, "to serve the people," and when it failed to do so it was "false to its promises" (C, IV, 4). The preface to the first edition of *Leaves* (1855) reads as a kind of manifesto on the interconnections between aesthetics and democratic politics, an account elaborated in more detail later in *Democratic Vistas* (1871). Whitman believed that grasping this interconnection was crucial to understanding his poetry. Those "who insist on viewing my poetry" as "literary performance," or as "aiming mainly toward art or aestheticism" (P, 671), invariably fail to understand it. Whitman disdained the growing tendency of literature to "magnify & intensify its own technism" and to "isolate itself from general & vulgar life, & to make a caste or order" (N, 1603). Opposing such tendencies in the first edition of *Leaves*, Whitman opened aesthetics to democratic politics, and democratic politics to aesthetics. Experimentally departing from both the "technism" of poetic form (most obviously the inherited conventions of lyric poetry) and the formalism of political institutions, Whitman hoped to stage an unmediated, challenging encounter with his audience. He attempted to poetically overcome the representational limitation of the very written text that connects and separates the poet from his public. Consider this famous passage from the "Song of Occupations":

Come closer to me,

Push close my lovers and take the best I possess, . . .

I was chilled with the cold type and cylinder and wet paper between us.

   (LG, 89)

Whitman likened his attempt to poetically move or "touch" the reader to the power of oratory and the spoken word in antebellum political culture. Discussing the power of oratory in the period, Emerson wrote that the orator's word should not be distinguished from action. "It is the electricity of action. It is action, as the general's word of command or chart of battle is action." Because oratory was closely associated with the crowds that often populate Whitman's poetry, some writers associated it with democratic unreason and the dangers of popular tyranny. Thoreau, for instance, took a more suspicious view of oratorical power when he wrote that the "orator yields to the inspiration of the transient occasion, and speaks to the mob before him, to those who can *hear* him; but the writer . . . who would be distracted by the event and the crowd which inspire the orator, speaks to the intellect and the heart of mankind, to all in any age who can *understand* him."[26] Whitman, in contrast, wanted the reader to hear his songs as much as understand them; he regularly situates himself within the clamor of the crowd rather than aspiring to rise above it. In his *American Primer* Whitman wrote that the ideal writer should be able to do with words "any thing, that man or woman or the natural powers can do" (AP, 598). Whitman wanted his words to touch his readers and move them toward democratic rejuvenation.

The connections that Whitman sought to establish with the reader, and to strengthen in the political culture of the time, were explicitly affective and erotic.[27] As Whitman wrote in the "Calamus" section of *Leaves of Grass*, he wanted readers to thrust him beneath their clothing, "to feel the throbs of their heart, to rest upon their hips" (LG, 271). Examining passages such as these, Allen Grossman has argued that Whitman's overriding concern in his poetry and its public orientation was with an "infinite distributability of affectionate presence." Whitman hoped to press in upon his readers as the surging crowds of Manhattan pressed in upon themselves and him, but—again in contrast to Emerson and Thoreau—he envisioned this proliferation of contact as stimulating difference rather than diminishing the individual. The urban crowds among which Whitman so often positions himself in his writings are his model carriers of "presence" and, as such, the markers of a representational limit. Grossman argues that Whitman's intention to rid transactions of "all representational mediation" is the reason for his interest in "phrenology, his dislike of political parties, poetic diction, mythology, and so on."[28]

Whitman's attempts to overcome political and written mediation in his poetry also illuminate the peculiar way that he invokes democracy in his writing. Instead of arguing for the legitimacy of democratic politics in the American setting, the goal of Whitman's work was to provoke and disseminate a democratic sensibility that shaped the experiences of individuals below the cognitive level of conviction or even persuasion. "I and mine do not convince by arguments, similes, rhymes. We convince by our presence" (LG, 303). The idea that one could "convince" by presence rather than argument relied on a vision of the "social and political" world as conserved not by "legislation, police, treaties, [or] dread of punishment," but by what Whitman called the "latent intuitional sense" (DV, 1013). By directing his poetic work to this infrasensible level of democratic life and practice, or to what Ralph Ellison would later call its "lower frequencies," Whitman hoped to invigorate individual and political capacities, to further encourage and enhance the individual and collective self-enactments he thought exemplary of American democracy.[29] His poems were to "arouse reason," but also to "suggest, give freedom, strength, muscle, candor" (N, 1563). "Your very flesh," he wrote in Leaves, "shall be a great poem and have the riches and fluency not only in its words but in the silent lines of its lips and face and between the lashes of your eyes and in every motion and joint of your body" (LG, 11). As his poetic translation of the vox populi became widespread, the autopoetic power that Whitman associates with democracy would become a part of the (electric) organization of the body (politic) itself.

Whitman's turn away from established channels of institutionalized politics in favor of aesthetic intervention into political life at the micropolitical level[30] has led some commentators to accuse him of abandoning faith in democratic politics altogether. One version of this argument suggests that Whitman's turn to aesthetics corresponds to a turn toward a "spiritual democracy," or an attempt by an élite class of poet-legislators "to overcome the practice of politics as a collective decision-making process."[31] In this reading Whitman's reference to "democratic despots" in

Democratic Vistas is understood as an all-too-literal reference to a despotic poetic class rather than to the self-enacting or autopoetic aspect of democratic politics itself. Others have more plausibly argued that an often unrecognized "dark side" taints Whitman's putatively democratic politics, his loathing of corrupt institutions "seep[ing] through to a disdain for the people themselves."[32] According to this interpretation Whitman exhibits the familiar conflict of "left-wing intellectuals" who want to celebrate the "common man" while often disdaining "actually existing people." Both readings attribute to Whitman a "Romantic" or "Rousseauian" longing for authentic and unalienated existence, a longing they then place at the heart of Whitman's critique of actually existing democracy.

Such arguments neglect Whitman's political and stylistic departures from earlier forms of political romanticism, departures which shape his claim to be a democratic poet. For Whitman, not only was poetry a kind of democratic action, but democratic action should itself be understood as a kind of poetry. Whitman in his poetry presented a "vulgar" or "promiscuous" democratic people to themselves as sublime and worthy of inspiring aesthetic appreciation and emulation rather than embarrassment or disgust.[33] He did so not to further enhance Americans' habitual self-regard but to invigorate the generous, autopoetic potentials already latent in the people. The highly individualized Romantic vision of the poet-legislator—best captured by Percy Bysshe Shelley's rapturous account of poets as the "unacknowledged legislators of the World"—attracted Whitman, but he ultimately rejected this vision, along with the lyric poetry associated with it, as didactic, élitist, and antidemocratic.[34] The heroic vision of the poet did appeal to Whitman in its idealism and in the emphasis that it placed on the world-making capacity of words. Emerson's essay "The Poet," which Whitman greatly admired, captured this capacity through its invocation of the poet as "the sayer, the namer. . . . He is a sovereign, and stands on the centre."[36] However, Whitman ultimately resisted this unitary, undemocratic vision of the poet-author-authority; his designation as the paradigmatic democratic poet emerges from his resistance to this familiar Romantic conception. Whitman is poorly read as "first, last and nothing else but a lyric poet, self-centered, individualistic, in the tradition of the great individualistic Romantic writers and poets."[35]

Whitman's most sustained confrontation with this Romantic vision is found in his writings on Thomas Carlyle. For Whitman, Carlyle's work best typified the antidemocratic temptation of modern times, and his response to Carlyle clearly articulates his own contrary vision of the form giving or autopoetic power of the people. Whitman agreed with Carlyle that theirs was a time of crisis and fundamental uncertainty: would it be "enoblement," Carlyle asked, or would it be "death?" Where Carlyle saw the greatest danger, however, Whitman saw promise and opportunity. Carlyle's disdain for the democratic masses, which he characterized as "swarmery" ("the gathering of men in swarms," from the German *Schwarmarei* and associated with the English term "enthusiasm"),[37] was dismissed by Whitman as a symptom of dyspepsia, the improper digestion of the spirit of the age.[38] Both writers were suspicious of quantitative or utilitarian visions of democracy, those which embraced the principle that the "Count of Heads" was "to be the Divine Court of Appeal on every question and interest of mankind."[39] But Whitman had faith in the ability of the people to resist their statistical reduction to so many "dreams or dots" (LG, 9). In "Shooting Niagara"—the essay to which Whitman's *Democratic Vistas* responds—Carlyle warned his "aristo" readers to avoid the impracticality of literature. He did this in part because his own attempts to unify aesthetics and politics (in *Chartism*, for example) had proved woefully ineffective.[40] No longer clinging to hopes for a heroic "literatus" (Whitman's term) or poet, Carlyle in *Shooting Niagara* longed for a new aristocratic union of title and nature. Carlyle expressed a wish that "the entire population" could "be thoroughly drilled," and called on the throne to bring this about, thereby taking a stand against the "dirt, disorder, nomadism, disobedience, folly and confusion" of democracy.[41] Whitman's poetry, in contrast, created a sublime "image-making work" of this very same democratic spectacle.

Whitman understood Carlyle's nostalgic longing for the heroic individual's reappearance as a futile though understandable temptation, which forced him to ask how democracy itself could produce the greatness of character usually associated with aristocratic culture, and not invariably diminish or threaten individual singularity. "My utmost pretension," Whitman wrote in *Specimen Days*, "is probably but to offset that old claim of the exclusively curative power of first-class individual men, as leaders and rulers, by the claims, and general movement and result, of ideas. Something of the latter kind seems to me the distinctive theory of America, of democracy, and of the modern—or rather I should say it *is* democracy, and it *is* the modern" (SD, 916). "Democracy," "America," and "the Modern" were for Whitman "convertible terms." His invocation of Hegel—implicit here, explicit elsewhere—guided Whitman further away from heroic individualists like Carlyle, not only to an understanding of the movement of ideas and spirit but also to embracing the insufficiency of the individual and the importance of the constitutive aspects of human relationality. Recent appreciations of Whitman's aesthetic individualism have underemphasized this aspect of his thought.[42]

In Hegel Whitman found the insight that truth is not in "any one party, or any one form of government" but in the "just relations of objects to each other" (SD, 920). The struggles between objects—the dialectic—reveal truth, Whitman writes, in the "endless process of Creative thought." This line of thinking brings Whitman to a question central to his own autopoetic understanding of democracy. "What is the fusing explanation and tie," Whitman asks, "what relationship between the (radical democratic) Me, the human identity of understanding, emotions, spirit, &c, on the one side, and the (conservative) Not Me, the whole material objective universe and laws, with what is behind them in time and space, on the other side?" (SD, 919). Whitman took from his admiring encounter with German idealism the opposition here between his "(radical democratic) Me" and the intransigent "conservative" existence of the material world. But why is the "Me" characterized by Whitman as "radical democratic" rather than, as we might expect, "free," or "moral?" If Romantic writers tended to see the poet as the text's sole originator and author/authority, Whitman works repeatedly to decenter this relationship. Even the poetic "Me" or "I" is not one, for Whitman, but many; it is democratic in its very plurality and in its "nomadism." As Whitman asks in *Leaves*, "Do I contradict myself? / Very well then . . . I contradict myself; / I am large . . . I contain multitudes" (LG, 87). Kateb has suggested that such moments in Whitman's work point to an inexhaustible inner reservoir of potentiality, and convincingly emphasizes the gap between the conscious (one might say representational) limitations of Whitman's "self" and the depths of his secularized understanding of "soul." For Kateb this is the basis of Whitman's ethics, for "to admit one's compositeness and ultimate unknowability is to open oneself to a kinship to others which is defined by receptivity and responsiveness to them."[43]

This abiding sense of inner strangeness that we recognize in others, and that leads us to be receptive of their singularity, is crucial to Kateb's identification of an Emersonian perfectionist ideal in Whitman's work. But for Whitman the inner strangeness that his "(radical democratic) Me" encounters results not from the primary ineffability of solitude but from the sublime potentialities of relational democratic life. The inexhaustible resources of potentiality that Kateb finds in Whitman's "democratic personality" do not lie first in the inner strangeness then open to the receptivity of another; instead this inner strangeness or uncanniness is better understood as a *product* of democratic encounter, as an effect of the multivoiced constitution of the democratic self. Whitman's account of the interconnection between democratic politics and democratic language richly explores this sublime effect of democracy (its production of a multitudinous democratic self), and Whitman hopes to further enact this effect by ventriloquizing the myriad and changing voices that constitute the vox populi. It is this attempt to poetically capture the sublimely polyphonic voice of the people, to serve as an aesthetic mediator to the people, that turns Whitman against lyric poetry and drives his poetic experimentalism.[44]

On the topic of polyvocality and the multitudinous self, Whitman has a striking affinity with the work of Mikhail Bakhtin, who is similarly concerned with the socially embedded forms of speech that occupy different and overlapping regions of a given language. Bakhtin calls this complex social background of meaningful speech production "heteroglossia." For Whitman a key distinction of the *American* language, which emerges from and helps (re)enact American democracy, was precisely its luxuriant proliferation of speech idioms. Whitman writes that "the immense diversity of race, temperament, character—the copious stream of humanity constantly flowing hither—must reappear in free rich growths of speech. . . . The opulence of race-elements is in the theory of America. Land of the Ensemble, to her consenting currents flow, and the ethnology of the States draws the grand outline of that hospitality and reception that must mark the new politics, sociology, literature, and religion" (N, 1661). The "theory of America" from which Whitman hopes to draw the orienting ethos of "hospitality" and "reception" emerges from its "immense diversity of race, temperament, character" and the "free rich growths of speech" that emanate from this diversity. Whitman's emphasis here is on a popular voice that always exceeds itself, that can never be coordinated into a final articulated unity or expression, and that is invariably experimental. "I consider *Leaves of Grass* and its theory," Whitman wrote in "A Backward Glance o'er Travel'd Roads," "to be experimental as, in the deepest sense, I consider our American republic itself to be" (P, 657). What Whitman claims in passages like this he formally enacts in the bold poetic experimentalism of *Leaves*, a text which according to one critic effectively "shunned all familiar marks of poetry of the time."[45] Whitman's innovations in poetic form are related to his attempts to poetically render the sublime cacophony of democratic speech. According to Allen Grossman, Whitman abandoned "poetic language" in favor of a "conjunctive principle" manifest in the "sequence of end-stopped, nonequivalent, but equipollent lines" that characterize the abandonment in *Leaves* of a "centralizing hypotactic grammar." This "grammar" is replaced in Whitman's poetry by what Grossman characterizes as "an unprecedented trope of inclusion."[46]

Whitman believed that the received traditions of European lyric poetry sought to avoid precisely this inclusive, heteroglossic dimension of language. Like Bakhtin, Whitman believed that lyrical poetic form evinced an undemocratically unitary theory of the subject as expressed by speech. To combat this conception of self Whitman initiated his radically innovative "democratic" changes within poetic discourse and form. (Bakhtin gave up on studying "discourse in poetry" altogether and turned instead to the novel.) For both writers an implicit and faulty understanding of the relationship between language and the self stood behind lyric poetry's aspirations and its attempt to cleanse language of heteroglot associations. It was not the poetry, in other words, but the assumptions about subjectivity behind the poetry that both writers found politically suspect. As Bakhtin writes, "In poetic genres, artistic consciousness—understood as a unity of all the author's semantic and expressive intentions—fully realizes itself within its own language; in them alone is such consciousness fully immanent, expressing itself in it directly and without mediation, without conditions and without distance. The language of the poet is *his* language, he is utterly immersed in it, inseparable from it, he makes use of each form, each word, each expression according to its unmediated power to assign meaning (as it were, 'without quotation marks'), that is as a pure and direct expression of his own intention."[47] Like Bakhtin, Whitman was acutely aware that speakers never come to language "without quotation marks," that in using language they acknowledge indebtedness to others, and that one cannot assume a "complete single-personed hegemony over [one's] own language."⁴⁸ Neither postulated "a simple and unmediated relationship of the speaker to his unitary and singular 'own' language."⁴⁹ Poetic language as conceptualized in the lyric mode had posited the individual as the fount of meaning, where Whitman and Bakhtin instead urged that the individual be grasped as an effect of the heteroglot currents of language itself.⁵⁰ As we saw above, this means that the "inner strangeness" one might encounter when "accounting with the unutterable" comes from an encounter with one or many internal others. "A person has no interior sovereign territory, he is wholly and always on the boundary; looking inside himself he looks into the eyes of another or with the eyes of another."⁵¹ This description resonates with Whitman's "(radical democratic) Me," irreducibly populated with a vast multitude of competing voices, or as Whitman noted in "Out of the Cradle Endlessly Rocking," "A thousand warbling echoes have started to life within me" (LG, 392).

This constitutively relational understanding of the self is what the influential interpretations of Whitman as a distinct but beholden Emersonian tend to neglect.⁵² Kateb, for example, finds particularly discomfiting Whitman's frequent references to "the love of comrades" and above all to "adhesiveness," and he rightly notes the ugly nativism that sometimes marks Whitman's work (particularly the writings on the Civil War). Kateb worries that Whitman's account of adhesiveness "threatens to suffocate the very individualism of personality which Whitman is trying to promote" with "an all-enfolding merger."⁵³ Thus for Kateb "Whitman's final lesson is solitude, not the adventures of human connectedness."⁵⁴ He asks us to choose between two Whitmans: the aesthetic individualist and the communitarian nationalist. The radical democratic Whitman shows this to be a false choice.

It is important to note that when Whitman invokes "adhesiveness" and the "love of comrades" he distinguishes them from isolating and mediating phenomena. There is "individualism, which isolates," but also "another half, which is adhesiveness or love, that fuses, ties, and aggregates, making the races comrades, and fraternizing all" (DV, 973). Whitman asserts his hope that his work dedicated to "ma femme" democracy will be able to "make divine magnetic lands / With the love of comrades, / With the life-long love of comrades" (LG, 272). "Adhesiveness" and "magnetism," odd terms to contemporary ears, were associated in antebellum America with the popular discourses of phrenology and mesmerism. Both discourses asserted that what bound individuals was infrasensible communication rather than common cognitive or representational commitments. Adhesiveness, Whitman reminds readers, cannot be found in "sounded and resounded words, chattering words, echoes, dead words" (LG, 274). For Whitman the importance of this infrasensible connection was crucial at a time when "the terrible doubt of appearances" became a cultural obsession and familiar bonds of trust and solidarity seemed threatened by the growth of impersonal market forces and a politics of distance and dissimulation; infrasensible attachment was the "latent intuitional sense" that *Leaves* attempted to tap.

Whitman hoped that his work could serve as a response to the political and epistemological crisis of looming civil war insofar as it could promote the magnetic, or electric, flows of shared sentiment and affirmation between people (but again, without reducing people to a common mind or substance). In "Calamus" Whitman responds to the "terrible doubt of appearances" in this way:

> I cannot answer the question of appearances or that of
>   Identity beyond the grave,
> But I walk or sit indifferent, I am satisfied,
> He ahold of my hand has completely satisfied me. (LG, 274–75)

This "love of man for his comrade," this "attraction of friend to friend," is where Whitman goes on to locate "the base of all metaphysics." If the specter of radical doubt, the impulse of skepticism, or its political corollary in corrosive mistrust, cannot be philosophically refuted with confidence, Whitman hoped that it might at least be tempered with comradely affection. Whitman's response to skepticism is not a renewed quest for certitude but something found in the ordinary gesture of holding a hand; skepticism is here assuaged by co-presence. It is clear from the above discussion of poetic presence that Whitman wanted his poetry to become something like that reassuring hand. This response to skepticism resides in the relations between people, in their being-*in*-common rather than being common.[55] Whitman is therefore misread as a theorist of socialization, or as simply offering his poetry as a "vehicle of social cohesion."[56] Mere social unification or national identification is foreign to Whitman's invocation of the inexhaustible plenitude of democratic life, to the people's "measureless wealth of power and capacity, their vast artistic contrasts of lights and shades," and to his aesthetic revaluation of American democracy's vulgar asymmetries and promiscuous inconsistencies into the register of the unrepresentable sublime. The "sublimest part of political history," Whitman wrote, "is currently issuing from the American people" (DV, 978).

III

Whitman's claim in *Leaves* that the "Americans of all nations at any time upon the earth, have probably the most poetical nature," and that "the United States are essentially the greatest poem" (LG, 5), would have sounded perverse in the mid-nineteenth century. Tocqueville's remarks, two decades earlier in *Democracy in America*, that America "pays less attention to literature than any other civilized country," or that only the writing of journalists could be described as "truly American," were characteristic of the European evaluation; it was the predominant image to which nineteenth-century American literature's declaration of cultural independence responded.[57] Tocqueville expressed a common view when he wrote that "Aristocracy, by keeping society fixed, favors the stability and endurance of positive religions as well as political institutions. . . . [and that] in this respect aristocracy favors poetry."[58] In a phrase that could have been Whitman's, however, Tocqueville also gestured to new literary possibilities in democracy: "democracy shuts the past to poetry, but opens the future."[59]

Whitman clearly identified American poetry with the future, but he significantly expanded his conception of the poetic to encompass individual and collective actions or performances. It was not simply that the American people provided rich material for poetry; they *were* poetry. Whitman addressed his work to the autopoetic nature of the people. In America, Whitman writes, "the performance, disdaining the trivial, unapproach'd in the tremendous audacity of its crowds and groupings, and the push of its perspective, spreads with crampless and flowing breadth, and showers its prolific and splendid extravagance" (LG, 5). Americans' "sublime" and "poetic" nature is related to this audacious collective performance, to democracy's "crampless and flowing breadth," which Whitman distinguishes from the solidity and "fossilism" of aristocratic political and literary institutions.[60] If other states in other times "indicate themselves in their deputies"—in their representatives—the "genius" of Whitman's America is "not best or most in its executives or legislatures, nor in its ambassadors or authors, or colleges or churches or parlors, nor even in its newspaper inventors—but always most in the common people" (LG, 5). The "poetical nature" of "the common people" corresponds to what Whitman describes as their capacity for "formative action" (DV, 993), action self-generated and transformative of the "fossilism" of received institutions. This is a capacity that Whitman associates with the people generally, but as he reminds his readers, "the people have only emerged in America" (P, 1087).

Like many of his contemporaries Whitman was captivated by the idea that human beings made their own history, while also being products of that history. Marx's famous observation in the third of his "Theses on Feuerbach"—"men are products of their circumstances and changed upbringing," but also the very force required to "change circumstances"[61]— resonates at several points in Whitman's work. While it is an overstatement to suggest that Whitman's democratic citizens "are free to act and create without historical restriction,"[62] it is true that Whitman primarily envisions the people as a creative, autopoetic power. Democracy, Whitman suggests, justifies itself through the works that it creates.

For Whitman language—"greater than buildings or ships or religions or paintings or music" (LG, 144)—was a crucial marker of the radical autopoetic power of the common people. Whitman understands language as an incarnation of "man's unconscious passionate creative energy," born of "passionate yearning" (N, 1626–28). For Whitman language is not born of description or definition, nor of an innate desire to know and take control of the world, but rather of a *creative* desire. This desire is moreover democratic, born of a kind of sublime democratic spontaneity. "Language is not an abstract construction of the learn'd, or of dictionary makers, but it is something arising out of the work, needs, ties, joys, affections, tastes, of long generations of humanity, and has bases broad and low, close to the ground. Its final decisions are made by the masses" (P, 1190). The democracy of language, its origin in the creative potentiality of the people, in the low and the ordinary, is one of the principal reasons why Whitman placed so much importance on slang. "Profoundly consider'd," slang "is the lawless germinal element, below all words and sentences, and behind all poetry" (P, 1189). Like his hero Jefferson, Whitman was a "friend of Neology," and like Tocqueville, Whitman believed that "the continual restlessness of democracy" was related to "endless changes of language."[63] The spontaneous creation and re-creation of language seems to Whitman most unhindered in a democracy, and it is clearly an important part of what makes the vox populi so "poetic" for him. It also traces the kind of democratic, as opposed to didactic or legislative, relationship that Whitman hoped to establish with his public. While Whitman did not aim to simply impose a democratic vision on his public, to assume the position of the sovereign-poet-legislator, he did work to poetically elicit the same democratic public that seemingly spoke through him. He sought to elicit an audience that could hear its own democratic voice in the songs of its poet.

Unlike some of his closest contemporaries (Michael Gilmore has singled out Hawthorne and Emerson), Whitman did not fear abandoning his words to the interpretive flux of a democratic public; he did not seek final control over his words and their significations.[64] The message of the great poets "to each man and woman" was "come to us on equal terms," because "what we enclose you enclose. What we enjoy, you may enjoy" (LG, 15). "Song of Myself" begins with the seeming egoism of "I celebrate myself, / and what I assume you shall assume." But Whitman continues: "For every atom belonging to me as good belongs to you" (LG, 27). In this assertion of common belonging, but not of a common substance—Kateb describes it as the recognition of common potentiality—a dialogical relationship and an agonistic if not antagonistic interaction ensue. Whitman does not transmit the information of his text into a passive mind— "we must not be sacks and stomachs," as Emerson wrote[65]—nor does he impose upon it a prophetic vision. Instead Whitman envisions the author and the reader struggling over the meanings conveyed.

> You shall no longer take things at second or third hand
>   . . . . nor look through the eyes of the dead
>   . . . . nor feed on the specters in books,
> You shall not look through my eyes either, nor take
>   Things from me,
> You shall learn to listen to all sides and filter them from yourself. (LG, 28)

Just as the institutions of democratic contest provide arenas for forming robust individuality, so does literature (albeit only of a certain kind) provoke the reader's democratic and poetic potential. As already argued, the circulation of Whitman's poetry aimed to affect readers on multiple levels of sensibility and disposition—so that they appreciate the democracy from which they spring as no longer disfigured but sublime—but never passively. Whitman envisions this process as a physical contest, mentioning the "gymnasiums" of "freedom's athletes" in confronting these texts and then describing practices of critical reading itself as a "gymnast's struggle." "The reader is to do something for himself, must be on the alert, must himself or herself construct indeed the poem, argument, history, metaphysical essay—the text furnishing the hints, the clue, the start or framework" (DV, 1016–17). The dialogic and physically transformative struggle to make a language one's own, to interact with the affective and representational hints and clues of a text, serves Whitman in *Democratic Vistas* as both an analogy and a practice of political education.

As a poet engaging with and situated within this surging poetic and democratic power of the people, Whitman does not attempt a usurpation of popular voice, nor does he simply play the role of ventriloquist. Rather than speak for the people, Whitman aims to speak to and among them: "A call in the midst of the crowd, / My own voice, orotund sweeping and final" (LG, 75). He notes his "dejection and amazement" that "few or none" have yet "really spoken to this people, created a single image-making work for them, or absorbed the central spirit and the idiosyncrasies which are theirs—and which, thus, in highest ranges, so far remain entirely uncelebrated, unexpressed" (DV, 978). Whitman notes that "literature, strictly speaking, has never recognized the people" (DV, 968). His pursuit of a poetic "image-making work" aimed to provide democracy with multiple images for imitation and adaptation—images taken from the sublime resources of "the people." The people in "their measureless wealth of latent power and capacity, their vast, artistic contrast of lights and shades" provide Whitman with his material. He is not imposing it upon them (heteronomically) but performing an aesthetic translation of what is already immanent to their democratic practices. "He strangely transmutes them, / They are not vile any more. . . . they hardly know themselves, they are so grown" (LG, 131). "The people are ungrammatical" and "untidy," but Whitman's work does not aim to clean them up or subject them to the laws of grammar (or codified rules of justice). Unlike Carlyle, who aimed to provide a voice for the mute force of

Chartism's popular crowds, Whitman's invocation of "the people" speaks from and among them. Like William Hazlitt, who opens his essay "What Is the People?" with the quick response "And who are you to ask that question?,"[66] Whitman refuses the division between the people and himself. As Larzer Ziff notes, Whitman makes the "democratic audience the author of the poems of its poet."[67] In this paradoxical claim to provide an aesthetic translation of the people's independent, but not self-identical, and sublime voice, the people are figured at once as the inexhaustible inspiration and the effect of poetic mediation. Whitman's work reveals the vox populi not to be a pregiven unity, or a national expression, but instead a provisional poetic effect or claim.

If Whitman's project was not to merely give aesthetic expression to the inarticulate yet existing sovereign voice of the people, neither was it to simply represent the people accurately. Poetry for Whitman should not aim just to accurately represent an independent reality, but to enact a new reality; again, there are passages that seem to conflict with this conclusion, as when Whitman writes in *Leaves* that the poet "swears to his art, I will not be meddlesome. . . . What I tell I tell for precisely what it is. . . . What I experience or portray shall go from my composition without a shred of my composition. You shall stand by my side and look in the mirror with me" (*LG*, 14). Or when Whitman claims that in *Leaves* "everything is literally photographed. Nothing is poeticized" (*N*, 1524). Such passages have led some to characterize Whitman as an "observer and reporter," even a proto–social scientist.[68] Whitman did try to capture (and identify with) the vast ensemble of American democracy in his open-ended lists and through his commitment to literature's under-represented. ("Of every hue and caste am I, of every rank and religion, A farmer, mechanic, artist, gentleman, sailor, quaker, / Prisoner, fancy-man, rowdy, lawyer, physician, priest"; *LG*, 204.) However, Whitman ultimately aspired to more than the mimetic realism of the photographic model; his resistance to "poeticizing" should not be confused with resistance to aesthetic translation *tout court*. In the categories of Romantic poetic representation described by M. H. Abrams, Whitman resisted both the mirror and the lamp.[69] Always in touch with his era's broader aesthetic movements, Whitman initially felt a deep affinity with the quest for mimetic realism that characterized much of antebellum painting, but like the painters he also longed for an ineffable truth that could not be captured by pursuing the ideal of the daguerreotype. According to David Reynolds, Whitman ultimately reviled this school's social complacency and its fetishizing of the actual.[70] Whitman's vivid portrayals of "interminable swarms of alert, turbulent, good-natured [and not so good-natured], independent citizens" are well known (DV, 978), but he also warns poets not to be captivated by the "study of the picture of things" (N, 1569). He urged readers to "confront the growing excess and arrogance of realism" (DV, 1009). This poetic capacity forms an important link between aesthetics and politics. If Whitman posits a surging creativity as central to his understanding of democracy, and embraces the vitality of the people over formal political institutions and law, that people is for Whitman forever without unified will or subjectivity. The people invoked by Whitman do not aim at the realization of a common essence or at the construction of such an essence, but are only realized through their continual political reinvention out of a collective reservoir of sublime potentiality.

The refusal by the people of final legibility, their resistance to serving as an originary and articulate principle, is due largely to what Whitman considers their constitutive futurity, the supersession of the existent that Whitman associates with "the growing excess and arrogance of realism" in the America of his time (DV, 1009). It is this futurity that underlies the people's worldly reality, their "main significance" (which Whitman opposed to the paradoxical "abstraction" of "realism"): "I count with such absolute certainty on the great future of the United States—different from, though founded on, the past—that I have always invoked that future, and surrounded myself with it, before or while singing my songs. (As ever, all tends to followings—America, too, is a prophecy. What, even of the best and most successful, would be justified by itself alone? By the present, or the material ostent alone? Of men or States, few realize how much they live in the future. That, rising like pinnacles, gives its main significance to all You and I are doing today)" (P, 1035). This is quite a remarkable parenthetical aside. The future gives significance to the present in that it guides and orients contemporary action, inhabiting that action and giving it meaning. Ernst Bloch in The Principle of Hope called this phenomenon "the Not-Yet-Conscious," which "fulfills the meaning of all men and the horizon of all being."[71] In drawing readers' attention to how the present is saturated with not only the past but the future, how contemporary actors inhabit a gap between them, Whitman claims to be even more "realistic" than narrow purveyors of "realism." Whitman believed that democracy engendered this experience in its citizens, a sense, to paraphrase Paine, that we have it in our power to begin the world anew. Whitman hoped to further enhance this sense of democratic capacity in his work, resisting the countervailing tendency to treat democratic life as somehow finished and always already accomplished.

While these concerns may seem a far remove from the prevailing concerns of contemporary democratic theory, there remain some illuminating continuities, which a brief concluding comparison with John Rawls's familiar theory of reflective equilibrium can reveal. Rawls's influential effort to construct a moral viewpoint from which questions of right can be impartially adjudicated builds on the moral orientations implicit in an existing liberal society's practices. While the later Rawls conceded the historicity of these practices, he nonetheless insisted on the existence of articulable formal principles that could be derived from the practical orientations, habits, and dispositions of the "background culture."[72] The Rawlsian democratic theorist must construct from these practices a coherent set of implied theoretical principles that can then orient the polity on questions of "basic justice." While critics have sometimes accused Rawls of offering "gifts to the demos" (Sheldon Wolin), or of illegitimately circumscribing citizens' ability to "reignite the radical democratic embers of the original position in the civic life of their society" (Jürgen Habermas), one of his central claims is that the constructed principles of justice are implicit within the society's practices, and therefore do not violate the people's legislative autonomy or capacity for democratic self-determination.[73] Rawls's constructivist project translates ethical practice into moral principle. "Reflective equilibrium" is then the process by which a polity reflectively tests itself against its underlying principles of justice, thus becoming more in line with these principles, and therefore more just (although Rawls importantly sees this as a continuing, open-ended process).[74] The reformative power of this democratic theory resides in its ability to compel (or, more generously, inspire) the polity to affirm and then act in accordance with its own implicit principles of justice.

Whitman imagined his poetry to operate in a remarkably analogous way, an analogy that may be based in his own familiarity with German Idealism. Yet for Whitman poetry's reformative power resided in the aesthetic transformation of a polity confronted with its own practices poetically rendered, rather than the moral transformation of a society confronted with the principles of justice implicit to its ethical practice. Whitman translates quotidian democratic practices into poetry and offers a poetic transcription of the polyvocality of the vox populi, thereby offering to the body politic an aesthetically transformed depiction of itself as sublime potentiality further enhancing its latent autopoetic power. Whitman's aesthetic re-presentation of the vox populi does not articulate a law to be obeyed so much as a capacity to be enacted; the people's capacity for regeneration becomes the affective source of its political bond. Whitman's poetry urges democratic citizens to take pleasure in the sublimity of their quotidian democratic life, to appreciate their unrefined and unfinished state — their autopoetic and "formative power" — rather than feel paralyzing "gaggery and guilt." In one of the anonymous reviews that Whitman wrote of *Leaves*, he suggested that through that work "the *interior* American republic shall also be declared free and independent" (R, 8). The "proof" of the poet's relation to the people he or she sings is not through the dynamics of recognition but in the way "the country *absorbs* him as affectionately as he has absorbed it" (LG, 26; my emphasis), and the "touch" of the poet tells only in "action" (LG, 22), in the further enactment of a democratic history as yet unfulfilled. While some have recently turned to Whitman to revitalize a sense of national pride or American mission,[75] he might be more productively invoked for his poetic understanding of democratic politics and for his provocation that our democratic history remains unwritten because that history has yet to be enacted.

Any interpretation of the political meaning of the term *people* ought to start from the peculiar fact that in modern European languages this term always indicates also the poor, the underprivileged, and the excluded. The same term names the constitutive political subject as well as the class that is excluded—de facto if not de jure—from politics.
GIORGIO AGAMBEN, "What Is a People?"[1]

§ 7 §

Staging Dissensus

Frederick Douglass and "We the People"

The aporia of ordinary language that Agamben positions at the heart of "the political meaning of the term *people*" goes strangely unacknowledged in most theoretical discussions of popular sovereignty, even though the people are generally construed as the basis of attempts to grasp the meaning of democratic legitimacy. In the familiar oppositions that govern most discussions in contemporary democratic theory—will and reason, legitimacy and legality, democracy and constitutionalism, majoritarianism and individual rights, the liberty of the ancients and the liberty of the moderns—the people are equated with the first half of each pairing, and the theoretical difficulty is taken to be how to best reconcile or resolve the opposing logics. Democratic theorists who resist the governing imperatives of this framework and instead attempt to conceptualize a political role for the people outside the institutions that legally organize them, or who embrace the productivity of paradox in democratic politics, are sometimes accused of "democratic mysticism."[2]

In this final chapter I build on the foregoing account of the postrevolutionary double inscription of the people. Through an exploration of select speeches and essays by the radical American abolitionist Frederick Douglass, I argue that we can learn important lessons about the peculiarities of democratic claims-making from an understanding of the people not as a unified subject, or what Ernesto Laclau calls a "social datum," or as a "legitimating fiction," or as "impersonal networks of intersubjective communication."[3] Rather, here I propose an understanding of the people as a form of political subjectification enacted through the simultaneous claiming of the two poles that Agamben describes: the people as at one and the same time the legitimating "fount of all political power" and that which lies beyond the pale of its authorizing claims. Unlike Agamben, however, I do not believe that this internal division need culminate in a "biopolitical plan to produce a people without fracture."[4] To the contrary, Douglass's speeches transmit an understanding of the people as a form of political subjectification enacted by what Jacques Rancière describes as "the part that has no part in the name of the whole."[5] My reading of Douglass is therefore inspired by Rancière's insight that "the fact that the people are internally divided is not . . . a scandal to be deplored . . . [so much as] the primary condition of the exercise of politics."[6]

I will initially focus my discussion on Douglass's most celebrated address, "The Meaning of July Fourth for the Negro," delivered on 5 July 1852 before a largely white antislavery society in Rochester, New York.[7] In this address Douglass exemplified the form of political subjectification that I call a constituent moment. As previously described, constituent moments enact felicitous claims to speak in the people's name, even though those claims explicitly break from the authorized procedures or norms for representing popular voice. The dilemmas of authorization that spring from these moments appear, as we have seen, in the formal political settings of constitutional conventions and political associations, as well as in the relatively informal political contexts of crowd actions, political oratory, and literature. While having no authorization to speak for the people, Douglass—an escaped slave, one *sans part*—nonetheless claimed to speak on their behalf. Douglass made this claim from an indeterminate or paradoxical position, insofar as he spoke at once as a slave—representing in his words "a people long dumb, not allowed to speak for themselves"—and as part of a political collectivity still without social determination.[8] This rhetorical positioning extracted Douglass from dominant categories of identification and classification (escaped African slave, racially determined or historically monumental invocations of the American people) while simultaneously setting the stage for a new political subject's emergence. In his Fourth of July address Douglass both spoke from outside the people to whom his speech was addressed and claimed to speak in their higher name.[9]

In doing so Douglass reveals in his Fourth of July address how democratic claims made by the part that has no part in the name of the whole reiterate in everyday rhetorical contexts dilemmas of popular authorization that democratic theorists have typically associated with, and isolated in, founding moments. "How can a people give birth to itself as a political subject?" becomes "Who are they—the uncounted, the subordinate, the low—to make claims at once *against and on the part of* the whole?" In both instances the grounds of authorization are absent, and the contingency underlying the existing system of rule is revealed. In both cases authorization arrives too late, after the fact of its proclamation. Throughout his work Douglass claims a continuity between the revolutionary events memorialized by the Fourth of July holiday—the events enacted by what he describes as "agitators and rebels, dangerous men"—and his own struggle against the organization of slave power (494).[10] Yet he establishes this connection in a manner generally overlooked by scholars who focus solely on analyzing the manifest content of Douglass's speech—emphasizing, for example, his appeal to natural law, liberalism, antislavery constitutionalism, or millennial providentialism—while neglecting the dramatic *staging* of the address itself.[11] Widely accepted interpretations of Douglass that turn on his unparalleled use of historically situated immanent critique, his rhetorical appeal to commonly held principles—"that all men are created equal," or "that they are endowed by their creator with certain unalienable rights"—to critique existing political practice overlook the break implied by the prior staging of these (only then) recognizable claims. Rancière's recent work on aesthetics and politics rigorously attends to this problem of staging. He describes this intervention into the political distribution of the sensible as a political poetics.[12]

I contend that an approach paying attention to this poetics or conflictual staging better captures the historical efficacy and challenge of
Douglass's celebrated forms of public address than do interpretations
that subsume his speeches into one ideological paradigm or another.
Such attempts wrongly presume an equality of the speaking subject or
a unified space of representation in assessing the meaning of Douglass's
address. This presumption is not only theoretically problematic, in that
it neglects the underlying dilemmas of authorization entailed by the
"peculiar situation" of Douglass's speech, but also contributes to a misunderstanding of the speech's historical effectivity.[13] By emphasizing the
absence of such an equal space of communicative exchange, Rancière's
work helps to illuminate aspects of Douglass's famous speech that most
attempts to slot it into familiar ideological paradigms have obscured. The
Douglass that emerges from this encounter offers important insights into
the fraught dynamics of democratic claims-making.

In the Fourth of July address Douglass staged what Rancière characterizes as the "*demonstration* proper to politics," which "is always both argument and opening up the world where argument can be received and
have an impact—argument about the very existence of such a world."[14]
One of Douglass's contemporaries, the poet James Russell Lowell, indicated this demonstrative dimension of Douglass's "argument," its prior
"opening up the world," when he wrote that "the very look and bearing
of Douglass are an irresistible logic against the oppression of his race."[15]
Such staging precedes and enables Douglass's argument; it enacts a prior
demonstration that is necessary for the audience to properly "hear" the
arguments of Douglass's speech as arguments that have a claim on them.
The demonstration must first *convert* them into the kind of people who
could themselves retrospectively authorize such a claim. This staging
first "makes visible that which had no reason to be seen"; it "lodges one
world into another."[16]

The emphasis on staging shifts the narrative focus of revolutionary
commemoration invoked in Douglass's address from juridical rights incompletely applied to the people incompletely enacted, from legal recognition to the democratic struggles that demand them. Thus understood,
Douglass's claims are much more radical and less easily assimilable than
familiar retrospective narratives of constitutional development allow—
that is, those narratives emphasizing the historical overcoming of contra-

dictions that purportedly existed between the universality of the rights declared in the Declaration of Independence or the preamble to the Constitution and the particularity of their historical application to "white, propertied, Christian, North American male heads of household."[17] Taking orientation from Douglass's example does not mean retrospectively confirming an underlying (or overlapping) liberal consensus but being more receptive to the emergent claims that fall outside this consensus. Douglass was deeply suspicious of retrospective appeals to common principle that animated the forces of reconciliation and solace, noting for example how the "cause of liberty may be stabbed by the men who glory in the deeds of [the] fathers" (494). In contrast to self-congratulatory narratives of historical reconciliation, Douglass offers a narrative of the American past that equates its full comprehension with ever-emergent forms of transformative democratic action and "unsettlement." Unlike familiar, dialectical narratives of unfolding universal rights, the enactment and reenactment of the people as presented by Douglass are not uniformly linear but rather a punctuated and unpredictable history of democratic claims-making—a changed emphasis with distinct theoretical consequences explored below.

Finally, this chapter's focus on staging also illuminates the connections between the formal and constitutional dimensions of Douglass's speeches—the dissensus that they enact within the representational space of political remembrance and constitutional law—and the contentions enacted in daily life over the reigning distribution of places and roles. In Rancière's words, staging "decomposes and recomposes the relationships between ways of *doing*, of *being*, of *saying* that define the perceptible organization of the community."[18] The concept of the staging of dissensus illuminates the interdependence of the macropolitical and micropolitical dimensions of Douglass's abolitionist politics. This chapter therefore explores Douglass's consideration of the power of claims enacted through practice as well as speech, through the transgressive occupation of different places and roles. It concludes by reflecting on how the civil rights activist and novelist James Baldwin—one of Douglass's great twentieth-century admirers—both extended and reiterated this conflictual staging in his own writing on America's ambivalent revolutionary inheritance.

I

Douglass's Fourth of July address, commonly celebrated as the greatest of abolition speeches, was delivered before five to six hundred people in Corinthian Hall, a neoclassical theater built in 1849, and Rochester's premier lecture hall; Susan B. Anthony, Ralph Waldo Emerson, Charles Dickens, William H. Seward, and William Lloyd Garrison all addressed audiences there. Douglass was asked to deliver the address by the Rochester Ladies' Anti-Slavery Society, and he was prominently billed as the featured speaker in the placards advertising the event. His address was preceded by an opening prayer and the customary reading of the Declaration of Independence by the Syracuse preacher Robert R. Raymond. What followed Raymond's somber invocation of the nation's founding principles was an unexpected break from the established protocols of epideictic Fourth of July address. Douglass—the era's most prominent black abolitionist—radically reappropriated America's revolutionary topoi.[19] He tapped a rhetorical countertradition that positioned the insurgent or escaped slave as the inheritor of America's "unfinished revolution."

Douglass navigated this speech situation's peculiar demands through a careful—and to his audience no doubt unexpected and shocking—series of rhetorical maneuvers.[20] His address enacted a powerful evasion of his audience's doctrine of assumptions, refusing the rhetorical commonplace and the obligatory commemoration of the "nation's jubilee." Rather than monumentalize the revolutionary generation's deeds, Douglass provocatively suggested that these deeds had been drained of their significance through the very acts of ceremonial repetition he was called on to perform: "The causes which led to the separation of the colonies from the British crown," Douglass remarked in his opening, "have never lacked for a tongue. They have been taught in your common schools, narrated at your firesides, unfolded from your pulpits, and thundered from your legislative halls, and are as familiar to you as household words . . . the American side of any question may be safely left in American hands" (494–95). Douglass's provocative separation of his own perspective from "the American side" marked a clear break from traditional Fourth of July oratory while also, eventually, claiming his own inheritance of the Revolution and of the people it declares. Through this rhetorical doubling

Douglass transformed the Revolution from a "rational, orderly, natural, conservative," and, most importantly, completed event to one "demanding sacrifice, unfinished."[21]

Douglass broke with the anticipated repertoires of Fourth of July address most dramatically by refusing the traditional identification of speaker and audience in a rhetorical invocation of a national and unified "we." His use of apostrophe, moreover, took this denial beyond the scope of his assembled audience to a wider if undefined public. Although he opened his speech with an appeal to his "fellow citizens," Douglass quickly proceeded to remark on the injustice hidden in this falsely unifying gesture. By establishing his own exclusion from the nation's annual festival of self-regard, by establishing a sharp boundary between "you" and "me," Douglass set himself apart from his audience. He thus rejected the self-celebration of the "good people" and struck an unexpectedly discordant note: "The purpose of this celebration is the Fourth of July. It is the birthday of your National Independence, and of your political freedom. This, to you, is what the Passover was to the emancipated people of God. It carries your minds back to the day, and to the act of your great deliverance" (496). Douglass's repeated *disidentification* creates a rhetorical perspective from which the audience can see itself anew—as a chosen people, yes, but internally divided, haunted by disavowed violence or injustice. Douglass not only emphasizes his inability to partake in the national celebration but suggests that the very cause and animating principles celebrated by his audience are the basis of his exclusion: "The sunlight that brought life and healing to you, has brought stripes and death to me. This Fourth of July is *yours*, not *mine*. *You* may rejoice, *I* must mourn" (496).

In refusing the anticipated assertion of a rhetorical commonplace, common principles, or a unitary "we," Douglass also called attention to the power organizing the speech situation itself, thereby staging the absence of a space of equal communicative exchange. Douglass elaborated on his understanding of "the peculiar relation subsisting" between him and the audience he was about to address in an oration given the following year to another largely white antislavery audience in New York. "I am a colored man, and this is a white audience. No colored man . . . can stand before an American audience without an intense and painful sense of the immense disadvantage under which he labors. . . . The ground which a colored man occupies in this country is every inch of it sternly disputed. . . . It is, perhaps, creditable to the American people . . . that they listen eagerly to the report of wrongs endured by distant nations. . . . But for my poor people enslaved—blasted and ruined—it would appear that America had neither justice, mercy nor religion. *She has no scales in which to weigh our wrongs—she has no standard by which to measure our rights*. Just here lies the difficulty of my cause. It is found in the fact that . . . we may not avail ourselves of admitted American principles. . . . Our position is anomalous, unequal, and extraordinary." [22] Douglass connects this immeasurable and extraordinary injustice to an incapacity of speaking and hearing. The absence of "scales" and "standard" to measure the wrongs of a "blasted and ruined" people, while facilitating the moral orientation toward *other* peoples, places these extraordinary anomalies below the threshold of recognition and justice, and renders African Americans incapable of having their claims heard as claims. They have *phônê* but no *logos*. [23] There are no common standards here capable of adjudicating between competing claims, no unitary space of representation; their wrongs cannot be resolved through judicial procedures. The "peculiar relation," the "anomalous, unequal, and extraordinary" position described in Douglass's address, is a consequence of being denied a place from which a claim can be made on behalf of "admitted American principles." If Douglass cannot avail himself of these principles, if he cannot speak from within or among the unified position of "we the people," then from where does he speak? What is the necessary supplement for registering his claims as claims?

The most obvious answer would be to say—and Douglass himself at times *does* say—that Douglass speaks on behalf of the enslaved, advocating "for a people long dumb, not allowed to speak for themselves." Douglass was widely proclaimed, as stated in the *New York Times* in 1872, "the representative orator of the colored race." [24] But Douglass's understanding of race—a lively and controversial topic in the scholarship—is inseparable from the relationship of the part with no part in relation to the whole. Douglass refused to speak from a racially unmarked position, and railed against those who did: "I utterly abhor and spurn with all contempt possible that cowardly meanness . . . which leads any colored man to repudiate his connection with his race . . . as a colored man I do speak—as a colored man I was invited here to speak—and

as a colored man there are peculiar reasons for my speaking. The man
struck is the man to cry out. I would place myself—nay, I am placed—
among the victims of American oppression. I view the subject from their
standpoint—and scan the moral and political horizon of the country
with their hopes, their fears, and their intense solicitude."[25] For Douglass race was a consequence of shared experiences of oppression and of
shared struggle *against* oppression: "*The man struck is the man to cry out.*"
Douglass claimed to speak from a particular position or perspective, but
the position could only be understood as a relation to the whole that excluded it. For Douglass there was no speaking position wholly removed
from the hegemonic, white "we the people" that oppressed and defined
him, but neither could he speak from within this position. Although
Douglass clearly rejected the "mystic racial chauvinism" that emerged
alongside racialized nineteenth-century conceptions of the nation, it is
misleading simply to ascribe to him a universalist position. Scholarly
attempts to position Douglass as the principal representative of the "assimilationist" tradition in African American political thought or that
criticize him as nineteenth-century America's greatest example of "racial
liberalism" elide the complexity of Douglass's rhetorical claims, reducing
them to a set of "positions."[26] That complexity, and the source of those
claims' power, lay in Douglass's *refusal* of the opposition between racial
particularism (a standpoint epistemology) and the supposed unmarked
universalism of racial liberalism. Douglass's staging of dissensus refuses
the terms of what Bernard Boxill has called the "two traditions in African
American political philosophy."[27]

The staging of Douglass's "we the people" is revealed in what
Eddie S. Glaude has described as Douglass's "ambiguously rich notion of
we'ness."[28] Douglass's rhetorical "we the people" highlights its politically
constructed character. He denies his public the captivating self-certitude
of a falsely unifying we, highlighting the we as a fragile and highly contested political achievement. Douglass refused to simply proclaim a we
on behalf of an already constituted political identity, whether the black
or the constitutionally organized white people. Douglass spoke on behalf
of a people that was not . . . yet. Doing so, he illuminated the politically
performative dimension of any claim to speak on behalf of a "we." The
"we," as Emile Benveniste argues, never speaks in its own name—a we
can never say we. The "we" is always a question of "drawing a line" and

"summoning a collective."[29] The political valence of this "summoning" is all the more acute when the "we" invoked is understood, as it was for Douglass, as "an original supreme Sovereign, [an] absolute and uncontrollable, earthly power," and when the claimant has no place within its authorizing claims.

Douglass's attachment to the authority of "we the people," along with his regular invocation of the tropes of American exceptionalism, have led many readers to contain the radicalism of his claims within a consensual or dialectically unfolding liberalism. Along with Martin Luther King's "Letter from the Birmingham City Jail" (1963), Douglass's Fourth of July address is commonly invoked as a paradigmatic instance of immanent critique in the dissenting traditions of American political thought.[30] The address is held up as a powerful example of what Michael Walzer calls "connected criticism." A connected critic, Walzer explains, "starts, say, from the views of justice embedded in the covenantal code . . . on the assumption that what is actual in consciousness is possible in practice, and then he challenges the practices that fall short of these possibilities."[31] According to this approach, Douglass exposes a *contradiction* between the universality of the principle and the historical particularity of its application. He affirms the underlying principles that are said to animate the "nation's jubilee"—the Declaration's "all men were created equal," for example, or the righteous morality of a humanistic Christianity—and then exposes the hypocrisy of declaring these principles in a country that accepted the conversion of black men, women, and children into slaveholder's property. Some find in this a reason to celebrate Douglass; others find in it reason to critique how his speeches reaffirmed an ideological hegemony even as they called for dissent—how, in Sacvan Bercovitch's words, they "enlisted radicalism itself in the cause of institutional stability."[32]

There is much textual support for this interpretation. As Douglass declares in the Fourth of July address, to the slave "your celebration is a sham; . . . your shouts of liberty and equality, hollow mockery; your prayers and hymns mere bombast, fraud, deception, impiety and hypocrisy—a thin veil to cover up crimes which would disgrace a nation of savages. There is not a nation on the earth guilty of practices, more shocking and bloody, than are the people of these United States, at this very hour" (498). After experiencing the force and precision of such devastating claims, it seems all too delicate to reduce these hypocrisies to mere "national inconsistencies," but Douglass repeatedly affirms the proclaimed principles of white Americans as the basis of his critique of their failure to live up to these principles. As he writes in his second autobiography *My Bondage, My Freedom* (1855): "The slaveholder . . . never lisps a syllable in commendation of the fathers of this republic . . . without inviting the knife to his own throat, and asserting the right of rebellion for his own slaves."[33] However, he also emphasizes the absence of "*scales in which to weigh our wrongs*," and "the fact that we may not avail ourselves of admitted American principles."

While the emphasis on immanent critique is true as far as it goes, and it surely explains some of the persuasive power of Douglass's rhetoric, it also overlooks the underauthorized performativity of his claims. The assimilationist or "racial liberal" interpretation of Douglass neglects the extent to which his enactment of the people would radically change the very people in whose name it is enacted. It neglects the complicated position from which Douglass spoke, as well as the explicitly thematized (in)audibility of his speech. Not only does Douglass return to the contested and constructed character of the authorizing "we," he also emphasizes that before any substantive appeal to principle can be claimed, the claim must first be heard *as* a claim. Douglass insists time and again that he is not asking for "mercy" or "pity," but to be heard as one with a claim—that is, one making "an *inconsiderate, impertinent and absurd claim to citizenship*."[34] As he said in 1853 in an address on behalf of the "Colored Convention": "Notwithstanding the impositions and deprivations which have fettered us—notwithstanding the disabilities and liabilities, pending and impending—notwithstanding the cunning, cruel, and scandalous efforts to blot out that right, we declare that we are, and of right ought to be *American citizens*. We claim this right, and we claim all the rights and privileges, and duties which, properly, attach to it."[35]

Approaches that focus solely on the substance of Douglass's claims (for example, his invocation of natural law) pay insufficient heed to the position from which he was making them, or on the staging of the claims.[36] Who is *he*, after all, to be speaking for *them*? In the Fourth of July address Douglass acted as both a subject who lacked the rights that he had (his division between *you* and *me*) and one who had the rights that he lacked (in his very speaking of these claims). Doing so, he staged the logic of dissensus: he "put two worlds in one and the same world."[37] In the Fourth of July address, and in many of Douglass's other speeches and texts from this volatile period leading up to the Civil War, the centrally reiterated, radical, and unavoidable claim is that Douglass *better* represents the destiny of the people he at once addresses and is excluded from than do their official representatives in Congress, their spokesmen in political parties, or the constitutional authority of the Supreme Court. It is in this sense that Douglass's address exemplifies a constituent moment.

II

The dilemma of popular authorization navigated in Douglass's rhetorical invocation of the "we" is also central to his understanding of constitutional authorization, or what I will characterize as Douglass's popular constitutionalism. Douglass addressed this dilemma most explicitly in a speech that he gave shortly after Chief Justice Roger B. Taney's infamous Dred Scott decision in 1857, which stated that all people of African descent, both free and slave, were not and could never be fully enfranchised citizens of the United States. The decision effectively overturned the Missouri Compromise of 1820, which had prevented the further spread of slavery into northern and western states, and legitimated the extension of slavery throughout the (soon-to-be-divided) union. It was therefore not only the constitutionality of the Missouri Compromise that was at issue, but the threatened nationalization of slavery itself.

Douglass's response to this disastrous decision not only took issue with the particulars of Taney's constitutional interpretation (in particular his narrowly juridical understanding of the Preamble's invocation of "We the People"), but also, and relatedly, questioned the judicial supremacy of the Supreme Court. Tapping revolutionary traditions of popular constitutionalism, Douglass refused to acknowledge the final authority of this latest judicial attempt to "settle" the slavery question. Douglass, like many black abolitionists who resisted William Lloyd Garrison's anticonstitutionalism, fully understood the invariant *politics* of constitutional interpretation. As Donald G. Nieman writes, many nineteenth-century "black leaders understood that the general language of the constitution made it a malleable document whose meaning was subject to redefinition through political and legal processes, that the polity was, in a sense, an ongoing constitutional convention."[38] The failure of settlement, and the perpetuation of political contest over the issue, rested for Douglass in the incomplete enactment of the people declared by the "RING-BOLT" of the nation's destiny, by the self-creating constituent power of the people. "Loud and exultingly have we been told that the slavery question is settled, and settled forever. You remember it was settled thirty-seven years ago, when Missouri was admitted into the Union. . . . Just fifteen years afterwards, it was settled again. . . . Ten years after this it was settled again by the annexation of Texas. . . . In 1850 [with the Fugitive Slave Law] it was again settled. This was called the final settlement. By it slavery was virtually declared to be the equal of Liberty. . . . Four years after this settlement, the whole question was once more settled, and settled by a settlement which unsettled all the former settlements."[39]

In sharp contrast to Garrisonian abolitionists, who construed the United States Constitution as a "covenant with death, and agreement with hell," Douglass had faith in a democratic politics of unsettlement that he believed the Constitution authorized. This faith emerged from a belief that the interpretive authority of the Constitution rested not with governmental agencies, or in the balanced relationship between them, but ultimately with "the people themselves."[40] Douglass's occasional invocation of the work of radical antislavery constitutionalists such as Lysander Spooner, William Goodell, Beriah Green, and Gerrit Smith situates him within this broad tradition of constitutional radicalism. Robert Cover, Wayne D. Moore, and William M. Wiecek have traced these traditions of popular constitutionalism within the abolitionist movement, and each has singled out the particular importance of Douglass.[41] "The collected writings of Frederick Douglass," David E. Schrader summarizes, "give us a kind of record of the dispute on constitutional interpretation within the abolitionist movement."[42] Douglass's reliance on the people's interpretive authority poses difficulties for scholars who have either admired or criticized his invocation of "original intent" as a basis of constitutional interpretation. As Douglass announced in his Fourth of July address, "I hold that every American citizen has a right to form an opinion of the constitution, and to propagate that opinion, and to use all honorable means to make his opinions the prevailing one" (505). The constitutional politics that Douglass advocated often revolved around what constituted such "honorable means," but the redemptive model of the Revolution, and its clear resonance with Douglass's struggle for independence as an escaped slave, highlighted the fraught nature of Douglass's political claims. "Douglass's greatest need," Robert Cover writes, "was for a vision of law that both validated his freedom and integrated norms with a future redemptive possibility for his people . . . [He embraced] a vision of an alternative world in which the entire order of American slavery would be without foundation in law."[43] For Douglass the Garrisonian refusal to make a constitutional claim in the people's name was ultimately an abdication of political responsibility. "Dissolve the Union, on this issue, and you delude the people of the free States with the false notion that their responsibilities have ceased, though the slaves remain in bondage."[44]

Douglass's popular constitutionalism led him not only to reject the judicial supremacy implied by Taney's decision; it was also the central objection that he made to the *substance* of the decision. Of particular importance to Douglass's argument was his rejection of Taney's basis for the denial of citizenship rights—that is, African ancestry. As Taney wrote in his decision: "The words 'people of the United States' and 'citizens' are synonymous terms. . . . They both describe the political body who . . . form the sovereignty. . . . The question before us is, whether the class of persons described in the plea in abatement [people of African ancestry] compose a portion of this people, and are constituent members of this sovereignty? We think they are not, and that they are not included . . . under the word 'citizens' in the Constitution, and can therefore claim none of the rights and privileges which that instrument provides for . . . citizens."[45] Douglass refuses this foundational equation of "the people" with "citizen," juridically defined (and for Taney, also racially defined). Turning to the Preamble's invocation of "We the People," Douglass writes in response: "We the people—not we the white people—not we, the citizens, or the legal voters—not we, the privileged class, and excluding all other classes but we the people; not we, the horses and cattle, but we the people—the men and women, the human inhabitants of the United States, do ordain and establish this Constitution, &c."[46] Douglass believed that the Preamble to the Constitution provided sufficient legal basis to eradicate slavery. As James A. Colaiaco writes, "Douglass considered the Preamble, like the Declaration of Independence, as a part of the nation's fundamental law. For him, the key to interpreting all sections and clauses of the constitution lay in comprehending its purpose in light of the language of the Preamble, which reveals the moral aspirations of the framers."[47] However, what Douglass emphasizes here is not simply "moral aspirations" but the people's political capacity for democratic self-creation. Douglass's faith in popular sovereignty has to be emphasized, particularly when considered alongside the period's usual invocation of popular sovereignty as a way of justifying slavery and the inviolability of states' rights (consider the popular sovereignty positions staked out by John Calhoun or Stephen Douglas). By locating constitutional authorship in "the human inhabitants of the United States," Douglass may seem to give the "people" a seemingly unambiguous referent in the territory's population, but the argument actually works to reveal again the always partial nature of any claim to speak in the people's name. In basing its authority in the people, Douglass's democratic constitutionalism continually condemned its own inevitable denial of inclusion and equality; it revealed the contestability of any boundary around the authorizing "we." "By claiming membership among 'the people,'" Wayne D. Moore has written, Douglass "*presumed* to be among those able to maintain (re-authorize) constitutional forms to represent the people's collective and separate political identities."[48] Douglass enacted the very popular and nonjuridical claiming that he argued for in the substance of his claim.

III

The language of presumption and claim highlights another important aspect of Douglass's work—and its connection to the form of political subjectification I am exploring here—in that it indicates his persistent refusal to *justify* his claim to speak in the name of "We the People." As noted above, Douglass frequently thematized the conditions required to hear of his claims *as claims*. He broke "the logic of expression," and refused to apply words "to their assigned mode of speaking."[49] This refusal is explicit in his Fourth of July address. Like many abolitionist writers—constitutionalists and anticonstitutionalists alike—Douglass was occasionally compelled to respond to critics who, while admiring the goals and principles of abolitionism, were nonetheless shocked by its manner and style. "I fancy I hear some one of my audience say," Douglass says in the Fourth of July address, "that you and your brother abolitionists fail to make a favorable impression on the public mind. Would you argue more, and denounce less . . . your cause would be much more likely to succeed" (497). The voices of deliberative moderation—then as now—tend to presume a speech situation of communicative parity. Yet as already discussed, according to Douglass it is the very parity of the speaking situation that cannot be presumed, its absence marking the "peculiarity" of his situation in relation to his audience. Because of this situation, appeals to reasoned argument are misplaced. Douglass continues: "At a time like this, scorching irony, not convincing argument, is needed. O! had I the ability, and could I reach the nation's ear, I would, to-day, pour out a fiery stream of biting ridicule, blasting reproach, withering sarcasm, and stern rebuke. For it is not the light that is needed, but fire. . . . The feeling of the nation must be quickened; the conscience of the nation must be roused; the propriety of the nation must be startled" (498). Quickened, roused, startled: Douglass's insights into the democratic importance of nondeliberative discourse and claims-making practices were not unique to him but a central component of abolition's public sphere.[50]

The distance between the abolitionist public sphere and the deliberative publics celebrated by recent theorists of political liberalism is further demonstrated in the radical Garrisonian Wendell Phillips's *Philosophy of the Abolition Movement* (1854), which explored the manner and language of abolitionist claims. Like Douglass in the Fourth of July address, Phillips responded to common charges that "in dealing with slaveholders and their apologists, we indulge in fierce denunciations, instead of appealing to their reason and common sense by plain statement and fair argument."[51] Also like Douglass, Phillips emphasized the importance of these radical denunciations to piercing the "crust of . . . prejudice or indifference."[52] Such claims, he writes, were essential not to "convincing" their public of the rightness of their cause but to "converting" them to it. "How else," Phillips asks, "shall a feeble minority . . . with no jury of millions to appeal to—denounced, vilified, and contemned—how shall we make way against the overwhelming weight of some colossal reputation?"[53] As with Douglass's claim to a people that was not . . . yet, Phillips engages here in an explicitly prophetic mode of speech: "We are weak here—out-talked, out-voted. You load our names with infamy, and shout us down. But our words bide their time. We warn the living that we have terrible memories, and that their sins are to never be forgotten."[54] Both men stake their claims on an authority that was to be only realized in the future; both enact through their address a prospective orientation to time.

Because of this fiery invocation of the divine and the fierce denunciation of the injustice of existing law, liberal theorists have, in William Rogers's words, traditionally "display[ed] a certain uneasiness and awkwardness in their treatment of antebellum reform movements like abolition."[55] Considering abolitionists' sensitivity to power in their acts of claims-making, their refusal to engage in common deliberation or dwell on public justifications, and their insistence on prophetic speech, it is curious that a number of contemporary democratic theorists, and particularly those taken with the reigning deliberative paradigm, have returned to the abolitionists as a case study. A particularly relevant example can be found in John Rawls's discussion of public reason in *Political Liberalism*. Rawls asks whether the abolitionists went against "the ideal of public reason." He then urges that readers view this important question "conceptually" and not "historically." When the question is so viewed, according to Rawls, abolitionists like Phillips and Douglass "did not go against the ideal of public reason; or rather they did not provided they thought, or on reflection would have thought (as they certainly could have thought), . . . that the comprehensive reasons they appealed to were required to give sufficient strength to the political conception to be subsequently realized."[56] In other words, given the particularity of their historical conditions, it was not *unreasonable* for the abolitionists to appeal to comprehensive moral views and to refuse to subject them to the bar of public reason. Such unreasonable participation in the public sphere is, Rawls suggests, sometimes necessary to better establish the conditions for a more just and well-ordered society (in which such unreasonable political enactments would presumably no longer be necessary). As Amy Gutmann and Dennis Thompson similarly argue, "some issues cannot even reach the political agenda unless some citizens are willing to act with passion, making statements and declarations rather than developing arguments and responses. When nondeliberative politics . . . are necessary to achieve deliberative ends, deliberative theory consistently suspends the requirements for deliberation."[57] In revisiting his arguments about public reason, Rawls argues even further that "new variations" of public reason must be allowed "from time to time" so that "claims of groups or interests arising from social change" will not be "repressed and fail to gain their appropriate political voice."[58] These claims, he avers, may even be based in particular comprehensive doctrines, with the "proviso" that "in due course proper political reasons . . . are presented" to justify or support their claim.[59]

The problem with these eminently reasonable arguments is that they confidently presume the possibility of easily assessing "deliberative ends" or "proper political reasons" in advance of the claims themselves. In contrast to Rawls, I think that these important questions should be viewed historically as well as conceptually. Viewed historically, the theoretical confidence of contemporary political liberals seems misplaced, and abolition provides a particularly acute example of the burdens of historical judgment. The conceptual confidence that these writers evince in a liberal political culture's ability to distinguish the temporarily unreasonable (but justified) from the simply unreasonable (and therefore illegitimate) depends on the ability to identify a kernel of justice, a "trace of reasonableness," within these claims. On this basis Rawls can argue that abolitionists like Douglass and Phillips *could* have argued according to the protocols of public reason, and that given the opportunities for proper reflection they *would* have argued in this way. But the confident identification of such claims' justice tends to be retrospective.

In *retrospect* the liberal political philosopher can see that these actions were easily subsumed within an unfolding and self-correcting constitutional tradition. This retrospection often does very little to support emerging political struggles. As William Connolly has argued, the dialectic of unfolding justice "always functions best as a retrospective description of movements that have already migrated from a place under-justice to a place on the register of justice/injustice."[60] The abolitionists certainly would not have passed the heuristic test that Rawls offers—"how would our arguments strike us presented in the form of a Supreme Court opinion? Reasonable? Outrageous?"[61] The abolitionist case in general, and Douglass's life and work in particular, suggest that such criteria not only fail to assist newly emergent democratic claims but may actively inhibit them. Robert Cover's analysis of how the legal order of slavery and its appeal to the rule of law undermined the legitimacy of claims for abolition is a powerful case study in this general dynamic.[62] Douglass himself was fully aware of it.

At several moments in Douglass's speeches he speaks out against the tendency to recall the principles of the past to reanimate reconciliation and inhibit the enactment of democratic "unsettlement." As Robert Fanuzzi has argued in his study of abolition's public sphere, Douglass and Garrison portrayed the movement as prophetically discordant with its own time. Abolition portrayed itself "as a rupture in the fabric of time, and as a suspension of orderly succession."[63] For Douglass this orientation was secured through a particular understanding of democratic "struggle" and "unsettlement" and his belief that contradictions of principle would not resolve themselves over time, but that liberties would have to be presumptuously claimed. This is what he means, I think, when in a lecture titled "The Do-Nothing Policy" (1856) he writes: "The open sesame for the colored man is action! action! action!"[64] Or when, in a speech on "West India Emancipation," he says: "If there is no struggle there is no progress. Those who profess to favor freedom yet depreciate agitation, are men who want crops without plowing up the ground. . . . They want the ocean without the awful roar of its many waters. . . . *Power concedes nothing without demand*. It never did and it never will. Find out just what any people will quietly submit to and you have found out the exact measure of injustice and wrong that will be imposed upon them and these will continue until they are resisted with either words or blow, or with both. The limits of tyrants are prescribed by the endurance of those whom they oppress."[65] This theme is central to *My Bondage and My Freedom*. In that text Douglass envisions an African American politics that rejects racial essentialism and that is born of agonistic political struggle. Douglass aspires not to bring African American life into conformity with the constitutive norms of the polity but to radically reimagine those norms. Douglass calls for neither recognition nor separation, but mutual transformation. It was moreover a transformative political struggle that he believed took place not only in the rhetorical contexts of political oration, nor in the formal contexts of legal interpretation, but also on the conflicted terrain of everyday life.

IV

Douglass's Fourth of July address, like Rancière's theory of political dissensus, emphasizes the continuity between the constitutional and the everyday, between formal, juridical power and politics and their more quotidian manifestations, between the macropolitical and the micropolitical. The struggle and "unsettlement" that Douglass called for in the 1850s was not simply directed at laws or government policies, or even at values, but at everyday activities, what Rancière describes as the "distribution of the sensible"—the regime of bodies, affects, and perceptions. Abolitionists commonly took this approach, directing reform efforts not just at citizens' opinion or policy reform. As Garrison put it in the "Prospectus" to his newspaper the *Liberator*, to "abolitionize" is to engage "the people, the whole people in the work; every man, woman and every child."[66] The abolitionists' opponents also recognized this attempt to link legal reform with a more thoroughgoing reform of the social body. Russell Sullivan, author of the widely read *Letters against the Immediate Abolition of Slavery* (1835), wrote that Garrison and the Anti-Slavery Society had "commenced the agitation of a legal, constitutional, and political reform . . . by measures adopted to inflame the passions of the multitude, inducing the women and children, the boarding school misses and factory girls . . . upon the avowed plan of turning the current of popular opinion."[67]

Among abolitionist writers Douglass may have had the most fully developed account of how slavery perpetuated itself not only through legal mechanisms, state power, and force but through a fully spiritualized despotism: "The whole relationship [of slavery] must not only demonstrate to [the slave's] mind its necessity, but also its absolute rightfulness."[68] At times Douglass's sophisticated account of the "organization of slave power" is reminiscent of a Gramscian theory of hegemony. The slaveholding powers, he writes in his essay on the Dred Scott decision, enjoy "the advantage of complete organization": "They are organized; and yet were not at the pains of creating their organizations. The State governments, where the system of slavery exists, are complete slavery organizations. The church organizations in those States are equally at the service of slavery; while the Federal Government, with its army and navy, from the chief magistracy in Washington, to the Supreme Court, and thence to the chief marshalship at New York, is pledged to support, defend, and propagate the crying curse of human bondage. The pen, the purse, and the sword are united against the simple truth, preached by humble men in obscure places."[69] Just as Douglass's constitutional claim to a "We the People" transcends the state's constituted authority and the Supreme Court's decision-making power, so did he call to combat the "organization of slave power" at the informal level of daily life by resisting the various roles and social practices that perpetuated it. Douglass returns often to the question of how the "organization of slavery" may be daily resisted. If, as Pierre Bourdieu quips, what is essential about the "objective consensus on the sense of the world *goes without saying because it comes without saying*,"[70] enacted challenges to the regime of the visible or the sayable—to Douglass's "complete organization of power"—occur not just through explicit invocations of an impossible authorization (claiming to speak in the name of a people that is not . . . yet) or a competing set of values or principles but also in practical activity or staging that works to bring that world into being.

Thus in addition to embracing the democratic value of sarcasm, irony, and denunciation, Douglass suggested that the claims made on behalf of those who have no part are also practically enacted, and in many ways acknowledged, by their opponents in everyday life. In a moving passage revealing how the "organization of slave power" is based in myriad daily acknowledgements that undermine the slaveowners's claim of natural white supremacy, Douglass offers a powerful example of how implied equality inhabits the very structure of hierarchical rule, thereby exposing the unsupportability of its claims and the contingency of its order: "Is it not astonishing that, while we are ploughing, planting, and reaping, using all kinds of mechanical tools, erecting houses, constructing bridges, building ships, working in metals of brass, iron, copper, silver, and gold; that while we are reading writing and ciphering, acting as clerks, merchants and secretaries, having among us lawyers, doctors, ministers, poets, authors, editors, orators, and teachers; that, while we are engaged in all manner of enterprises common to other men, digging gold in California, capturing the whale in the Pacific, feeding cattle on the hill side, living, moving, acting, thinking, planning, living in families as husbands, wives, and children, and, above all, confessing and worshipping the Christian's God, and looking hopefully for life and immortality beyond the grave, we are called upon to prove that we are men!" (497). This is not argument so much as it is showing. The "proof" of slave equality, denied in ideology and speech, may be nonetheless detected in everyday acts of acknowledgement that may implicitly corrode these discursive justifications. In a perceptive comment on this passage, Patchen Markell has argued that Douglass here is not calling for recognition, nor simply the debunking of the "false belief in the nonhumanity of the slave." Instead the passage reveals "a contradiction within the actual, a disavowal on the part of the slaveholder of part of the meaning of their own practices."[71] The implicit equality of making the command to comprehending subjects undermines the command's self-evident legitimacy.

That former slaves could also be "lawyers, doctors, ministers, poets, authors, editors, orators, and teachers" unsettled the functional distribution of proper roles, eschewing sociological reductionism and highlighting the constructed quality of place. Douglass appreciated the power of enacting suspensions of these assigned modes of speaking and being, even those "assigned" to him by his erstwhile white abolitionist supporters. In *My Bondage, My Freedom* Douglass describes his painful break with Garrison and other advocates of moral suasion in just this way. While Garrison and others initially lionized Douglass and relied heavily on his personal experience in slavery to mobilize support for their cause, they actively resisted his attempts to do more than speak from personal experience, his attempts not to be reduced to "experience" and "testimony." Douglass described white abolitionist attempts to pin him down to his "simple narrative" as yet another effort to keep blacks in their place. "Give us the facts," said one of his white abolitionist supporters, "we will take care of the philosophy."[72] For Douglass this well-meaning advice from white abolitionists relying on the sentimental authenticity of his experience was all too reminiscent of the meticulous orchestration of subservience and place under the "organization of slave power."

Already in his first autobiography, the *Narrative of the Life of Frederick Douglass* (1845), Douglass emphasized at some length how the cruel slaveowner the Rev. Rigby Hopkins demanded and violently enforced small and daily acts of subservience and groveling deference from his slaves. "A mere look, word, or motion—a mistake, accident, or want of power—are all matters for which a slave may be whipped at any time."[73] Of course the Jim Crow laws quickly established throughout the American South in the wake of emancipation and failed Reconstruction also recognized the quotidian dimensions of domination, and worked to more carefully legislate the micropolitical segregation of races, further insinuating white supremacy into the fabric of everyday life. This quotidian domination became a central site for the staged confrontations of the civil rights movements in the following century, when claims to enact a people that is not yet took the form of proliferating acts of civil disobedience aimed to intervene at this micropolitical level as well as at the level of the formal institutions of government and law.

Just over a century after Douglass's Fourth of July address, James Baldwin, in an essay titled "They Can't Turn Back" (1960), elegantly captured the quotidian dimensions of what Rancière calls the order of the "police," which "stems as much from the assumed spontaneity of social relations as from the rigidity of state functions," while also suggesting how this order might be challenged and transformed (an enacted "redistribution of the sensible") through political activity which "shifts a body from the place assigned to it or changes a place's destination."[74] Baldwin did so by recounting the intricate orchestration of power through gesture and manner in the postwar South:

> I am the only Negro passenger at Tallahassee's shambles of an airport. It is an oppressively sunny day. A black chauffeur, leading a small dog on a leash, is meeting his white employer. He is attentive to the dog, covertly very aware of me and respectful of her in a curiously watchful, waiting way. She is middle aged, beaming and powdery faced, delighted to see both the beings who make her life agreeable. I am sure that it has never occurred to her that either of them has the ability to judge her or would judge her harshly. She might almost, as she goes toward her chauffeur, be greeting a friend. No friend could make her face brighter. If she were smiling at me that way I would expect to shake her hand. But if I should put out my hand, panic, bafflement, and horror would then overtake that face, the atmosphere would darken, and danger, even the threat of death, would immediately fill the air.
>
> On such small signs and symbols does the southern cabbala depend . . . The system of signs and nuances covers the mined terrain of the *unspoken — the forever unspeakable — and everyone in the region knows his way across* the field. This knowledge that a gesture can blow up a town is what the South refers to when it speaks of its "folkways."[75]

Baldwin's imagined outstretched hand may be construed as a claim made by those without part, a claim of equal reciprocity, a claim threatening the practical choreography of gesture and movement that reproduces the reigning order of places and roles; by Baldwin's account the simple act of outstretching a hand could have the effect of speaking the unspoken, revealing the contingency underlying the "mined terrain" of the social "field" as it threatens to "blow up" the town. It is notable that the darkening of the atmosphere described by Baldwin is occasioned not by an enemy who sets out to threaten or destroy but by a friend of sorts—a loyal servant who makes life "agreeable." Baldwin imagines not a direct challenge to the order that comes from without—a challenge much more easily legible and therefore combatable—but one that comes uncannily from within the "terrain of the unspoken." Like Douglass's invocation a century earlier of the "anomalous, unequal, and extraordinary" position of blacks in America, for whom there is no available "scale" or "standard," Baldwin's imagined action allows us to glimpse the "evidence of things not said."[76]

In *The Fire Next Time* (1963), Baldwin made clear that the stakes of the civil rights movement, and its ultimate claims, lay in bringing into being a new people, a new political subject, and it is here that I think the continuities between Baldwin and Douglass are most striking, and that their work is most productive when viewed from the perspective of constituent moments. Baldwin, writing a century after the emancipation of the slaves failed to overturn the system of white supremacy, had a much greater appreciation than Douglass of the difficulties and the resistance to what he described as "history's strangest metamorphosis"; there is a tragic dimension in Baldwin's writing rarely present in Douglass's redemptive prose. Baldwin suggests that the mutually transformative dimension of the civil rights movement—its prophetic invocation of a people yet to come—explained the depth of southern white horror and resistance to the movement. For Baldwin the movement's ultimate claims were not simply about recognizing a formally excluded social group but a vertiginous challenge to the identities of both groups and the staging of the possible emergence of a new political subject (what Rancière calls a "third people").[77] In the preface to *The Fire Next Time*, Baldwin writes, "The danger in the minds of most white Americans, is the loss of their identity. Try to imagine how you would feel if you woke up one morning to find the sun shining and all the stars aflame. You would be frightened because it is out of the order of nature. Any upheaval in the universe is terrifying because it so profoundly attack's one's sense of one's own reality. Well, the black man has functioned in the white man's world as a fixed star, as an immovable pillar: and as he moves out of his place, heaven and earth are shaken to their foundations."[78] Baldwin's invocation of how the black man's moving out of his place shakes the foundations of the order of nature is at once figurative and literal; he suggests the close correlation between social and literal place, and how challenges to the former often imply reorganizing the latter. It is the vertigo produced by the exposure of the contingency of the order, on Baldwin's account, that helps to explain the fury elicited to sustain it.

African American college students who began sitting in at segregated lunch counters in Greensboro, North Carolina, in February 1960, and soon thereafter in Nashville and throughout the South, shattered the prevailing southern myth of "good race relations" and dramatized the shifting of the "fixed star" of race through the occupation of places where they should not be seen. As the historian Jason Sokol has recently written, the system of southern racial segregation, codified in Jim Crow laws and buttressed by everyday behavior, was directly confronted by the spatial tactics of the movement's acts of civil disobedience. The occupation of different spaces in the movement's quest to reorganize social roles so scrambled prevailing white southern understandings of the affectionate relations between the races that most white southerners immediately attributed the activism to the influence of outside agitators—communists, the NAACP, northern liberals, and so on—seeking comfort in the idea that this challenge came from outside rather than from within. Sokol suggests that this physical occupation and the interruption of the choreography of power in the South brought home to white southerners their world's fraying fabric. Sokol quotes one white woman as saying, "the Negroes I now knew bore little resemblance to the Negro I had envisaged since childhood. . . . No greater dislocation of my thought and emotion could have resulted if I had been catapulted to another planet."[79] Rancière theorizes this dynamic when he writes, "Political subjectification redefines the field of experience that gave to each their identity with their lot. It decomposes and recomposes the relationships between ways of *doing*, of *being*, of *saying* that define the perceptible organization of the community, the relationship between where one does one thing and those where one does something else, the capacities

associated with this particular *doing* and those required for another."[80]
The redistribution of the sensible that Rancière associates with this form
of political subjectification sets a condition for the emergence of a new
political subject, and it is just this political subject, this "strangest metamorphosis" into a "third people," that Baldwin invokes in his account
of "liberation." Baldwin expressly did not mean by that term the emancipation of a given identity but the struggle to be free from the grip of
inherited identities, the enactment of a new identity through mutually
transformative political struggle.[81] "The possibility of liberation which
is always real is also always painful, since it involves such an overhaul-
ing of all that gave us our identity. The Negro who will emerge out of
this present struggle—whoever, indeed, this dark stranger may prove
to be—will not be dependent, in any way at all, on any of the props and
crutches which help form our identity now. And neither will the white
man. We will need every ounce of moral stamina we can find. For everything is changing from our notion of politics to our notion of ourselves,
and we are certain, as we begin history's strangest metamorphosis, to
undergo the torment of being forced to surrender far more that we ever
realized we had accepted."[82] In denying that this transformative process
can be achieved without effecting the transformation of all parties to
this shared inheritance of racial injustice, Baldwin, like Douglass before
him, invoked a key political dilemma whose authority can only ever be
prospective. Rather than base his claims in already constituted identities and subjects, or simply on behalf of underlying principles on which
existing parties can seemingly agree, he makes his claims in the name of
the people that is not . . . yet. In his famous call to "achieve our country,"
Baldwin too remains firmly within the mythos of American exceptionalism, as his thought limns what Emerson called "this new yet unapproachable America," and what Langston Hughes invoked when he wrote, "let
America be America again / the land that has never been yet."[83] Far from
being a sign of ritualized consensus, in which such dissenting claims
surreptitiously reinforce the reigning distribution of places and roles,
these claims ask their audience not to simply reconfirm and reapply their
existing moral commitments—to affirm the grounds of an overlapping
consensus—but to abandon a part of themselves, to be besides themselves, to become subject of a collective transformation and to "undergo
the torment of being forced to surrender far more that we ever realized

we had accepted."[84] This is not to reaffirm a consensual rite of assent so much as to confront, time and again, that rite's inevitable failure.

As mentioned above, Douglass's Fourth of July address was actually delivered on the fifth of July. In the nineteenth century black Americans celebrated a number of holidays and commemorations—New Year's Day festivals, West Indies Emancipation Day, New York Abolition Day, and others—that both marked their isolation from white America and hopefully commemorated unfulfilled movements of slave insurrection and emancipation.[85] These "freedom celebrations" quite literally staged a dissensus within the prevailing order of commemoration. On 4 July 1827 the state of New York outlawed slavery, and beginning in the following year numerous black communities began holding festive public celebrations to commemorate the event. To dramatize the "fundamental contradiction between the nation's commitment to democratic ideals and the practices of racial exclusion,"[86] most of these communities celebrated the holiday on 5 July. Doing so, they drew attention to a time out of joint. Douglass's Fourth of July address, like the "holiday" on which it was performed, was an unusual commemoration insofar as it did not monumentalize the past or celebrate the already achieved independence of "we the people." Instead, it set the stage for the emergence of another people, a "third people."[87] Douglass offered a monument not to the past but to the future; his speech, and the holiday on which it was delivered, provided his audience—a virtual people—with a paradoxical commemoration of what will have been.

In the concluding sentence of *Invisible Man*, Ralph Ellison's nameless narrator asks the reader: "Who knows, but that on the lower frequencies I speak for you?"[88] From the perspective of constituent moments we might understand this question as an elementary or inaugurating political gesture, particularly when the claim is made by the invisible and the uncounted. Ellison's question dramatizes how in democratic contexts we are always caught taking the risk of speaking in one another's names, as well as our inability to know if these claims are authorized until we make them, until we attempt to tap the "lower frequencies" of the audience of our address. We can never know in advance who is implicated by our claims to community.[89] That Ellison's questioning narrator is known only by his invisibility also dramatizes the peculiarity of the position from which such claims are made: the Invisible Man asks his question from an obscure hole in a basement, one flooded with the stolen energy of "Monopolated Light & Power."

Democracy may require us to imagine ourselves as speaking for others, to base our claims in an authority that always comes after the fact, but it does not provide rules to adjudicate impartially between those claims, or definitively to determine their legitimacy before the fact of their enunciation. The people never emerge to speak in their own name. As Danielle Allen has written, "The people exists finally only in the imagination of democratic citizens who must think [and feel] themselves into this body in order to believe that they act through it."[90] Douglass's Fourth of July address suggests that to speak for others on the "lower frequencies" is not simply to tap a system of shared values, much less to speak from a position of delegated authority, but to stage a strange scene of interlocution, to stage a dissensus. Ellison's Invisible Man also claims to speak for an audience that cannot hear him, to stand for an audience that cannot see him. Although the political meaning of the people has always carried the double valence of the unified political subject and those excluded from politics, the term also contains another double meaning. The people has meant both the ordinary folk and a source of political redemption and renewal. The uncanny persistence of these founding dilemmas, these constituent moments, in the democratic scenarios of everyday life may enliven a sense not only of their precariousness but of their still untapped potentials. On the lower frequencies, we may still have it in our power to begin the world anew.

The understanding of time, and of human life experienced in time . . . is an important part of . . . society's understanding of itself—of its structure and what legitimates it, of the modes of action which are possible to it and in it. There is a point at which histori-cal and political theory meet.   J. G. A. POCOCK, *Politics, Language, and Time*[1]

The restorative power of democracy is still part of the American political consciousness.   SHELDON WOLIN, "Fugitive Democracy"[2]

Conclusion

Prospective Time

America was the first modern republic to openly declare itself based in the authoritative voice of the people, but because of the heterogeneity of its population, the expanse of its different territories, and its lack of a single shared tradition or common past it was also the western country perhaps least capable of creating consensus over the location or meaning of that voice. The more that power was proclaimed in the people's name during the postrevolutionary years, the more the people seemed to re-cede from clear view.[3] While the Revolution ostensibly made Americans "one people," it also inaugurated a history of political contention over the meaning and extent of that term. The Revolution may have promised an important source of common belief and behavior, it may have been what Douglass called the "RING-BOLT to the chain of [the] nation's destiny," but it was also a source constituted by paradox, an unreachable origin that offered no absolute criteria to adjudicate the competing claims made on behalf of the people who claimed to have been enacted by it.

"Democratic politics," Danielle Allen writes, "cannot take shape until 'the people' is imaginable," but the people also become imaginable in and through democratic politics.[4] In postrevolutionary America this imagining often took the form of competing narratives of the Revolution. Attempts to narrate the historical significance of the Revolution, and thus to define the people in whose name it was proclaimed, began even before the War of Independence ended in 1783. Competing claims to the revolutionary inheritance profoundly shaped the contours of early American political culture, and do so still. Even the post-mnemonic tendencies of our political present return repeatedly to the orienting example of America's revolutionary past. I have offered a different account of that narrative relation, suggesting that such returns proliferate on formal and informal political registers, taking up different points of beginning and conclusion over a history of democratic claims-making. The return to the "restorative power of democracy" is never finally resolved by recovering a lost unity of intent, or by affirming the self-correcting political tradition to which it gave rise. The narrative focus on constituent moments, returning time and again to underauthorized but felicitous claims to speak in the people's name, aims to diminish the captivating hold of dangerous democratic fantasies of "the people as one."[5] It does so by emphasizing the democratic productivity of a people never at one with itself.

Focusing on the fraught felicity of democratic *claims* transmits an orientation to political time that is neither nostalgic nor naïvely futurist or teleological. Instead such a focus conveys a sense of prospective time in which the conditions of the felicitous constituent claim are shaped but never determined by the past or by law, and where the authorizing people remains forever a people that is not . . . yet. The Revolution is the animating center of this narrative, but by its very nature this point of historical origin can neither anchor nor contain the constituent people, nor can the laws or procedures of democratic decision making that they establish. Constituent moments enliven us to how popular constituent capacities are not based in the instituting actions of the distant past — although they often energetically draw on the memories of these actions — but continually elicited in the midst of our political life.

Habermas's recent work on political founding, imagination, and constitutional development offers a clarifying contrast to this last point. In a provocative essay on the role of paradox in contemporary democratic theory, Habermas responds to Frank Michelman's critique of some of the founding precepts of his deliberative theory of political liberalism.[6] According to Michelman, Habermas's attempt to articulate a democratic theory that sustains the "radical democratic embers" of collective will formation and "public autonomy," while equally affirming the inviolability of individual rights and "private autonomy" guaranteed by law, founders on its claim to be practically situated in time; that is, it founders on requiring procedural legitimacy of even the popular constituent assemblies that give birth to a constitutional tradition or found a republic.[7] Habermas "makes political rightness dependent from the start," Michelman writes, "on validation supposed to be obtainable only through the constant availability of broadly participatory, actual democratic political processes to take up any question of fundamental law" (M 160).

This open procedural validity is an impossible requirement that could never be met in practical contexts (say, in a constitutional convention) because those who constitute the self-governing community—the people—cannot themselves be democratically determined or authorized in advance, but only provisionally claimed. Before the praxis of deliberation can get under way one must address the logically prior problem of determining the relevant agent of democratic decision making; as I have argued throughout, this determination cannot itself be democratically resolved. Whereas Habermas's theory emphasizes the inalienability of deliberative praxis (one of the elements that distinguishes procedural from substantive justice), the normative bounds of this praxis would themselves have to result from free and open democratic deliberation to meet his criterion for legitimacy. "But the question of what is . . . an adequate or proper process is one that must itself fall under right reason's jurisdiction." There is a failure of democratic nerve at this moment in Habermas's work, a "dispiriting meltdown of popular sovereignty" (M 183). Michelman rightly notes that "the relatively concrete terms and conditions of a democratic debate that is *fair* and *open to all* . . . are themselves reasonably contestable and actually contested . . . the judgments of sundry putatively free and equal persons will not be indifferent to how the contests are resolved" (M 163). As I have argued, such struggles characterized much of postrevolutionary American politics, and, most relevant here, they frequently marked the debates over constitutional ratification.[8] If constituent power determines the rules or criteria through which we distinguish between the legitimate and illegitimate representations of the people's authorizing voice, to what rules or criteria do we appeal to distinguish between the legitimate and illegitimate claims of constituent power?

Constituent power poses the possibility of constitutional revision and reform that cannot be captured by the procedural rules of recognition governing that reform. Here democratic contest troubles the organizing legal procedures of democratic change. Because for Habermas the validity-conferring procedure of democratic examination of the laws must itself be legally constituted, the problematic legality-of-law question poses the familiar problem of infinite regress: "If it takes a legally constituted democratic procedure to bring forth valid fundamental laws, then the (valid) laws that frame *this* lawmaking event must themselves be the product of a conceptually prior procedural event that was itself framed by valid laws that must, as such, have issued in their turn from a still prior (properly) legally constituted event. And so on, it would appear, without end" (M 164). Michelman argues that constitution-making moments seem invariably marked by illegality, or perhaps alegality (although Michelman insists that such constituent moments of higher lawmaking are internally regulated by their "jurisgenerative" spirit).[9] Considering the practical dimension of Habermas's discourse theory and its emphasis on historical praxis over the constructivist procedures of individualized practical reason, it is fair to ask, as Michelman does, "where in history can this 'originary' constitutive moment ever be fixed or anchored?" The prerequisites of Habermas's theory seem to propel it in a quest for rational foundations that it can never fully justify on its own terms.

It is here that Habermas's theory enlists a somewhat undertheorized—and not fully justified—imagined relation of present actors to the revolutionary past. Without historical elaboration, and veiling the contestations that mark these constituent moments, Habermas's theory presents a consensual and stylized account of "founding acts" at odds with the account given here, but one that shares some interesting parallels with Arendt's analysis as discussed (and criticized) in chapter 1. Both Arendt and Habermas base the authority of the constitution in its capacity to be amended and augmented. Unlike Arendt, however, Habermas's insistence on context-transcending validity claims cannot halt at the point of the "admirable" and enabling "blindness" that she attributed to early Americans, their supposedly salutary forgetting of the authorizing dilemmas of constituent power. Nonetheless, Habermas does offer something like a theoretical reiteration of what Arendt characterized as the revolutionaries' "capacity to look upon yesterday with the eyes of centuries to come."[10] Rather than construe this capacity as a "blindness" or affirm constitutional "reverence," either of which would illegitimately enlist heteronomic supports into Habermas's systematic theory of democratic autonomy, Habermas attempts to embrace and redirect the gap in legitimacy that Michelman identifies. The problem is that he can only do so by putting the supplement of imagination and historical narrative at the heart of his theory. His "interpretation of constitutional history as a learning process" rests on "the nontrivial assumption that later generations will start with the same standards as did the founders" (H 775). But what are those standards?

Habermas seeks to articulate the "reasonable trace" of the "assemblies of Philadelphia and Paris," which we can "see *in retrospect* as an entirely new beginning" (H 768; my emphasis). It is through this (narratively) reconstructed tradition of constitutional revision that Habermas seeks to respond to Michelman's criticism and resolve the problem of infinite regress. The paradox, Habermas writes, "resolves itself in the dimension of historical time, *provided one conceives* the constitution as a project that makes the founding act into an ongoing process of constitution-making that continues across generations" (H 768; my emphasis). Habermas redeploys this regressive movement within the supposedly pre-political procedures that Michelman's critique may politicize. "I propose that we understand the regress itself as the understandable expression of the future-oriented character, or openness, of the democratic constitution: in my view, a constitution that is democratic—not just in its content but also according to its source of legitimation—is a tradition-building project with a clearly marked beginning in time. All the later generations have the task of actualizing the still untapped normative substance of the system of rights laid down in the original document of the constitution" (H 774). The "tapping" of this originary "normative substance" is contained within procedures and rules of recognition that constituent moments reveal as highly contestable. While Michelman does not dwell on this point in his critique, he brings this dilemma clearly into view. For all of Habermas's talk of openness and "future-oriented" democratic transformation, the tracks of constitutional development are laid out in advance and are purportedly immanent to the democratic practice of deliberation.

While Habermas proclaims that the "polity's groundless discursive self-constitution" is "not immune to contingent interruptions and historical regressions," it must be understood "in the long run as a self-correcting learning process." The formal procedures or acts that structure its origi-nary articulation — "the assemblies of Philadelphia and Paris" — must not be viewed as constraints marked by political conflict but "conceived" as enabling (consensual?) origins containing a "trace" of rationality. It would seem that the historical *story* told about the meaning of these founding assemblies is essential to viewing them in this way. Historical narration establishes an unbroken relation of the past to the present in its retrospective unification of these moments; but in doing so it also quietly selects and distinguishes between the claims that "count" and those that do not. Habermas's response to Michelman confronts the dilemmas of authorization posed by this paradox, but in doing so it also makes histori-cal narration and the imagined relation to the past essential to his theory. It is by means of this "nontrivial" imagined relation that we can conceive of ourselves as the inheritors of this tradition with its "same standards." The imagined relation enables the inheritors of this constitutional tra-dition to see it as their own, as a self-correcting democratic process of constitutional development. "The descendents can learn from past mis-takes only if they are 'in the same boat' as their forebears," Habermas writes (H 775). "All participants must be able to recognize the project as *the same* through history and judge it from *the same* perspective" (H 775). For Habermas's theory of "tapping," the Revolution must be understood as fully realized — justified and fulfilled — by the Constitution. But this is controversial, positioning readers "inside the frame we are supposed to be judging."[11]

American political history reveals controversies hidden by Habermas's account because competing claims to the inheritance of the Revolution, and to the people it enacts, have often taken the form of different histori-cal narratives — different ways of situating contemporary Americans in relation to their revolutionary past and therefore defining the significance of their revolutionary inheritance. As elaborated in chapter 1, Arendt was keenly aware of this contested inheritance in *On Revolution*, and she engaged in political theorizing through contested narrative redescription. The "revolutionary spirit" and "public happiness" that Arendt admired in the Revolution was "lost through the failure of thought and remembrance," and she envisioned her work as one of critical recovery.[12]

The politics of narrative redescription do not only signal that academic interpretations of the Revolution are invariably political—that Progressives, for example, saw social conflict and economic manipulation in the Revolution and founding, while cold war liberals saw a broad, principled consensus around liberalism.[13] Rather, these narratives may offer a more deeply formative relation to the past, a public hermeneutic and perspective that have allowed citizens to "interpret the present experience of the collectivity, reconnect it to past symbols, and carry it forward."[14] These bundled images, stories, and legends compose the political imaginary that both contests and makes "possible common practices and a widely shared sense of legitimacy."[15] These narratives declare the Revolution's central aims, reading its events for prophetic signs of historical progress, and direct and orient political action by way of these signs. They play an important role in creating, sustaining, and revising the political community's sense of time, not only figuring its relation to its past but also shaping its sense of duration and political temporality, outlining the possibilities inscribed in its present, and drawing the horizon of its future aspirations. Revolutionary redescription, often written in the Providential mode, has therefore been a part of American politics and political theorizing since the Revolution itself; histories of the Revolution have been indelibly interwoven with the history of the Revolution.

In one of the very first of these histories, David Ramsay's *History of the American Revolution* (1789), the Philadelphia Convention and the ratification of the new federal Constitution were figured as the culminating fulfillment of the Revolution. Ramsay waited until ratification was complete before he published his history, so that his text could provide the Constitution with a historical pedigree in the events of the Revolution, which he retrospectively figured as Providentially preordained. In doing so Ramsay was able to portray the Constitution's Anti-Federalist opponents as betrayers rather than upholders of the Revolution, which he defined as the outcome of reasoned deliberation rather than an unruly enthusiasm for liberty. Like other Federalists, notably Madison in *Federalist* no. 45, Ramsay insisted that national unity was a prevailing aim of the Revolution. As Michael Lienesch has put the point, Ramsay and other early "constitutional historians" of the Revolution "made the Revolution look distinctly less revolutionary than before . . . their arguments tended to place the Revolutionary War within a sequence of events culminating in the Constitutional convention, effectively picturing a violent revolt as a deliberate reform. . . . This was a radical reinterpretation, through which a theory of politics inspired by Revolutionary passion became in retrospect an idea of government informed by Constitutional reason."[16]

Federalist interpretations of the Revolutionary past were countered by Anti-Federalist appropriations that emphasized local governance, actual representation, and vigilant citizenship as the core principles of the "Spirit of '76." Mercy Otis Warren's three-volume *History of the American Revolution* (1805) offers perhaps the best example of the opposition narrative. These appropriations and reappropriations continued to shape political debate in the years that followed, particularly around the question of who constituted the people. The return to national origin in competing narratives of the Revolution authorized very different forms of politics, and different forms of political identity. For some of the nineteenth-century proponents of Manifest Destiny, the Revolution evinced the civilizing movement of a racialized Anglo-Saxon identity westward and authorized the displacement and destruction of "inferior" races. For the emerging movements of the working class in the 1820s and 1830s, the Revolution was proclaimed against the rising aristocracy of capital. United in their differences, all shared the sense, to quote Benjamin Rush, that "THE REVOLUTION IS NOT OVER!"[17] Rush, as we saw in chapter 3, invoked this unfinished state to authorize projects of social discipline, but it also became the ground of resistance to such projects.

During the nineteenth century invocations of the "unfinished work" of the Revolution became a remarkably common trope of political resistance reiterated by former slaves and abolitionists, small landowners, women, socialists, and the poor. Some have argued that the ubiquitous trope of the unfinished revolution worked to convert dissent into consensus, as all political conflict was woven into the unbroken fabric of cultural continuity. Sacvan Bercovitch, this position's most persuasive advocate, argues that the "rhetoric of continuing revolution" offered an idiom through which hegemonic cultural values—"the American ideology"—could be transmitted even through the claims of dissenting constituencies. Cultural and political dissent in these terms merely worked to reaffirm and enforce the values to which it purportedly objected. According to Bercovitch, this was enabled by the revolutionary translation of "the Enlightenment rhetoric of 'the people'" into the biblical figuration of "the chosen people," which allowed "propertied, white, Anglo-Saxon males" to at once embrace and contain the leveling consequences of the people.[18] The notion of "chosen people," according to Bercovitch, substantializes the people in a similar way to the nation and aims to cover over its animating paradoxes. But it has not been fully successful in doing so; the containment was not as complete and hegemonic as Bercovitch suggests.

Competing stories of Revolution gave shape to changing self-understandings of the nation and to the dissenting movements of its political history. It is in part through these plural "stories of peoplehood," anchored in the principles and the events of the Revolution, that these competing claims are articulated and navigated but never finally overcome. Competing claims to speak in the people's name—particularly those constituent moments that break from authorized representations of popular voice—have returned time and again to competing accounts of the Revolution to authorize their claims. "The designation of origins," as Anne Norton has succinctly put the point, is invariably "a political act."[19]

The problem of the people enacted *through* representation but always escaping capture *by* representation is a formal dilemma of democratic legitimacy—the paradox of politics—and one that is continually renavigated not by logic or argument, but through competing narratives of collective belonging. As Frank Ankersmit has shown, the irresolvable demands of political representation are clearly intermeshed with the dilemmas of literary and historical representation, particularly narratives that bring unification to the people in whose name democracy is proclaimed.[20] This is one of the reasons that the history of historiography should be understood, in J. G. A. Pocock's words, as a part of the history of political thought. But it also suggests that contemporary democratic theory, to more forthrightly engage the paradoxes that lie at its heart, must account for its own reliance on the (contestable) narrative cohesion of the people. Most democratic theorists have simply bracketed the question, either through the deontological suspension of the question of collectivity, or by way of the communitarian affirmation of existing historical communities with a common sense of good. Most contemporary democratic theorists have either presumed the existence of a "closed society," one that individuals enter by birth and leave by death—the Kantian solution—or taken this cohesion as a historical achievement and affirmed the normative potential of their unifying traditions—the Hegelian solution. In both cases the grounding assumption of the pre-existence of the people, however normatively problematic, seems to free the theory from having to account for the people's formation, and therefore from the normative significance of the historical narratives that give a people shape. Rogers Smith is surely right in his recent call for democratic theorists to be more attentive to the normative dimensions of "stories of peoplehood," and to more clearly and openly conceptualize how such stories must be understood as intrinsic and internal to democratic theorizing.[21]

Of course narratives of founding have been a perennial preoccupation of political theorists, particularly those within the republican tradition. There is a rich tradition of theoretical reflection on how stories of founding bind the political present to the authority of the past.[22] The stories that republics tell about their political founding are "more than literary superstructure," as Melissa Mathes has put it: "these stories are integral to the construction of the republic's political identity."[23] This tradition had a powerful impact on American political thought during the revolutionary and postrevolutionary years. As Douglas Adair has argued, many American founders saw themselves as lawgivers in the Greco-Roman sense, and they were well aware of how the stories of their actions would shape the politics that followed.[24] The republican deification of the virtuous founders, followed by inevitable corruption and decline and the need for a return to founding principles, established a powerful framework for the political orientation of early Americans, which Pocock has captured in his elaboration of the "Machiavellian moment." This "moment," which can refer to the moment of founding or to the later moments of political response to corruption and crisis through a return to founding principles, is crucially about the internal relationship between historical consciousness and political action. It is a moment in "conceptualized time in which the republic was seen as confronting its own temporal finitude, as attempting to remain morally and politically stable in a stream of irrational events conceived as essentially destructive of all systems of secular stability."[25] According to historians like Pocock, Bailyn, Wood, Banning, and Murrin, this profoundly retrospective relation to the political present—this "archaism at the heart of modernity"—provided a conceptual lens through which colonial rebels understood their struggles with the Parliament, and propelled their actions toward Revolution.

Of course the "republican synthesis," originally formulated as a rejection of the liberal consensualism of Louis Hartz and others, has been challenged anew by another generation of liberal interpretations focusing on natural law, rights, and sovereignty. The "Machiavellian moment" has been perhaps predictably countered by the reassertion of the "Lockean moment."[26] Even though the juridical and contractual dimensions of Lockean interpretations of the Revolution and founding do not emphasize the historical to the same extent as the civic republicans—they do not emphasize the internal relationship between historical narrative and political theorizing—they too rely on a narrative of Revolution to stabilize their theory of democratic legitimacy. Although it has been argued that contract theories demand "collective amnesia," the affirmation of a "memoryless person," and a need to "relieve individuals and society of the burden of the past by erasing the ambiguities,"[27] attempts to read the founding as a contractual moment also rely on narrative components. Instead of understanding the Revolution as an act of restoration, the recovery of lost constitutional liberties, or the renewal of a corrupted virtue, they understand it as an originary moment of dramatic consent. The largely exhausted historiographic debates between "liberal" and "civil republican" interpretations of the Revolution and founding were at least in part about different paradigms of history—competing accounts of historical self-understanding.

There is a sort of unification—sometimes presented as a dialectical *Aufhebung*—of these two historical paradigms in prevailing narratives of American constitutional development, narratives shared by legal theorists and popular understanding. Following Bruce Ackerman's work, we can call them "constitutional moments," insofar as they emphasize the dialectical unfolding of constitutional principles. These narratives emphasize a return to founding principles — the Declaration's affirmation of "life liberty and the pursuit of happiness," or the Preamble's statement of constitutional ends — to more fully tap their unrealized potential. They affirm these principles as what John Quincy Adams called "the vital essence, the pith, the marrow, and the substance of our constitutional law."[28] Although these narratives still anchor contemporary democratic politics in the time of the founding, thereby establishing an authoritative and unbroken legal tradition to this time, they replace the nostalgic longing for a lost virtue with an emphasis, as with Habermas, on original rights insufficiently tapped; in the place of Polybian cycles of corruption and regeneration there is the progressive history of self-correcting constitutional development. "Constitutional moments" seem to still draw, albeit somewhat surreptitiously, from the Providential narrative of America's special mission, but this narrative typically subsumes the transcendental authority within an immanent and unfolding constitutional history. This historical narrative was given its most powerful articulation in the speeches of Abraham Lincoln, but it is widely available in more rhetorically prosaic and theoretically elaborated forms as well.

This constitutionalization of the Providential tropes that have traditionally structured American political self-understanding has profoundly affected political movements seeking to extend rights to formally and informally disenfranchised constituencies — the women's suffrage and civil rights movements being the most obvious examples. This powerful narrative offers a vision of constitutional revision that is at once eminently juridical in its orientation and self-congratulatory in its evaluation. It invites us to look back on an unjust past and console ourselves for the injustice by admiring our contemporary state of affairs. These are narratives of solace.[29]

As we saw in chapter 7, the retrospective appeal to a constitutional "system of rights" waiting to be tapped "ever more fully" that characterizes "constitutional moments" may also have the unintended but very real effect of actively inhibiting the emergence of new democratic claims from below the threshold of justice. Retrospective narratives of rights tapping and constitutional development affirm, in William Connolly's words, "that the most recent identities are also the most true, natural or advanced." In doing so they tend to transmit to their contemporaries an implicit guarded self-satisfaction, discouraging these narratives' inheritors "from cultivating that partial, comparative sense of contingency in their own identities from which responsiveness to new claims," to new "emergent identities," might proceed. The retrospective orientation to a constitutionally authorized system of rights may be at once indispensable to the further enactment of democratic claims and an obstacle to that enactment.[30] It may hinder struggles not immediately recognized or articulated within the reigning idioms of constitutionalism. A narrative supplement focused on what Douglass called "unsettlement" is needed, one that an emphasis on constituent moments can provide.

All these "moments" evidence the claim that political theorizing relies on narrative not as mere ornamentation, or as an "unwelcome *obiter dicta*," but as something internal to its enterprise. As Joshua Dienstag has argued, theorists are "plotters" in both senses of the term.[31] The narrative orientation to the Revolution and its inheritance suggested by a focus on constituent moments differs significantly from the Machiavellian, the Lockean, and the constitutional orientations. It aspires to create a different relationship to the revolutionary past, and to at least potentially enable a renewed attentiveness to the possibilities of a more democratic future. Constituent moments emphasize how appeals to the voice of the people have had political efficacy in postrevolutionary contexts, even while breaking from the established rules for representing that voice, and emphasize the extent to which the people are a provisional *achievement* of claims-making rather than their pre-existing ground. These narratives may therefore transmit a prospective rather than a retrospective orientation to time, an orientation enlivened by a sensitivity to the unanticipated and the emergent. While this sensibility resonates with the Providential, prophetic, and anticipatory tropes of American political thought and culture, it is not reducible to them. It weaves into these narratives an emphasis on the importance of the apparently underauthorized claim for furthering the cause of democracy. A narrative oriented around constituent moments does not aim to resolve the indeterminacy of popular enactment—how a people gives birth to itself as a people—but to sustain this indeterminacy as a way of revitalizing or dramatizing incipient democratic energies.

Constituent moments may do this in part by reversing the narrative emphasis of rights and struggle. Rather than place narrative emphasis on the universal underlying principles that supposedly animate the historically specific struggle for rights, they shift the emphasis to the historically contingent struggle itself. Rather than focus on juridical rights incompletely applied, these narratives emphasize the people incompletely enacted, shifting the narrative focus of American history from legal application or recognition to the democratic struggles that demand them. Bruce Ackerman's influential work on "moments of higher lawmaking" has reintroduced the importance of political appeals to the sovereignty of the people in the history of American constitutional development. Ackerman's narrative has helped to instill a sense of democratic efficacy irreducible to a narrowly construed proceduralism. His persuasive narrative of American constitutional history situates contemporaries in relation to their revolutionary past in such a way that constitutional reform need not abide by formal amendment rules, for example. Ackerman's focus on "refounding" has emphasized the extent to which the postrevolutionary inheritance is not a simple unbroken history of constitutional development, but a history punctuated by ruptures of the people's higher lawmaking power.

In contrast to Ackerman's appeal to the people's higher lawmaking power, the narrative focus on constituent moments emphasizes more than dramatic moments of constitutional lawmaking and constitutional realignment. Constituent moments need not mark, to quote Ackerman, "a radical break" from the political past, a "drastic change" and a new beginning.[32] Instead a narrative focus on constituent moments proliferates the dilemmas of authorization across an entire history of democratic claims-making—in such formal political contexts as constitutional conventions and presidential politics, and also in the relatively informal contexts of crowd protest, political oratory, and poetry.

Constituent claims need not register on the level of constitutional reform to have a real political efficacy. If Ackerman's influential narrative helps to engender a sense of political efficacy by pluralizing the moments of refounding, it still folds these moments into a single narrative of punctuated constitutional development. The focus on constituent moments works against such narratives of national unification. While taking their "source" in the inheritance of the Revolution, constituent moments emphasize the dilemmatic and contested structure of that source, proliferating these small dramas of self-authorization across a protean and plural history. To attend to the everyday possibility that constituent moments will reappear—rather than waiting for the coming of an epochal act of constitutional moments—is to be alert and open to the possibility of their reemergence, a disposition perhaps akin to what Walter Benjamin called the "weak messianism" that infuses the political present.[33]

Thus a narrative focus on constituent moments has the virtue of establishing lines of continuity between the macropolitical and the micropolitical, and lines of connection and solidarity among different forms of democratic insipience across time. It is also the narrative that determines the events, rather than vice versa. So what would count as a relevant event in such a history? Consider the following examples, chosen for the historically and institutionally variable ways in which they enact the dilemmas of authorization characteristic of constituent moments; these examples are intended as provocations for further thinking rather than definitive interpretations of the events.

—In June 1774 a group of citizens in Philadelphia proposed to the legally constituted Pennsylvania legislature that it appoint a local committee of correspondence, modeled on the committees that had emerged in the previous decade, to coordinate and mobilize resistance to the Coercive Acts. When the legislature refused to authorize the formation of such a committee, its proponents independently called a meeting of the freeholders and freemen of the city and county of Philadelphia. On the self-created authority of that meeting, a committee of correspondence was "officially" declared.[34]

—In the spring of 1841 Thomas W. Dorr led a protest movement against the government of Rhode Island, targeting the constrictive terms of its constitutional charter of 1663, which allowed only landowners to vote. Tapping into the long-simmering grievances of the disenfranchised majority, Dorr and others formed the Rhode Island Suffrage Association, and then organized an extralegal "People's Convention" which drafted an entirely new state constitution without property qualifications for voting (but excluding all nonwhites from citizenship). The unauthorized vote on the proposed constitution in early 1842 won over fourteen thousand votes, a clear majority. After this popular—but illegal—ratification, an election was held in which Dorr ran and won the office of governor. A "People's Legislature" was also elected. To defend the new government

Dorr led a failed raid on the state arsenal. Soon after this fiasco a Law and Order militia was organized to crush the rebellion. Dorr was imprisoned and then pardoned, but the movement ultimately took its case to the Supreme Court, arguing for the legitimacy of the People's Government. In the resulting decision, *Luther v. Borden*, the Court first formulated the "political questions" doctrine. On questions of war and revolution it would defer to the political branches of government, keeping open the question of political legitimacy.[35]

— In August 1971 a group of antiwar activists — many of them members of the "Catholic Left" — broke into a draft board office in Camden, New Jersey. Arrested by the FBI while destroying and removing draft board files, the "Camden 28" went to court two years later for what Chief Justice Brennan described as one of the "great trials of the twentieth century." Openly affirming their participation in the illegal break-in, but highlighting the untenable moral situation forced upon them by "the madness . . . perpetuated [in Vietnam] by our government in the name of the American people," the activists argued that the popular jury had the power to nullify the laws they were accused of breaking in the name of a higher authority. Instructed by the presiding judge to acquit only if they found the government's actions "offensive to the basic standards of decency and shocking to the universal sense of justice," the jury acquitted the activists of every count brought against them.[36]

— At the opening of the Fifth International AIDS Conference in Montreal in 1989 — at the time the largest medical conference ever held — members of ACT UP, AIDS Action Now, and Réaction SIDA invaded the Palais de Congrès, seized the podium, and "officially" opened the conference "on behalf of persons living with AIDS in Canada and around the world." Resisting the medical establishment's customary exclusion of those actually stricken by disease from important deliberations concerning strategy, policy, and treatment, the spokesman for the activists claimed from the podium that "this conference has now changed international AIDS conferences forever." This self-proclaimed "official" convocation elicited loud support from thousands of invited and authorized participants. International AIDS conferences were never the same again.[37]

— In March and April 2006, millions of people protested in cities and towns throughout the United States against proposed anti-immigrant legislation in Congress; one million demonstrators were estimated to fill the streets of Los Angeles alone. Many of the participants in these actions were formally noncitizens who nonetheless enacted a claim to speak on behalf of the (authorized and enfranchised) people; they, "the undocumented" and their supporters, enacted a political power that they did not yet officially have. "We Are America," some of the signs provocatively read. Conservative opponents of the marches reduced the openness of their democratic claims to narrow identity claims and emphasized the illegitimacy of having "illegals" participate in the political process of a foreign country. Some suggested that the proliferation of Mexican flags was evidence of the "*reconquista*" movement's designs to retake the American Southwest. Others suggested that the marchers were like a "stranger living in your basement," wrongly "demanding" rather than "requesting" their rights. Liberal supporters, by contrast, emphasized that the marchers only wanted to be included and formally integrated into the polity to which they already contributed economically. Both opponents and supporters neglected the extent to which the unpredicted constituent capacity of these marchers staged the appearance of a new political subject.[38]

A narrative focus on constituent moments emphasizes the emergent singularity of these rich and varied instances of democratic claims making, rather than quickly subsuming them within one self-correcting history of constitutional development anchored to a "myth of a single people and a single narrative."[39] While in the United States constituent moments were first enacted and then enabled by the Revolution, they may ultimately work to dispel the captivating spectacle of the founding moment that has typically drawn the attention of political theorists. This captivation may leave us "small . . . wordless, abashed, say crushed," and for more than a mere "moment."[40] The preoccupation with "founding" should perhaps be supplemented by the ongoing and enacted pursuit of a "finding," a search after our answerability to the claims made by others upon us and by us upon them, and to an acknowledgment of our being engaged in the everyday complexities of what Stanley Cavell calls the "claims to community."[41]

A focus on constituent moments may at once deflate the dramatically exceptional significance of the founding moment while simultaneously infusing the democratic everyday with the possibility of the extraordinary. Rather than resignation in the face of power, or the anticipation of exceptional rupture, constituent moments may help us find and engender small dramas of self-authorization within the midst of everyday life. This attentiveness may sensitize us to opportunities for democratic enactment in unexpected places and at unexpected times, not only in the official political venues of elections and party politics, but also here, now.

Notes

INTRODUCTION Constituent Moments

1. Lefort, *The Political Forms of Modern Society*, 303–4.
2. Adams, *The Papers of John Adams*, vol. 4, 208–12.
3. Cited in Sullivan, *Life of James Sullivan with Selections from His Writings*, 75–77.
4. Dahl, *After the Revolution*, 60.
5. See Näsström, "The Legitimacy of the People."
6. Adams, *Papers of John Adams*, vol. 4, 209.
7. Rodgers, "The People," *Contested Truths*, 80–111, 84.
8. Wolin, "Norm and Form," 37.
9. Throughout this book I draw on Jacques Rancière's conception of subjectification. For Rancière, subjectification (*la subjectivation*), as opposed to subjection, refers to the enactment of a political subject premised on breaking from the reigning categories of identification. The people are the political subject of democracy. "Constituent moments" refer to a mode of subjectification premised on speaking on behalf of a people that is not . . . yet. There are other forms of political subjectification, other modes through which one is enacted as a

subject of politics. Aggregative democrats, for example, reduce political subjectification to acting publicly on personal interests or preferences. Deliberationists focus on engagement in reasoned public argument over issues of collective
concern. See Rancière, *Dis-agreement*, 35–42; and Rancière, "Politics, Identification, and Subjectivization."

10. Michael Hardt's and Antonio Negri's "multitude," which they oppose to
the sovereign logic of "the people," offers one recent attempt to theorize immanent collective agency free of the "trap" of representation. The people, on their
account, are unitary and "closed," while the multitude is "an open, inclusive
concept" composed of "innumerable internal differences that can never be reduced to a single or unitary identity." For reasons that will become clear, I agree
with Ernesto Laclau that the attending faith in "the expression of a spontaneous
tendency to converge" and act is little more than a metaphysical wish signaling
the "eclipse of politics." See Hardt and Negri, *Multitude*, xiv; Laclau, *On Populist
Reason*, 240.

11. See Derrida, "Force of Law."

12. Tocqueville, *Democracy in America*, 60.

13. McGee, "In Search of 'the People,'" 239.

14. Cited in Pierre Rosanvallon, "Revolutionary Democracy," *Democracy Past
and Future*, 79–97, 83.

15. Margaret Canovan, however, offers a useful historical and conceptual
analysis in *The People*.

16. See for example Bourdieu, "The Uses of the People," *In Other Words*, 150–
55.

17. Riker, *Liberalism against Populism*, 238.

18. John Winthrop, "A Modell of Christian Charity," 14.

19. Bailyn, *Ideological Origins of the American Revolution*.

20. Michael Kazin, *The Populist Persuasion*.

21. Larry D. Kramer, *The People Themselves*.

22. James Wilson, "James Wilson's Opening Address, Pennsylvania Ratifying
Convention (November 24, 1787)," *The Debate on the Constitution*, ed. Bailyn,
vol. 1, 791–803, 802.

23. Smith, *Civic Ideals*, 38–39.

24. Derrida, "Declarations of Independence," 10.

25. Burke, "Revolutionary Symbolism in America," 87–94, 89.

26. Ibid.; on Burke's theory of symbolic action see *Language as Symbolic
Action*, 2–100.

27. On Burke's theory of identification see *A Rhetoric of Motives*, 55–65.

28. Burke, "Revolutionary Symbolism in America," 93. I take the phrase
"double inscription" from Emilios A. Christodoulidis, "Against Substitution:
The Constitutional Thinking of Dissensus," *The Paradox of Constitutionalism*, ed.
Loughlin and Walker, 189–208. The people's double inscription can be traced
back to ancient political thought. M. I. Finley has described the classical "ambi-

guity of the word *demos*": "On the one hand, it meant the citizen body as a whole
. . . on the other hand it meant the common people, the many, the poor." Finley,
Politics in the Ancient World, 1–2.

29. The audience reactions to Burke's address are published as "Discussions
and Proceedings," *American Writers' Congress*, ed. Hart, 165–71, 168–69.

30. See for example Laclau, "Why Do Empty Signifiers Matter to Politics?,"
Emancipation(s), 36–46; and "Why Constructing a People Is the Main Task of
Radical Politics."

31. See "Discussions and Proceedings," 167–68.

32. The people's constituent power is therefore not wholly absorbed within
the form of the constitution (the "juridical containment thesis"), nor does it
unfold dialectically across a history of constitutional development ("the mutual
articulation thesis"), nor does it exist as a wholly independent "outside" power
("the radical potential thesis"). Instead it is at once enabled by and in excess
of the constitutional power founded in its authority ("the irresolution thesis").
This helpful typology is outlined by Loughlin and Walker in their introduction
to *The Paradox of Constitutionalism*, 1–8.

33. See Austin, *How to Do Things with Words*; and "Performative Utterances,"
Philosophical Papers, 233–52. Theoretical explorations of the difference I identify here can be found in Derrida, "Signature Event Context," *Margins of Philosophy*, 307–30; and Judith Butler, *Excitable Speech*, 141–63.

34. Whelan, "Democratic Theory and the Boundary Problem"; Morone, *The
Democratic Wish*, 44.

35. Tocqueville, *Democracy in America*, 31.

36. Paine, "Rights of Man," *Political Writings*, 59–263, 166.

37. Paine, "Common Sense," *Political Writings*, 1–45, 45.

38. Ibid., 44.

39. See for example Murrin, "A Roof without Walls," 344.

40. Edward Larking explores Paine's rhetorical strategies for eliciting a unified revolutionary public in *Thomas Paine and the Literature of Revolution*.

41. I am grateful to Bonnie Honig for many illuminating discussions on the
politics of the future anterior.

42. Adams, *The First American Constitutions*, 65; Dippel, "The Changing Idea of
Popular Sovereignty in Early American Constitutionalism"; Morgan, *Inventing
the People*, 237–87; and Wills, "James Wilson's New Meaning for Sovereignty."

43. Wood, *The Creation of the American Republic*, 64–74.

44. Reid, "In a Defensive Rage."

45. Morgan, *Inventing the People*, 135.

46. Maier, *From Resistance to Revolution*, 66.

47. Kramer, *The People Themselves*, 91.

48. Constituent power is discussed further in chapter 1. For a useful introduction to the concept see Kalyvas, "Popular Sovereignty, Democracy, and the
Constituent Power."

49. Wilson, "James Wilson's Opening Address."

50. See Bruce Ackerman, "Higher Lawmaking," *Responding to Imperfection*, ed. Levinson, 63–88.

51. Wood, *The American Revolution*, 159.

52. Morgan, *Inventing the People*, 255.

53. Wood, *The Creation of the American Republic*, 345; Gordon S. Wood, *Representation in the American Revolution*, 2.

54. In addition to Wood see John Phillip Reid, *The Concept of Representation in the Age of the American Revolution*.

55. Burke, *On Empire, Liberty, and Reform*, 55.

56. Morone, *The Democratic Wish*, 44.

57. Adams, "A Dissertation on the Canon and Feudal Law," *The Political Writings of John Adams*, 3–21, 14.

58. See for example Fliegelman, *Declaring Independence*; and Gustafson, *Representative Words*.

59. On a "taking" theory of citizenship see Honig, *Democracy and the Foreigner*, 98–103.

60. Stimson, *The American Revolution in the Law*, 48.

61. Cited in Wood, *The American Revolution*, 42.

62. Ibid., 44. For a detailed account of the transfer of authority from the king to the formal representatives of an independent people see Marston, *King and Congress*.

63. See Pauline Maier, *American Scripture*, 46–96.

64. Wood, *The Creation of the American Republic*, 319.

65. Wolin, "The People's Two Bodies," 12.

66. Morone, *The Democratic Wish*, 55.

67. Wood, *The Creation of the American Republic*, 314.

68. Tocqueville, *Democracy in America*, 58.

69. Ryerson, *The Revolution Is Now Begun*.

70. Conroy, "Development of a Revolutionary Organization," 220.

71. See for example Miller, "The Ghostly Body Politic," 104, 115.

72. Wolin, "Transgression, Equality, Voice," 80.

73. Rosanvallon, "Revolutionary Democracy," *Democracy Past and Future*, 92.

74. Wood, *The Creation of the American Republic*, 398.

75. I explore the provisionality of "we" in greater detail in chapter 8.

76. Harris, "Civil Society in Post-Revolutionary America," 203.

77. See Ankersmit, *Aesthetic Politics*.

78. Tilly, *Popular Contention in Great Britain*, 340–92; George Rudé, *The Crowd in History*, 31.

79. Sprengel, *1700's in America*, 57.

80. Kant, *The Conflict of the Faculties*, 153–71.

81. During the "Age of Revolutions" artists struggled with the difficulties of representing the people in painting, theater, and literature. As many scholars

of the French Revolution have shown, these aesthetic or stylistic debates illuminate similar dimensions to the debates over political representation. See De Baecque, "The Allegorical Image of France"; Hunt, "The Imagery of Radicalism," *Politics, Culture, and Class in the French Revolution*, 87–122; and Rosanvallon, "Revolutionary Democracy," *Democracy Past and Future*.

82. Wood, *The Creation of the American Republic*, 370.

83. Cover, *Justice Accused*, 27.

84. Benjamin Rush, "Address to the People of the United States," *The Documentary History of the Ratification of the Constitution*, ed. Kaminski, Saladino, and Jensen, vol. 13, 45–49, 46.

85. See for example Bouton, *Taming Democracy*, and the essays in Young, ed., *The American Revolution*.

86. Morone, *The Democratic Wish*, 63.

87. Ibid., 52.

88. James Morone argues that the "democratic wish" of unmediated popular power, which he calls "the most important false hope in American history," has been dialectically entwined with the expansion of the administrative state. Historical appeals to the people's voice have been appeals above interest, and while Morone admires the "democratic wish" as the only real alternative to interest-based politics, he bemoans its effects. For him the "final irony of the American state-building process is that "democratic aspirations built a bureaucracy largely beyond popular control." Morone understands these appeals to the people as efforts to transcend contention, not as a crucial resource of ongoing democratic contention. He too quickly reduces "the people" to "that united, consensual collectivity of classical republicanism." Ibid., 29, 7, 53.

89. See Handlin and Handlin, eds., *The Popular Sources of Political Authority*, 1–54.

90. Wood, *The Creation of the American Republic*, 306–343.

91. Wood, *The American Revolution*, 23.

92. Black, *The Association*, 29.

93. Burgh, *Political Disquisitions*.

94. James Wilson, "Of the Study of Law in the United States," *Works of James Wilson*, vol. 1, 76–79, 79.

95. Morgan, *Inventing the People*, 281.

96. Wood, *The Creation of the American Republic*, 562.

97. Ibid. See also John P. McCormick, "People and Elites in Republican Constitutions, Traditional and Modern," *The Paradox of Constitutionalism*, ed. Loughlin and Walker, 107–28.

98. Holmes, *Passions and Constraint*, 8–9.

99. Ibid., 9.

100. "Federalist No. 40," *The Federalist*, ed. Cooke, 256–60, 265.

101. Hart, *The Concept of Law*, 75.

102. Holmes, *Passions and Constraint*, 148.

103. Jeremy Waldron, "Disagreement and Precommitment," *Law and Disagreement*, 255–81, 268.

104. Wolin, "Norm and Form," 30.

105. Wolin, "The People's Two Bodies," 12.

106. Hofstadter, *The American Political Tradition and the Men Who Made It*, 6.

107. Anne Norton, "Transubstantiation: The Dialectic of Constitutional Authority."

108. See for example Lance Banning, "Republican Ideology and the Triumph of the Constitution, 1789 to 1793"; Hannah Arendt, *On Revolution*, 198.

109. "In this sovereign interpellation," Michael Warner writes, "the people are always coming across themselves in the act of consenting to their own coercion" (112). Voice, I argue in contrast, persists as a supplementary unsettlement in the representational space of the Constitution. We may be the people of the constitutional text, but the enactment of the people also exceeds its own self-authorized representations. See Warner's essay "Textuality and Legitimacy in the Printed Constitution," *The Letters of the Republic*, 97–117, 112.

110. Ackerman, *We the People*, 169.

111. Andrew Arato, "Carl Schmitt and the Revival of the Doctrine of Constituent Power in the United States."

112. Ackerman, *We the People*, 193.

113. Ibid., 179.

114. Rancière, *Dis-agreement*, 22.

115. Lovejoy, "'Desperate Enthusiasm.'"

116. Benhabib, "Democracy and Difference," 85.

117. Habermas, "Constitutional Democracy," 776; Rawls, *Political Liberalism*, 231–54.

CHAPTER 1   Revolution and Reiteration

1. Hannah Arendt, *The Life of the Mind*, 210.

2. Arendt, *On Revolution*, 198. Further references cited parenthetically in the body of the text.

3. Arendt, "Understanding and Politics," 391. On Arendt's use of historical narrative as a post-metaphysical mode of political theorizing see Benhabib, "Hannah Arendt and the Redemptive Power of Narrative"; Lisa Disch, *Hannah Arendt and the Limits of Philosophy*, 106–40; and David Luban, "Explaining Dark Times: Hannah Arendt's Theory of Theory."

4. Arendt, *The Life of the Mind*, 212.

5. Arendt, "Walter Benjamin: 1892–1940," *Men in Dark Times*, 153–206, 205. The distinction between "absolute validity," associated with determinate, moral judgment, and "exemplary validity," associated with reflective, aesthetic (and for Arendt, political) judgment, is discussed in Arendt's *Lectures on Kant's Political Philosophy*, 72–77; also see McClure, "The Odor of Judgment."

6. Arendt's relationship to democratic politics is not self-evident. For a portrait of Arendt as an antidemocratic thinker see Wolin, "Hannah Arendt"; for a more generous assessment, and one focused on *On Revolution*, see Isaac, "Oases in the Desert."

7. Patchen Markell has persuasively challenged approaches to Arendt's work that emphasize the ruptural or anarchic dimensions of her account of "beginnings." "The point of her critique of rule and her recovery of beginning," he writes, "is not to celebrate those phenomena that are conventionally taken to be rule's opposites . . . but to prise apart phenomena that the idea of 'rule' has taught us to see as inseparably connected." Markell is surely right that Arendt's understanding of freedom cannot be equated with pure "undetermined spontaneity." However, Arendt's juridical interpretation of continuous authority in *On Revolution*, along with the attending contrast between law and power, does not easily correspond with Markell's insightful interpretation—based primarily in a reading of *The Human Condition*—of beginning as "practical attunement" or "attention and responsiveness to worldly events." Nor does it easily correspond with the political experiences of postrevolutionary America. Constituent power in postrevolutionary America was not only a willful, rule-making, legislative power but also a rule-interpreting, responsive, tending one. See Markell, "The Rule of the People," 5.

8. Readers who emphasize the extra-institutional aspects of Arendt's conception of the political tend to draw upon the Greek, agonistic, and aesthetic dimensions of her theory of political action. See for example Villa, "Beyond Good and Evil."

9. Arendt, *The Human Condition*, 205.

10. See for example Rawls, *Political Liberalism*, 415.

11. I therefore disagree with Antonio Negri's claim that "Arendt has given us the clearest image of constituent power in its radicalness and strength," but agree with him that in her narrative of the American Revolution "the antagonistic event disappears." Negri, *Insurgencies*, 18–19. See also Kalyvas, "Taming the Extraordinary: Hannah Arendt," *Democracy and the Politics of the Extraordinary*, 187–300.

12. In addition to the abovementioned work of Negri and Kalyvas, two other important essays engage directly with Arendt's critique of constituent power in *On Revolution*. See Ingram, "Novus Ordo Seclorum"; and Scheurman, "Revolutions and Constitutions." I clarify my differences with these interpretations below.

13. Waldron, "Arendt's Constitutional Politics," 203.

14. On the productivity of paradox in contemporary democratic theory see Keenan, *Democracy in Question*. For an interpretation of Arendt arguing that she affirms the paradox of authorization associated with founding moments, albeit in a less encompassing manner than Jacques Derrida, see Honig, "Declarations of Independence."

15. Ricoeur, "The Political Paradox."

16. Honig, "Between Deliberation and Decision." Some theorists wrongly ascribe a decisionistic element to Arendt's work. See for example Martin Jay, "The Political Existentialism of Hannah Arendt"; and Wolin, *The Politics of Being*, 35–40. Andreas Kalyvas has persuasively critiqued these claims in "From the Act to the Decision."

17. Wellmer, "Arendt on Revolution," 227.

18. Arendt's turn to storytelling as a mode of political theorizing may itself be understood as an attempt to deflate the captivating grip of such formal paradoxes on the theoretical imagination. She suggests as much when she writes that the real "significance" of republican stories of founding is as exemplars of "how the human mind attempted to solve the problem of beginning" (*On Revolution*, 205). While others have stressed the centrality of narrative in Arendt's work as a mode of political theorizing, none, so far as I know, have emphasized its significance for navigating the central dilemmas of self-authorization continually reiterated in contemporary democratic theory. Remembrance and imagination are essential elements of Arendt's theory of constitutional authority in *On Revolution*. I return to this question in the book's conclusion.

19. Honig, "Declarations of Independence," 97.

20. Wolin's understanding of the layered complexity of postrevolutionary political cultures, along with his related conceptions of political "birthright" and constitutional "tending," resonates with the central themes of this chapter. While Wolin appreciates much more than Arendt the significance of the Anti-Federalist challenge to the Federalist position, both theorists depict constitutional tending practices as much less agonistic than they actually were. The fraught and contestable nature of democratic *claims* to speak in the people's name are largely absent from both of their accounts. See Sheldon S. Wolin, "Tending and Intending a Constitution," *The Presence of the Past*, 82–100.

21. Shannon Stimson, *The American Revolution in the Law*, 11.

22. R. R. Palmer, *The Age of the Democratic Revolution*, 216, 222. Arendt relied extensively on Palmer's history of the revolutions but disagreed with some of his central conclusions. Most importantly for this chapter, Arendt rejected the continuity that Palmer identified between the "constituted bodies" of prerevolutionary France and America. Arendt insisted on a qualitative distinction between the "free consociations" of colonial America and the "feudal" institutions of prerevolutionary France to emphasize the authoritative continuity of the former and the radical discontinuity of the latter. See Arendt, *On Revolution*, 311–12 n. 2.

23. Wood, *The American Revolution*, 159; Adams, *The First American Constitutions*, 65. While political theorists (including Arendt and Schmitt) have often associated constituent power with Emmanuel Joseph Sieyès and his distinction in "What Is the Third Estate?" between *pouvoir constituent* and *pouvoir constitué*, most historians of political thought now emphasize the concept's emergence during the English Civil War and Glorious Revolution. See Franklin, *John Locke*

and the Theory of Sovereignty; and Forsyth, "Thomas Hobbes and the Constituent Power of the People." Egon Zweig argues that constituent power can be traced back to the writings of Plato and Aristotle, insofar as the concept presumes a distinction between fundamental law and everyday ordinance. Egon Zweig, *Die Lehre vom Pouvoir constituant*, 119.

24. "Eighteenth-century Americans," Larry Kramer writes, "had an expansive image of popular constitutionalism. They took for granted the people's responsibility not only for making, but also for interpreting and enforcing their constitutions." Kramer, *The People Themselves*, 53. Shannon Stimson similarly writes, "the American Revolution was not only about widening the participation in making law—sovereignty—but also about widening the space for reflective judgment about laws once made." Stimson, *The American Revolution in the Law*, 53.

25. However, this common way of posing the problem—the tension between popular will and the law—actually masks a deeper paradox. The people—as the slippage between people and nation would indicate—is taken as a given here. As I have emphasized, the primary dilemma of constituency revolves around how a people is constituted as a self-authorizing collective entity in the first place. Bernard Yack has explored the conceptual and the historical relationship between popular sovereignty, with its impossible referent of the people's will, and the emergence of identarian nationalism. According to Yack, nineteenth-century nationalism emerges in response to pressures internal to the discourse of popular sovereignty, especially those revolving around the fraught identification of the people's constituent power. "For if the people precede the establishment and survive the dissolution of political authority [constituted power], then they must share something beyond a relationship to that authority . . . the nation provides precisely what is lacking in the concept of the people: a sense of where to look for the prepolitical basis of the community." Yack, "Popular Sovereignty and Nationalism," 524. Carl Schmitt translates this historical emergence into a theoretical necessity, again masking the dilemmas of constituency. "Nation and people are often treated as equivalent concepts," Schmitt writes, but "the word 'nation' is clearer and less prone to misunderstanding. It denotes, specifically, the people as a unity capable of political action. . . . The theory of the people's constituent power presupposes the conscious willing of political existence, therefore, a nation." Schmitt, *Constitutional Theory*, 127.

26. Sieyès, "What Is the Third Estate?," 136. I leave aside whether this is an accurate portrayal of Sieyès's view. Both Schmitt and Arendt neglect Sieyès's central claim, for example, that "prior to the nation and above the nation there is only natural law" (136).

27. William Scheuerman also emphasizes the Schmittian dimensions of Arendt's understanding of constituent power, and suggests that Arendt's critique of the concept was in fact a surreptitious critique of Schmitt. "Arendt and Schmitt," he writes, "both emphasize the ways in which the spirit of the

revolutionary moment inevitably haunt the political and legal institutions that it helped bring to birth. *Yet Arendt suggests that we need neither to accept Schmitt's vision of revolutionary politics as a mere exercise in arbitrary willfulness nor to accept the vision of dictatorship that logically follows from it.*" Scheuerman, "Revolutions and Constitutions," 253; emphasis in original. I wholly agree. I disagree, however, both with Scheuerman's characterization of Arendt's alternative position and with the normative commitments that underwrite his approach. A fuller elaboration of Arendt's position, which I offer here, provides a critical perspective on Scheuerman's corrective. Arendt is not *refuting* claims of political paradox but trying to release readers from the captivation of its terms. Where Scheuerman sees conceptual incompleteness, I see a shift in theoretical strategy. The paradox *and the definitive resolution* that Scheuerman recommends remain equally captive to the "question of absolute validity" that Arendt thought a category mistake when applied to the political realm. Both invoke the need for an absolute. For Arendt, when Americans got tangled in the absolute they were being untrue to their experiences. Scheuerman misses this central aspect of Arendt's account of the Revolution and consequently wants to correct her "deeply enigmatic appropriation of the revolutionary legacy" (254). Scheuerman is rightly critical of some of Arendt's historical claims—focusing particularly on her account of the French Revolution—but he too quickly concedes constituent power to Schmitt's understanding of the concept. While Scheuerman's essay seeks to salvage the French Revolution's Enlightenment legacy from what he sees as its grotesque caricature in the work of both Schmitt and Arendt, I turn to the American Revolution to find an alternative understanding of constituent power to that endorsed by Schmitt and criticized by Arendt.

28. Schmitt, *Constitutional Theory*, 125.

29. Ibid.; on this point see Renato Christi, "Carl Schmitt on Sovereignty and Constituent Power," *Law as Politics*, ed. Dyzenhaus, 179–93.

30. Ibid., 126.

31. William Scheuerman, "Revolutions and Constitutions," 254.

32. Schmitt, *Constitutional Theory*, 127.

33. Arendt, *The Life of the Mind*, 206.

34. Arendt, *Between Past and Future*, 296 n. 21.

35. Schmitt called this the "Jacobin argument" of democracy, according to which there exists an "authoritative identification of a minority as the people . . . and the decisive transfer of the concept from the quantitative into the qualitative." Schmitt, *The Crisis of Parliamentary Democracy*, 31. Jon Cowans offers a detailed exploration of this dynamic in *To Speak for the People*.

36. The people on this understanding have a normative and even legal constitution, while the mob is associated with the violent irrationality of force. Arendt notes the ultimate difficulty of distinguishing between the two, and emphasizes how this difficulty plagues the work of thinkers she otherwise admired like Clemenceau and Zola. Arendt, *The Origins of Totalitarianism*, 203, 107. Margaret Canovan has insightfully explored Arendt's use of the terms "people," "mob,"

and "masses," although I disagree with some of her conclusions regarding Arendt's wholly positive and normative invocation of the people. See Canovan, "The People, the Masses, and the Mobilization of Power."

37. On Arendt's creative appropriation of Tocqueville's analysis see Dana Villa, "Tocqueville and Arendt: Public Freedom, Plurality, and the Preconditions of Liberty," *Public Freedom*, 85–107.

38. Arendt, "What is Authority?," *Between Past and Future*, 91–141, 140.

39. Arendt, *The Life of the Mind*, 208.

40. Arendt, "Lying in Politics," *Crisis of the Republic*, 3–47, 6.

41. Kalyvas, *Democracy and the Politics of the Extraordinary*, 230.

42. Derrida, "Force of Law."

43. Maier mentions Arendt's work as an influence and begins *From Resistance to Revolution* by quoting Tocqueville: "The Revolution of the United States was the result of a mature and reflecting preference for freedom . . . its course was marked . . . by a love of order and law." Andrew Arato has also emphasized the revolutionary insistence on continuous legality. See Andrew Arato, *Civil Society, Constitution, and Legitimacy*.

44. I limit my claims about Arendt's distinction between popular power and law to her discussion in *On Revolution*. She develops a more capacious understanding of legality beyond the narrowly procedural in *Eichmann in Jerusalem* as well as in "Civil Disobedience" (which I discuss below). See Lida Maxwell, "The Demands of Justice: Courts and Publics in Hannah Arendt's *Eichmann in Jerusalem*," paper presented at the conference of the American Political Science Association, September 2007.

45. Stimson, *The American Revolution in the Law*, 48.

46. Arendt, however, is not the only theorist to emphasize early America's abolition of sovereignty. For example, Judith Shklar writes: "In America, sovereignty was replaced by politics as a continuous, legally directed process . . . The will of the people is an appeal to legitimacy, not sovereignty." Shklar, "The Federalist as Myth," 942.

47. Anti-Federalist writers regularly criticized the Philadelphia Convention's disregard for legality, particularly its creation of constitutional ratifying conventions that suspended the mode of amendment established under the Articles of Confederation. Anti-Federalists believed that this set a dangerous precedent in extralegality. As one Anti-Federalist wrote: "the same reasons which you *now* urge for destroying the *present* federal government, may be urged for *abolishing the system* which you now propose to adopt; and as the *method prescribed* by the *articles* of confederation is *now totally disregarded* by you, as *little regards* may be shewn by you to the *rules prescribed* for the amendment of the *new system*." Cited in Storing, *What the Anti-Federalists Were for*, 8. On this question see my "'Unauthorized Propositions.'"

48. "The Federalist No. 40 [February 8, 1788]," *The Federalist*, ed. Cooke, 258–67.

49. Arendt, *On Revolution*, 96–106; Arendt, *The Human Condition*, 278–84;

The *locus classicus* for this argument is Nietzsche, "How the 'Real World' at Last Became a Myth," *Twilight of the Idols*, 50–51.

50. Arendt, "What Is Authority?," *Between Past and Future*, 122.

51. Burns, "Hannah Arendt's Constitutional Thought," 173.

52. This question has been revived in recent scholarship urging the non-exclusivity of article V in directing the constitutional amendment process in the United States. See Bruce Ackerman, "Higher Lawmaking," *Responding to Imperfection*, ed. Levinson, 63–88; and Akhil Reed Amar, "Popular Sovereignty and Constitutional Amendment," *Responding to Imperfection*, 89–116.

53. "The space of appearances," Arendt writes, "comes into being whenever men are together in the manner of speech and action, and therefore predates and precedes all formal constitution of the public realm and the various forms of government, that is the various forms in which the government can be organized." Arendt, *The Human Condition*, 230.

54. This is precisely how Kant defuses the right to revolution, by denying the authority of a constituent power outside the legal organization of the state. As Christine Korsgaard explains, "for the people to be able to judge the supreme political authority with the force of law, they must already be viewed as united under a general legislative Will; hence they can and may not judge otherwise than the present chief of state wills." See Korsgaard, "Taking the Law into Our Own Hands," 311.

55. As Warner argues, "what was needed for legitimacy, the Americans came to believe, was the derivative afterward of writing rather than the [volatile and seemingly nonmediated] speech of the people. By articulating a nonempirical agency to replace empirical realization of the people, writing became the hinge between a delegitimizing revolutionary politics and a nonrevolutionary already legal signification of the people; it masked the contradiction between the two." As this book argues, Warner overstates the finality of this masking. Warner, "Textuality and Legitimacy in the Printed Constitution," *The Letters of the Republic*, 97–117, 104.

56. Kramer, *The People Themselves*, 233.

57. For Arendt's critique of Boorstin see *On Revolution*, 219. The centrality of "experience" to Arendt's thought is indicated in a late interview. When Arendt was asked, "What is the subject of your thought?," she replied: "Experience! Nothing else! And if we lose the ground of experience we get into all kinds of theories." See "On Hannah Arendt," *Hannah Arendt*, ed. Hill, 308.

58. Arendt, "What Is Freedom?," *Between Past and Future*, 143–72, 164–65.

59. Ibid., 165.

60. Ludwig Wittgenstein, *On Certainty*, 62.

61. "One needs to look beyond her theoretical framework," Andreas Kalyvas claims, to take "a step beyond Arendt," to understand how these principles remain immanent to constituent action. Habermas offers the "inescapable procedural presuppositions of the practice of original self-constitution, whereby

citizens view themselves as the authors of the law they also are subjects as addressees." Kalyvas, "Popular Sovereignty, Democracy, and the Constituent Power," 236. This enhanced proceduralism is not best understood as an advance. Arendt's thought on these questions is not "incomplete": she instead offers a thoroughgoing political critique of such appeals to "absolute validity."

62. Seyla Benhabib, "Toward a Deliberative Model of Democratic Legitimacy," *Democracy and Difference*, 67–94, 78.

63. See Ingram, "Novus Ordo Seclorum," 249.

64. Arato, *Civil Society, Constitution, and Legitimacy*, 247.

65. Ibid., 333.

66. Arendt, *The Life of the Mind*, 210.

67. Arendt, "What Is Freedom?," 153. "The performing arts . . . have indeed a strong affinity with politics. Performing artists—dancers, play-actors, musicians, and the like—need an audience to show their virtuosity, just as acting men need the presence of others before whom they can appear; both need a publicly organized space for their work" (154). Bonnie Honig elaborates on Arendt's departure from substantive principle and command morality through her distinction between *virtú* and virtue. See Honig, *Political Theory and the Displacement of Politics*, 1–17.

68. Ibid., 152–53.

69. See Hannah Arendt, "Montesquieu's Revision of the Tradition."

70. For good discussions of the motivation deficit in neo-Kantian political thought see Bennett, "'How Is It, Then, That We Still Remain Barbarians?'"; Krause, "Desiring Justice"; and Markell, "Making Affect Safe for Democracy?"

71. Honig, "Declarations of Independence."

72. In this, my interpretation aligns with Alan Keenan, "Promises, Promises: The Abyss of Freedom and the Loss of the Political in the Work of Hannah Arendt," *Democracy in Question*, 76–101.

73. Arendt, *Eichmann in Jerusalem*, 243.

74. Hannah Arendt, "Civil Disobedience," *Crisis of the Republic*, 49–102, 96.

75. Ibid., 99.

76. Ibid.

77. Waldron, "Arendt's Constitutional Politics," 203.

78. Arendt, *Between Past and Future*, 3.

CHAPTER 2 Crowds and Communication

1. Riggs, ed., *The Anarchiad*, 6–7.

2. Samuel Adams, "Letter to Noah Webster, April 30, 1784," *The Writings of Samuel Adams*, 303–6.

3. George Washington, "Circular to State Governments," *Writings*, 516–26, 526.

4. Smith, *The Dominion of Voice*, 50. Jennet Kirkpatrick focuses on the violent American legacies of such acts in *Uncivil Disobedience*.

5. Pauline Maier, *From Resistance to Revolution*, 4. Emphasizing the centrality of crowds to the political culture of the period, Arthur Schlesinger has written that "mass violence played a dominant role at every significant turning point in the events leading up to the War for Independence." Schlesinger, "Political Mobs and the American Revolution," 244.

6. Tilly, *Popular Contention in Great Britain*.

7. Habermas, *The Structural Transformation of the Public Sphere*, 132.

8. John Adams, "A Dissertation on the Canon and Feudal Law," *The Political Writings of John Adams*, 3–21, 7.

9. Ibid., 4.

10. Ibid., 18.

11. In *Knowledge Is Power* (1989) Richard D. Brown explores in detail how information spread throughout the colonies, while his later book *The Strength of a People* (1996) elaborates how this diffusion was justified by the civic republican ideology of the "informed citizen."

12. Bailyn, *Ideological Origins of the American Revolution*, 21.

13. Ferguson, *The American Enlightenment*, 28–30.

14. Thomas Jefferson, "Letter to Edward Carrington, January 16, 1787," *Political Writings*, 152–54, 153.

15. Manning, *The Key of Liberty*, 165–66.

16. Benjamin Rush, "Of the Mode of Education Proper in a Republic," *Essays*, ed. Meranze, 5–12, 9.

17. Adams, "A Dissertation on the Canon and Feudal Law," *The Political Writings of John Adams*, 15.

18. Ibid., 13.

19. Schmitt, *The Crisis of Parliamentary Democracy*, 35.

20. Trenchard and Gordon, *Cato's Letters*, 111.

21. The debate between proponents of the "liberal" and "civic republican" interpretive paradigms has largely subsided in recent years. Joyce Appleby usefully recounts the main lines of argument in *Liberalism and Republicanism in the Historical Imagination*.

22. Describing this communicative imperative as a demand for social transparency, Foucault writes, "Fear haunted the latter half of the eighteenth-century, the fear of darkened spaces, of the pall of gloom which prevents the full visibility of things, men and truths. It sought to break up the patches of darkness that blocked the light, eliminate shadowy areas of society, demolish the unlit chambers where arbitrary political acts, monarchical caprice, religious superstitions, tyrannical and priestly plots, epidemics and the illusions of ignorance were fomented." Foucault, *Power/Knowledge*, 153.

23. Bailyn, *Ideological Origins of the American Revolution*, 18–19.

24. Cooke, *Language and Reason*, 166.

25. Habermas, *The Structural Transformation of the Public Sphere*, 54.

26. Ibid., 8.

27. Ibid., 26.

28. Ibid.,108.

29. Jürgen Habermas, "Popular Sovereignty as Procedure," *Between Facts and Norms*, 463–90, 486.

30. "Federalist No. 10," *Federalist*, ed. Cooke, 56–65, 62.

31. Warner, *The Letters of the Republic*, 38.

32. Ibid., 61.

33. Ibid., 172.

34. Warner, "The Mass Public and the Mass Subject."

35. Fliegelman, *Declaring Independence*; Gustafson, *Eloquence Is Power*; Looby, *Voicing America*.

36. Looby, *Voicing America*, 44.

37. Cited in Fliegelman, *Declaring Independence*, 94–95.

38. See Lovejoy, "'Desperate Enthusiasm'"; Ruttenburg, *Democratic Personality*; and Stout, "Religion, Communication, and the Ideological Origins of the American Revolution." Ruttenburg argues that the "aggressive uncontainability" of itinerant speech during the Great Awakening was crucial to the formation of an expansive "democratic personality" in eighteenth-century American political culture.

39. Ruttenburg, *Democratic Personality*, 83–119.

40. Revolutionary print and crowd publics were often related by the combined effect they had on undermining colonial authority. Peter Oliver, for example, wrote in 1781 that "News Papers" were the weapons of the patriots' "Warfare." But their insults "were vociferated in the Streets, & echoed back from the Press which the Faction had consecrated for such purposes . . . from the Labors of their Brain would often issue a Bonfire, a Mob, & tarring and feathering." Oliver, *Origin and Progress of the American Rebellion*, 97. Similarly, the *Anarchiad* parodies the postrevolutionary press by urging its readers to "Wake, scribble, print; arouse thee from thy den, / And raise conventions with thy blust'ring pen!"; Riggs, ed., *The Anarchiad*, 10. Later sociologists of the crowd would, to the contrary, ontologize the difference between the crowd and the public, with the crowd organized around shared feeling and the public on the "ability to think and reason with others." Robert E. Park, "The Crowd and the Public," 80.

41. Ong, *Orality and Literacy*.

42. Stout, "Religion, Communication, and the Ideological Origins of the American Revolution," 528.

43. This is the argument advanced by Alessandro Portelli in *The Text and the Voice*.

44. Riggs, ed., *The Anarchiad*, 25.

45. No theorist has done more to put affect back on the agenda of contemporary theory than Gilles Deleuze. For a lucid account of affect and communica-

tion in a Deleuzian vein see Massumi, "The Autonomy of Affect"; and Connolly, *The Ethos of Pluralization*. Don Herzog explores the role of affect in the political debate of late-eighteenth- and early-nineteenth-century England in *Poisoning the Mind of the Lower Orders*, 140–243.

46. Massumi, "The Autonomy of Affect," 228.

47. Literary historians in particular have turned to the significance of non-representational modes of communication in late-eighteenth-century American political culture by exploring the language of sentimentality. See Burgett, *Sentimental Bodies*; Stern, *The Plight of Feeling*; and Tomkins, *Sensational Designs*.

48. Jonathan Edwards, "Concerning the Nature of the Affections, and Their Importance in Religion," *A Jonathan Edwards Reader*, 138–71, 148.

49. Ibid., 141.

50. Ibid., 145.

51. Cited in Yarbrough, "Jonathan Edwards on Rhetorical Authority," 397.

52. Hugh Blair, *An Abridgement of Lectures on Rhetoric*, 143.

53. Ibid., 154.

54. Rousseau, "Essay on the Origin of Languages Which Treats of Melody and Musical Imitation," 157.

55. Kristin Boudreau, "Early American Criminal Narratives and the Problem of Public Sentiments," 249.

56. David Hume, *A Treatise of Human Nature*, 579.

57. Waldstreicher, *In the Midst of Perpetual Fetes*, 54. Charles Tilly emphasizes the importance of conceptualizing crowds as performances or repertoires rather than groups or social entities. See for example Tilly, *Contentious Performances*, 1–30.

58. Oliver, *Origin and Progress of the American Rebellion*, 65.

59. Smith, *The Dominion of Voice*, 27.

60. Cornell, *The Other Founders*, 116.

61. The early modern background of Anglo-American crowd repertoires is explored in Gilje, *Rioting in America*; Hobsbawm, *Primitive Rebels*; Rudé, *The Crowd in History*; Thompson, "The Moral Economy of the English Crowd in the Eighteenth Century"; Tilly, *Popular Contention in Great Britain*; and Underdown, *Revel, Riot, and Rebellion*. See also the essays collected in Pencak, Dennis, and Newman, eds., *Riot and Revelry in Early America*.

62. The diversity of crowd actions in eighteenth-century America is explored in detail in Paul A. Gilje, *Road to Mobocracy*; Hoerder, *Crowd Action in Revolutionary Massachusetts*; Jacob and Jacob, eds., *Origins of Anglo-American Radicalism*; Lemisch, "Jack Tar in the Streets"; Maier, *From Resistance to Revolution*; Nash, *The Urban Crucible*; St. George, *Conversing by Signs*, 205–96; and Wood, "A Note on Mobs in the American Revolution."

63. Hoerder discusses LeBon's influence on historians in *Crowd Action in Revolutionary Massachusetts*, 1–36.

64. Thompson, "The Moral Economy of the English Crowd," 188.

65. Rudé, *The Crowd in History*, 31.

66. Gilje, *Rioting in America*, 21.

67. Cited in Mills, *The Crowd in American Literature*, 24.

68. Gordon S. Wood, *Representation in the American Revolution*, 1.

69. Adams, "A Dissertation on the Canon and Feudal Law," *The Political Writings of John Adams*, 14.

70. Waldstreicher, *In the Midst of Perpetual Fetes*, 12.

71. Wood, *The Radicalism of the American Revolution*, 89.

72. Reid's analysis emphasizes the defensive and downplays the constituent and self-authorizing nature of crowd claims. He argues that the revolutionary crowd "always represented or was protected by some agent of lawful, constitutional authority." The claim that "it was the Whig control of certain governmental institution for enforcing law and not any theory of popular sovereignty that gave the Whig crowd its legitimacy" may be true of the jurists that are the focus of Reid's study, but it mischaracterizes the emergent understanding of legitimate self-authorization attending revolutionary and postrevolutionary crowd actions. Reid, "In a Defensive Rage," 1060, 1089.

73. Jared Sparks, *The Life of Gouverneur Morris*, 22–25.

74. As reflected in the claim, for example, that in postrevolutionary America "writing was the dominant mode of the political," or that the period saw a "powerful drift from immanence to representation in both literature and society." Warner, *The Letters of the Republic*, 67; Ziff, *Writing in the New Nation*, xi.

75. Smith, *The Dominion of Voice*, 11.

76. Nicolaus Mills emphasizes Adams's attempt to theorize such a distinction in "The Revolutionary Crowd of Adams and Jefferson," *The Crowd in American Literature*, 18–40.

77. Cited in Reid, "In A Defensive Rage," 1052.

78. John Adams, *Legal Papers of John Adams*, vol. 3, 250.

79. Paine, "Dissertations on Government, the Affairs of the Bank, and Paper Money," *The Thomas Paine Reader*, 167–200, 168.

80. Ibid., 23.

81. Ibid., 19.

82. Adams, "Novanglus," *The Works of John Adams*, vol. 4, 3–180, 82.

83. Adams, *Legal Papers of John Adams*, vol. 3, 269.

84. Adams, "Autobiography to 1776," *Diary and Autobiography of John Adams*, vol. 3, 253–449, 292.

85. Cited in Mills, "The Revolutionary Crowd of Adams and Jefferson," 27.

86. Abigail Adams, "Letter to Thomas Jefferson, January 29, 1787," *The Adams-Jefferson Letters*, ed. Cappon, 168–69, 168.

87. Adams, "Diary, December 17, 1773," *Diary and Autobiography of John Adams*, vol. 2, 85–86, 85.

88. Wood, *The Creation of the American Republic*, 398.

89. Cited in John K. Alexander, "Fort Wilson Incident of 1779: A Case Study of the Revolutionary Crowd," 589.

90. Cited in Alexander, "The Fort Wilson Incident of 1779," 604.

91. Rosswurm, "As a Lyen Out of His Den," 315.

92. Benjamin Rush, "An Account of the Influence of the Military and Political Events of the American Revolution on the Human Body," 188.

93. Joyce Appleby, James R. Jacob, and Margaret C. Jacob, "Introduction to the Paperback Edition," *The Origins of Anglo-American Radicalism*, ed. J. R. Jacob and M. C. Jacob, 1–16, 8.

94. "The Carlisle Riot and Its Aftermath, 26 December 1787–20 March 1788," *The Documentary History of the Ratification of the Constitution*, ed. Jensen, Kaminski, and Saladino, vol. 2, *Pennsylvania*, 670–708. See also Cornell, "The Carlisle Riot: The Constitutionalism of the Crowd," *The Other Founders*, 109–20.

95. "An Old Man," *Carlisle Gazette*, 2 January 1788, repr. in "The Carlisle Riot and Its Aftermath," 670–73, 671.

96. Ibid., 672.

97. "One of the People," *Carlisle Gazette*, 9 January 1788, repr. in "The Carlisle Riot and Its Aftermath," 674–78, 676.

98. "An Old Man," *Carlisle Gazette*, 2 January 1788, repr. in "The Carlisle Riot and Its Aftermath," 672.

99. Ibid.

100. "Another of the People," *Carlisle Gazette*, 16 January 1788, repr. in "The Carlisle Riot and Its Aftermath," 679–84, 680.

101. Ibid., 679.

102. "One of the People," *Carlisle Gazette*, 9 January 1788, repr. in "The Carlisle Riot and Its Aftermath," 675.

103. Ibid.

104. Ibid., 677.

105. Ibid., 676.

106. Cited in Mills, *The Crowd in American Literature*, 26.

107. Thomas Jefferson, "Letter to Abigail Adams, February 22, 1787," *The Adams-Jefferson Letters*, ed. Cappon, 172–73, 173.

108. See Russell L. Hanson, *Democratic Imagination in America*, 54–91; and Robert W. Shoemaker, "'Democracy' and 'Republic' as Understood in Late Eighteenth-Century America."

109. Nash, *The Urban Crucible*, 22.

110. Shoemaker, "'Democracy' and 'Republic as Understood in Late Eighteenth-Century America,'" 18.

111. Adams, "A Defense of the Constitutions of the United States of America," *The Political Writings of John Adams*, 105–303, 299.

112. Ziff, *Writing in the New Nation*, 32; Ruttenburg, *Democratic Personality*, 392.

113. See McClelland, *The Crowd and the Mob*, 107.

114. Adams, *Legal Papers of John Adams*, vol. 3, 246.

115. Shaw, *American Patriots and the Rituals of Revolution*, 9.

116. Ibid., 15.

117. Wolin, "Fugitive Democracy."

118. Rancière, *Dis-agreement*, 11–12.

119. Ibid., 36.

CHAPTER 3   Sympathy and Separation

1. Benjamin Rush, "Address to the People of the United States," *The Documentary History of the Ratification of the Constitution*, ed. Kaminski, Saladino, and Jensen, vol. 13, 45–49, 47.

2. Rousseau, "Essay on the Origin of Languages Which Treats of Melody and Musical Imitation," 72.

3. Benjamin Rush, "Observations on the Fourth of July Procession in Philadelphia," *Documentary History of the Ratification of the Constitution*, ed. Kaminski, Saladino, and Jensen, vol. 18, 261–69.

4. Rush himself wrote that he "abhors titles and everything that belongs to the *pageantry* of government." Such pageantry is "spurious, dramatic, and artificial, no Reality belonging to it." *Letters of Benjamin Rush*, vol. 1, 513–15, 514; "A Thought on Monarchy and Aristocracy," *The Autobiography of Benjamin Rush*, 197–200, 198.

5. Jay Fliegelman takes the term "soft compulsion" from John Quincy Adams's lectures on rhetoric. It captures what Fliegelman describes as "a new model of political submission," representing "not rational assent but a new mesmerist mixture of voluntarism and involuntarism." See Fliegelman, *Declaring Independence*, 39–42, 40.

6. Rush, "Observations on the Fourth of July Procession in Philadelphia," 262.

7. Susan G. Davis emphasizes this performatively mimetic dimension of political parades and processions, revealing how these spectacles not only reflected social order but actively shaped it. See Davis, *Parades and Power*.

8. Edmund Burke, *A Philosophical Enquiry into the Sublime and Beautiful*, 115.

9. Rush, "Observations on the Fourth of July Procession in Philadelphia," 266.

10. Meranze, *Laboratories of Virtue*, 169.

11. Davidson, *Revolution and the Word*, 109. See also Barnes, *States of Sympathy*; and Stern, *The Plight of Feeling*.

12. John Mullan, *Sentiment and Sociability*, 27.

13. Foucault, "Space, Knowledge, Power," *Essential Works of Foucault*, vol. 3, 349–64, 361.

14. Michael Walzer argues that liberalism is characterized by the "art of separation," by which he means "a certain way of drawing the map of the social and political world." The art of separation I invoke here is more literal. Rush's art of

separation involves the spatial choreography of citizens. See Walzer, "Liberalism and the Art of Separation," 315. On the "art of sympathy" see Radner, "The Art of Sympathy in Eighteenth-Century British Moral Thought."

15. Jay Fliegelman explores the paradoxes of educating to independence in *Prodigals and Pilgrims*.

16. Brown, *The Power of Sympathy*, 63.

17. Rush, *The Autobiography of Benjamin Rush*, 43.

18. Ibid., 46.

19. Benjamin Rush, "Letter to Ebenezer Howard, November 8, 1765," *Letters of Benjamin Rush*, vol. 1, 18–19, 18; Rush, *The Autobiography of Benjamin Rush*, 46.

20. Rush claimed that in 1790 he "determined never again to influence the opinions and passion of my fellow citizens upon political subjects." Benjamin Rush, "Letter to John Adams, March 23, 1805," *Letters of Benjamin Rush*, vol. 2, 892–93, 893. See also Schutz and Adair, eds. *The Spur of Fame*.

21. Forget, "Evocations of Sympathy," 282.

22. Lawrence, "The Nervous System and Society in the Scottish Enlightenment"; Reill, *Vitalizing Nature in the Enlightenment*, 122–23.

23. Benjamin, "On the Mimetic Faculty," *Reflections*, 333–36.

24. Cited in Radner, "The Art of Sympathy in Eighteenth-Century British Moral Thought," 204 n. 1.

25. See Farr, "Political Science and the Enlightenment of Enthusiasm"; Frank, "'Besides Our Selves'"; Heyd, *"Be Sober and Reasonable"*; Klein, "Sociability, Solitude, and Enthusiasm"; and Pocock, "Enthusiasm."

26. Lord Shaftesbury, *Characteristics of Men, Manners, Opinions, Times*, 10.

27. Cited in Forget, "Evocations of Sympathy," 285.

28. Frederick Beiser explores these critiques, and Hutcheson's response to them, in *The Sovereignty of Reason*, 307–18.

29. Hume, *Enquiries concerning the Human Understanding and concerning the Principles of Morals*, 224.

30. Radner, "The Art of Sympathy in Eighteenth-Century British Moral Thought," 192.

31. Benjamin Rush, "Letter to Granville Sharp, 9 July, 1774," "The Correspondence of Benjamin Rush and Granville Sharp," ed. Woods, 6–8.

32. Benjamin Rush, "An Enquiry into the Effects of Public Punishments upon Criminals and upon Society," 6, repr. in *Essays*, ed. Meranze, 79–94.

33. Rush, *Two Essays on the Mind*, 2, 13.

34. See Eric T. Carlson and Meredith M. Simpson, "Benjamin Rush's Medical Use of the Moral Faculty."

35. Mullan, *Sentiment and Sociability*, 24.

36. Forget, "Evocations of Sympathy," 291; Lawrence, "The Nervous System and Society in the Scottish Enlightenment," 26.

37. Rush, *Lectures on the Mind*, 238.

38. James Rodgers, "Sensibility, Sympathy, Benevolence," 140.

39. Reill, *Vitalizing Nature in the Enlightenment*, 140.

40. Lawrence, "The Nervous System and Society in the Scottish Enlightenment," 33; Henry Homes (Lord Kames), *Essays on the Principles of Morality and Natural Religion*, 17.

41. Rush, *Lectures on the Mind*, 238–39.

42. Forget, "Evocations of Sympathy," 283.

43. Rush, *Lectures on the Mind*, 244.

44. On the connection between eighteenth-century theories of nerves and the culture of sensibility see Banfield, *The Culture of Sensibility*, 1–36.

45. Forget, "Evocations of Sympathy," 302.

46. Benjamin Rush, "Three Lectures upon Animal Life," 52.

47. See D'Elia, *Benjamin Rush*, 9–19, 91–101.

48. Rush, "On the Mode of Education Proper in a Republic," *Essays*, ed. Meranze, 5–12, 8–9. See also Rush, *Letters of Benjamin Rush*, vol. 1, 582–85.

49. D'Elia, "The Republican Theology of Benjamin Rush," 188.

50. Abzug, "Benjamin Rush and Revolutionary Christian Reform," *Cosmos Crumbling*, 11–29, 15.

51. Ibid., 20.

52. Rush, *Letters of Benjamin Rush*, vol. 2, 785.

53. Ibid., vol. 1, 584 n. 13.

54. Cited in Wasserman, "Benjamin Rush on Government and the Harmony and Derangement of the Mind," 640. For a discussion of how eighteenth-century faculty psychology offered a similarly "powerful analogy . . . between the construction of a polity and the construction of the self," see Howe, *The Making of the American Self*, 78–106, 79.

55. Rush, *Lectures on the Mind*, 479.

56. D'Elia, *Benjamin Rush*, 68.

57. Rush, *Two Essays on the Mind*, 35.

58. See Foucault, *Discipline and Punish*, 76. Foucault writes that in eighteenth-century medical politics "society's control over individuals was accomplished not only through consciousness or ideology, but also in the body and with the body . . . The body is a biopolitical reality; medicine is a biopolitical strategy." Foucault, "The Birth of Social Medicine," *Essential Works of Foucault*, vol. 3, 134–56, 137.

59. Schutz and Adair, eds., *The Spur of Fame*, 19–20, 20.

60. Rush, *The Autobiography of Benjamin Rush*, 81.

61. Ibid., 89.

62. Rush, *Letters of Benjamin Rush*, vol. 1, 388.

63. The tragic unfolding of the French Revolution and the bitter partisan politics of the Early Republic's first decade led Rush away from his postrevolutionary projects of social reform and toward a renewed faith in the power of Christian conversion. "All systems of political order and happiness seem of

late years to have disappointed their founders and advocates," he wrote to John Adams in 1806. "My only hope for suffering and depressed humanity is derived from a belief in a new and divine order of things which we are told will be introduced . . . by the influence of the gospel upon individuals and nations." Schutz and Adair, eds. *The Spur of Fame*, 24–25, 25, 57.

64. Benjamin Rush, "Introductory Lecture," *Sixteen Introductory Lectures*, 363–95, 363.

65. D'Elia, *Benjamin Rush*, 18; Rush, *The Autobiography of Benjamin Rush*, 114.

66. Franco Venturi, *Utopia and Reform in the Enlightenment*, 71.

67. See Wood, *The Radicalism of the American Revolution*, 95–109.

68. Rush, *The Autobiography of Benjamin Rush*, 197.

69. Rush, *Two Essays on the Mind*, 111.

70. Cited in Eric T. Carlson and Jeffrey L. Wollock, "Benjamin Rush on Politics and Human Nature," 75.

71. Rush, *Letters of Benjamin Rush*, vol. 1, 460–61.

72. Ibid., 454.

73. Benjamin Rush, "Address to the People of the United States," 46.

74. Rush, *Letters of Benjamin Rush*, vol. 1, 137.

75. In 1777 these essays were assembled in a pamphlet entitled *Observations upon the Present State of the Government of Pennsylvania*.

76. Ibid., 15.

77. Rush, *Lectures on the Mind*, 717.

78. See Alexander, "The Fort Wilson Incident of 1779."

79. Rush, *Letters of Benjamin Rush*, vol. 1, 244.

80. Benjamin Rush, "An Account of the Influence of the Military and Political Events of the American Revolution on the Human Body," *Medical Inquiries and Observations upon Diseases of the Mind*, 186–96, 188.

81. Ibid., 189–90.

82. Ibid., 194.

83. Ibid., 196.

84. Rush, "Of the Mode of Education Proper in a Republic," *Essays*, ed. Meranze, 5.

85. Ibid., 9. For other discussions of this aspect of Rush's work see Michael Meranze's introduction to Rush's *Essays*, i–xxxi; Takaki, "Republican Machines," *Iron Cages*, 17–27; and Terrell, "'Republican Machines.'"

86. D'Elia, *Benjamin Rush*, 128.

87. See Sandel, *Democracy's Discontent*, 129–33, 321–25.

88. Bloch, *Visionary Republic*, 75–115.

89. Rush, *Letters of Benjamin Rush*, vol. 1, 620.

90. Benjamin Rush, "Letter to William Peterkin, November 27, 1784," "Further Letters of Benjamin Rush," 27.

91. See Clarence J. Glacken, *Traces on the Rhodian Shore*.

92. Crèvecoeur, *Letters from an American Farmer*, 75.

93. Rush, *Letters of Benjamin Rush*, vol. 1, 315.

94. Rush calls Hartley's associationism "the germ of [his own] system of physiology." See Rush, *The Autobiography of Benjamin Rush*, 94. See also D'Elia, "Benjamin Rush, David Hartley and the Revolutionary Uses of Psychology."

95. For a useful summary of Hartley's theory of association see Barbara Bowen Oberg, "David Hartley and the Association of Ideas."

96. Rush, *Two Essays on the Mind*, 36.

97. Ibid., 29.

98. Ibid., 27.

99. Ibid., 21.

100. Ibid., 36.

101. Rush, "Of the Mode of Education Proper in a Republic," *Essays*, ed. Meranze, 9.

102. Haakonssen, *Medicine and Morals in the Enlightenment*, 200.

103. Benjamin Rush, "The Study of Medical Jurisprudence," *Sixteen Introductory Lectures*, 363–95, 363.

104. Rush, *Two Essays on the Mind*, 37. Rush eventually abandoned this Enlightenment faith in the perfectibility of man, reaffirming the more pessimistic teachings of his New Lights upbringing. See note 63, above.

105. Hofstadter, "The Founding Fathers: An Age of Realism," *The American Political Tradition and the Men Who Made It*, 3–22.

106. Rush, "Thoughts upon the Amusements and Punishments, Which Are Proper for Schools," *Essays*, ed. Meranze, 34–43, 42.

107. Rush, "Of the Mode of Education Proper in a Republic," *Essays*, ed. Meranze, 9.

108. Michael Meranze and Thomas Dumm both suggest this reading. See Dumm, *Democracy and Punishment*, 87–112; and Meranze's introduction to Rush's *Essays*, i–xxxi.

109. Michel Foucault, "Governmentality," *The Foucault Effect*, 87–104, 95.

110. Rush, *Two Essays on the Mind*, 40.

111. Rush, "Directions for Conducting a Newspaper," *Selected Writings of Benjamin Rush*, ed. Runes, 396–98, 397.

112. Rush, "A Plan of a Peace Office for the United States," *Essays*, ed. Meranze, 106–9.

113. Rush, "An Address to the Ministers of the Gospel of Every Denomination in the United States upon Subjects Interesting to Morals," *Essays*, ed. Meranze, 67–72, 68–69.

114. Rush, *Letters of Benjamin Rush*, vol. 1, 244.

115. Benjamin Rush, "The French Fête in Philadelphia in Honor of the Dauphin's Birthday," 259.

116. Waldstreicher, *In the Midst of Perpetual Fetes*, 18.

117. Rush, "An Enquiry into the Effects of Public Punishments upon Criminals and upon Society," 6.

118. Ibid., 11.

119. Benjamin Rush, *An Address to the Inhabitants of the British Settlements in American upon Slave Keeping*, 29.

120. Rush, "An Enquiry into the Effects of Public Punishments upon Criminals and upon Society," 12.

121. Rush also emphasized his need to resist sympathetic identification with infected patients for fear of contamination, thereby making sympathy and contagion almost synonymous. "I . . . use every precaution . . . to prevent taking the infection. I even strive to subdue my sympathy for my patients; otherwise I should sink under the accumulated loads of misery." Rush, *Letters of Benjamin Rush*, vol. 2, 641.

122. Rush, "An Enquiry into the Effects of Public Punishments upon Criminals and upon Society," 11–12.

123. Meranze, *Laboratories of Virtue*, 127.

124. Sullivan, "The Birth of the Prison," 337.

125. Rush, *Letters of Benjamin Rush*, vol. 1, 512.

126. Rush, *The Autobiography of Benjamin Rush*, 185.

127. See Eric Slauter, "Being Alone in the Age of the Social Contract."

128. Rush, *Letters of Benjamin Rush*, vol. 2, 824.

129. Radner, "The Art of Sympathy in Eighteenth-Century British Moral Thought," 192.

130. Wood, "Interests and Disinterestedness in the Making of the Constitution," 81.

131. Adams, "Defense of the Constitutions of Government of the United States," *The Works of John Adams*, vol. 4, 587–88.

132. James Madison, "The Vices of the Political System of the United States," *The Papers of James Madison*, vol. 9, 348–57, 357.

133. "The Federalist no. 52" [8 February 1788], *The Federalist*, ed. Cooke, 353–59, 355.

134. "The Federalist no. 55" [13 February 1788], *The Federalist*, ed. Cooke, 372–78, 374.

135. Plato, *The Republic*, 492.

136. See McClelland, *The Crowd and the Mob*.

137. Richard K. Matthews argues that this passage provided the "linchpin to [Madison's] entire edifice," but that this "linchpin" relied upon an "unchallenged philosophical assumption." I agree with Matthews concerning the passage's importance but believe that there was a more fully developed discourse behind it than he recognizes. See Matthews, *If Men Were Angels*, 24, 66.

138. Benjamin Rush, "Address to the People of the United States," 48.

CHAPTER 4 Spaces of Insurgent Citizenship

1. Democratic Society of Pennsylvania, "'Address to the Patriotic Societies of the United States' October 9th, 1794," *The Democratic-Republican Societies, 1790–1800*, ed. Foner, 93–96, 96.

2. "Order," *Columbia Centinel* (Boston), 3 September 1794.

3. George Washington, "Sixth Annual Address to Congress, November 19, 1794," *Writings*, 887–95, 889.

4. "George Washington to Burges Ball, September 25, 1794," *Writings*, 884–885, 884. On 5 August 1794 Hamilton wrote Washington a lengthy analysis of the uprising in western Pennsylvania, in which he also attributed significant responsibility to the agitations of the societies at Washington Town and Mingo Creek. These societies, Hamilton wrote, were "justly chargeable with the excesses, which have been from time to time committed; serving to give consistency to an opposition which has at length matured to a point, that threatens the foundations of Government & of the Union; unless speedily and effectually subdued." See "Alexander Hamilton to George Washington, August 5, 1794," *Papers of Alexander Hamilton*, vol. 12, 24–58, 32. The Whiskey Rebellion was in fact supported by several members of the societies at Washington Town and Mingo Creek, but that does not mean that the rebellion was an outcome of the societies' activities. In fact most societies immediately condemned the rebellion, while remaining firm opponents to the Federalist policies they believed had incited it. While most societies continued to argue for the right to organize the citizenry politically and to contest acts of government, they rejected irregular and illegal opposition to existing law. In the rebellion's wake the societies distanced themselves from direct resistance and more openly accepted the legitimacy of formal governmental procedures and laws. Self-created societies came to be seen as legitimate so long as they did not directly challenge the authority of duly constituted government and law. On the response of the societies to the Whiskey Rebellion see Chesney, "How Can the Law Regulate Loyalty without Imperiling It?"; Davis, "Guarding the Republican Interest"; and Koschnik, "The Democratic Societies of Philadelphia and the Limits of the American Public Sphere."

5. See Brooke, "Ancient Lodges and Self-Created Societies," 273–359; John L. Brooke, "Consent, Civil Society, and the Public Sphere in the Age of Revolution and the Early American Republic," *Beyond the Founders*, ed. Jeffrey L. Pasley, Andrew W. Robertson, and David Waldstreicher, 207–50; Foner, Introduction, *The Democratic-Republican Societies*, 3–52; Elkins and McKitrick, *The Age of the Federalists*, 451–88; Harris, "Civil Society in Post-Revolutionary America"; Link, *Democratic-Republican Societies*; Schoenbachler, "Republicanism in the Age of Democratic Revolution"; Sioli, "The Democratic-Republican Societies at the End of the Eighteenth Century"; and Alfred F. Young, *The Democratic Republicans of New York: The Origins, 1763–1797*.

6. "Thomas Jefferson to James Madison, December 28, 1794," *The Republic of Letters*, ed. Smith, 867.

7. "James Madison to James Monroe, December 4, 1794," in *The Papers of James Madison*, vol. 15, 409.

8. See for example Hofstadter, *The Idea of a Party System*, 92–95; and Link, *Democratic-Republican Societies*, 125–55.

9. I take the phrase, if not the exact inflection I give it here, from Holston, "Spaces of Insurgent Citizenship."

10. On the decline of deferential republicanism see Beeman, "Deference, Republicanism and the Emergence of Popular Politics in Eighteenth-Century America"; Kirby, "Early American Politics"; Pocock, "The Classical Theory of Deference." For a broader discussion of the democratization of character in the 1790s see Appleby, *Capitalism and a New Social Order*, esp. 51–79. For a provocative study of the coexistence of populist and élitist-deferential forms of republicanism, and the invisibility of this distinction to many historians responsible for the "republican revival," see McCormick, "Machiavelli against Republicanism."

11. Rawls, *Political Liberalism*, xvi–xvii.

12. Michel Foucault, "Polemics, Politics, and Problematizations," *Essential Works of Foucault*, vol. 3, 111–21.

13. Ames, "Speech in the Convention of Massachusetts, January 15, 1788," *Works of Fisher Ames*, vol. 1, 541–47, 546.

14. "Resolutions Adopted to Commemorate the 1783 British Evacuation of New York City, November 26, 1794," *The Democratic-Republican Societies*, ed. Foner, 204–5, 204.

15. Eugene Link estimated that forty-two societies were created between 1793 and 1798. Matthew Schoenbachler has more recently suggested that "more than fifty" were established in the last decade of the eighteenth century. See Link, *Democratic-Republican Societies*, 13–15; Schoenbachler, "Republicanism in the Age of Democratic Revolution," 237.

16. Cobbett, "The History of Jacobinism: Its Crimes, Cruelties, and Perfidies," *Peter Porcupine in America*, 182–218, 194.

17. "Minutes of the Democratic Society of Philadelphia, October 9th, 1794," *The Democratic-Republican Societies*, ed. Foner, 93–96, 94.

18. See Bailyn, "A Note on Conspiracy," *Ideological Origins of the American Revolution*, 144–59; and Wood, "Conspiracy and the Paranoid Style." The Federalists also contributed to this political culture of conspiracy, which reached a zenith in Federalist writing on the secret machinations of the Bavarian Illuminati against the American government, especially in the political sermons of Jedidiah Morse.

19. "Columbus," *Columbia Centinel* (Boston), 30 November 1793.

20. Foner, "Introduction," *The Democratic-Republican Societies*, 20.

21. Brooke, "Ancient Lodges and Self-Created Societies," 314. See also Durey, *Transatlantic Radicals and the Early American Republic*.

22. "Address to the Free and Independent Citizens of the United States, December 29, 1794," *The Democratic-Republican Societies*, ed. Foner, 59–63, 60.

23. On the history of extraparliamentary association in Britain see Black, *The Association*; and Clark, *British Clubs and Societies*. For the revolutionary reiteration of these associations in the late eighteenth century and the early nineteenth see Epstein, *Radical Expression*; and Parssinen, "Association, Convention, and Anti-Parliament in British Radical Politics."

24. On the *sociétés populaires* see Johnson, *The Paradise of Association*; and Tominaga, "Voice and Silence of Public Space."

25. Parssinen, "Association, Convention, and Anti-Parliament in British Radical Politics," 504.

26. Burgh, *Political Disquisitions*; Obadiah Hulme, *An Historical Essay on the English Constitution*.

27. Burgh, *Political Disquisitions*, 506.

28. "German Republican Society Address to Citizen Genêt, May 17, 1793," *The Democratic-Republican Societies*, ed. Foner, 55–56.

29. Brooke, "Ancient Lodges and Self-Created Societies," 284, 296.

30. Kloppenberg, "The Virtues of Liberalism," 24.

31. Ibid., 25.

32. Suzette Hemberger offers a provocative interpretation of the persistence of these dilemmas post-founding in "A Government Based on Representations."

33. Sharp, *American Politics in the Early Republic*, 124–25.

34. For a study of how early Americans navigated the tensions between the local, regional, and national conceptions of the people see Beer, *To Make a Nation*.

35. Morgan, *Inventing the People*, 13–15.

36. On the imperatives of early American "consensual literature" see Ferguson, *The American Enlightenment*, 1–21. For a rhetorical account of how this demand for consensus contributed to the vehemence and nondeliberative character of postrevolutionary political discourse see Shiffman, "Construing Disagreement."

37. See for example Sharp, *American Politics in the Early Republic*.

38. "George Washington to Burges Ball, September 25, 1794," *Writings*, 885.

39. See Wiebe, *The Opening of American Society from the Adoption of the Constitution to the Eve of Disunion*, 73–74.

40. "The People," *Columbia Centinel* (Boston), 24 March 1794.

41. "ORDER," *Columbia Centinel* (Boston), 3 September 1794.

42. John W. Malsberger offers a useful survey in "The Political Thought of Fisher Ames."

43. Ames, "Speech in the Convention of Massachusetts, January 15, 1788," *Works of Fisher Ames*, vol. 1, 543.

44. Ibid., 546.

45. Joseph De Maistre also explored the nonsovereignty of the unrepresented multitude: "the people are the sovereign that cannot exercise sovereignty." "The Study of Sovereignty," *The Works of Joseph de Maistre*, 93–128, 93.

46. See Noah Webster, "The Revolution in France," *Political Sermons of the American Founding Era*, ed. Sandoz, vol. 2, 1237–99, 1273. This sentiment was strengthened after Washington's condemnation of the societies' role in the Whiskey Rebellion. It even gained the support of some of the society members themselves. Moderate members of the Tammany Society of New York, for example, gave their unqualified support to Washington: "The public's right to associate, speak and publish sentiments are only excellent as a revolutionary means, when a government is to be overturned. An exercise of this right in a free and happy country like this resembles the sport of firebrands; it is phrenzy, and this phrenzy is in proportion to the party zeal of the self-created associations." Cited in Appleby, *Capitalism and a New Social Order*, 65.

47. Ames, "Debate over the Propriety of Replies to the President's Speeches, November 26, 1794," *Works of Fisher Ames*, vol. 2, 1053–71, 1057.

48. Ibid., 1070.

49. On the constitutional appeal of the transatlantic radical of the 1790s see Epstein, "The Constitutionalist Idiom," *Radical Expression*, 3–28. On popular constitutionalism in the American context see Kramer, *The People Themselves*.

50. James Madison, "Who Are the Best Keepers of the People's Liberties?," *The Papers of James Madison*, vol. 14, 426–27, 426.

51. "German Republican Society Address to Citizen Genêt, May 17, 1793," *The Democratic-Republican Societies*, ed. Foner, 55–56.

52. "Democratic Society of New York Address to 'Fellow Freemen,' January 26, 1795," *The Democratic-Republican Societies*, ed. Foner, 192–98, 194.

53. "German Republican Society of Philadelphia Address to the Free and Independent Citizens of the United States, December 29, 1794," *The Democratic-Republican Societies*, ed. Foner, 59–63, 62.

54. "Federalist No. 51," *The Federalist*, ed. Cooke, 347–53, 347–48.

55. "Alexander Hamilton to George Washington, September 2nd, 1794," *Papers of Alexander Hamilton*, vol. 17, 180–90, 187.

56. "Alexander Hamilton to George Washington, August 5th, 1794," *Papers of Alexander Hamilton*, vol. 17, 24–58, 40.

57. "Tully No. III," *Papers of Alexander Hamilton*, vol. 17, 159–62, 160.

58. "Tully No. I," *Papers of Alexander Hamilton*, vol. 17, 132–35, 135.

59. Hemberger, "A Government Based on Representations," 328.

60. Wood, *The Creation of the American Republic*, 398.

61. Cited in Appleby, *Capitalism and a New Social Order*, 68.

62. "Jefferson to Madison, December 28, 1794," *The Republic of Letters*, ed. Smith, 867.

63. Pynchon, *Mason & Dixon*, 395.

64. Cited in Link, *Democratic-Republican Societies*, 175.

65. McDonald, *The Presidency of George Washington*, 133. See also Smelser, "The Federalist Period as an Age of Passion"; and Howe, "Republican Thought and the Political Violence of the 1790s."

66. Brooke, "Ancient Lodges and Self-Created Societies," 275.

67. James Madison, "Virginia Convention Speech, June 20, 1788," *The Papers of James Madison*, vol. 11, 159–65, 163.

68. Tunis Wortman, *Oration on the Influence of Social Institutions upon Human Morals and Happiness*, 5.

69. Fliegelman, *Prodigals and Pilgrims*, 12.

70. John Locke, *Some Thoughts Concerning Education and Of the Conduct of the Understanding*, 12. See James Tully, "Governing Conduct: Locke on the Reform of Thought and Behavior."

71. See Link, "Schools of Political Knowledge," *Democratic-Republican Societies*, 156–74, 164.

72. "Republican Society of Lancaster, Constitution and Address, January 3rd, 1795," *The Democratic-Republican Societies*, ed. Foner, 119–22, 120.

73. Burgh, *Political Disquisitions*, vol. 3, 4.

74. "German Republican Society of Philadelphia Address to the Democratic Society of Pennsylvania, February 20th, 1794," *The Democratic-Republican Societies*, ed. Foner, 57–58, 57.

75. "German Republican Society of Philadelphia Address to Friends and Fellow Citizens, April 11th, 1793," *The Democratic-Republican Societies*, ed. Foner, 53–55, 53.

76. See Pocock, "The *Vita Activa* and the *Vivere Civile*," *The Machiavellian Moment*, 49–80.

77. For a persuasive account of the historical interdependence of these supposedly contrasting theoretical paradigms see Kloppenberg, *The Virtues of Liberalism*.

78. Dworkin, "Rights as Trumps."

79. Democratic Society of Pennsylvania, "'Address to the Patriotic Societies of the United States' October 9th, 1794," *The Democratic-Republican Societies, 1790–1800*, ed. Foner, 96.

80. Arendt, "The Perplexities of the Rights of Man," *The Origins of Totalitarianism*, 290–302; Lefort, *Democracy and Political Theory*, 37.

81. Gouverneur Morris, *Diary and Letters of Gouverneur Morris*, vol. 2, 450–51.

82. Cobbett, "The History of Jacobinism: Its Crimes, Cruelties, and Perfidies," *Peter Porcupine in America*, 182–216, 194.

83. Epstein, *Radical Expression*, 147–66.

84. See Brown, *Toussaint's Clause*, 45–65.

85. Ames, "Debate over the Propriety of Replies to the President's Speeches, November 26, 1794," *Works of Fisher Ames*, vol. 2, 1056.

86. Waldstreicher, *In the Midst of Perpetual Fetes*, 17–107.

87. On the contrasting political styles of the Federalists and the Democratic Republicans see Brooke, "Ancient Lodges and Self-Created Societies," 305–9; Waldstreicher, "Federalism, the Styles of Politics, and the Politics of Style"; and Waldstreicher, "Why Thomas Jefferson and African Americans Wore Their Politics on Their Sleeves." Robert Hariman discusses republicanism not as a coherent conceptual system or ideology but as stylistic repertoire, rhetoric, and sensibility in *Political Style*, 95–140.

88. Foner, ed., *The Democratic-Republican Societies*, 84.

89. Simon Schama, *The Embarrassment of Riches*, 221–22.

90. Cited in Wood, *Revolutionary Characters*, 53.

91. On the ritual and symbolic resources of the American Revolution see Shaw, *American Patriots and the Rituals of Revolution*; and Waldstreicher, *In the Midst of Perpetual Fetes*, 177–245.

92. See Foner, Introduction, *The Democratic-Republican Societies*, 17.

93. Warner, "Textuality and Legitimacy in the Printed Constitution," *The Letters of the Republic*, 97–117.

94. Sean Wilentz, *The Rise of American Democracy*, 58.

95. Cited in Ibid.

96. Sheldon S. Wolin, "Contract and Birthright," *The Presence of the Past*, 137–50, 150.

97. Jacques Rancière, *On the Shores of Politics*, 61.

98. Tocqueville, *Democracy in America*, 58.

99. Putnam, *Bowling Alone*, 19–23.

100. Lynn M. Sanders, "Against Deliberation."

101. Gutmann and Thompson, *Democracy and Disagreement*, 50–51. I elaborate on these points in chapter 7.

102. Sparks, "Dissident Citizenship," 77. On this point see also Iris Marion Young, "Activist Challenges to Deliberative Democracy."

103. Wolin, *Politics and Vision*, 606.

CHAPTER 5   Hearing Voices

1. Morgan, *Inventing the People*, 153.

2. Brown, *Wieland and Memoirs of Carwin the Biloquist*, 300–301. Further references cited parenthetically in the body of the text.

3. Williams, *Voice, Trust, and Memory*, 133.

4. Derrida, *Of Grammatology*, 140.

5. See for example Spivak, "Can the Subaltern Speak?"

6. Wolin, "Transgression, Equality, Voice," 68.

7. Ibid., 69.

8. Ibid., 87.

9. Wolin, "Norm and Form," 55. Similarly Jacques Rancière: "in his resolute

hatred of democracy, Plato delves much further into the foundations of politics and democracy than those tired apologists who assure us lukewarmly that we should love democracy 'reasonably,' meaning 'moderately.'" Rancière, *Disagreement*, 10.

10. Tomkins, "What Happens in *Wieland*," *Sensational Designs*, 40–62, 56, 61.

11. See for example Lovejoy, *Religious Enthusiasm in the New World*, 222.

12. I use the phrase "transportive interpellation" to capture the authoritative relationship of the interpellative scene, but also to emphasize that the hailed subjects are to be carried *beyond themselves* as a necessary prerequisite of the authoritative effect. In Brown's novel this transport is effected through the active elicitation of the involuntary imagination. The classical account of interpellation as "hailing" is Althusser, "Ideology and Ideological State Apparatuses," 170–77.

13. Roland Barthes, *The Grain of the Voice*, 184.

14. As in Brown's depiction of the "rhapsodist," Clara is portrayed in *Wieland* as one with a "thoughtful mind . . . equally remote from the giddy raptures of enthusiasm, and the sober didactic strain of dull philosophy." Brown, *Rhapsodist and Other Uncollected Writings*, 5.

15. The scene and the novel's title refer to Christoph Martin Wieland, *The Trial of Abraham*. For a discussion of the influence of this work on *Wieland* see Axelrod, *Charles Brockden Brown*, 61–64. For a wonderful discussion of Wieland's influence on Enlightenment politics of the eighteenth century, and in particular his work on the private lodge's resistance to the monopoly of state power and its competing claims of authorization, see Koselleck, *Critique and Crisis*, 86–97.

16. Looby, *Voicing America*, 100.

17. Barthes, *The Grain of the Voice*, 183–84.

18. Voice is linked in Brown's novel to the transportive power of the sublime. Peter De Bolla has emphasized this transportive power in his analysis of the discourse of the sublime: "Our persuasion we can usually control, but the influence of the sublime brings power and irresistible might to bear, and reign supreme over every hearer . . . sublimity flashes forth at the right moment scatters everything before it like a thunderbolt, and at once displays the power of the orator in all its plenitude." De Bolla, *The Discourse of the Sublime*, 37.

19. "The passions have their gestures, but they also have their accents; and these accents, which thrill us, these tones of voice that cannot fail to be heard, penetrate to the very depths of the heart, carrying there the emotions they wring from us, forcing us in spite of ourselves to feel what we hear." Rousseau, "Essay on the Origin of Languages Which Treats of Melody and Musical Imitation," 5.

20. Burgh, *Art of Speaking*, 12.

21. Ibid., 29.

22. Fliegelman, Introduction to Brown, *Wieland*, vii–xlii, xiv. See also Gustafson, *Eloquence Is Power*.

23. Gustafson, *Eloquence Is Power*, xvii.

24. The Anti-Federalist writer "Brutus" captures this interconnected sense of the problematic of representation in his defense of a "resemblance" model of representation. "A representation of the people of America, if it be a true one, must be *like* the people . . . They are the sign—the people are the thing signified." "Brutus III," *The Documentary History of the Ratification of the Constitution*, ed. Kaminski, Saladino, and Jensen, vol. 14, 199–24, 122.

25. Cahill, "An Adventurous and Lawless Fancy," 32.

26. Publius eloquently demonstrates the contrast between fact-based political deliberation and political judgment disfigured by the distorting role of the imagination. "The moment we launch into conjectures about the usurpation of the federal Government," he writes, "we get into an unfathomable abyss, and fairly put ourselves out of the reach of all reasoning. Imagination may range at pleasure till it gets bewildered amidst the labyrinths of an enchanted castle, and knows not on which side to turn to extricate itself from the perplexities into which it so rashly adventured." "Federalist No. 31," *The Federalist*, ed. Cooke, 193–98, 197.

27. James Madison, "Jay's Treaty (April 6, 1796)," *The Papers of James Madison*, vol. 16, 290–301.

28. Cited in Lienesch, *New Order of the Ages*, 163–64.

29. Proverbs 28:18.

30. Clark, *Charles Brockden Brown*, 169, 174.

31. Brown shares this emphasis with Edmund Burke, who in his *Reflections on the Revolution in France* famously asserted continuities between enlightenment and enthusiasm in contrast to their usual opposition in the eighteenth-century Anglophone thought. See Pocock, "Edmund Burke and the Redefinition of Enthusiasm."

32. Ziff, "A Reading of *Wieland*," 51.

33. "Thomas Jefferson to James Madison (September 6, 1789)," *Political Writings*, 593–98, 593.

34. Shklar, "Democracy and the Past," 174; and Holland, *The Body Politic*, 3.

35. On the "heresy of the free spirit" see Cohn, *The Pursuit of the Millennium*.

36. Schwarz, *Knaves, Fools, Madmen, and that Subtile Effluvium*.

37. Chauncey, *Enthusiasm Described and Cautioned against*, 3.

38. Ferguson, *Solitude and the Sublime*.

39. For a description of the Yates family murders on which Brown modeled his narrative see Axelrod, *Charles Brockden Brown*, 53–68.

40. John Adams, *Correspondence between the Honorable John Adams, Late President of the United States, and the Late William Cunningham, Esquire*, 19.

41. "In the midst of the frenetic political and philosophical climate of the 1790s," Edmund Cahill writes, "Brown finds the technologies of aesthetic ex-

perience to be highly complex and ambiguous, but also assumes the imagination's eminent ability to comprehend such complexity and ambiguity, and to elaborate its central relation to the national polity and social transformation." Cahill, "An Adventurous and Lawless Fancy," 33.

42. Disraeli, *Curiosities of Literature*.

43. On the dangerous and reformative power of early American novels see Davidson, *Revolution and the Word*; and Martin, *The Instructed Vision*.

44. Brown, "Walstein's School of History," 35.

45. In his *Notes on the State of Virginia* Jefferson emphasizes the centrality of imagination to the moral formation of the self. He invokes the purported lack of imagination among people of African descent as a basis of natural inferiority. Jefferson, *Notes on the State of Virginia*, 138–39.

46. Jefferson, "Letter to Robert Skipwith, August 3, 1771," *Political Writings*, 233–35, 234.

47. Jefferson, "Letter to Peter Carr, August 10, 1787," *Political Writings*, 252–56, 253.

48. Martin, *The Instructed Vision*.

49. For a detailed biographical account of Brown's response to the inheritance of the American Revolution and the "Jacobin" politics of the 1790s see Kafer, *Charles Brockden Brown's Revolution and the Birth of the American Gothic*.

50. For an insightful discussion of "postrevolutionary nostalgia" see Looby, *Voicing America*, 174–80.

51. Ferguson, *Solitude and the Sublime*, 1.

52. Benjamin Rush, "The Effects of the American Revolution on the Mind and Body of Man," in Dagobert D. Runes, ed., *Selected Writings of Benjamin Rush*, 325–33, 331.

53. "Charles Brockden Brown to Thomas Jefferson, December 15, 1789," cited in Clark, *Charles Brockden Brown*, 163.

54. For a discussion of Brown's relationship to Godwin, see Kafer, *Charles Brockden Brown's Revolution and the Birth of the American Gothic*, 132–66.

55. Tomkins, "What Happens in *Wieland*," *Sensational Designs*, 61.

56. Wood, *The Creation of the American Republic*, 534.

57. James Wilson, "Opening Address, Pennsylvania Ratifying Convention (November 24, 1787)," *The Debate on the Constitution*, ed. Bailyn, vol. 1, 791–806, 793. In a more imperious tone Publius wrote: "The fabric of the American Empire ought to rest on the solid basis of THE CONSENT OF THE PEOPLE. The streams of national power ought to flow immediately from that pure original fountain of all legitimate authority." "Federalist No. 22," *The Federalist*, ed. Cooke, 135–46, 146.

58. James Wilson, "Opening Address, Pennsylvania Ratifying Convention (November 24, 1787)," *The Debate on the Constitution*, ed. Bailyn, vol. 1, 801–2.

59. Kramer, *The People Themselves*, 133.

60. Durey, *Transatlantic Radicals and the Early American Republic*.

61. For a reading of *Wieland* that emphasizes the consequences of Carwin's foreignness see Samuels, "Wieland."

62. See the essays anthologized in Arensberg, ed., *The American Sublime*.

63. Brown makes this point most explicit in a preface written to his novel *Edgar Huntly, or, Memoirs of a Sleep-Walker* (1799): "Puerile superstition and exploded manners; Gothic castles and chimeras, are the material usually employed for this end [of calling forth passions and engaging the sympathy of the reader]. The incidents of Indian hostility, and the perils of western wilderness, are far more suitable; and, for a native of America to overlook these, would admit of no apology." Brown, *Edgar Huntley*, 3. Brown explores the sublimity of crowd actions in his short story "Thessalonica: A Roman Story."

64. See for example Elkins and McKitrick, *The Age of Federalism*, 451–88; Sharp, *American Politics in the Early Republic*, 69–91.

65. Burke captured this invocation of the traditional sublime in *Reflections on the Revolution in France* and his invocation of the "pleasing illusions which made power gentle and obedience liberal." "Our liberty becomes a noble freedom it carries an imposing and majestic aspect. It has a pedigree and illustrating ancestors. It has its bearings and its ensigns armorial. It has its gallery of portraits; its monumental inscriptions; its records, evidences, and tithes." Edmund Burke, *Reflections on the Revolution in France*, 67. The distinction between a democratic and a traditional sublime to which I am gesturing here parallels the argument made by Stephen White in *Edmund Burke*, 76–79.

66. Verba, "The 1993 James Madison Award Lecture," 678.

67. Godwin, *Enquiry concerning Political Justice*, 247.

68. Honig, "The Genres of Democracy," *Democracy and the Foreigner*, 107–22.

69. MacCannell, "Fascism and the Voice of Conscience," 136.

70. On the uncanny relation to law see Honig, "Between Deliberation and Decision."

CHAPTER 6 "Aesthetic Democracy"

1. Walt Whitman, *Democratic Vistas*, 984. Subsequent references to Whitman's work will be cited in the text with the following abbreviations:

AP   *An American Primer*

C   *With Walt Whitman in Camden*

DV   *Democratic Vistas* in *Poetry and Prose*, 953–1018

E   "The Eighteenth Presidency!" in *Poetry and Prose*, 1331–49

LG   *Leaves of Grass* (multiple editions) in *Poetry and Prose*, 5–145 [1855]; 165–672 [1891–92]; 677–696 [1860, 1865]

N   *Notebooks and Unpublished Prose Manuscripts*

P   *Poetry and Prose*

R   *Walt Whitman: The Contemporary Reviews*
SD *Specimen Days & Collect*
W   *Walt Whitman's Workshop*

2. Matthiessen, *From the Heart of Europe*, 90; Kateb, *The Inner Ocean*, 240.

3. The contrast between autopoetic and autonomic emphasizes the aesthetic over juridical concerns in Whitman's work, while also emphasizing his creative and transformative conception of democratic politics. As Jacques Rancière's work has shown, to affirm the poetic dimension of politics is to understand political enactment in terms of a "reconfiguration of the sensible." In Whitman's work it is the very perceptual self of "democratic self determination" that is continually reformed and recreated. See Jacques Rancière, *The Politics of Aesthetics*, 12–18. The theme of revisionary poetic politics is obviously related to Whitman's preoccupation with revising his own body of work in the multiple editions of *Leaves of Grass*. For a discussion that traces this theme through the different editions see Michael Moon, *Disseminating Whitman*.

4. Slavoj Žižek has explored the significant transformation of the politics of "the people" into the politics of "a people." For Žižek the "sublime enthusiasm" of *the* people is an "open" but "brief, passing moment," "not yet hegemonized by any positive ideological project." See Žižek, *Tarrying with the Negative*, 1.

5. Harold Bloom offers the best general discussion of Emerson's and Whitman's distinct conceptions of the "American Sublime" in "Emerson and Whitman"; See also Kronick, "On the Border of History." I cannot offer an extended discussion of the sublime here, but Kateb provides a useful summary statement: "the sublime refers to such aspects of artworks, nature, and human social phenomenon as the unbounded or boundless; the indefinite, indeterminate, or infinite; the transgressive; the overwhelming or overpowering . . . the awe-inspiring, wondrous, astonishing, or unexpectedly mysterious; and the uncanny." Kateb, "Aestheticism and Morality: Their Cooperation and Hostility," *Patriotism and Other Mistakes*, 117–49, 129.

6. Rancière, *Dis-agreement*, 10.

7. Kateb, "Aestheticism and Morality," 143. Kateb rightly emphasizes Whitman's attempt to "show that nearly everyone and everything is worthy of aesthetic attitudes and feeling," but Whitman goes beyond this aesthetic affirmation of the "world as it is" to engender an enlivening sense of the people's poetic power, their capacity for "formative action."

8. Whitman's persistent loyalty to the Founding generation is emphasized by Daniel Aaron in his essay "Whitman and the Founding Fathers."

9. For a good account of Whitman's involvement with the "Young America" movement see David Reynolds's *Walt Whitman's America*, 81–82.

10. Ibid., 26.

11. Jerome Loving emphasizes Whitman's party activism and its influence on his literary work. See Loving, "The Political Roots of *Leaves of Grass*," 97–119.

12. Webster, *The Letters of Noah Webster*, 504.

13. Reynolds, *Walt Whitman's America*, 306.

14. See for example Fanuzzi, *Abolition's Public Sphere*.

15. This distinction is extensively elaborated in Sean Wilentz's influential study of working-class politics in antebellum America. See Wilentz, *Chants Democratic*. A detailed account of the centrality of reform movements to antebellum political culture is provided in Walters, *American Reformers*.

16. Thoreau, "A Plea for Captain John Brown," *Civil Disobedience and Other Essays*, 31–48, 37.

17. Emerson, "New England Reformers," *Essays: First and Second Series*, 361–79, 363.

18. Emerson, "Self-Reliance," *Selected Essays*, 175–204, 179.

19. Emerson, "Speech on Affairs in Kansas," *Complete Works of Ralph Waldo Emerson*, vol. 6, 255–63, 259–60.

20. Emerson, "Nature," *Selected Essays*, 35–82, 52.

21. Cited in Erkkila, *Whitman the Political Poet*, 103.

22. Kateb, *The Inner Ocean*, 240.

23. See Brown, *The Strength of a People*, esp. 119–53.

24. Erkkila, *Whitman the Political Poet*, 92.

25. Donald E. Pease argues that the "doctrine of the body electric" was Whitman's democratic translation of the early modern discourse of the King's Two Bodies. Through this doctrine Whitman "develops a correspondence between an individual's inner impulses and the democratic masses." See his "Walt Whitman and the Vox Populi of the American Masses," 110.

26. Emerson, "Eloquence," *Complete Works of Ralph Waldo Emerson*, vol. 8, 111–21, 115; Thoreau, *Walden*, 404.

27. The erotic dimensions of Whitman's understanding of politics, and the political dimensions of his understanding of eros, have been explored by Michael Moon. Whitman's "body politics," Moon writes, "is designed to reconstitute the readers' very subjectivity in relation not only to the author's but to their own and everyone else's bodily existence . . . Whitman revises readerly subjectivity in the direction of a heightened, transforming sense of the constructedness and hence the dense politicality of all bodily experiences, erotic and otherwise." Moon, *Disseminating Whitman*, 4.

28. Grossman, "The Poetics of Union in Whitman and Lincoln," 208.

29. I take "infrasensible" from William Connolly's explorations of these topics. See his *Neuropolitics* and *Why I Am Not a Secularist*. Ellison invokes democracy's "lower frequencies" in the final line of *Invisible Man*.

30. Deleuze and Guattari, *A Thousand Plateaus*, 208–31.

31. Goldhammer, "Walt Whitman," 62.

32. Ellis, *The Dark Side of the Left*, 73.

33. Martha Nussbaum emphasizes this aspect of Whitman's thought, arguing that he "attempts to create a democratic counter-cosmos, in which hierarchies of souls are replaced by the democratic body of the United States." See "Demo-

cratic Desire," 656. I disagree with Nussbaum, however, when she writes that Whitman's poetry aimed to diminish the public's disgust at their own promiscuous embodiment only because it was a "barrier to the full equality and mutual respect of all citizens." Whitman's poetics of citizenship aimed at a transformative political praxis that cannot be reduced to the formalism of reciprocity or mutual respect, but also cannot be simply opposed to it. Also see Nussbaum, *Hiding from Humanity*, 117.

34. Cited in Abrams, *Natural Supernaturalism*, 384.

35. James, *American Civilization*, 51.

36. Emerson, "The Poet," *Essays: First and Second Series*, 217–38, 219.

37. Carlyle, "Shooting Niagara," 202.

38. "One may include among the lessons of his life—even though that stretch'd to amazing length—how behind the tally of genius and morals stands the stomach, and gives a sort of casting vote." Whitman, *SD*, 168.

39. Carlyle, "Shooting Niagara," 200.

40. For a discussion of Carlyle's attempts to speak *for* the masses see Plotz, "Crowd Power," 90.

41. Carlyle, "Shooting Niagara," 235.

42. In addition to Kateb's work, already cited, see Morton Schoolman's rewarding chapters on Whitman in *Reason and Horror*, 185–250.

43. Kateb, *The Inner Ocean*, 252.

44. By asserting the close interconnection between Whitman's radically democratic politics and his formal poetic innovations, I depart from critics who have attempted to isolate the one from the other. For a good discussion of this tendency in the critical literature see Bellis, "Against Representation."

45. Kenneth M. Price, *Whitman and Tradition*, 53.

46. Grossman, "The Poetics of Union in Whitman and Lincoln," 193–95.

47. Bakhtin, "Discourse in the Novel," 285.

48. Ibid., 297.

49. Ibid., 269.

50. Ibid., 288.

51. Ibid., 287.

52. Relatedly, Kateb has little to say about language's role in constituting the self in Whitman's work, to which I will turn again below. Stephen White perceptively explains Kateb's general avoidance of such in *Sustaining Affirmation*, 35.

53. Kateb, *The Inner Ocean*, 259.

54. Ibid., 266.

55. See Nancy, *The Inoperative Community*, 57–58.

56. This argument is made by Samuel H. Beer in "Liberty and Union."

57. Larzer Ziff, *Literary Democracy*.

58. Tocqueville, *Democracy in America*, 483.

59. Ibid., 485.

60. In an insightful aphorism from *The Gay Science*, Nietzsche similarly de-

scribes "really democratic" ages as those where individuals replace faith in fixed social hierarchies with faith in their own performative capacities: "everybody experiments with himself, improvises, makes new experiments, enjoys his experiments; and all nature ceases and becomes art." Nietzsche, *The Gay Science*, 303.

61. Marx, "Theses on Feuerbach," *The Marx-Engels Reader*, 143–45, 144.

62. Goldhammer, "Walt Whitman," 41.

63. Tocqueville, *Democracy in America*, 478–82.

64. Michael Gilmore, *American Romanticism and the Marketplace*.

65. Emerson, *Representative Men*, 8.

66. Hazlitt, "What Is the People?," 3.

67. Larzer Ziff, "Whitman and the Crowd," 586.

68. Samuel Beer argues that Whitman should be taken "seriously as a social scientist." See Beer, "Liberty and Union," 363.

69. M. H. Abrams, *Mirror and the Lamp*.

70. Reynolds, *Walt Whitman's America*, 286.

71. Ernst Bloch, *Principle of Hope*, vol. 1, 5–6.

72. Rawls, *Political Liberalism*, 14.

73. Wolin, "The Liberal/Democratic Divide"; Habermas, "Reconciliation through the Public Use of Reason."

74. Rawls, *Political Liberalism*, 97.

75. Most notably Rorty, "American National Pride: Whitman and Dewey," *Achieving Our Country*, 3–38.

CHAPTER 7 Staging Dissensus

1. Agamben, "What Is a People?," 29.

2. Holmes, *Passions and Constraint*, 167. Good examples of contemporary democratic theorists who affirm the productivity of paradox are Christodoulidis, "The Aporia of Sovereignty"; Connolly, *Political Theory and Modernity*; and Keenan, *Democracy in Question*.

3. For a canonical treatment of the people as a unified subject see Michelet, *The People*. By "social datum" Laclau refers to both the people as a sociological entity and the variety of social scientific attempts to empirically quantify the people through voting procedures, opinion polls, demographic studies, etc. See Laclau, *On Populist Reason*, 224. Edmund Morgan shows how during the seventeenth century political "representatives invented the sovereignty of the people in order to claim it for themselves." In treating the people as a political fiction used to further expand the reach of state power, Morgan offers a one-sided account of the governmental logics of this fiction, neglecting how it enabled and inspired forms of popular contention against the state. Morgan, *Inventing the People*, 49–50; Habermas offers a picture of "desubstantialized" popular sov-

ereignty: "Subjectless and anonymous, an intersubjectively dissolved popular sovereignty withdraws into democratic procedures and the demanding communicative presuppositions of their implementation." This democratic theory transubstantiates the people into a quite different form of democratic mysticism. See Habermas, "Popular Sovereignty as Procedure," *Between Facts and Norms*, 466–81, 486.

4. Agamben, "What Is a People?," 33.

5. Rancière, *Dis-agreement*, 1–19. Laclau's recent work positions his theory of articulation and the political logic of the empty signifier on very similar terrain as Rancière. "It is in the contamination of the universality of the *populus* by the partiality of the *plebs*," Laclau writes, "that the peculiarity of the 'people' as a historical actor lies." Laclau, *On Populist Reason*, 224.

6. Rancière, "Who Is the Subject of the Rights of Man?," 7.

7. Frederick Douglass, "What to the Slave Is the Fourth of July?" Subsequent references will be parenthetically cited in the body of the text.

8. Douglass, *Life and Times of Frederick Douglass*, 375.

9. Alan Keenan has identified the paradoxical dimension of this task: "To lay the conditions for the people to become a people, one must appeal to the sense of the people *as* a people; yet the success of that appeal depends on those conditions already being in place, or at the very least being imaginable. The paradoxical task of the legislator—or rather, of all democratic political actors—then, is to make an appeal that sets the conditions for its own proper reception; one must appeal to the political community in such a way that its members will accept the regulations that will make them into the kind of (general) people able to 'hear' such an appeal." Keenan, *Democracy in Question*, 52.

10. Douglass makes this connection frequently in his writings, as when he writes that if the slave "kills his master, he imitates only the heroes of the revolution." See *My Bondage and My Freedom*, 283.

11. For an interpretation of Douglass that emphasizes natural law and "Lockean liberalism" see Boxhill, "Two Traditions in African American Political Philosophy"; on antislavery constitutionalism see Moore, *Constitutional Rights and Powers of the People*; on prophecy and millennial providentialism see Glaude, *Exodus!*; Rogers, *We Are All Together Now*; and Shulman, *American Prophecy*.

12. In his insistence on the inescapably "poetic" or aesthetic dimensions of politics Rancière critiques Habermas's attempt in *The Philosophical Discourse of Modernity* to deflate the literary, poetic, metaphorical, or "world-disclosive" dimensions of language as secondary to the inherent telos of speech (mutual understanding). In addition to *Dis-agreement*, 43–60, see Rancière, "Dissenting Words," 113–26; Habermas, *The Philosophical Discourse of Modernity*, 185–210. Nikolas Kompridis had brilliantly elaborated on Habermas's politically disabling neglect of "world disclosive" speech in *Critique and Disclosure*.

13. The presence of the body inflects the meaning of the oration and the dissensus that it stages, something lost in most interpretations. For an interesting

discussion of this issue see Fanuzzi, "Frederick Douglass's Public Body," *Abolition's Public Sphere*, 83–128.

14. Rancière, *Dis-agreement*, 56. Rancière offers the example of the plebian secession at Aventin to explain this point: "The patricians at Aventin do not understand what the plebians say; they do not understand the noises that come out of the plebians' mouths, so that, in order to be audibly understood and visibly recognized as legitimate speaking subjects, the plebians must not only argue their position but must also construct the scene of argumentation in such a manner that the patricians must recognize it as a world in common. It is necessary to 'invent a scene.'" Rancière, "Dissenting Words," 125, 116.

15. Cited in Colaiaco, *Frederick Douglass and the Fourth of July*, 24.

16. Rancière, "Ten Theses on Politics," 11.

17. Benhabib, "Democracy and Difference," 85.

18. Rancière, *Dis-agreement*, 40.

19. Jacqueline Bacon, "'Do You Understand Your Own Language?'"

20. For an elaboration of the established repertoires and topoi of the nineteenth-century Fourth of July address see Bodnar, "Public Memory in Nineteenth-Century America: Background and Context," *Remaking America*, 21–38; and Howard H. Martin, "The Fourth of July Oration."

21. See Jasinsky, "Rearticulating History in Epideictic Discourse," 78.

22. Frederick Douglass, "A Nation in the Midst of a Nation: An Address Delivered in New York, New York, on 11 May 1853," *The Frederick Douglass Papers*, ed. Blassingame, vol. 2, 423–40, 424–25.

23. Rancière, *Dis-agreement*, 21–42.

24. Cited in Colaiaco, *Frederick Douglass and the Fourth of July*, 5.

25. Douglass, "A Nation in the Midst of a Nation," 427–28.

26. This familiar interpretation of Douglass is elaborated in Boxhill, "Two Traditions in African American Political Philosophy." Charles W. Mills takes a similar approach in his savaging of Douglass's "inspiring" but "naïve" view of American racial politics in "Whose Fourth of July? Frederick Douglass and 'Original Intent,'" *Frederick Douglass*, ed. Lawson and Kirkland, 100–142, 105. The familiar binary of assimilationism and separatism obscures much of the nuance in writers like Douglass, DuBois, Ellison, and Baldwin.

27. Boxhill, "Two Traditions of African American Political Philosophy."

28. Glaude, *Exodus!*, 115. Consider the following passage: "We are Americans, and as Americans, we would speak to Americans. We address you not as aliens nor as exiles, humbly asking to be permitted to dwell among you in peace; but we address you as American citizens asserting their rights on their own native soil." Douglass, "The Claims of Our Common Cause," *Frederick Douglass: Selected Speeches and Writings*, ed. Foner, 260–71, 261.

29. Or, as Robert Musil put it: "we are a we to which reality does not correspond." Cited in Rosanvallon, *Democracy Past and Future*, 91. I am grateful to Emilios Christodoulidis for drawing my attention to Benveniste's work on this

question. See Christodoulidis, "Against Substitution," *Paradox of Constitution-alism*, ed. Martin Loughlin and Neil Walker, 189–210, 200–206. On the political dilemmas of "we" see also Clarkson, "Who Are 'We?'"; and van Roermund, "First-Person Plural Legislature."

30. I agree with Nikhil Pal Singh's recent critique of familiar attempts to retrospectively assimilate black political thinkers like Douglass and King into an unbroken tradition of "shared national identity across time," as the "fulfillment of a project" and the "completion of a destiny." What Singh says of King and his legacy is also true of Douglass: their "black freedom dreams had a habit of exceeding the sanctioned boundaries and brokered compromises of the established political order." See Singh, *Black Is a Country*, 5.

31. Walzer, *The Company of Critics*, 19.

32. Bercovitch, *Rites of Assent*, 50.

33. Douglass, *My Bondage and My Freedom*, 65.

34. Douglass, "The Claims of Our Common Cause," *Frederick Douglass: Selected Speeches and Writings*, ed. Foner, 264.

35. Ibid.

36. Frank M. Kirkland also urges readers of Douglass to pay more attention to the "rhetorical and communicative settings in which Douglass is engaged." See his "Enslavement, Moral Suasion, and the Struggles for Recognition," *Frederick Douglass*, ed. Lawson and Kirkland, 243–310, 244.

37. Rancière, "Who Is the Subject of the Rights of Man?," 6.

38. Donald G. Nieman, *Promises to Keep*, viii.

39. "The Dred Scott Decision," *Frederick Douglass*, ed. Foner, 344–58, 347.

40. This motto was printed on the masthead of Garrison's radical abolitionist newspaper the *Liberator*.

41. Cover, *Justice Accused*; Moore, *Constitutional Rights and Powers of the People*; Wiecek, *The Sources of Antislavery Constitutionalism in America*.

42. See David E. Schrader, "Natural Law in the Constitutional Thought of Frederick Douglass," *Frederick Douglass*, ed. Lawson and Kirkland, 85–99, 85.

43. Cover, "Nomos and Narrative," 137.

44. "The Dred Scott Decision," *Frederick Douglass*, ed. Foner, 352.

45. An unabridged version of Chief Justice Taney's Dred Scott decision may be found on the website of the Library of Congress. The most definitive discussion of the Dred Scott case is Fehrenbacher, *The Dred Scott Case*.

46. "The Dred Scott Decision," *Frederick Douglass*, ed. Foner, 354.

47. Colaiaco, *Frederick Douglass and the Fourth of July*, 103.

48. Moore, *Constitutional Rights and Powers of the People*, 63–64; my emphasis.

49. Rancière, "Jacques Rancière: Literature, Politics, Aesthetics," 5.

50. See Fanuzzi, *Abolition's Public Sphere*; and Joel Olson, "The Freshness of Fanaticism: The Abolitionist Defense of Zealotry."

51. Phillips, "Philosophy of the Abolition Movement," 246.

52. Ibid., 249.

53. Ibid., 247.

54. Ibid., 248. For a broader treatment of the central role of prophetic discourse in the dissenting traditions of American political thought, especially as those traditions bear on questions of race, see Shulman, *American Prophecy*.

55. Rogers, *We Are All Together Now*, 17.

56. Rawls, *Political Liberalism*, 247–54.

57. Amy Gutmann and Dennis Thompson, *Why Deliberative Democracy?*, 51. See also Gutmann and Thompson, *Democracy and Disagreement*, 133–37.

58. John Rawls, "The Idea of Public Reason Revisited," *Law of Peoples*, 129–80, 142–43.

59. Ibid., 152.

60. Connolly, *The Ethos of Pluralization*, 186.

61. Rawls, *Political Liberalism*, 254.

62. Cover, *Justice Accused*.

63. Fanuzzi, *Abolition's Public Sphere*, xix.

64. Douglass, "The Do-Nothing Policy," *Frederick Douglass*, ed. Foner, 342–44, 355.

65. "West India Emancipation," *Frederick Douglass*, ed. Foner, 358–68, 367. Douglass's insistence that quiescence does not in any way indicate the absence of domination clearly resonates with the "power debates" and the critique of pluralism that preoccupied American political scientists in the 1970s. The best study to emerge from these debates, and the one that provides the clearest sense of the stakes of these debates for democratic theory and for democratic politics, is John Gaventa, *Power and Powerlessness*.

66. Cited in Fanuzzi, *Abolition's Public Sphere*, xii–xiii.

67. Ibid., xiv.

68. Douglass, *My Bondage and My Freedom*, 337.

69. "The Dred Scott Decision," *Frederick Douglass*, ed. Foner, 345–46.

70. Bourdieu, *Outline of a Theory of Practice*, 167.

71. Markell, "The Potential and the Actual," 36.

72. Douglass, *My Bondage and My Freedom*, 266.

73. Frederick Douglass, *Narrative of the Life of Frederick Douglass*, 111.

74. Rancière, *Dis-agreement*, 29–30. "The police is thus first an order of bodies that defines the allocation of ways of doing, ways of being, ways of saying, and sees that those bodies are assigned by name to a particular place and task; it is an order of the visible and the sayable that sees that a particular activity is visible and another is not, that this speech is understood as discourse and another as noise" (29).

75. Baldwin, "They Can't Turn Back," *Collected Essays*, 622–37, 623.

76. For a wonderful exploration of this theme in Baldwin's work as it relates to debates in contemporary democratic theory, see Balfour, *The Evidence of Things Not Said*.

77. Rancière, *Dis-agreement*, 88.

78. Baldwin, "The Fire Next Time," *Collected Essays*, 291–348, 294.

79. Sokol, *There Goes My Everything*, 63.

80. Rancière, *Dis-agreement*, 40.

81. See Balfour, *The Evidence of Things Not Said*, 135–39.

82. Baldwin, "The Dangerous Road before Martin Luther King," *Collected Essays*, 638–58, 658.

83. "Achieving our country" comes from the final sentence of Baldwin's "The Fire Next Time," 346; Emerson, "Experience," *Essays: First and Second Series*, 241–62, 255; Hughes, "Let America Be America Again," *Collected Poems of Langston Hughes*, 189.

84. Sacvan Bercovitch has made the strongest case for the all-absorbing hegemony of the figure of the "unfinished mission" in American political cultures from the seventeenth century through the Revolution and to the present day, claiming that through the ubiquitous Jeremiadic imperatives of the chosen people all varieties of political dissent and resistance are invariably enlisted in the forces of a narrow cultural continuity. It is a provocative thesis. However, the formalism of Bercovitch's approach, his presumption that such a ritualized identity exists apart from competing claims to speak on its behalf, too quickly enfolds these different historical enactments within a largely undifferentiated "ritual" of collective belonging. He is insufficiently attentive to how "the" ritualized invocation gets refigured and contested through these claims, that no ritual exists independently of these alternative claimings. The possible failure of the ritual is its own condition of possibility. See Bercovitch, *Rites of Assent*.

85. Gravely, "The Dialectic of Double-Consciousness in Black American Freedom Celebrations"; Shane White, "It Was a Proud Day: African Americans, Festivals, and Parades in the North, 1741–1834."

86. Glaude, *Exodus!*, 86.

87. Rancière, *Dis-agreement*, 88.

88. Ellison, *Invisible Man*, 581.

89. I take this formulation from the work of Stanley Cavell. See his *The Claim of Reason*, 22.

90. Danielle Allen, *Talking to Strangers*, 68.

CONCLUSION Prospective Time

1. Pocock, *Politics, Language, and Time*, 233.

2. Wolin, "Fugitive Democracy," 43.

3. According to Anders Stephenson, postrevolutionary Americans had "no readily available mythology of ethnogenesis to which one could appeal." See his *Manifest Destiny*, 20.

4. Allen, *Talking to Strangers*, 69.

5. Claude Lefort, *Democracy and Political Theory*, 13.

6. Michelman, "How Can the People Ever Make the Laws?"; Habermas, "Constitutional Democracy." Further references placed parenthetically in the text preceded by M and H. See also Frank Michelman, "Always under Law?"; and Frank Michelman, "Can Constitutional Democrats Be Legal Positivists?"

7. Jürgen Habermas, *The Inclusion of the Other*, 69.

8. For an elaboration of this point see my "'Unauthorized Propositions.'"

9. Michelman, "Law's Republic."

10. Arendt, *On Revolution*, 198.

11. Bonnie Honig, *Emergency Politics*, 36.

12. Arendt, *On Revolution*, 221.

13. For a useful overview see Alan Gibson, *Interpreting the Founding*.

14. Wolin, "Contract and Birthright," *The Presence of the Past*, 137–50, 141.

15. Charles Taylor, "What Is a 'Social Imaginary?,'" *Modern Social Imaginaries*, 23–30, 23.

16. Lienesch, *New Order of the Ages*, 166.

17. Benjamin Rush, "Address to the People of the United States," *The Documentary History of the Ratification of the Constitution*, ed. Kaminski, Saladino, and Jensen, vol. 13, 46–49, 49.

18. Bercovitch, *Rites of Assent*, 43–46.

19. Norton, *95 Theses on Politics, Culture, Method*, 133.

20. Ankersmit, *Aesthetic Politics*, 21–63.

21. Smith, *Stories of Peoplehood*.

22. See for example Arendt, "What Is Authority?," *Between Past and Future*, 91–142.

23. Mathes, *Rape of Lucretia and the Founding of Republics*, 8. See also Smith, *Politics and Remembrance*.

24. Adair, *Fame and the Founding Fathers*.

25. Pocock, *The Machiavellian Moment*, viii.

26. Breen, *The Lockean Moment*.

27. Wolin, "Contract and Birthright," *The Presence of the Past*, 144.

28. Cited in Jacobus Tenbroek, *Antislavery Origins of the Fourteenth Amendment*, 63.

29. See Jacobson, *Pride and Solace*.

30. Connolly, *Why I Am Not a Secularist*, 71; *The Ethos of Pluralization*, 184.

31. Dienstag, *Dancing in Chains*, 15.

32. Ackerman, *We the People*, 204–5.

33. Walter Benjamin, "Theses on the Philosophy of History," *Illuminations*, 253–64, 254.

34. Adams, *The First American Constitutions*, 31.

35. Thompson, "Is There Anything 'Legal' About Extralegal Action?"

36. *The Camden 28*.

37. Keenan, "Remember Jacques Derrida (Part 2)."

38. Beltran, "Achieving the Extraordinary"; Charles Krauthammer, "Immigrants Must Choose," *Washington Post*, 14 April 2006, § A, 17.

39. Wolin, "*E Pluribus Unum*: The Representation of Difference and the Reconstitution of Collectivity," *The Presence of the Past*, 120–36, 136.

40. Cavell, "Finding as Founding," 105.

41. Cavell, *The Claim of Reason*, 27.

Bibliography

Aaron, Daniel. "Whitman and the Founding Fathers." *Mickle Street Review*
10 (1988), 5–1.
Abrams, M. H. *The Mirror and the Lamp: Romantic Theory and the Critical
Tradition.* New York: Oxford University Press, 1971.
———. *Natural Supernaturalism: Tradition and Revolution in Romantic
Literature.* New York: W. W. Norton, 1973.
Abzug, Robert H. *Cosmos Crumbling: American Reform and the Religious
Imagination.* New York: Oxford University Press, 1994.
Ackerman, Bruce. *We the People: Foundations.* Cambridge: Harvard University
Press, 1991.
Adair, Douglas G. *Fame and the Founding Fathers: Essays by Douglas Adair,*
ed. T. Colburn. New York: W. W. Norton, 1974.
Adams, John. *Correspondence between the Honorable John Adams and William
Cunningham, 1803–1812,* ed. E. M. Cunningham. Boston: True and Greene,
1823.
———. *The Works of John Adams,* vols. 1–10, ed. Charles Francis Adams.
Boston, 1850.

———. *Diary and Autobiography of John Adams*, vols. 1–4, *Diary (1755–1804) and Autobiography (through 1780)*, ed. L. H. Butterfield, Leonard C. Faber, and Wendell D. Garrett. Cambridge: Harvard University Press, 1961.

———. *Legal Papers of John Adams*, vols. 1–3, ed. L. Kinvin Wroth and Hiller B. Zobel. Cambridge: Harvard University Press, 1965.

———. *Papers of John Adams*, ed. Robert Joseph Taylor, Mary-Jo Kline, and Gregg L. Lint. Cambridge: Belknap, 1977.

———. *The Political Writings of John Adams*, ed. George Wescott Carey. Washington: Regnery, 2000.

Adams, Samuel. *The Writings of Samuel Adams*, ed. Harry A. Cushing. New York: G. P. Putnam and Sons, 1908.

Adams, Willi Paul. *The First American Constitutions: Republican Ideology and the Making of the State Constitutions in the Revolutionary Era*. Chapel Hill: University of North Carolina Press, 1980.

Agamben, Giorgio. "What Is a People?" *Means without End: Notes on Politics*, ed. C. Casarino, 29–36. Minneapolis: University of Minnesota Press, 2000.

Alexander, John K. "The Fort Wilson Incident of 1779: A Case Study of the Revolutionary Crowd." *William and Mary Quarterly* 31 (1974), 589–612.

Allen, Danielle. *Talking to Strangers: Anxieties of Citizenship since Brown v. Board of Education*. Chicago: University of Chicago Press, 2004.

Althusser, Louis. "Ideology and the Ideological State Apparatuses: (Notes toward an Investigation)." *Lenin and Philosophy and Other Essays*, trans. B. Brewster, 127–86. New York: Monthly Review Press, 1971.

Ames, Fisher. *Works of Fisher Ames*, vols. 1–2, ed. W. B. Allen. Indianapolis: Liberty, 1983.

Ankersmit, F. R. *Aesthetic Politics: Political Philosophy beyond Fact and Value*. Palo Alto: Stanford University Press, 1996.

Appleby, Joyce Oldham. *Capitalism and a New Social Order: The Republican Vision of the 1790s*. New York: New York University Press, 1984.

———. *Liberalism and Republicanism in the Historical Imagination*. Cambridge: Harvard University Press, 1992.

Arato, Andrew. "Carl Schmitt and the Revival of the Doctrine of Constituent Power in the United States." *Cardozo Law Review* 21 (1999), 1739–47.

———. *Civil Society, Constitution, and Legitimacy*. New York: Rowman and Littlefield, 2000.

Arendt, Hannah. "Understanding and Politics." *Partisan Review* 20 (1953), 377–392.

———. *The Human Condition*. Chicago: University of Chicago Press, 1958.

———. *The Origins of Totalitarianism*. Cleveland: World, 1958.

———. *Eichmann in Jerusalem: A Report on the Banality of Evil*. London: Faber and Faber, 1963.

———. *Men in Dark Times*. New York: Harcourt Brace Jovanovich, 1968.

———. *Crisis of the Republic*. New York: Harcourt Brace Jovanovich, 1972.

————. *Between Past and Future.* New York: Penguin, 1977.

————. *The Life of the Mind: One Volume Edition.* New York: Harcourt Brace Jovanovich, 1978.

————. *Lectures on Kant's Political Philosophy.* Chicago: University of Chicago Press, 1982.

————. *On Revolution.* New York: Penguin, 1990.

————. "Montesquieu's Revision of the Tradition." *The Promise of Politics,* ed. Jerome Kohn, 63–69. New York: Schocken, 2005.

Arensberg, Mary. *The American Sublime.* Albany: State University of New York Press, 1986.

Austin, J. L. *How to Do Things with Words.* Cambridge: Harvard University Press, 1975.

————. *Philosophical Papers,* ed. J. O. Urmson and G. J. Warnock. Oxford: Oxford University Press, 1979.

Axelrod, Alan. *Charles Brockden Brown: An American Tale.* Austin: University of Texas Press, 1983.

Bacon, Jacqueline. ""Do You Understand Your Own Language?' Revolutionary Topoi in the Rhetoric of African-American Abolitionists." *Rhetoric Society Quarterly* 28, no. 2 (1998), 55–75.

Bailyn, Bernard. *Ideological Origins of the American Revolution.* Cambridge: Harvard University Press, 1974.

————, ed. *The Debate on the Constitution: Federalist and Antifederalist Speeches, Articles and Letters during the Struggle over Ratification,* vols. 1–2. New York: Library of America, 1993.

Bakhtin, Mikhail. "Discourse in the Novel." *The Dialogic Imagination: Four Essays,* ed. Vadim Liapunov, trans. Kenneth Bostrom, 259–422. Austin: University of Texas Press, 1981.

Baldwin, James. *Collected Essays.* New York: Library of America, 1998.

Balfour, Lawrie. *The Evidence of Things Not Said: James Baldwin and the Promise of American Democracy.* Ithaca: Cornell University Press, 2001.

Banfield, G. J. Barker. *The Culture of Sensibility: Sex and Society in Eighteenth-Century England.* Chicago: University of Chicago Press, 1992.

Banning, Lance. "Republican Ideology and the Triumph of the Constitution, 1789–1793." *William and Mary Quarterly,* 31, no. 2 (1974), 167–88.

————. *The Jeffersonian Persuasion.* Ithaca: Cornell University Press, 1978.

Barnes, Elizabeth. *States of Sympathy: Seduction and Democracy in the American Novel.* New York: Columbia University Press, 1997.

Barthes, Roland. *The Grain of the Voice: Interviews, 1962–1980,* trans. Linda Coverdale. Berkeley: University of California Press, 1991.

Beeman, Richard R. "Deference, Republicanism and the Emergence of Popular Politics in Eighteenth-Century America." *William and Mary Quarterly* 49, no. 3 (1992), 401–30.

Beeman, Richard R, Stephen Botein, and Edward D. Carter II, eds. *Beyond*

Confederation: Origins of the Constitution and American National Identity.
Chapel Hill: University of North Carolina Press, 1987.

Beer, Samuel H. "Liberty and Union: Walt Whitman's Idea of the Nation."
Political Theory 12, no. 3 (1984), 331–60.

———. *To Make a Nation: The Rediscovery of American Federalism.* Cambridge:
Belknap, 1993.

Beiser, Frederick. *The Sovereignty of Reason: The Defense of Rationality in the
Early English Enlightenment.* Princeton: Princeton University Press, 1996.

Bellis, Peter J. "Against Representation: The 1855 Edition of Leaves of Grass."
Centennial Review 43, no. 1 (1999), 71–94.

Beltran, Christina. "Achieving the Extraordinary: Hannah Arendt, Immigrant
Action and the Space of Appearance." *Political Theory,* forthcoming.

Benhabib, Seyla. "Hannah Arendt and the Redemptive Power of Narrative."
Social Research, 1990, 167–96.

———, ed. *Democracy and Difference: Contesting the Boundaries of the Political.*
Princeton: Princeton University Press, 1996.

———. "Democracy and Difference: Reflections on the Metapolitics of
Lyotard and Derrida." *Journal of Political Philosophy* 2 (1995), 1–23.

Benjamin, Walter. *Illuminations: Essays and Reflections.* New York: Schocken,
1969.

———. *Reflections: Essays, Aphorisms, Autobiographical Writings,* ed. Peter
Demetz. New York: Schocken, 1978.

Bennett, Jane. "'How Is It, Then, That We Still Remain Barbarians?' Foucault,
Schiller, and the Aestheticization of Ethics." *Political Theory* 24, no. 4
(1996), 653–72.

Bercovitch, Sacvan. *Rites of Assent: Transformations in the Symbolic Construction
of America.* New York: Routledge, 1993.

Black, Eugene Charlton. *The Association: British Extraparliamentary Political
Organization, 1769–1793.* Cambridge: Harvard University Press, 1963.

Blair, Hugh. *An Abridgement of Lectures on Rhetoric.* Cambridge: Cambridge
University Press, 1802.

Bloch, Ernst. *The Principle of Hope,* trans. Paul Knight, Neville Plaice, and
Stephen Plaice. Cambridge: MIT Press, 1995.

Bloch, Ruth H. *Visionary Republic: Millennial Themes in American Thought,
1756–1800.* New York: Cambridge University Press, 1985.

Bloom, Harold. "Emerson and Whitman: The American Sublime." *Poetry and
Repression: Revisionism from Blake to Stevens,* 253–56. New Haven: Yale
University Press, 1976.

Boas, George. *Vox Populi: Essays in the History of an Idea.* Baltimore: Johns
Hopkins University Press, 1969.

Bodnar, John. *Remaking America: Public Memory, Commemoration, and
Patriotism in the Twentieth Century.* Princeton: Princeton University Press,
1992.

Boudreau, Kristin. "Early American Criminal Narratives and the Problem of Public Sentiments." *Early American Literature* 32, no. 3 (1997), 249–69.

Bourdieu, Pierre. *Outline of a Theory of Practice.* Cambridge: Cambridge University Press, 1977.

———. *In Other Words: Essays towards a Reflexive Sociology.* Palo Alto: Stanford University Press, 1990.

Bouton, Terry. *Taming Democracy: "The People," the Founders, and the Troubled Ending of the American Revolution.* New York: Oxford University Press, 2007.

Boxhill, Bernard. "Two Traditions in African American Political Philosophy." *Philosophical Forum* 24, nos. 1–3 (1992), 119–35.

Breen, T. H. *The Lockean Moment.* New York: Oxford University Press, 2001.

Brooke, John L. "Ancient Lodges and Self-Created Societies: Voluntary Associations and the Public Sphere in the Early Republic." *Launching the "Extended Republic": The Federalist Era,* ed. R. Hoffman and P. J. Albert, 273–377. Charlottesville: University Press of Virginia, 1996.

Brown, Charles Brockden. *Rhapsodist and Other Uncollected Writings.* Gainesville: Scholars' Facsimiles and Reprints, 1977.

———. "Thessalonica: A Roman Story." *Somnambulism and Other Stories,* ed. Alfred Weber, 25–52. Frankfurt am Main: Peter Lang, 1987.

———. "Walstein's School of History. From the German of Krants of Gotha." *Literary Essays and Reviews,* ed. Alfred Weber, Wolfgang Schafer, and John R. Holmes, 31–38. Frankfurt am Main: Peter Lang, 1987.

———. *Edgar Huntly, or Memoirs of a Sleep-Walker,* ed. Norman S. Grabo. New York: Penguin, 1988.

———. *Wieland and Memoirs of Carwin the Biloquist,* ed. J. Fliegelman. New York: Penguin, 1991.

Brown, Gordon S. *Toussaint's Clause: The Founding Fathers and the Haitian Revolution.* Jackson: University Press of Mississippi, 2005.

Brown, Richard D. *The Strength of a People: The Idea of an Informed Citizenry in America, 1650–1870.* Chapel Hill: University of North Carolina Press, 1996.

Brown, William Hill. *The Power of Sympathy.* New York: Penguin, 1997.

Burgett, Bruce. *Sentimental Bodies: Sex, Gender and Citizenship in the Early Republic.* Princeton: Princeton University Press, 1998.

Burgh, James. *Political Disquisitions; or, an Enquiry into Public Errors, Defects, and Abuses,* vols. 1–3. Philadelphia: Robert Bell, 1775.

———. *Art of Speaking, Containing an Essay in Which Are Given Rules for Expressing Properly the Principal Passions and Humours, Which Occur in Reading or Public Speaking.* Baltimore, 1804.

Burke, Edmund. *Reflections on the Revolution in France.* Indianapolis: Hackett, 1987.

———. *A Philosophical Enquiry into the Sublime and Beautiful.* New York: Penguin, 1998.

————. *On Empire, Liberty, and Reform: Speeches and Letters*, ed. David Bromwich. New Haven: Yale University Press, 2000.

Burke, Kenneth. "Revolutionary Symbolism in America." *American Writers' Congress*, ed. Hart, 87–94.

————. *Language as Symbolic Action: Essays on Life, Literature, and Method.* Berkeley: University of California Press, 1966.

————. *A Rhetoric of Motives.* Berkeley: University of California Press, 1969.

Burns, Robert. "Hannah Arendt's Constitutional Thought." *Amor Mundi: Explorations in the Faith and Thought of Hannah Arendt*, ed. James W. Bernauer, 157–85. Boston: Martinus Nijhoff, 1987.

Butler, Judith. *Excitable Speech: A Politics of the Performative.* New York: Routledge, 1997.

Cahill, Edward. "An Adventurous and Lawless Fancy: Charles Brockden Brown's Aesthetic State." *Early American Literature* 36, no. 1 (2001), 31–70.

Camden 28. Anthony Giachino. EEC Media, 2007.

Canovan, Margaret. "The People, the Masses, and the Mobilization of Power: The Paradox of Hannah Arendt's 'Populism.'" *Social Research* 69, no. 2 (2002), 403–22.

————. *The People.* New York: Polity, 2005.

Cappon, J. L., ed. *The Adams-Jefferson Letters: The Complete Correspondence between Thomas Jefferson and Abigail and John Adams.* Chapel Hill: University of North Carolina Press, 1959.

Carlson, Eric T., and Meredith M. Simpson. "Benjamin Rush's Medical Use of the Moral Faculty." *Bulletin of the History of Medicine* 39, no. 1 (1965), 22–33.

Carlson, Eric T., and Jeffrey L. Wollock. "Benjamin Rush on Politics and Human Nature." *Journal of the American Medical Association* 236, no. 1 (1976), 73–77.

Carlyle, Thomas. "Shooting Niagara: And After?" *Critical and Miscellaneous Essays*, 200–241. London: Chapman and Hall, 1894.

Cavell, Stanley. *The Claim of Reason: Wittgenstein, Skepticism, Morality and Tragedy.* New York: Oxford University Press, 1979.

————. "Finding as Founding." *This New yet Unapproachable America: Lectures after Emerson after Wittgenstein*, 77–118. Albuquerque: Living Batch, 1989.

Chauncey, Charles. *Enthusiasm Described and Cautioned against.* Boston: Draper for Eliot and Blanchard, 1742.

Chesney, Robert M. "How Can the Law Regulate Loyalty without Imperiling It? Democratic-Republican Societies, Subversion, and the Limits of Legitimate Political Dissent in the Early Republic." *North Carolina Law Review* 82 (2004), 1525–79.

Christodoulidis, Emilios A. "The Aporia of Sovereignty: On the Representation of the People in Constitutional Discourse." *King's College Law Journal* 12, no. 1 (2001), 111–33.

Clark, David Lee. *Charles Brockden Brown: Pioneer Voice of America*. Durham: Duke University Press, 1952.

Clark, Peter. *British Clubs and Societies, 1580–1800: The Origins of the Associational World*. New York: Oxford University Press, 2000.

Clarkson, Carrol. "Who Are 'We'? Don't Make Me Laugh." *Law and Critique* 18, no. 3 (2007), 361–74.

Cmiel, Kenneth. *Democratic Eloquence: The Fight over Popular Speech in Nineteenth Century America*. Berkeley: University of California Press, 1990.

Cobbett, William. *Peter Porcupine in America: Pamphlets on Republicanism and Revolution*, ed. David A. Wilson. Ithaca: Cornell University Press, 1994.

Cohn, Norman. *The Pursuit of the Millennium: Revolutionary Millenarians and Mystical Anarchists of the Middle Ages*. New York: Oxford University Press, 1961.

Colaiaco, James A. *Frederick Douglass and the Fourth of July*. New York: Palgrave Macmillan, 2006.

Connolly, William E. *Political Theory and Modernity*. New York: Blackwell, 1988.

———. *The Ethos of Pluralization*. Minneapolis: University of Minnesota Press, 1995.

———. *Why I Am Not a Secularist*. Minneapolis: University of Minnesota Press, 1999.

———. *Neuropolitics: Thinking, Culture, Speed*. Minneapolis: University of Minnesota Press, 2002.

Conroy, David W. "Development of a Revolutionary Organization, 1765–75." *A Companion to the American Revolution*, ed. Jack P. Greene and J. R. Pole, 216–21. Malden, Mass.: Blackwell, 2003.

Cooke, Jacob E., ed. *The Federalist*. Middletown, Conn.: Wesleyan University Press, 1961.

Cooke, Maeve. *Language and Reason: A Study of Habermas's Pragmatics*. Cambridge: MIT Press, 1997.

Cornell, Saul. *The Other Founders: Anti-Federalism and the Dissenting Tradition in America, 1788–1828*. Chapel Hill: University of North Carolina Press, 1999.

Cover, Robert. *Justice Accused: Antislavery and the Judicial Process*. New Haven: Yale University Press, 1975.

———. "Nomos and Narrative." *Narrative, Violence, and the Law: The Essays of Robert Cover*, ed. Martha Minow, 95–172. Ann Arbor: University of Michigan Press, 1995.

Cowans, Jon. *To Speak for the People: Public Opinion and the Problem of Legitimacy in the French Revolution*. New York: Routledge, 2001.

Crèvecoeur, J. Hector St. John de. *Letters from an American Farmer*, ed. S. Manning. New York: Oxford University Press, 1997.

Dahl, Robert Alan. *After the Revolution: Authority in a Good Society*. New Haven: Yale University Press, 1970.

Davidson, Cathy N. *Revolution and the Word: The Rise of the Novel in America.* New York: Oxford University Press, 1986.

Davis, Jeffrey A. "Guarding the Republican Interest: The Western Pennsylvania Democratic Societies and the Excise Tax." *Pennsylvania History* 67 (2000), 43–62.

Davis, Susan G. *Parades and Power: Street Theatre in Nineteenth-Century Philadelphia.* Berkeley: University of California Press, 1988.

De Baecque, Antoine. "The Allegorical Image of France, 1750–1800: A Political Crisis of Representation." *Representations* 47 (1994), 111–43.

De Bolla, Peter. *The Discourse of the Sublime: Readings in History, Aesthetics, and the Subject.* New York: Basil Blackwell, 1989.

Deleuze, Gilles, and Felix Guattari. *A Thousand Plateaus: Capitalism and Schizophrenia.* Minneapolis: University of Minnesota Press, 1987.

D'Elia, Ronald. "The Republican Theology of Benjamin Rush." *Pennsylvania History* 33, no. 2 (1966), 187–203.

———. "Benjamin Rush, David Hartley and the Revolutionary Uses of Psychology." *Proceedings of the American Philosophical Society* 114 (1970), 109–18.

———. *Benjamin Rush, Philosopher of the American Revolution.* Philadelphia: Transactions of the American Philosophical Society, 1974.

Derrida, Jacques. *Of Grammatology.* Baltimore: Johns Hopkins University Press, 1974.

———. "Signature Event Context." *Margins of Philosophy*, trans. Alan Bass, 307–30. Chicago: University of Chicago Press, 1982.

———. "Declarations of Independence." *New Political Science* 15 (1986), 7–17.

———. "Force of Law: The Mystical Foundations of Authority." *Deconstruction and the Possibility of Justice*, ed. D. Cornell, M. Rosenfeld, and D. G. Carlson, 3–67. New York: Routledge, 1992.

Dienstag, Joshua. *Dancing in Chains: Narrative and Memory in Political Theory.* Palo Alto: Stanford University Press, 1997.

Dippel, Horst. "The Changing Idea of Popular Sovereignty in Early American Constitutionalism: Breaking Away from European Patterns." *Journal of the Early Republic* 16, no. 1 (1996), 21–45.

Disch, Lisa. *Hannah Arendt and the Limits of Philosophy.* Ithaca: Cornell University Press, 1996.

Disraeli, Isaac. *Curiosities of Literature: Consisting of Anecdotes, Characters, Sketches, and Observations, Literary, Critical, and Historical.* London: Printed for J. Murray, 1791.

Douglass, Frederick. *Life and Times of Frederick Douglass: His Early Life as a Slave, His Escape from Bondage, and His Complete History.* New York: Collier, 1962.

———. *The Frederick Douglass Papers*, ser. 1, *Speeches, Debates, and Interviews*, ed. John W. Blassingame. New Haven: Yale University Press, 1982.

———. *Narrative of the Life of Frederick Douglass, an American Slave*. New York: Penguin, 1982.

———. "What to the Slave Is the Fourth of July?" *The American Intellectual Tradition*, vol. 1, *1630–1865*, ed. Hollinger and Capper, 492–506.

———. *Frederick Douglass: Selected Speeches and Writings*, ed. Philip S. Foner. Chicago: Lawrence Hill, 1999.

———. *My Bondage and My Freedom*. New York: Penguin, 2003.

Dumm, Thomas. *Democracy and Punishment: Disciplinary Origins of the United States*. Madison: University of Wisconsin Press, 1987.

Durey, Michael. *Transatlantic Radicals and the Early American Republic*. Lawrence: University of Kansas Press, 1997.

Dworkin, Ronald. "Rights as Trumps." *Theories of Rights*, ed. Jeremy Waldron, 153–67. New York: Oxford University Press, 1984.

Dyzenhaus, David, ed. *Law as Politics: Carl Schmitt's Critique of Liberalism*. Durham: Duke University Press, 1998.

Edwards, Jonathan. *A Jonathan Edwards Reader*, ed. J. E. Smith, H. S. Stout, and K. P. Minkema. New Haven: Yale University Press, 1995.

Elkins, Stanley, and Eric McKitrick. *The Age of Federalism: The Early American Republic, 1788–1800*. New York: Oxford University Press, 1993.

Ellis, Richard J. *The Dark Side of the Left: Illiberal Egalitarianism in America*. Lawrence: University of Kansas Press, 1998.

Ellison, Ralph. *Invisible Man*. New York: Vintage, 1995.

Emerson, Ralph Waldo. *Complete Works of Ralph Waldo Emerson*, vols. 1–12. Boston: Houghton Mifflin, 1903–4.

———. *Selected Essays*, ed. Larzer Ziff. New York: Penguin, 1982.

———. *Essays: First and Second Series*. New York: Library of America, 1990.

———. *Representative Men*. Cambridge: Harvard University Press, 1996.

Epstein, James A. *Radical Expression: Political Language, Ritual, and Symbol in England, 1790–1850*. New York: Oxford University Press, 1994.

Erkkila, Betsy. *Whitman the Political Poet*. New York: Oxford University Press, 1989.

Fanuzzi, Robert. *Abolition's Public Sphere*. Minneapolis: University of Minnesota Press, 2003.

Farr, James. "Political Science and the Enlightenment of Enthusiasm." *American Political Science Review* 82, no. 1 (1988), 51–69.

Fehrenbacher, Don E. *The Dred Scott Case: Its Significance in American Law and Politics*. New York: Oxford University Press, 1978.

Ferguson, Frances. *Solitude and the Sublime: Romanticism and the Aesthetics of Individuation*. New York: Routledge, 1992.

Ferguson, Robert A. *The American Enlightenment, 1750–1820*. Cambridge: Harvard University Press, 1994.

Finley, M. I. *Politics in the Ancient World*. Cambridge: Cambridge University Press, 1991.

Fliegelman, Jay. *Prodigals and Pilgrims: The American Revolution against Patri-archal Authority, 1750–1800.* Cambridge: Cambridge University Press, 1982.

———. *Declaring Independence: Jefferson, Natural Language and the Culture of Performance.* Palo Alto: Stanford University Press, 1993.

Foner, Philip S., ed. *The Democratic-Republican Societies, 1790–1800: A Documentary Sourcebook of Constitutions, Declarations, Addresses, Resolutions, and Toasts.* Westport, Conn.: Greenwood, 1976.

Forget, Evelyn L. "Evocations of Sympathy: Sympathetic Imagery in Eighteenth-Century Social Theory and Physiology." *History of Political Economy* 35 (2003), 282–308.

Forsyth, Murray. "Thomas Hobbes and the Constituent Power of the People." *Political Studies* 24, no. 2 (1981), 191–203.

Foucault, Michel. *Discipline and Punish: The Birth of the Prison.* New York: Vintage, 1979.

———. *Power/Knowledge: Selected Interviews and Other Writings, 1972–1977,* ed. C. Gordon. New York: Pantheon, 1980.

———. *Essential Works of Foucault, 1954–1984,* vols. 1–3, ed. James Faubion and Paul Rabinow. New York: New Press, 1984.

———. *The Foucault Effect: Studies in Governmentality with Two Lectures by and an Interview with Michel Foucault,* ed. G. Burchell, C. Gordon, and P. Miller. Chicago: University of Chicago Press, 1991.

Frank, Jason. "'Besides Our Selves': An Essay on Enthusiastic Politics and Civil Subjectivity." *Public Culture* 17, no. 3 (2005), 371–92.

———. "Unauthorized Propositions: *The Federalist Papers* and Constituent Power." *Diacritics* 32, nos. 2–3 (2007), 103–20.

Franklin, Julian H. *John Locke and the Theory of Sovereignty: Mixed Monarchy and the Right of Resistance in the Political Thought of the English Revolution.* Cambridge: Cambridge University Press, 1978.

Furet, François. *Interpreting the French Revolution.* New York: Cambridge University Press, 1981.

Gaventa, John. *Power and Powerlessness: Quiescence and Rebellion in an Appalachian Valley.* Urbana: University of Illinois Press, 1982.

Gibson, Alan Ray. *Interpreting the Founding: Guide to the Enduring Debates over the Origins and Foundations of the American Republic.* Lawrence: University Press of Kansas, 2006.

Gilje, Paul A. *Road to Mobocracy: Popular Disorder in New York City, 1763–1834.* Chapel Hill: University of North Carolina Press, 1987.

———. *Rioting in America.* Bloomington: Indiana University Press, 1996.

Gilmore, Michael T. *American Romanticism and the Marketplace.* Chicago: University of Chicago Press, 1988.

Glacken, Clarence J. *Traces on the Rhodian Shore: Nature and Culture in Western Thought from Ancient Times to the End of the Eighteenth Century.* Berkeley: University of California Press, 1976.

Glaude, Eddie S. *Exodus! Religion, Race, and Nation in Early Nineteenth-Century Black America*. Chicago: University of Chicago Press, 2000.

Godwin, William. *Enquiry concerning Political Justice*. New York: Penguin, 1985.

Goldhammer, Jesse R. "Walt Whitman: Democracy's Janus-Faced Poet." *Critical Sense*, 1996, 37–67.

Gravely, William. "The Dialectic of Double Consciousness in Black American Freedom Celebrations." *Journal of African American Philosophy* 67, no. 4 (1982), 302–17.

Griswold, Rufus W. *The Republican Court, or, American Society in the Days of Washington*. New York: D. Appleton, 1854.

Grossman, Allan. "The Poetics of Union in Whitman and Lincoln: An Inquiry toward the Relationship of Art and Policy." *The American Renaissance Reconsidered: Selected Papers from the English Institute, 1982–83*, ed. Walter Benn Michaels and Donald E. Pease, 183–208. Baltimore: Johns Hopkins University Press, 1985.

Gustafson, Sandra M. *Eloquence Is Power: Oratory and Performance in Early America*. Chapel Hill: University of North Carolina Press, 2000.

Gustafson, Thomas B. *Representative Words: Politics, Literature, and the American Language, 1776–1865*. Cambridge: Cambridge University Press, 1992.

Gutmann, Amy, and Dennis Thompson. *Democracy and Disagreement*. Cambridge: Harvard University Press, 1996.

———. *Why Deliberative Democracy?* Princeton: Princeton University Press, 2004.

Haakonssen, Lisbeth. *Medicine and Morals in the Enlightenment: John Gregory, Thomas Percival, and Benjamin Rush*. Amsterdam: Rodopi, 1997.

Habermas, Jürgen. *The Philosophical Discourse of Modernity: Twelve Lectures*. Cambridge: MIT Press, 1987.

———. *The Structural Transformation of the Public Sphere: An Inquiry into a Category of Bourgeois Society*. Cambridge: MIT Press, 1992.

———. "Reconciliation through the Public Use of Reason: Remarks on John Rawls's Political Liberalism." *Journal of Philosophy* 92, no. 3 (1995), 109–31.

———. *Between Facts and Norms: Contributions to a Discourse Theory of Law and Democracy*. Cambridge: MIT Press, 1996.

———. *The Inclusion of the Other: Studies in Political Theory*. Cambridge: MIT Press, 1998.

———. "Constitutional Democracy: A Paradoxical Union of Contradictory Principles?" *Political Theory* 29, no. 6 (2001), 766–81.

Hamilton, Alexander. *Papers of Alexander Hamilton*, vols. 1–27, ed. Harold Syrett. New York: Columbia University Press, 1961–87.

Handlin, Mary, and Oscar Handlin, eds. *The Popular Sources of Political Authority: Documents on the Massachusetts Constitution of 1780*. Cambridge: Belknap, 1966.

Hanson, Russell L. *The Democratic Imagination in America: Conversations with Our Past*. Princeton: Princeton University Press, 1985.

Harding, Samuel Banister. *Select Orations Illustrating American Political History*. New York: Macmillan, 1909.

Hardt, Michael, and Antonio Negri. *Multitude: War and Democracy in the Age of Empire*. New York: Penguin, 2004.

Hariman, Robert. *Political Style: The Artistry of Power*. Chicago: University of Chicago Press, 1995.

Harris, Marc L. "Civil Society in Post-Revolutionary America." *Empire and Nation: The American Revolution in the Atlantic World*, ed. Eliga H. Gould and Peter S. Onuf, 197–216. Baltimore: Johns Hopkins University Press, 2004.

Hart, H. L. A. *The Concept of Law*. London: Oxford University Press, 1961.

Hart, Henry, ed. *American Writers' Congress*. New York: International, 1935.

Hazlitt, William. "What Is the People?" *Selected Writings*, ed. John Cook, 3–28. New York: Oxford University Press, 2009.

Heimart, Alan. *Religion and the American Mind, from the Great Awakening to the Revolution*. Cambridge: Harvard University Press, 1966.

Hemberger, Suzette. "A Government Based on Representations." *Studies in American Political Development* 10 (1996), 289–332.

Herzog, Don. *Poisoning the Minds of the Lower Orders*. Princeton: Princeton University Press, 1998.

Heyd, Michael. *"Be Sober and Reasonable": The Critique of Enthusiasm in the Seventeenth and Early Eighteenth Centuries*. Leiden: E. J. Brill, 1995.

Hill, Melvyn A., ed. *Hannah Arendt: The Recovery of the Public World*. New York: St. Martin's, 1979.

Hobsbawm, Eric. *Primitive Rebels*. Manchester: Manchester University Press, 1964.

Hoerder, Dirk. *Crowd Action in Revolutionary Massachusetts, 1765–1780*. New York: Academic, 1977.

Hofstadter, Richard. *The Idea of a Party System: The Rise of Legitimate Opposition in the United States, 1780–1840*. Berkeley: University of California Press, 1969.

———. *The American Political Tradition and the Men Who Made It*. New York: Vintage, 1989.

Holland, Catherine. *The Body Politic: Foundings, Citizenship, and Difference in the American Political Imagination*. New York: Routledge, 2001.

Hollinger, David A., and Charles Capper. *The American Intellectual Tradition*, vol. 1, *1630–1865*. New York: Oxford University Press, 1993.

Holmes, Stephen. *Passions and Constraint: On the Theory of Liberal Democracy*. Chicago: University of Chicago Press, 1995.

Holston, James. "Spaces of Insurgent Citizenship." *Cities and Citizenship*, ed. James Holston, 155–76. Durham: Duke University Press, 1999.

Homes, Henry, Lord Kames. *Essays on the Principles of Morality and Natural Religion*. Edinburgh, 1751.

Honig, Bonnie. "Declarations of Independence: Arendt and Derrida on the Problem of Founding a Republic." *American Political Science Review* 85 (1991), 97–113.

———. *Political Theory and the Displacement of Politics*. Ithaca: Cornell University Press, 1993.

———. *Democracy and the Foreigner*. Princeton: Princeton University Press, 2001.

———. "Between Deliberation and Decision: Political Paradox in Democratic Theory." *American Political Science Review* 101 (2007), 17–44.

———. *Emergency Politics*. Princeton: Princeton University Press, forthcoming.

Howe, Daniel Walker. *The Making of the American Self: Jonathan Edwards to Abraham Lincoln*. Cambridge: Harvard University Press, 1997.

Howe, John R. "Republican Thought and the Political Violence of the 1790's." *American Quarterly* 19, no. 2 (1967), 147–65.

Hughes, Langston. *The Collected Poems of Langston Hughes*. New York: Alfred A. Knopf, 1994.

Hulme, Obadiah. *An Historical Essay on the English Constitution*. London: Edward and Charles Dilly, 1771.

Hume, David. *Enquiries concerning the Human Understanding and concerning the Principles of Morals*, ed. L. A. Selby-Brigg. Oxford: Clarendon, 1966.

———. *A Treatise of Human Nature*, ed. P. H. Nidditch. New York: Oxford University Press, 1978.

Hunt, Lynn. *Politics, Culture, and Class in the French Revolution*. Berkeley: University of California Press, 1984.

Ingram, David. "Novus Ordo Seclorum: The Trial of (Post) Modernity or the Tale of Two Revolutions." *Hannah Arendt: 20 Years Later*, ed. Larry May and Jerome Kohn, 221–49. Cambridge: MIT Press, 1997.

Isaac, Jeffrey C. "Oases in the Desert: Hannah Arendt on Democratic Politics." *American Political Science Review* 88, no. 1 (1994), 156–68.

Isaac, Rhys. "Dramatizing the Ideology of the Revolution: Popular Mobilization in Virginia, 1774–1776." *William and Mary Quarterly* 33 (1976), 357–85.

Jacob, Margaret, and James Jacob, eds. *Origins of Anglo-American Radicalism*. London: George Allen and Unwin, 1984.

Jacobson, Norman. *Pride and Solace: The Functions and Limits of Political Theory*. Berkeley: University of California Press, 1978.

James, C. L. R. *American Civilization*. New York: Basil Blackwell, 1993.

Jasinsky, James. "Rearticulating History in Epideictic Discourse: Frederick Douglass's 'The Meaning of the Fourth of July to the Negro.'" *Rhetoric and Political Culture in Nineteenth Century America*, ed. Thomas Benson, 71–89. East Lansing: Michigan State University Press, 1997.

Jay, Martin. "The Political Existentialism of Hannah Arendt." *Partisan Review* 45, no. 2 (1978), 348–68.

Jefferson, Thomas. *Notes on the State of Virginia*, ed. W. Peden. Chapel Hill: University of North Carolina Press, 1989.

———. *Political Writings*, ed. J. Appleby and T. Ball. Cambridge: Cambridge University Press, 1999.

Jensen, Merrill, John P. Kaminski, and Gaspare J. Saladino, eds. *The Documentary History of the Ratification of the Constitution*, vols. 1–18. Madison: Historical Society of Wisconsin, 1976–.

Johnson, Martin Phillip. *The Paradise of Association: Political Culture and Popular Organizations in the Paris Commune of 1871*. Ann Arbor: University of Michigan Press, 1996.

Kafer, Peter. *Charles Brockden Brown's Revolution and the Birth of American Gothic*. Philadelphia: University of Pennsylvania Press, 2004.

Kalyvas, Andreas. "From the Act to the Decision: Hannah Arendt and the Question of Decisionism." *Political Theory* 32, no. 3 (2004), 320–46.

———. "Popular Sovereignty, Democracy, and the Constituent Power." *Constellations* 12, no. 2 (2005), 223–44.

———. *Democracy and the Politics of the Extraordinary: Max Weber, Carl Schmitt, and Hannah Arendt*. New York: Cambridge University Press, 2008.

Kant, Immanuel. *The Conflict of the Faculties*, trans. Mary J. Gregor. Lincoln: University of Nebraska Press, 1992.

Kateb, George. *The Inner Ocean: Individualism and Democratic Culture*. Ithaca: Cornell University Press, 1992.

———. *Patriotism and Other Mistakes*. New Haven: Yale University Press, 2006.

Kazin, Michael. *The Populist Persuasion: An American History*. New York: Basic, 1995.

Keenan, Alan. *Democracy in Question: Democratic Openness in a Time of Political Closure*. Palo Alto: Stanford University Press, 2003.

Keenan, Thomas. "Remember Jacques Derrida (Part 2): Drift: Politics and the Simulation of Real Life." *Grey Room* 1, no. 21 (2006), 94–111.

Kirby, John B. "Early American Politics: The Search for Ideology: An Historical Analysis and Critique of the Concept of 'Deference.'" *Journal of Politics* 23 (1970), 808–38.

Kirkpatrick, Jennet. *Uncivil Disobedience: Studies in Violence and Democratic Politics*. Princeton: Princeton University Press, 2008.

Klein, Lawrence E. "Sociability, Solitude, and Enthusiasm." *Enthusiasm and Enlightenment in Europe, 1650–1850*, ed. Lawrence E. Klein and Anthony J. LaVopa, 153–77. San Marino, Calif.: Huntington Library Press, 1998.

Kloppenberg, James T. "The Virtues of Liberalism: Christianity, Republicanism, and Ethics in Early American Political Discourse." *Journal of American History* 74 (1987), 9–33.

———. *The Virtues of Liberalism*. New York: Oxford University Press, 1998.

Kompridis, Nikolas. *Critique and Disclosure: Critical Theory between Past and Future*. Cambridge: MIT Press, 2006.

Koschnik, Albrecht. "The Democratic Societies of Philadelphia and the Limits of the American Public Sphere, 1793–1795." *William and Mary Quarterly* 58, no. 3 (2001), 1–31.

Koselleck, Reinhart. *Critique and Crisis: Enlightenment and the Pathogenesis of Modern Societies*, trans. Keith Tribe. Cambridge: MIT Press, 1988.

Korsgaard, Christine. "Taking the Law into Our Own Hands: Kant on the Right to Revolution." *Reclaiming the History of Ethics: Essays for John Rawls*, ed. Christine M. Korsgaard and Barbara Herman, 297–328. New York: Cambridge University Press, 1997.

Kramer, Larry D. *The People Themselves: Popular Constitutionalism and Judicial Review*. New York: Oxford University Press, 2004.

Kramnick, Isaac. *Republicanism and Bourgeois Radicalism: Political Ideology in Late Eighteenth Century England and America*. Ithaca: Cornell University Press, 1990.

Krause, Sharon. "Desiring Justice: Motivation and Justification in Rawls and Habermas." *Contemporary Political Theory* 4 (2005), 363–85.

Kronick, Joseph. "On the Border of History: Whitman and the American Sublime." *The American Sublime*, ed. Mary Arensberg, 51–82.

Laclau, Ernesto. *Emancipation(s)*. New York: Verso, 1996.

———. *On Populist Reason*. New York: Verso, 2005.

———. "Why Constructing a People Is the Main Task of Radical Politics." *Critical Inquiry* 32, no. 4 (2006), 646–80.

Larking, Edward. *Thomas Paine and the Literature of Revolution*. New York: Cambridge University Press, 2005.

Lawrence, Christopher. "The Nervous System and Society in the Scottish Enlightenment." *Natural Order: Historical Studies in Scientific Culture*, ed. Barry Barnes and Steven Shapin, 19–40. Beverly Hills: Sage, 1979.

Lawson, Bill E., and Frank M. Kirkland, eds. *Frederick Douglass: A Critical Reader*. Malden, Mass.: Blackwell, 1999.

Lefort, Claude. *Democracy and Political Theory*, trans. David Macey. Minneapolis: University of Minnesota Press, 1988.

———. *The Political Forms of Modern Society: Bureaucracy, Democracy, Totalitarianism*. Cambridge: MIT Press, 1986.

Lemisch, Jessie. "Jack Tar in the Streets: Merchant Seamen in the Politics of Revolutionary America." *William and Mary Quarterly* 25 (1968), 371–407.

Levinson, Sanford, ed. *Responding to Imperfection: The Theory and Practice of Constitutional Amendment*. Princeton: Princeton University Press, 1995.

Lienesch, Michael. *New Order of the Ages: Time, the Constitution, and the Making of Modern American Political Thought*. Princeton: Princeton University Press, 1988.

Link, Eugene P. *Democratic-Republican Societies, 1790–1800*. New York: Octagon, 1942.

Locke, John. *Some Thoughts concerning Education and of the Conduct of the Understanding*, ed. Ruth Grant and Nathan Tarcov. Indianapolis: Hackett, 1996.

Looby, Christopher. *Voicing America: Language, Literary Form, and the Origins of the United States*. Chicago: University of Chicago Press, 1996.

Loughlin, Martin, and Neil Walker, eds. *The Paradox of Constitutionalism: Constituent Power and Constitutional Form*. Oxford: Oxford University Press, 2007.

Lovejoy, David. "'Desperate Enthusiasm': Early Signs of American Radicalism." *Origins of Anglo-American Radicalism*, ed. Jacob and Jacob, 214–25.

———. *Religious Enthusiasm in the New World: Heresy to Revolution*. Cambridge: Harvard University Press, 1985.

Loving, Jerome. "The Political Roots of Leaves of Grass." *Historical Guide to Walt Whitman*, ed. D. Reynolds, 97–119. New York: Oxford University Press, 2000.

Luban, David. "Explaining Dark Times: Hannah Arendt's Theory of Theory." *Social Research* 50, no. 1 (1983), 215–48.

MacCannell, Juliet Flower. "Fascism and the Voice of Conscience." *The Hysteric's Guide to the Future Female Subject*, 127–52. Minneapolis: University of Minnesota Press, 1999.

Madison, James. *The Papers of James Madison*, ed. W. T. Hutchinson and William M. E. Rachal, Robert A. Rutland, et al. Chicago: University of Chicago Press, 1962–.

Maier, Pauline. *From Resistance to Revolution: Colonial Radicals and the Development of American Opposition to Britain, 1765–1776*. New York: W. W. Norton, 1972.

———. *American Scripture: Making the Declaration of Independence*. New York: Vintage, 1998.

Maistre, Joseph Marie, comte de. *The Works of Joseph de Maistre*, ed. and trans. Jack Lively. New York: Schocken, 1971.

Malsberger, John W. "The Political Thought of Fisher Ames." *Journal of the Early Republic* 2, no. 1 (1982), 1–20.

Manning, William. *The Key of Liberty*. Cambridge: Harvard University Press, 1993.

Markell, Patchen. "Making Affect Safe for Democracy? On 'Constitutional Patriotism.'" *Political Theory* 28, no. 2 (2000), 38–63.

———. "The Rule of the People: Arendt, *Archê*, and Democracy." *American Political Science Review* 100, no. 1 (2006), 1–14.

———. "The Potential and the Actual: Mead, Honneth and the I." *Recognition and Power: Axel Honneth and the Tradition of Critical Social Theory*, ed. Bert van der Brink and David Owen, 100–135. New York: Cambridge University Press, 2007.

Marston, Jerrilyn Greene. *King and Congress: The Transfer of Political Legitimacy, 1774–1776*. Princeton: Princeton University Press, 1987.

Martin, Howard H. "The Fourth of July Oration." *Quarterly Journal of Speech* 44, no. 4 (1958), 393–401.

Martin, Terence. *The Instructed Vision: Scottish Common Sense Philosophy and the Origins of American Fiction*. Bloomington: Indiana University Press, 1961.

Marx, Karl. "Theses on Feuerbach." *The Marx-Engels Reader*, ed. Robert C. Tucker, 143–45. New York: W. W. Norton, 1978.

Maslan, Susan. "Resisting Representation: Theatre and Democracy in Revolutionary France." *Representations* 52 (1995), 27–51.

Massumi, Brian. "The Autonomy of Affect." *Deleuze: A Critical Reader*, ed. Paul Patton, 217–39. New York: Blackwell, 1996.

Mathes, Melissa M. *Rape of Lucretia and the Founding of Republics: Readings in Livy, Machiavelli, and Rousseau*. University Park: Pennsylvania State University Press, 2000.

Matthews, Richard K. *If Men Were Angels: James Madison and the Heartless Empire of Reason*. Lawrence: University of Kansas Press, 1995.

Matthiessen, F. O. *From the Heart of Europe*. New York: Oxford University Press, 1948.

McClelland, J. S. *The Crowd and the Mob: From Plato to Canetti*. London: Unwin Hyman, 1989.

McClure, Kirstie. "The Odor of Judgment: Exemplarity, Propriety, and Politics in the Company of Hannah Arendt." *Hannah Arendt and the Meaning of Politics*, ed. Craig Calhoun and John McGowan, 53–84. Minneapolis: University of Minnesota Press, 1997.

McCormick, John P. "Machiavellian Democracy: Controlling Elites with Ferocious Populism." *American Political Science Review* 95, no. 2 (2001), 297–313.

———. "Machiavelli against Republicanism: On the Cambridge School's 'Guicciardinian Moments.'" *Political Theory* 31, no. 5 (2003), 615–43.

McDonald, Forrest. *The Presidency of George Washington*. Lawrence: University of Kansas Press, 1988.

McGee, Michael C. "In Search of 'the People': A Rhetorical Alternative." *Quarterly Journal of Speech* 61, no. 3 (1975), 235–49.

Meranze, Michael. *Laboratories of Virtue: Punishment, Revolution, and Authority in Philadelphia, 1760–1835*. Chapel Hill: University of North Carolina Press, 1996.

Michelet, Jules. *The People*, trans. John P. McKay. Urbana: University of Illinois Press, 1973.

Michelman, Frank I. "Law's Republic." *Yale Law Journal* 97 (1988), 1493–1537.

———. "Always under Law?" *Constitutional Commentary* 12, no. 2 (1995), 227–47.

———. "How Can the People Ever Make the Laws? A Critique of

Deliberative Democracy." *Deliberative Democracy: Essays on Reason and Politics*, ed. James Bohman and William Rehg, 145–72. Cambridge: MIT Press, 1997.

———. "Can Constitutional Democrats Be Legal Positivists? Or Why Constitutionalism?" *Constellations* 2, no. 3 (2006), 293–308.

Miller, Joshua. "The Ghostly Body Politic: Federalist Papers and Popular Sovereignty." *Political Theory* 16, no. 1 (1988), 99–119.

Mills, Nicolaus. *The Crowd in American Literature*. Baton Rouge: Louisiana State University Press, 1986.

Moon, Michael. *Disseminating Whitman: Revision and Corporeality in Leaves of Grass*. Cambridge: Harvard University Press, 1991.

Moore, Wayne D. *Constitutional Rights and Powers of the People*. Princeton: Princeton University Press, 1996.

Morgan, Edmund S. *Inventing the People: The Rise of Popular Sovereignty in England and America*. New York: W. W. Norton, 1989.

Morone, James A. *The Democratic Wish: Popular Participation and the Limits of American Government*. New York: Basic, 1990.

Morris, Gouverneur. *Diary and Letters*, ed. Anne Cary. New York: C. Scribner's Sons, 1888.

Mullan, John. *Sentiment and Sociability: The Language of Feeling in the Eighteenth Century*. New York: Oxford University Press, 1988.

Murrin, John M. "A Roof without Walls: The Dilemma of American National Identity." *Beyond Confederation*, ed. Beeman, Botein, and Carter, 333–48.

Nancy, Jean-Luc. *The Inoperative Community*, trans. Peter Connor, Lisa Barbus, Michael Holland, and Simona Sawhney. Minneapolis: University of Minnesota Press, 1991.

Nash, Gary B. *The Urban Crucible: Social Change, Political Consciousness, and the Origins of the American Revolution*. Cambridge: Harvard University Press, 1979.

Näsström, Sofia. "The Legitimacy of the People." *Political Theory* 35, no. 5 (2007), 624–58.

Negri, Antonio. *Insurgencies: Constituent Power and the Modern State*, trans. Maurizia Boscagli. Minneapolis: University of Minnesota Press, 1999.

Newman, Simon P. *Parades and the Politics of the Street: Festive Culture in the Early American Republic*. Philadelphia: University of Pennsylvania Press, 1997.

Nieman, Donald G. *Promises to Keep: African Americans and the Constitutional Order, 1776 to the Present*. New York: Oxford University Press, 1991.

Nietzsche, Friedrich. *Twilight of the Idols*, trans. R. J. Hollingdale. New York: Penguin, 1968.

———. *The Gay Science*, trans. Walter Kaufmann. New York: Vintage, 1974.

Norton, Anne. "Transubstantiation: The Dialectic of Constitutional Authority." *University of Chicago Law Review* 55, no. 2 (1988), 458–72.

————. *95 Theses on Politics, Culture and Method*. New Haven: Yale University Press, 2004.

Nussbaum, Martha. "Democratic Desire: Walt Whitman." *Upheavals of Thought: The Intelligence of Emotions*, 645–78. Cambridge: Cambridge University Press, 2001.

————. *Hiding from Humanity: Disgust, Shame, and the Law*. Princeton: Princeton University Press, 2004.

Oberg, Barbara Bowen. "David Hartley and the Association of Ideas." *Journal of the History of Ideas* 37, no. 3 (1976), 441–54.

Oliver, Peter. *Origin and Progress of the American Rebellion*, ed. D. Adair, and J. A. Shutz. Palo Alto: Stanford University Press, 1961.

Olson, Joel. "The Freshness of Fanaticism: The Abolitionist Defense of Zealotry." *Perspectives on Politics* 5, no. 4 (2007), 685–701.

Ong, Walter J. *Orality and Literacy: The Technologizing of the Word*. New York: Routledge, 1988.

Paine, Thomas. *The Thomas Paine Reader*, ed. Isaac Kramnick and Michael Foot. New York: Penguin, 1987.

————. *Political Writings*, ed. Bruce Kuklick. Cambridge: Cambridge University Press, 1989.

Palmer, R. R. *The Age of the Democratic Revolution: The Challenge*. Princeton: Princeton University Press, 1959.

Park, Robert E. "The Crowd and the Public." *The Crowd and the Public and Other Essays*, ed. H. Elsner, 3–84. Chicago: University of Chicago Press, 1972.

Parssinen, T. M. "Association, Convention, and Anti-Parliament in British Radical Politics, 1771–1848." *English Historical Review* 88 (1973), 504–33.

Pasley, Jeffrey L., Andrew W. Robertson, and David Waldstreicher, eds. *Beyond the Founders: New Approaches to the Political History of the Early American Republic*. Chapel Hill: University of North Carolina Press, 2003.

Pease, Donald E. "Walt Whitman and the Vox Populi of the American Masses." *Visionary Compacts: American Renaissance Writings in Cultural Context*, ed. Walter Benn Michaels and Donald E. Pease, 108–57. Madison: University of Wisconsin Press, 1987.

Pencak, William, Mathew Dennis, and Paul Douglas Newman, eds. *Riot and Revelry in Early America*. University Park: Pennsylvania State University Press, 2002.

Phillips, Wendell. "Philosophy of the Abolition Movement." *Against Slavery: An Abolitionist Reader*, ed. Mason Lowance, 246–51. New York: Penguin, 2000.

Pitkin, Hanna Fenichel. *The Concept of Representation*. Berkeley: University of California Press, 1972.

Plato. *The Republic*, ed. Desmond Lee. New York: Penguin, 1962.

Plotz, John. "Crowd Power: Chartism, Carlyle, and the Victorian Public Sphere." *Representations* 70, no. 1 (2000), 87–114.

Pocock, J. G. A. *Politics, Language, and Time: Essays on Political Thought and History*. Chicago: University of Chicago Press, 1971.

———. *The Machiavellian Moment: Florentine Political Thought and the Atlantic Republican Tradition*. Princeton: Princeton University Press, 1975.

———. "The Classical Theory of Deference." *American Historical Review* 81, no. 3 (1976), 516–23.

———. "Edmund Burke and the Redefinition of Enthusiasm: The Context as Counter-Revolution." *The French Revolution and the Creation of Modern Political Culture*, vol. 3, *The Transformation of Political Culture, 1789–1848*, ed. F. Furet and M. Ozouf, 19–35. Oxford: Pergamon, 1989.

———. "Enthusiasm: The Antiself of Enlightenment." *Enthusiasm and Enlightenment in Europe, 1650–1850*, ed. Lawrence E. Klein and Anthony J. LaVopa, 7–28. San Marino, Calif.: Huntington Library Press, 1998.

Pole, J. R. *Political Representation in England and the Origin of the American Republic*. Berkeley: University of California Press, 1979.

Portelli, Alessandro. *The Text and the Voice: Writing, Speaking and Democracy in American Literature*. New York: Columbia University Press, 1994.

Price, Kenneth M. *Whitman and Tradition: The Poet and His Century*. New Haven: Yale University Press, 1990.

———, ed. *Walt Whitman: The Contemporary Reviews*. Cambridge: Cambridge University Press, 1996.

Putnam, Robert D. *Bowling Alone: The Collapse and Revival of American Community*. New York: Simon and Schuster, 2000.

Pynchon, Thomas. *Mason & Dixon*. New York: Henry Holt, 1997.

Radner, John B. "The Art of Sympathy in Eighteenth-Century British Moral Thought." *Studies in Eighteenth-Century Culture*, ed. Roseann Runte, 189–210. Madison: University of Wisconsin Press, 1979.

Rancière, Jacques. "Politics, Identification, and Subjectivization." *The Identity in Question*, ed. John Rajchman, 63–72. New York: Routledge, 1995.

———. *On the Shores of Politics*, trans. Liz Heron. London: Verso, 1995.

———. *Dis-agreement: Politics and Philosophy*, trans. Julie Rose. Minneapolis: University of Minnesota Press, 1999.

———. "Dissenting Words: A Conversation with Jacques Rancière." *Diacritics* 30, no. 2 (2000), 113–26.

———. "Jacques Rancière: Literature, Politics, Aesthetics: Approaches to Democratic Disagreement." *SubStance* 92 (2000), 3–24.

———. "Ten Theses on Politics." *Theory and Event* 5, no. 3 (2001) [available online at Project Muse].

———. *The Politics of Aesthetics*, trans. Gabriel Rockhill. New York: Continuum, 2004.

———. "Who Is the Subject of the Rights of Man?" *South Atlantic Quarterly* 103, nos. 2–3 (2004), 297–310.

Rawls, John. *Political Liberalism*. New York: Columbia University Press, 1993.

―――. *Law of Peoples*. Cambridge: Harvard University Press, 2001.

Reid, John Phillip. "In a Defensive Rage: The Uses of the Mob, the Justification in Law, and the Coming of the American Revolution." NYU *Law Review* 49 (1974), 1043–91.

―――. *The Concept of Representation in the Age of the American Revolution*. Chicago: University of Chicago Press, 1989.

Reill, Peter Hanns. *Vitalizing Nature in the Enlightenment*. Berkeley: University of California Press, 2005.

Reynolds, David S. *Walt Whitman's America: A Cultural Biography*. New York: Alfred A. Knopf, 1995.

Rice, Grantland S. *Transformation of Authorship in America*. Chicago: University of Chicago Press, 1997.

Ricoeur, Paul. "The Political Paradox." *Legitimacy and the State*, ed. William E. Connolly, 250–72. New York: New York University Press, 1984.

Riggs, Luther G., ed. *The Anarchiad: A New England Poem*. Gainesville, Fla.: Scholars' Facsimiles and Reprints, 1967.

Riker, William H. *Liberalism against Populism: A Confrontation between the Theory of Democracy and the Theory of Social Choice*. Long Grove, Ill.: Waveland, 1988.

Rodgers, Daniel T. *Contested Truths: Keywords in American Politics since Independence*. Cambridge: Harvard University Press, 1998.

Rodgers, James. "Sensibility, Sympathy, Benevolence: Physiology and Moral Philosophy in Tristram Shandy." *Languages of Nature: Critical Essays on Science and Literature*, ed. Ludmilla J. Jordanova, 117–58. New Brunswick: Rutgers University Press, 1986.

Rogers, William. *We Are All Together Now: Frederick Douglass, William Lloyd Garrison and the Prophetic Tradition*. New York: Routledge, 1995.

Rorty, Richard. *Achieving Our Country: Leftist Thought in 20th Century America*. Cambridge: Harvard University Press, 1998.

Rosanvallon, Pierre. *Democracy Past and Future*, ed. Samuel Moyn. New York: Columbia University Press, 2006.

Rosswurm, Steven. "'As a Lyen Out of His Den': Philadelphia's Popular Movement, 1776–80." *Origins of Anglo-American Radicalism*, ed. Margaret Jacob and James Jacob, 300–323.

Rousseau, Jean-Jacques. "Essay on the Origin of Languages Which Treats of Melody and Musical Imitation." *On the Origin of Languages*, trans. John H. Moran, 5–83. Chicago: University of Chicago Press, 1966.

Rubenfeld, Jed. *Freedom and Time: A Theory of Constitutional Self-Government*. New Haven: Yale University Press, 2001.

Rudé, George F. E. *The Crowd in History: A Study of Popular Disturbances in France and England, 1730–1848*. New York: John Wiley and Sons, 1964.

Rush, Benjamin. *An Enquiry into the Effects of Public Punishments upon Criminals and upon Society*. Philadelphia: Joseph James, 1787.

————. *Medical Inquiries and Observations upon Diseases of the Mind.* Philadelphia, 1789.

————. *Three Lectures upon Animal Life.* Philadelphia: Budd and Bartram, 1799.

————. *Sixteen Introductory Lectures, to Courses of Lectures upon the Institutes and Practices of Medicine.* Philadelphia, 1811.

————. "The French Fête in Philadelphia in Honor of the Dauphin's Birthday, 1782." *Pennsylvania Magazine of History and Biography* 21 (1897), 257–62.

————. *Selected Writings of Benjamin Rush*, ed. Dagobert D. Runes. New York: Philosophical Library, 1947.

————. *The Autobiography of Benjamin Rush: His Travels through Life Together with his Commonplace Book for 1789–1813*, ed. George W. Corner. Princeton: Princeton University Press, 1948.

————. *Letters of Benjamin Rush*, vols. 1–2, ed. L. H. Butterfield. Princeton: Princeton University Press for the American Philosophical Society, 1951.

————. "Further Letters of Benjamin Rush." *Pennsylvania Magazine of History and Biography* 78, no. 1 (1954), 3–45.

————. *Two Essays on the Mind.* New York: Brunner Mazel, 1972.

————. *Lectures on the Mind*, ed. Eric T. Carlson, Jeffrey L. Wollock, and Patricia S. Noel. Philadelphia: American Philosophical Society, 1981.

————. *Essays: Literary, Moral and Philosophical*, ed. M. Meranze. Schenectady, N.Y.: Union College Press, 1988.

Ruttenburg, Nancy. *Democratic Personality: Popular Voice and the Trial of American Authorship.* Palo Alto: Stanford University Press, 1998.

Ryerson, Richard Alan. *The Revolution Is Now Begun: The Radical Committees of Philadelphia, 1765–1776.* Philadelphia: University of Pennsylvania Press, 1978.

St. George, Robert Blair. *Conversing by Signs: Poetics of Implication in Colonial New England Culture.* Chapel Hill: University of North Carolina Press, 1998.

Samuels, Shirley. "Wieland: Alien and Infidel." *Early American Literature* 25, no. 1 (1990), 44–66.

Sandel, Michael J. *Democracy's Discontent: America in Search of a Public Philosophy.* Cambridge: Harvard University Press, 1996.

Sanders, Lynn M. "Against Deliberation." *Political Theory* 25, no. 3 (1997), 347–76.

Sandoz, Ellis. *Political Sermons of the American Founding Era, 1730–1805*, vols. 1–2. Indianapolis: Liberty Fund, 1998.

Schama, Simon. *The Embarrassment of Riches: An Interpretation of Dutch Culture in the Golden Age.* New York: Vintage, 1997.

Scheurman, William E. "Revolutions and Constitutions: Hannah Arendt's Challenge to Carl Schmitt." *Law as Politics*, ed. Dyzenhaus, 252–80.

Schlesinger, Arthur. "Political Mobs and the American Revolution, 1765–1776." *Proceedings of the American Philosophical Society* 99 (1955), 244–50.

Schmitt, Carl. *The Crisis of Parliamentary Democracy*, trans. Ellen Kennedy. Cambridge: MIT Press, 1992.

———. *Constitutional Theory*, trans. Jeffrey Seitzer. Durham: Duke University Press, 2008.

Schoenbachler, Mathew. "Republicanism in the Age of Democratic Revolution: The Democratic-Republican Societies of the 1790's." *Journal of the Early Republic* 18 (1998), 237–61.

Schoolman, Morton. *Reason and Horror: Critical Theory, Democracy, and Aesthetic Individuality*. New York: Routledge, 2001.

Schutz, John A., and Douglas Adair, eds. *The Spur of Fame: Dialogues of John Adams and Benjamin Rush*. San Marino, Calif.: Huntington Library Press, 1966.

Schwartz, Hillel. *Knaves, Fools, Madmen, and That Subtile Effluvium: A Study of the Opposition to the French Prophets in England, 1706–1710*. Gainesville: University of Florida Press, 1978.

Shaftesbury, Anthony Ashley Cooper, Earl of. *Characteristics of Men, Manners, Opinions, Times*, ed. Lawrence E. Klein. New York: Cambridge University Press, 1999.

Sharp, John Roger. *American Politics in the Early Republic: The New Nation in Crisis*. New Haven: Yale University Press, 1993.

Shaw, Peter. *American Patriots and the Rituals of Revolution*. Cambridge: Harvard University Press, 1981.

Shiffman, Gary. "Construing Disagreement: Consensus and Invective in 'Constitutional' Debate." *Political Theory* 30, no. 2 (2002), 175–203.

Shklar, Judith. "The Federalist as Myth." *Yale Law Journal* 90, no. 4 (1981), 942–53.

———. "Democracy and the Past: Jefferson and His Heirs." *Redeeming American Political Thought*, ed. Stanley Hoffman and Dennis F. Thompson, 171–86. Chicago: University of Chicago Press, 1998.

Shoemaker, Robert W. "'Democracy' and 'Republic' as Understood in Late Eighteenth-Century America." *American Speech* 41, no. 2 (1966), 83–95.

Shulman, George. *American Prophecy: Race and Redemption in American Political Culture*. Minneapolis: University of Minneapolis Press, 2008.

Sieyès, Emmanuel Joseph. "What Is the Third Estate?" *Political Writings*, ed. Michael Sonenscher, 92–162. Indianapolis: Hackett, 2003.

Singh, Nikhil Pal. *Black Is a Country: Race and the Unfinished Struggle for Democracy*. Cambridge: Harvard University Press, 2004.

Sioli, Marco M. "The Democratic-Republican Societies at the End of the Eighteenth Century: The Western Pennsylvania Experience." *Pennsylvania History* 60 (1993), 288–304.

Slauter, Eric. "Being Alone in the Age of the Social Contract." *William and Mary Quarterly* 62, no. 1 (2004), 81–122.

Sloan, Douglas. "From Nottingham Academy to the 'Edinburgh of America':

Benjamin Rush." *The Scottish Enlightenment and the American College Ideal*, 185–224. New York: Teachers College Press, 1971.

Smelser, Marshall. "The Federalist Period as an Age of Passion." *American Quarterly* 10, no. 4 (1958), 391–419.

Smith, Bruce James. *Politics and Remembrance: Republican Themes in Machiavelli, Burke, and Tocqueville*. Princeton: Princeton University Press, 1985.

Smith, James Morton, ed. *The Republic of Letters: The Correspondence between Thomas Jefferson and James Madison, 1776–1826*, vols. 1–3. New York: W. W. Norton, 1995.

Smith, Kimberly K. *The Dominion of Voice: Riot, Reason, and Romance in Antebellum Politics*. Lawrence: University Press of Kansas, 1999.

Smith, Rogers M. *Civic Ideals: Conflicting Visions of Citizenship in U.S. History*. New Haven: Yale University Press, 1997.

———. *Stories of Peoplehood: The Politics and Morals of Political Membership*. Cambridge: Cambridge University Press, 2003.

Sokol, Jason. *There Goes My Everything: White Southerners in the Age of Civil Rights, 1945–1975*. New York: Alfred A. Knopf, 2006.

Sorel, Georges. *Reflections on Violence*, ed. Jeremy Jennings. Cambridge: Cambridge University Press, 1999.

Sparks, Holloway. "Dissident Citizenship: Democratic Theory, Political Courage, and Activist Women." *Hypatia* 12, no. 4 (1997), 74–110 [special issue on citizenship].

Sparks, Jared. *The Life of Gouverneur Morris, with Selections from his Correspondence and Miscellaneous Papers*, vol. 1. Boston: Gary and Bowen, 1832.

Spivak, Gayatri Chakravorty. "Can the Subaltern Speak?" *Marxism and the Interpretation of Culture*, ed. Cary Nelson and Lawrence Grossberg, 271–313. Urbana: University of Illinois Press, 1988.

Sprengel, M. C. *1700's in America: Historical Genealogical Calendar or Yearbook of the Most Noteworthy Recent Worldwide Events Containing for 1784 the History of the North American Revolution*, trans. Henz Dutt and Karin Dutt. Cape Girardeau: Southeast Missouri State University Press, 2004.

Stephenson, Anders. *Manifest Destiny: American Expansion and the Empire of Right*. New York: Farrar, Straus and Giroux, 1999.

Stern, Julia A. *The Plight of Feeling: Sympathy and Dissent in the Early American Novel*. Chicago: University of Chicago Press, 1997.

Stimson, Shannon C. *The American Revolution in the Law: Anglo-American Jurisprudence before John Marshall*. Houndmills: Macmillan, 1990.

Storing, Herbert J. *What the Anti-Federalists Were for*. Chicago: University of Chicago Press, 1981.

Stout, Harry S. "Religion, Communication, and the Ideological Origins of the American Revolution." *William and Mary Quarterly* 34 (1997), 519–41.

Sullivan, James. *Life of James Sullivan with Selections from His Writings*, ed. Thomas C. Amory. Boston: Phillips, Sampson, 1859.

Sullivan, Robert R. "The Birth of the Prison: The Case of Benjamin Rush." *Eighteenth-Century Studies* 31, no. 3 (1998), 333–44.

Takaki, Ronald. *Iron Cages: Race and Culture in Nineteenth-Century America*. New York: Alfred A. Knopf, 1979.

Taylor, Charles. *Modern Social Imaginaries*. Durham: Duke University Press, 2004.

TenBroek, Jacobus. *The Antislavery Origins of the Fourteenth Amendment*. Berkeley: University of California Press, 1951.

Terrell, Colleen. "'Republican Machines': Franklin, Rush and the Manufacture of Civic Virtue in the Early American Republic." *Early American Studies* 1, no. 2 (2003), 100–132.

Thompson, E. P. "The Moral Economy of the English Crowd in the Eighteenth Century." *Customs in Common: Studies in Traditional Popular Culture*, 185–258. New York: New Press, 1993.

Thompson, P. M. "Is There Anything Legal about Extralegal Action? The Debate over Dorr's Rebellion." *New England Law Review* 36 (2002), 385–432.

Thoreau, Henry David. *A Week on the Concord and Merrimack Rivers, Walden; or, Life in the Woods, the Maine Woods, Cape Cod*. New York: Library of America, 1985.

———. *Civil Disobedience and Other Essays*. New York: Dover, 1993.

Tilly, Charles. *Popular Contention in Great Britain, 1758–1834*. Cambridge: Harvard University Press, 1995.

———. *Contentious Performances*. Cambridge: Cambridge University Press, 2008.

Tocqueville, Alexis de. *Democracy in America*, ed. J. P. Mayer, trans. George Lawrence. New York: Harper Collins, 1988.

———. *The Old Regime and the Revolution*, trans. Alan S. Kahan. Chicago: University of Chicago Press, 1998.

Tominaga, Shigeki. "Voice and Silence of Public Space: Popular Societies in the French Revolution." *Public Space and Democracy*, ed. Marcel Hénaff and Tracy B. Strong, 79–94. Minneapolis: University of Minnesota Press, 2001.

Tomkins, Jane. *Sensational Designs: The Cultural Work of American Fiction, 1790–1860*. New York: Oxford University Press, 1985.

Trenchard, John, and Thomas Gordon. *Cato's Letters: or, Essays on Liberty, Civil and Religious, and Other Important Subjects*, ed. R. Hamoway. Indianapolis: Liberty Fund, 1995.

Tully, James. "Governing Conduct: Locke on the Reform of Thought and Behavior." *An Approach to Political Philosophy: Locke in Contexts*, 179–241. Cambridge: Cambridge University Press, 1993.

Underdown, David. *Revel, Riot, and Rebellion: Popular Politics and Culture in England, 1603–1660*. New York: Oxford University Press, 1985.

Van Roermund, Bert. "First-Person Plural Legislature: Political Reflexivity and Representation." *Philosophical Explorations* 6 (2003), 235–50.

Venturi, Franco. *Utopia and Reform in the Enlightenment.* Cambridge: Cambridge University Press, 1971.

Verba, Sidney. "The 1993 James Madison Award Lecture: The Voice of the People." *PS: Political Science and Politics* 26, no. 4 (1993), 677–86.

Villa, Dana. "Beyond Good and Evil: Arendt, Nietzsche, and the Aestheticization of Political Action." *Political Theory* 20, no. 2 (1992), 274–308.

———. *Public Freedom.* Princeton: Princeton University Press, 2008.

———, ed. *The Cambridge Companion to Hannah Arendt.* New York: Cambridge University Press, 2000.

Waldron, Jeremy. *Law and Disagreement.* New York: Oxford University Press, 1999.

———. "Arendt's Constitutional Politics." *The Cambridge Companion to Hannah Arendt,* ed. Dana Villa, 201–19.

Waldstreicher, David. "Federalism, the Styles of Politics, and the Politics of Style." *Federalists Reconsidered,* ed. Doran Ben-Atar and Barbara B. Oberg, 99–117. Charlottesville: University of Virginia Press, 1998.

———. *In the Midst of Perpetual Fetes: The Making of American Nationalism, 1776–1820.* Chapel Hill: University of North Carolina Press, 1998.

———. "Why Thomas Jefferson and African Americans Wore Their Politics on Their Sleeves: Dress and Mobilization between American Revolutions." *Beyond the Founders: New Approaches to the Political History of the Early American Republic,* ed. Jeffrey L. Pasley, Andrew W. Robertson, and David Waldstreicher, 79–106. Chapel Hill: University of North Carolina Press, 2004.

Walters, Ronald G. *American Reformers, 1815–1860.* New York: Hill and Wang, 1978.

Walzer, Michael. "Liberalism and the Art of Separation." *Political Theory* 12, no. 3 (1984), 315–30.

———. *The Company of Critics: Social Criticism and Political Commitment in the Twentieth Century.* New York: Basic, 1988.

Warner, Michael. *The Letters of the Republic: Publication and the Public Sphere in Eighteenth Century America.* Cambridge: Harvard University Press, 1990.

———. "The Mass Public and the Mass Subject." *Habermas and the Public Sphere,* ed. Craig Calhoun, 377–401. Cambridge: MIT Press, 1992.

Washington, George. *Writings,* ed. J. Rhodehammel. New York: Library of America, 1997.

Wasserman, Manfred J. "Benjamin Rush on Government and the Harmony and Derangement of the Mind." *Journal of the History of Ideas* 33, no. 4 (1972), 639–42.

Webster, Noah. *The Letters of Noah Webster,* ed. H. M. Warfel. New York: Library Publishers, 1953.

Wellmer, Albrecht. "Arendt on Revolution." *The Cambridge Companion to Hannah Arendt*, ed. Dana Villa, 220–44.

Whelan, Frederick G. "Democratic Theory and the Boundary Problem." *Liberal Democracy*, ed. J. Roland Pennock and J. W. Chapman, 13–42. New York: New York University Press, 1983.

White, Shane. "'It Was a Proud Day': African Americans, Festivals, and Parades in the North, 1741–1834." *Journal of American History* 81, no. 1 (1994), 13–50.

White, Stephen. *Sustaining Affirmation: The Strengths of Weak Ontology in Political Theory*. Princeton: Princeton University Press, 2000.

———. *Edmund Burke: Modernity, Politics and Aesthetics*. New York: Rowman and Littlefield, 2002.

Whitman, Walt. *An American Primer*. Boston: Small, Maynard, 1904.

———. *With Walt Whitman in Camden*, ed. Horace Traubel. New York: Mitchell Kennerly, 1914.

———. *Walt Whitman's Workshop: A Collect of Unpublished Prose Manuscripts*, ed. Clifton Joseph Furness. New York: Russell and Russell, 1964.

———. *Notebooks and Unpublished Prose Manuscripts*. New York: New York University Press, 1984.

———. *Specimen Days and Collect*. New York: Dover, 1995.

———. *Poetry and Prose*, ed. J. Kaplan. New York: Library of America, 1996.

Wiebe, Robert H. *The Opening of American Society: From the Adoption of the Constitution to the Eve of Disunion*. New York: Alfred A. Knopf, 1984.

Wiecek, William M. *The Sources of Antislavery Constitutionalism in America, 1760–1848*. Ithaca: Cornell University Press, 1977.

Wieland, Christoph Martin. *The Trial of Abraham*. Norwich: John Trumbell, 1787.

Wilentz, Sean. *Chants Democratic: New York City and the Rise of the American Working Class, 1788–1850*. New York: Oxford University Press, 1984.

———. *The Rise of American Democracy: Jefferson to Lincoln*. New York: W. W. Norton, 2005.

Williams, Melissa S. *Voice, Trust, and Memory: Marginalized Groups and the Failings of Liberal Representation*. Princeton: Princeton University Press, 1998.

Wills, Garry. "James Wilson's New Meaning for Sovereignty." *Conceptual Change and the Constitution*, ed. Terence Ball and J. G. A. Pocock, 99–106. Lawrence: University of Kansas Press, 1988.

Wilson, James. *Works of James Wilson*, vols. 1–2, ed. James DeWitt Andrews. Chicago: Callaghan, 1896.

———. *Law Lectures*. Cambridge: Harvard University Press, 1967.

Winthrop, John. "A Modell of Christian Charity." *The American Intellectual Tradition*, vol. 1, *1630–1865*, ed. Hollinger and Capper, 6–15.

Wittgenstein, Ludwig. *On Certainty*, ed. G. E. M. Anscombe and G. H. von Wright. New York: Harper and Row, 1972.

Wolin, Richard. *The Politics of Being*. New York: Columbia University Press, 1990.

Wolin, Sheldon S. "The People's Two Bodies." *Democracy* 1, no. 1 (1981), 9–24.

———. "Hannah Arendt: Democracy and the Political." *Salmagundi* 60 (1983), 3–19.

———. *The Presence of the Past: Essays on the State and the Constitution*. Baltimore: Johns Hopkins University Press, 1989.

———. "Norm and Form: The Constitutionalizing of Democracy." *Athenian Political Thought and the Reconstruction of American Democracy*, ed. J. P. Euben, J. R. Wallach, and J. Ober, 29–58. Ithaca: Cornell University Press, 1994.

———. "Transgression, Equality, Voice." *Dēmokratia: A Conversation on Democracies, Ancient and Modern*, ed. Josiah Ober and Charles Hendrick, 68–92. Princeton: Princeton University Press, 1995.

———. "Fugitive Democracy." *Democracy and Difference: Contesting the Boundaries of the Political*, ed. Seyla Benhabib, 31–45. Princeton: Princeton University Press, 1996.

———. "The Liberal/Democratic Divide: On Rawls's Political Liberalism." *Political Theory* 24, no. 1 (1996), 97–119.

———. *Politics and Vision*. Expanded edition. Princeton: Princeton University Press, 2004.

Wood, Gordon S. "A Note on Mobs in the American Revolution." *William and Mary Quarterly* 23 (1966), 635–42.

———. *The Creation of the American Republic, 1776–1787*. Chapel Hill: University of North Carolina Press, 1969.

———. *Representation in the American Revolution*. Charlottesville: University Press of Virginia, 1969.

———. "Conspiracy and the Paranoid Style: Causality and Deceit in the Eighteenth Century." *William and Mary Quarterly* 39 (1982), 401–41.

———. Democratization of the American Mind." *The Moral Foundations of the Republic*, ed. Robert Horowitz. Charlottesville: University Press of Virginia, 1986.

———. "Interests and Disinterestedness in the Making of the Constitution." *Beyond Confederation*, ed. Beeman, Botein, and Carter, 69–112.

———. *The Radicalism of the American Revolution*. New York: Alfred A. Knopf, 1992.

———. *The American Revolution: A History*. New York: Modern Library, 2003.

———. *Revolutionary Characters: What Made the Founders Different*. New York: Penguin, 2006.

Woods, John A., ed. "The Correspondence of Benjamin Rush and Granville Sharp, 1773–1809." *Journal of American Studies* 1, no. 1 (1954).

Wortman, Tunis. *Oration on the Influence of Social Institutions upon Human Morals and Happiness*. New York: C. C. Van Alen, 1796.

Yack, Bernard. "Popular Sovereignty and Nationalism." *Political Theory* 29, no. 4 (2001), 517–36.

Yarbrough, Stephen R. "Jonathan Edwards on Rhetorical Authority." *Journal of the History of Ideas* 47 (1986), 395–408.

Young, Alfred F. *The Democratic Republicans of New York: The Origins, 1763–1797.* Chapel Hill: University of North Carolina Press, 1967.

———, ed. *The American Revolution: Explorations in American Radicalism.* DeKalb: Northern Illinois University Press, 1976.

Young, Iris Marion. "Activist Challenges to Deliberative Democracy." *Political Theory* 29, no. 5 (2001), 670–90.

Ziff, Larzer. "A Reading of *Wieland*." PMLA 77 (1962), 51–57.

———. *Literary Democracy: The Declaration of Cultural Independence in America.* New York: Penguin, 1982.

———. "Whitman and the Crowd." *Critical Inquiry* 10, no. 2 (1984), 579–91.

———. *Writing in the New Nation: Prose, Print and Politics in the Early United States.* New Haven: Yale University Press, 1991.

Žižek, Slavoj. *Tarrying with the Negative: Kant, Hegel, and the Critique of Ideology.* Durham: Duke University Press, 1993.

———. *The Ticklish Subject: The Absent Center of Political Ontology.* New York: Verso, 1999.

Zweig, Egon. *Die Lehre vom Pouvoir constituant: Ein Beitrag zum Staatsrecht der französischen Revolution.* Tübingen, 1909.

Index

Page numbers in *italics* refer to illustrations.

Abolitionists, 185, 186, 213, 214, 220, 221, 222–27, 228, 230

Abrams, M. H., 205

Absolute validity: avoidance of, 55–56; of constituent power, 34, 43, 45, 47, 50, 54–55, 64, 135; exemplary validity vs., 34, 42, 260 n. 5; revolutionaries and, 34, 42, 45–50, 61, 263–64 n. 27, 266–67 n. 61

Abzug, Robert, 111

Accountability, 15, 85, 88, 130, 145–46

"Account of the Influences of the Military and Political Events of the American Revolution on the Human Body, An" (Rush), 116

Ackerman, Bruce, 31–32, 247–49, 250

ACT UP, 252

Adair, Douglas, 246

Adams, Abigail, 89–90, 96

Adams, John Quincy: on canon and feudal laws, 70; on circulation of knowledge, 70–71; on consent of people, 1; on constitution, 56, 248; on crowd activity, 96; on democracy, 97, 112, 172; on government despotism, 85; on judiciousness of people, 89; on land, 125; on legitimacy of people, 2–3, 87–88; on new claims, 150; on representation, 14, 85

Adams, Samuel, 11, 67

Adams, Willi Paul, 13, 45

Addison, Joseph, 106

"Address to the People of the United States" (Rush), 101

Adhesiveness, 199–200

Aesthetics: dangers of, 172; democracy and, 37–38, 182–83, 185, 190, 191, 193, 201; imagination and, 174; individuality and, 189, 196; political, 102, 152, 174, 178, 211

Affect, affectation, 68, 77–80, 82, 101–2, 192

Agamben, Giorgio, 209, 210

Age of realism, 119

Age of Revolutions, 37, 84, 150, 158, 258–59 n. 81

AIDS Action Now, 252

Alien and Sedition Acts (1798), 71, 176, 177

Allen, Danielle, 236, 238

American Communist Party, 6

Americanism, 5

American Primer (Whitman), 192

American Revolution: as act of restoration, 247; constituent power and, 12, 42; crowd gatherings and, 35; early texts and, 9–10; mutual promising and, 34, 44, 45, 48, 59, 60, 61, 63, 64, 65; new order and, 50–51; pageantry of, 20; political freedom and, 58; popular sovereignty and, 10; public happiness and, 58; realized in Constitution, 242, 243; significance of, 237–38; unfinished, 244–45; unification and, 9

Ames, Fisher, 132, 138, 151

Anarchiad, 67, 69, 77, 100

Anarchy: crowd actions and, 35, 96, 103; democracy as, 97; fear of, 35, 97, 103, 114, 142; postrevolutionary politics and, 114, 116–17

Anglo-American Enlightenment, 144

Anthony, Susan B., 214

Anti-Federalists: Antifederal Club parody, 148–49, 150; as conservatives, 27–28; on constituent power, 55; on constitution, 175, 243; local government emphasized by, 244; on Philadelphia Convention, 141; rioting by, 93–95; as voice of people, 53–54

Antinomianism, 169, 187, 189–90

Antislavery groups, 210, 228. See also Abolitionists

Arato, Adnrew, 62

Arendt, Hannah: on American political genius, 31, 41, 55, 58–59; on American Revolution, 34, 44, 45, 48, 50, 52; augmentation theory of, 45, 52, 56–57, 63, 64; on civil disobedience, 65; on constituent power, 41–66; on constitution, 52–61; on dilemmas' validity, 34; on experience, 58–59; on French Revolution, 34, 44, 45, 50, 52; on grammar of action, 59–60; on heteronomy of beginnings, 61; historical narrative used by, 34, 41, 243; on mutual promising, 34, 44, 45, 48, 59, 60, 61, 63, 64, 65; on political past, 41–42; on principles, 62–63; on revolutionary politics, 42, 48–49; on rights, 147; on Schmitt, 49; on Sièyes, 47, 48, 49

Articles of Confederation, 27

Art of Speaking (Burgh), 162

Assimilation, 217, 219

Augmentation theory, 45, 52, 56–57, 63, 64

Aurora, 190

Austin, J. L., 8

Authority, authorization: civil, 174–75; constituent moments and, 51; constituent power and, 37, 44,

240; crowd action and, 33, 68, 83–84; Democratic-Republican Societies and, 36; dilemmas in, 33, 34, 36, 37, 57, 78, 84, 87, 90, 95, 176, 210, 211, 212, 220, 242, 250, 251; of eloquence, 162, 163; feudalism and, 73; imagination and, 166, 178–79; interpretive, 54; mystical foundations of, 3; of people, 1–2, 7–8, 11, 16, 19–20, 24, 30, 34, 36–37, 43–44, 51–53, 57, 63, 98, 137; popular will and, 34; public, 7; religion and, 46, 56; representation and, 20, 82; sovereign, 5, 10, 98; sublimity of, 180; textuality and, 76, 169, 170–71; tradition and, 41, 56; unauthorized, 8; voice and, 76–77, 81–82, 160, 162–63, 178; of *vox Dei*, 170–72; of *vox populi*, 3, 75–76, 78, 82, 137, 166, 175, 188. *See also* Constituent moments; Self-authorization

Autobiography of the Life of Frederick Douglass, 230

Autonomy: boundaries of, 37; collective, 43; democratic, 72, 181, 241; imagination and, 164–65, 166; public vs. private, 239

Bache, William, 111
Bailyn, Bernard, 70, 72, 133
Bakhtin, Mikhail, 83, 197, 198
Baldwin, James, 39, 213, 231–34
Barlow, Joel, 67, 77
Barthes, Roland, 158, 161
Beard, Charles, 31
Beginnings, 61
Benhabib, Seyla, 43
Benjamin, Walter, 106, 251
Benveniste, Emile, 217–18
Bercovitch, Sacvan, 218, 245, 297 n. 84
Biloquism, 169
Black, Eugene, 134

Black, Joseph, 106
Blacks, freed, 5
Blackstone, William, 15
Blair, Hugh, 79–80
Bloch, Ernst, 206
Bloody Kansas events, 185, 188
Bodily mimesis theory, 35, 103, 107
Bodin, Jean, 28
Boorstin, Daniel, 59
Boston Massacre (1770), 88–89
Boston Tea Party (1773), 90
Bourdieu, Pierre, 4, 229
Boxill, Bernard, 217
Bradford, Ebenezer, 144
Brennan, William J., 252
British Constitution, 16
Brooke, John L., 135, 143
Brooklyn Eagle, 190
Brown, Charles Brockden, 37, 156, 157–81; on imagination, 173–74, 178–79, 180; influence on, 169; on popular voice, 181
Brown, John, 187
Brown, Richard, 191
Brown, William Hill, 104
Burgh, James, 27, 105, 135, 145, 162
Burke, Edmund, 14, 103, 178, 288 n. 65
Burke, Kenneth, 6–7, 28

Cahill, Edward, 164
Caleb Williams (Godwin), 174
Calhoun, John, 223
Calvinism, 79, 110, 159, 165, 167
Camden 28, 252
Camisards, 168–69
Carlisle riots (1787), 93–94
Carlyle, Thomas, 195–96
Carr, Peter, 173
Cato's Letters (Trenchard and Gordon), 72
Cavell, Stanley, 253
Censorship, 71
Char, René, 66

Chauncey, Charles, 169

Chodowiecki, Daniel Nicolas, 20–24, 150

Cicero, 162, 170

Citizen Mungo, 150

Citizenship, 37, 99, 116; independent, 191; insurgent, 36, 131, 143, 147, 155; poetics of, 183, 189, 190; practices of, 144; rights, 222; self-authorized, 143; spatial choreography and, 36, 102–4, 124, 127

City upon a Hill, 4

Civil disobedience, 8, 65, 233

Civil rights movement, 232

Claims-making, 3, 8, 11, 216, 219, 222, 223, 225, 228–29, 238, 249

Class: conception of people and, 28; domination and, 7; egalitarianism and, 92–93; people as, 5

Cobbett, William, 132, 149

Coercive Acts, 251

Colaiaco, Jams A., 222

Collective action, 17, 19; temporality of, 22, 24

Colonial authorities, 5, 15

Colonial governors: authority of, 11, 139; colonial interests and, 163; sovereignty and, 13; suppression by, 105

Colored Convention, 219

Columbia Centinel, 128

Commentaries on the Laws of England (Blackstone), 15

Committee on Correspondence, 134

Common Sense (Paine), 9–10, 113

Communicative rationality, 62

Communism, 6

Compact, notion of, 60

Concept of Law (Hart), 29

Condorcet, Marquis de, 119

Conflict of the Faculties, The (Kant), 22

Connecticut Wits, 67, 100

Connolly, William, 226, 248–49

Conscientious objectors, 65

Consent principle, 2

Conservatives, 27–28

Constituencies: alien, 3; dilemmas of, 14, 19, 24, 31, 130; representation of, 2. See also People

Constituent moments: crowd actions and, 35, 68, 84, 90; defined, 8, 18, 210; dilemmas in, 34, 37, 84, 250–51; examples of, 251–53; history of, 31; inheritance of, 25; narratives and, 246–51, 253; people as one and, 238; revolutionary roots of, 32; self-authorization and, 51, 250–51, 254; self-representation and, 8–9; tapping and, 241–42, 248

Constituent power: abolition of, 53; absolute validity of, 34, 43, 45, 47, 50, 54–55, 64, 135; authorization and, 37, 44, 240; autopoetic, 183, 193, 195, 202; colonial resistance and, 13, 25; constituted power vs., 46–47; constitution making and, 45; as contribution to political ideas, 44; criticism of, 42; crowds and, 86, 98–99; dilemmas in, 34, 43, 55, 58, 61, 63–64, 241; law vs., 52, 53, 55, 60, 62, 66; mobilized multitude and, 49; mystical, 29–30; nation as, 48; paradoxes of, 51; people as, 12, 18, 24–25, 31, 32, 101, 115; popular sovereignty and, 12, 25; restorative, 27; self-created societies and, 133; sublime and, 183

Constitution, U.S.: amendments to, 58, 240–41; article V, 24, 32; Federalists and, 27; infinite regress and, 241; partisan politics and, 102; Preamble of, 222–23; ratification of, 31, 52, 93, 101, 175, 243; as realization of Revolution, 242, 243; reverence for, 56; seat of power

and, 53–54; source of law and, 54;
writtenness of, 57–58

Constitutionalism: constituent
power and, 45; constitutional
augmentation theory and, 45, 52,
56–57, 63, 64; constitutional resistance and, 140–41; *constituto libertatis* and, 48; conventions and, 24;
defenders and enforcers of, 5, 11–
12; democratic will and, 29, 209;
liberal, 48; negative, 29; popular,
5, 12, 16, 24, 34, 66, 130, 139, 221;
popular voice and, 28, 167; positive, 28; postrevolutionary American, 5, 25, 52–53, 57, 239–40; self-
authorization and, 30, 32, 43, 57

Constitutional law: freedom and,
222; legality of, 240; people as
source of, 46, 52, 53, 73, 250;
political representation and, 13, 16;
popular will and, 49, 54; power vs.,
52, 53, 55, 60, 62, 66; rule of, 5;
theological identification with, 46

Constitutional moments, 31–33, 248,
251

Constitutional Theory (Schmitt), 48

Continental Congress, 1, 2; as representative of people, 13, 17

"Contract and Birthright" (Wolin),
153

Conventions, 24, 26

Cooke, Maeve, 73

Cooper, Anthony Ashley, third earl of
Shaftesbury, 106–7, 168

Cooper, Samuel, 111

Corinthian Hall, 214

Coughlin, Father, 7

Council of Censors, 115

Cover, Robert, 24, 221, 222, 226

Creation of the American Republic, The
(Wood), 90

Crèvecoeur, J. Hector St. John de, 118

Crowd actions: affect and, 77–78, 82;

authorization and, 33, 68, 86, 98,
271 n. 72; constituent moments
and, 35, 68, 90; constituent power
and, 86, 98–99; critics of, 797;
direct-action, 20, 24, 69, 83, 84,
85, 91; fear of, 88; inarticulacy and,
100; legitimation and, 83–85, 86,
87, 90–91, 92; motivation for, 83;
postrevolutionary politics and,
35, 68–69, 96, 100; psychological
theories of, 68–79; religious sermons and, 78–79; representative,
20, 69, 84–85, 88–90; revolutionary politics and, 35; self-created
associations and, 33, 67–68, 92;
voice of people and, 97; volatility
of, 35

Cullen, William, 104, 105, 106, 108–
10

Cultural nationalism, 184

Curiosities of Literature (Disraeli), 173

Dahl, Robert, 2

Declaration of Independence, 9, 101,
213

*Defense of the Constitutions of Govern-
ment of the United States* (Adams),
125

D'Elia, Donald, 110, 117

Deliberative theory, 43, 62, 69, 73, 75,
154–55, 163, 225, 238–40, 242

Democracy: aesthetic, 37–38, 182–
83, 185, 190, 191, 193, 201; agonistic, 36, 63, 64, 189; autonomy and,
72, 181; as basis of legitimacy, 62;
as check on governmental power,
4; as distemper, 112; excesses of,
31, 113, 115, 117; of language, 202–
3; meaning of, 182, 183, 185; as no
government, 97; people's identity
and, 1; popular sovereignty and,
99; regenerative, 189; restorative
power of, 237; spiritual, 193; as volcano, 138–39; will of, 29–30, 32

Democracy and Political Theory (Lefort), 1

Democracy in America (Tocqueville), 4, 50, 154, 201

Democratic-Republican Societies: American life politicized by, 143; censorial role of, 145–46; on civic education, 144–46; on constant action, 146–47; constitutional resistance and, 140–41; declamations in, 151; described, 128–29; on Federalist policies, 132–33; Federalists and, 137–39, 140, 147–53, 176; on inclusive citizenship, 152–53; insurgent citizenship and, 131, 143, 147, 155; liberty and, 134; membership in, 132; opposition to, 128–29, 142–43, 147–53; popular authorization and, 36, 129; on popular culture, 144; on popular sovereignty, 135–37, 154, 175; precedents of, 134; on vigilance and watchfulness, 147; as voice of people, 52–53, 134, 135, 138. *See also* Self-created societies

Democratic Review, 184

Democratic Society of Pennsylvania, 128, 130, 148–49, 150, 151

Democratic Vistas (Whitman), 182, 190, 194

Demophilus, 15–16

Derrida, Jacques, 9, 52, 63, 156

Dickens, Charles, 214

Dienstag, Joshua, 249

Direct-action crowd, 20, 24, 69, 83, 84, 85, 91

Discourse ethics, 72–73

Discrimination, 5

Disquisitions (Burgh), 27

Disraeli, Isaac, 173

Dissensus, 38–39, 211–12, 213, 215, 217, 219–20, 227, 229, 236

Dissent: consensus vs., 234, 244–45; democratic theory and, 155; legitimate, 129, 138; traditions in, 218

Dissertation on the Canon and Feudal Law (Adams), 14

Divine voice (*Vox Dei*), 3, 37, 46, 47, 98, 157–58, 166, 168, 170–72, 179, 181

Dorr, Thomas W., 251–52

Douglas, Stephen, 223

Douglass, Frederick, 37; background of, 210–11; on claims, 216, 219, 223, 228–29; on Constitution, 221–23; disidentification of, 215; on law and freedom, 222; on organization of slave power, 211, 228–29, 230; on popular sovereignty, 223; on public reason, 225–26; on race, 216–17; on Revolution, 237; on slavery question, 221; staging dissensus by, 38–39, 211–12, 213, 215, 217, 219–20, 227, 229, 236; on third people, 39; on unsettlement, 38, 213, 221, 227, 228, 249; as voice of people, 210–11; we the people and, 216, 217–18, 220, 222, 223, 225, 228–29

Dred Scott decision, 220, 228

Dunciad (Pope), 69, 100

Durey, Michael, 177

Economic hardship, 91–92

Education: civic, 144–46; public, 143, 191

Edwards, Jonathan, 79

Egalitarianism, 92–93

Eichmann in Jerusalem (Arendt), 64

"Eighteenth Presidency, The!" (Pierce), 186

Ellison, Ralph, 39, 193, 235–36

Emerson, Ralph Waldo, 187, 188, 189, 190, 192, 194, 203, 214, 234

Enthusiasm, 106–7, 167–70

"Enthusiasm Described and Cautioned against" (Chauncey), 169

Epstein, James, 150
Equality, 19, 63, 212, 218, 223, 229–
    30, 290–91 n. 33
Equal voice, 2
Erkkila, Betsy, 191
Eroticism, 192
Essay on Human Understanding
    (Locke), 118
Essay on the Origin of Languages
    (Rousseau), 101, 161

Fanuzzi, Robert, 227
Faulkner, Ephraim, 91–92
Federalist Papers, 55, 74, 244
Federalists: on confidence in govern-
    ment, 130; on constitution, 27, 93,
    95, 175; democratic rhetoric by,
    27–28; Revolution interpreted by,
    244; self-created associations and,
    36, 95, 132, 137–39, 141, 147–53, 176
Ferguson, Adam, 105, 117–18
Ferguson, Frances, 174
Feudalism, 73
Fifth International AIDS Conference,
    252
Fire Next Time, The (Baldwin), 232–34
Fliegelman, Jay, 75, 144, 162, 163, 273
    n. 5
Foederal Procession, 101–3
Forget, Evelyn, 105
Forgetting, 119, 241
Fort Wilson event, 91–92, 116
Foucault, Michel, 104, 131, 268 n. 22
Franco-American alliance, 133
Franklin, Benjamin, 122, 143
Freedom, 42–43, 50, 51, 52, 57–58,
    60, 66, 215, 222
Freeman, Joe, 7
Freemasons, 143
Free press, 71–72
Free-Soil movement, 185, 186
French Prophets, 168–69
French Revolution, 20, 34, 44, 45,
    48–50, 55, 133, 275 n. 63

Freneau, Phillip, 139
Friends of Government, 93
Fugitive Slave Law, 185, 221
Furet, François, 49

Garrison, William Lloyd, 214, 220,
    221, 227, 228, 230
Genêt, Edmond Charles, 133
Genuine Principles of the Ancient Saxon
    or English Constitution, The (De-
    mophilus), 15–16
George III, king of England, 98
German idealism, 196, 208
German Republican Society of Phila-
    delphia, 140, 145, 146–47
Gettysburg Address, 38
Gilmore, Michael, 203
Glaude, Eddie S., 217
Glorious Revolution, 15, 26
Godwin, William, 170, 174, 180
Gold, Mike, 7
Goodell, William, 221
Good-evil tension, 72
Gordon, Thomas, 72
Government: abolition of, 9; censor-
    ship by, 71; despotism of, 85, 87;
    mobs and, 82
Governmental power: checks on, 4,
    140; encroaching, 5; over people,
    28; people as justification for, 5;
    transference of authority and, 13
Grain of the Voice, The (Barthes), 158
Grammar of action, 59–60
Great Awakening, 76, 78
Green, Beriah, 221
Green Mountain Boys, 25
Grenville, George, 13
Grossman, Allen, 192–93, 198
Gustafson, Sandra, 75, 163
Gutmann, Amy, 225

Habermas, Jürgen: on American his-
    tory, 38; deliberative theory of, 43,
    69, 73, 238–40; democratic theory

Habermas, Jürgen (*continued*)
of, 74, 207, 238–39, 240–42, 292–
93 n. 3; on infinite regress, 241–42;
influence of, 35; on public delib-
eration, 69, 73; on public sphere,
36, 68, 72–74, 163; Rancière's
critique of, 293 n. 12; on self-
constitution, 266–67 n. 61, 266
n. 61; tapping theory of, 242, 248
Haitian Revolution (1791), 150
Hamden (pseudonym). *See* Rush,
Benjamin
Hamilton, Alexander, 132, 140–41,
154, 279 n. 4
Hanson, Alexander, 24
Hardt, Michael, 256 n. 10
Harper's Ferry raid, 187
Hart, H. L. A., 29
Hartley, David, 118
Hartz, Louis, 247
Hawthorne, Nathaniel, 203
Hazlitt, William, 205
Hegel, G. W. F., 196, 246
Helvétius, Claude Adrien, 119
Henry, Patrick, 76, 77
Heteroglossia, 197, 198
Historical narratives, 34, 41, 241,
246–51
History of the American Revolution
(Ramsay), 243
History of the American Revolution
(Warren), 244
Hitchborn, Benjamin, 54
Hitler, Adolf, 7
Hobbes, Thomas, 45, 106
Hobsbawm, E. J., 83
Hofstadter, Richard, 31
Holland, Catherine, 168
Holmes, Stephen, 28–31
Honig, Bonnie, 43, 63, 179
Hopkins, Lemuel, 67
Hopkins, Rigby, 230
Hughes, Graham, 65
Hughes, Langston, 234

Hulme, Obadiah, 135
Human Condition, The (Arendt), 55,
59, 261 n. 7
Hume, David, 81, 106, 107, 108
Humphreys, David, 67
Hutcheson, Francis, 81, 106, 107
Hutchinson, Thomas, 90

Identity: historical narrative and,
41; loss of, 232–34; of people in
democracy, 1, 30; political, 9;
power of, 6; racialized, 244; unification and, 12
Imagination: aesthetics and, 174;
authority and, 166, 178–79; autonomy and, 164–65, 166; dangers
of, 172, 173–74; democratic theory
and, 39; literature and, 173; popular sovereignty and, 136; power of,
173; public authority and, 37, 158;
reason and, 162, 171, 173; revelation and, 167; sympathetic, 108,
124; transformative power of, 164
Immigration, 185, 252–53
Imperial Crisis, 11, 13
Independence: local declarations of,
17; representation and, 19–20; as
unifying, 9
Indigenous peoples, 5
Individuality, 188, 189, 196, 199, 209
Ingram, David, 62
"Inquiry into the Influences of Physical Causes upon Morals" (Rush),
119
Invisibility, 235–36
Invisible Man (Ellison), 235–36

Jackson, Andrew, 184
Jacobin Clubs, 36, 134, 176
Jay's Treaty (1794), 133, 151
Jefferson, Thomas: on Brown's *Wieland*, 172–74; democratic societies
on, 132; on democratic societies,
71, 129, 142; on democratic voice,
9–10; on Henry, 76, 77; on lit-

erature and imagination, 173; on living vs. dead, 168; politics of perpetual newness and, 168; on Shays's rebellion, 96; as unifying symbol, 184; "we" used by, 10, 19
Jim Crow laws, 65, 230, 233
Johnson, Samuel, 105
Judicial supremacy, 57, 66

Kalyvas, Andreas, 51, 266 n. 61
Kansas-Missouri Act (1854), 185
Kant, Immanuel, 20, 22, 246
Kateb, George, 182, 183, 189, 190, 196–97, 199, 203
Keenan, Alan, 293 n. 9
King, Martin Luther, Jr., 218
Kloppenburg, James, 136
Knowledge, free circulation of, 70–72, 191
Knox, William, 16
Korsgaard, Christine, 266 n. 54
Kramer, Larry, 12, 58, 176, 263 n. 24

Laclau, Ernesto, 7, 43, 210, 256 n. 10, 292 n. 3, 293 n. 5
Laurens, Henry, 91
Law. See Constitutional law
Lawson, George, 45
Leaves of Grass (Whitman), 182, 185, 190, 191, 196, 201, 205
Le Bon, Gustave, 83
Lee, Richard Henry, 11
Lefort, Claude, 1, 147
Left, revolutionary, 6
Letters against the Immediate Abolition of Slavery (Sullivan), 228
Levellers, 45
Liberalism: consensus in, 243; constitutionalism and, 28, 48; general liberal principle, 72; natural law, 5; resigned, 4
Liberty: Antifederal club and, 149–50; contagion of, 24; Declaration on, 248; early American history of, 70; intellectual, 159; knowledge and, 71; passion for, 114–16, 147, 244; people as keepers of, 139, 143–44, 146–47; popular virtue and, 144; safeguarding, 128, 209; self-created societies and, 129–30, 132, 134–35, 139, 152; slavery and, 218, 221; of speech, 72; suppression of, 105, 140, 143; tumults in, 87
Lienesch, Michael, 244
Life of the Mind, The (Arendt), 41, 62
Lincoln, Abraham, 38, 248
Locke, John, 45, 118, 144, 247
London Corresponding Society, 134
Looby, Christopher, 75–76, 160
Louis XIV, king of France, 168
Lowell, James Russell, 212
Ludlow (pseudonym). See Rush, Benjamin
Luther v. Borden, 252
Lynching, 5

Macaulay, Catherine, 105
Machiavelli, Niccolò, 63, 246, 247
Madison, James, 27, 28, 55, 120, 125–26, 129, 139, 144, 244; on popular voice and constitution, 167, 175
Magnetism, 200
Maier, Pauline, 13, 52, 68
Mandeville, Bernard, 106
Manning, William, 71
Markell, Patchen, 230, 261 n. 7
Market, 73, 200
Marx, Karl, 202
Marxism, 7, 83
Mason & Dixon (Pynchon), 142
Massachusetts Ratifying Convention, 24, 132
Massumi, Brian, 78
Mathes, Melissa, 246
Matthews, Richard K., 278 n. 137
Matthiessen, F. O., 182
McCannell, Juliet, 181
McDonald, Forrest, 136, 143

McKean, Thomas, 94
"Meaning of July Fourth for Negroes, The" (Douglass), 210, 211, 212, 216–17, 236; audience for, 214–15; claims in, 223; as constituent moment, 220; as immanent critique, 218–19; setting of speech, 214
Memoirs of Carwin the Biloquist (Brown), 156, 177
Meranze, Michael, 35, 123
Mesmerism, 200
Michelman, Frank, 239, 240, 241, 242
Miller, Samuel, 167
Mirabeau, Marquis de, 4
Missouri Compromise (1820), 185, 220
Mobocracy, 116–17, 121
Modernity: archaism in, 247; political, 43; tradition and, 59, 247
Montesquieu, Baron de, 63, 117
Moon, Michael, 290 n. 27
Moore, Wayne D., 221, 223
Morality: sentimentalism, 106, 107–8, 109, 119, 173; sympathy and, 107; tradition and, 41
Morgan, Edmund, 11, 13, 156
Morone, James, 17, 25
Morris, Gouverneur, 86–87, 147
Mouffe, Chantal, 43
Munro, Alexander, *secundus*, 106
Myth: constituent power as, 29–30; people as, 5; political movements and, 5

Nash, Gary, 96
National Gazette, 139
Nationalism, revolutionary, 47
Negri, Antonio, 256 n. 10, 261 n. 11
New Scottish school of rhetoric, 80
Nieman, Donald G., 220
Nietzsche, Friedrich, 291–92 n. 60
Nihilism, 55
Normative proceduralism, 62

Norton, Anne, 31, 245
Novanglus (Adams), 89
Nussbaum, Martha, 290–91 n. 33

Oliver, Andrew, 90
Oliver, Peter, 82, 269 n. 40
On Revolution (Arendt), 41, 43, 44, 45–46, 51, 52, 56, 57–59, 65, 243
On the Shores of Politics (Rancière), 153
Opinion polls, 4, 54
Oppression: free knowledge vs., 70; symbol of people and, 5
Oration, 76–77, 162–63, 192, 215, 227
Other, 181
Otis, James, 11

Paine, Thomas, 9–10, 19, 88, 98, 113, 133, 184
Palmer, Robert R., 44, 136
Pamphleteers, 53, 72
Parliamentary sovereignty, 15–16, 17
Parssinen, T. M., 134
Passion, 80–81, 108, 116, 125–26, 244
Patriot élite, 86, 92, 96, 113
Peale, Charles Wilson, 115
Pease, Donald E., 290 n. 25
Penal reform, 122–24
Pennsylvania Constitution, 92, 102, 113, 114–15
Pennsylvania Ratifying Convention, 175
Penn, Thomas, 86
People: ambiguity of, 141–42; authority of, 1–2, 7–8, 11, 16, 19–20, 24, 30, 34, 36–37, 43–44, 51–53, 57, 63, 98, 137, 163; as basis of democracy, 1; chosen, 245; in communist propaganda, 6; as constituency, 2, 31; defense of constitution and, 5, 11–12; double inscription of, 7–9, 30, 37, 38, 64, 210; as empty signifier, 7; extempore conduct by, 92, 116, 147; as fictional notion, 4; French Revolution and, 49–50;

identity of, 1; inability to speak of, 6; as judge, 53; as justification for power, 5; legitimacy of, 2–3; leveling consequences of, 2–3, 245; mob vs., 50; as one, 237–38; poetic construction of, 183; poetry and, 191, 201–2, 203, 205; as political claim, 3; political order and, 7–8; as *populus*, 5; reign of, 4; revolutionary origins of, 9; as rule-bound electorate, 29; social basis of, 28; as social class, 5; in socialist propaganda, 6; spatial choreography and, 36, 102–4, 124, 127; sublimity of, 183; as symbol, 4, 6; third, 39, 232, 235; transubstantiation of, 31; as term, 128, 209; will of, 29–30, 49, 54, 87, 88, 120, 136. *See also* Constituencies; Constituent moments; Constituent power; Popular sovereignty; *Vox populi*

Persuasion, 74, 80, 193, 219

Peterkin, William, 117

Philadelphia: Foederal Procession in, 101–3; penal reform in, 122–24

Philadelphia Convention, 31, 55, 125, 141, 175, 243

Phillips, Wendell, 224, 225, 226

Philosophy of the Abolition Movement (Phillips), 224

Phrenology, 200

Pierce, Franklin, 186

Pitt, William, 87

Pocock, J. G. A., 136, 237, 245, 246

Poet-legislators, 193, 194

Pole, J. R., 136

Political aesthetics, 102, 152, 174, 178, 211

Political Disquisitions (Burgh), 135, 145

Political freedom, 42–43, 50, 51, 52, 57–58, 60, 66, 215, 222

Political Liberalism (Rawls), 38

Political theology, 46, 47–48

Politics, postrevolutionary American. *See* Postrevolutionary American politics

Politics, revolutionary American. *See* Revolutionary American politics

Polls, 4, 54

Pope, Alexander, 69, 100

Popular politics: enhanced legal authority and, 25; extra-legal participants and, 175; flourishing of, 176; instability of people and, 3; legality of law and, 66; legitimate form of, 91, 247; quasi-physiological theory of, 116; self-created forms of, 92

Popular sovereignty: colonial debates and, 15; complexity of, 156; constituent power and, 12, 25, 27; as creative concept, 44, 154; democracy and, 99; democratic societies and, 135–37; dilemmas in, 10, 28–29, 60–61, 65; emerging claims and, 18; establishment of, 98; faith in, 223; meltdown of, 239; political imagination and, 136; political meaning of people and, 209; representation and, 129, 135, 157–58; resistance and, 12

Popular voice. *See Vox populi*

Populism, 4

Porter, Allen, 7

Postrevolutionary American politics: affect and, 78; anarchy and, 114; authority of people and, 1–2, 7–8, 24, 34, 43–44, 51–53, 57, 63, 163; constitutionalism and, 5, 25, 52–53, 57, 239–40; corruption and, 119–20; crowd phenomena and, 35, 68–69, 96, 100; dilemmas of voice and, 37, 158, 160; disembodied public and, 74; natural law liberalism and, 5; popular sovereignty and, 10, 14; public sphere and, 72–73; representation and, 10, 14, 69, 85; texts vs. voice in, 163

Potestas in populo, 59

Pouvoir constituent. See Constituent power

Poverty, 50

Power. *See* Constituent power; Governmental power

Power of Sympathy, The (Brown), 104

Price, Richard, 113

Principle of Hope, The (Bloch), 206

Principles, 62

Print culture: expansion of, 70–72; materiality of, 75; public sphere and, 73–74, 163

Proclamation of Neutrality (1793), 133

Procrustes, 30

Progressives, 243

Proletariat, 6

Propaganda: communist, 6; reform, 27; socialist, 6

Public opinion polls, 4, 54

Public sphere: debate in, 70–71, 74; model for, 72–73; need for, 69–70; oration in, 76–77; print works and, 73–74, 163; research on, 36

Publius, 140, 286 n. 26

Pufendorf, Samuel von, 89

Puritan New England, 4

Putnam, Robert, 143

Pynchon, Thomas, 142

Race: assimilation and, 217; identity and, 232–34, 244; inequality and, 186; understanding of, 216–17

Racism, 5, 233

Radner, John, 108

Ramsay, David, 243–44

Rancière, Jacques, 35, 38, 99–100, 153, 181, 201, 211, 212, 213, 227–28, 233–34, 255–56 n. 9, 293 n. 12

Rawls, John, 38, 207, 225, 226

Raymond, Robert R., 214

Réaction SIDA, 252

Realism, 119, 205–7

Reason: Constitutional, 244; dis-

embodiment of, 74; as guidance, 159, 162; human nature and, 118; imagination and, 162, 171, 173; individualized, 240; limitations of, 79, 81–82; passion and, 116, 126; political, 100; public, 62, 87–88, 225–26; of state doctrine, 65; voice and, 162; will and, 209

Reflections on the Revolution in France (Burke), 288 n. 65

Reform politics, 186–87

Reid, John Phillip, 86

Reid, Thomas, 81

Reill, Peter Hans, 109

Religion: authority and, 46, 56; enthusiasm for, 167–70

Representation: actual, 14, 15, 17; arguments over, 13; authority and, 20; constitutional law and, 13, 16; crisis in, 14, 35, 86, 97, 181, 188; crowds and, 20, 69, 84–85, 88–90; defined, 138; equal voice and, 2; feudalism and, 73; limits of, 27; mediation of, 77; principles of, 2; regional vs. national, 136; representative crowd and, 20, 69, 84, 88–90; revolution and, 19–20; sovereign people and, 10; taxation and, 13, 90; virtual, 13–14, 85, 96; *vox populi* and, 64, 69, 74, 135, 137, 156–57, 164, 181, 245, 249; wariness of, 85–86

Republican machines, 36, 71, 104, 107, 117, 120, 130

Republican principles, 2, 105, 112, 139, 247

Republican Society, 92, 115

Republican Society of Lancaster, 145

Resistance: constituent power and, 12–13, 18, 25; democratic societies and, 130

Revelation, 110, 112, 167, 171

Revolutionary American politics:

common sense and, 58; constituent power and, 45, 53; crowd and, 35; mutual promising and, 34, 44, 45, 48, 59, 60, 61, 63, 64, 65; problem of beginning and, 42

Revolutions: absolute validity and, 34, 42, 45–50, 61, 263–64 n. 27, 266–67 n. 61; left and, 6; as political event, 42; popular voice and, 37; revolution principle, 53; unifying acts and, 9

Reynolds, David, 185, 206

Rhetoric, 27, 79–80, 82, 162, 171, 219, 245

Rhode Island Suffrage Association, 251

Rights of man, 20, 38, 135, 146, 213, 248–49

Rights of Man, The (Paine), 9, 133

Riker, William, 4

Riots, 68, 83, 88–89, 94

Rochester Ladies' Anti-Slavery Society, 214

Rodgers, Daniel T., 3

Rogers, William, 225

Rosanvallon, Pierre, 19

Rousseau, Jean-Jacques, 46, 80, 101, 161

Rudé, George, 20, 83, 84

Rush, Benjamin, 24; analogical reasoning of, 111–12; on anarchia, 116–17; background of, 101, 104–5, 110; on body vs. soul, 112; on circulation of knowledge, 71; on democratic excess, 113, 115, 117; on extempore conduct, 92, 116, 147, 244; on Foederal Procession, 101–3; on government, 113–14; on imagination, 174; institutional reforms by, 120–21; on mobocracy, 116–17, 121; on penal reform, 122–24; Pennsylvania Constitution opposed by, 102, 113, 114–15; on power and

people, 101 pseudonyms of, 113, 114; religious faith of, 110–11; on republican machines, 36, 71, 104, 107, 120, 130; on social reform, 113, 130; on solitude, 122, 124; on spatial choreography, 35, 102–4, 124, 127; U.S. Constitution backed by, 127

Ruttenburg, Nancy, 76

Sanders, Lynn, 154–55

Schama, Simon, 152

Scheuerman, William, 48, 263–64 n. 27

Schmitt, Carl, 6, 43, 47–49, 50, 72

Schools for Political Knowledge, 144–45

Schrader, David E., 221

Scott, Dred, 220, 228

Scottish Enlightenment, 106, 108, 117–18

Scottish school of rhetoric, 80

Self-authorization: citizenship as, 143; constituent moments and, 51, 250–51, 254; constitutional order and, 30, 33; of crowd, 86, 271 n. 72; dilemmas in, 3, 30, 43–44, 51, 57, 62, 129, 262 n. 18, 263 n. 25; racialized articulation of people and, 150; voice of people and, 32, 137, 157

Self-captivation, 164

Self-created societies: crowds and, 33, 67–68, 92; Federalists and, 36, 95, 137–39, 141; judgment and, 115; opposition to, 36, 68, 128–29; radicalized, 134–35; resistance by, 11, 13, 17; as voice of people, 17–18, 24, 25, 53–54, 135, 137, 157. *See also* Democratic-Republican Societies

Self-enactment, 18, 36, 37, 38, 193

Seward, William H., 214

Shaftesbury, Third Earl of (Cooper, Anthony Ashley), 106–7, 168

Shaw, Peter, 98

Shays, Daniel, 25, 90, 114

Shays's Rebellion (1787), 52, 67, 71, 89–90, 96

Sheffield Society of Constitutional Information, 134

Shelley, Percy Bysshe, 194

Shklar, Judith, 168

Sieyès, Abbé, 46–47, 48, 49

Slavery: equality and, 218; expansion of, 185; fanaticism and, 186; Haitian Revolution and, 150; nationalization of, 220; in New York, 235; organizational powers and, 211, 228–29, 230; perpetuation of, 221, 228; rebellion and, 219. *See also* Abolitionists

Smith, Adam, 81, 106, 108, 117–18

Smith, Gerrit, 221

Smith, Kimberly, 68, 82, 87

Smith, Rogers, 5, 246

Social class: conception of people and, 28; domination and, 7; egalitarianism and, 92–93; people as, 5

Socialism, 6

Social transparency, 72

Society for Promoting Political Inquiries, 122

Society of Cincinnati, 138, 143

Socrates, 126, 171

Sokol, Jason, 233

Solitude, 122, 124, 169, 197, 199

Sons of Liberty, 11, 133, 134

Sorel, George, 6

Sovereignty. *See* Parliamentary sovereignty; Popular sovereignty

Spirit of the Laws (Montesquieu), 117

Spooner, Lysander, 221

Sprengel, M. C., 20, 22

Staging of dissensus, 38–39, 211–12, 213, 215, 217, 219–20, 227, 229, 236

Stamp Act (1765), 11, 13, 20, 21, 23, 67, 90, 105

State constitutions, 25–26, 55, 175, 251

Steele, Richard, 106

Sterne, Laurence, 173

Stimson, Shannon, 53

Stout, Harry, 77

Structural Transformation of the Bourgeois Public Sphere (Habermas), 69

Subjectification, 9, 45, 145, 210, 223, 233–34

Sugar Act (1764), 11

Sullivan, James, 1–2

Sullivan, John L., 184

Sullivan, Robert, 123, 228

Supreme Court, U.S., 57, 65, 220, 226, 228–29, 252

Symbolism: of founding fathers, 184, 246; of people, 4, 6; revolutionary, 152

Sympathy: active, 122–23; affect and, 68; art of, 108, 124; channeling of, 118; contagious, 106, 107, 126; of contiguity, 109, 120; corporeal communicative economy and, 109–10; defined, 81, 107, 109; as *facultas incognita*, 110; imagination and, 108, 124; law and order and, 81; medico-political understanding of, 103, 105, 110, 117, 119; between orator and audience, 80; political organization of, 36; power of, 104; proximity and, 104, 106, 122, 124, 127; public punishments and, 122–23; regulation of, 108; separation and, 104, 106, 107–8, 124–25; spatial reform and, 104, 125; theories of, 35–36, 103–4, 105–6, 109–11, 119

Tammany Society, 132, 144

Taney, Roger B., 220, 222

Tax policies: resistance to, 11; by unrepresented authority, 13, 90

Temples of Liberty, 152

"They Can't Turn Back" (Baldwin), 231

Thompson, Dennis, 225

Thompson, E. P, 83

Thoreau, Henry David, 187, 192

Tilly, Charles, 20, 69, 84

Time, 237

Tocqueville, Alexis de, 4, 9, 49, 50, 135, 154, 201

Tompkins, Jane, 174

Trade, 17, 73, *149*, 151

Transatlantic radicalism, 133, 177

"Transgression, Equality, Voice" (Wolin), 19

Travels through Life (Rush), 104

Treatise on Human Nature (Hume), 81

Trenchard, John, 72

Trumbull, John, 67

Ultraism, 186, 188, 189

Ulysses, 30

Universality vs. particularity, 38, 217, 218

Universal pragmatics, 62

Unsettlement, democratic, 7, 38, 213, 221, 227, 228, 249

Ventriloquism and voice, 37, 157–58, 163–66, 172, 175, 177, 179, 181, 204

Verba, Sidney, 179

Vigilantism, 5, 25

Violence, 5

Virginia Chronicle, 142

Virginia Ratifying Convention, 144

Virtú, 63

Voice of God. *See* Vox Dei

Voice of people. *See* Vox populi

"Voice of the People, The" (Verba), 179

Volk, das, 7

Voting rights, 2, 115

Vox Dei, 3, 37, 46, 47, 98, 157–58, 166, 168, 170–72, 179, 181

Vox populi: absolute power of, 55; authority of, 3, 75–76, 78, 82, 137, 175, 188; collective self-presence and, 181; constitutionalization of, 28, 167, 175; crowd activity and, 97; democratic theory of, 156–57; dilemmas of, 37, 158; inarticulacy of, 100; latency and, 5–6; locating, 35; mobility of, 158; order and, 179; poetry and, 38, 183, 193, 203, 204, 205; polyvocality of, 208; populism and, 4; potency of, 5; representation and, 64, 69, 74, 135, 137, 156–57, 181, 249; self-created associations and, 17, 24, 25, 53–54, 134, 135, 137, 138, 157; sovereignty and, 16; sublime and, 77, 160, 164, 177, 179, 182, 183, 194, 197–98, 201, 205; textualization of, 57–58; ventriloquism and, 37, 157–58, 163–66, 172, 175, 177, 179, 181, 204; as *vox Dei*, 3, 37, 46, 47, 98, 157–58, 166, 179. *See also* Constituent power; People

Waldron, Jeremy, 30, 43, 66

Waldstreicher, David, 96, 122, 151–52

Walzer, Michael, 218, 273–74 n. 14

Warner, Michael, 57–58, 75, 153, 163, 260 n. 109

Warren, Mercy Otis, 244

Washington, George: criticisms of, 132, 152; on self-created societies, 36, 68, 128, 129, 137; as unifying symbol, 184

Webster, Noah, 139, 184

"We the People," 10, 141; authority of, 18, 31, 58, 95; Douglass and, 216, 217–18, 220, 222, 223, 225, 228–29

Whately, Thomas, 13–14

"What Is Freedom?" (Arendt), 63

"What Is the People?" (Hazlitt), 205

"What to the Slave Is Your Fourth of July" (Douglass), 38

Whigs: good-evil tension and, 72; history of, 2; popular resistance discourse, 12, 18

Whiskey Rebellion (1794), 53, 128, 130, 141, 176, 177, 179

Whitefield, George, 78–79, 110

White supremacy, 229, 231, 232

Whitman, Walt: on adhesiveness, 199–200; on aesthetic democracy, 37–38, 182–83, 185, 190, 191, 194, 201; affect in works of, 192; antinomianism and, 187, 189–90; on arenas of freedom, 189, 204; on Carlyle, 195–96; ethics of, 196; influences on, 184; on inner strangeness, 196–97, 199; on institutions, 187–88; language of, 197–99, 202–3; mediation in works of, 192, 193; poetic experimentation of, 198; as poetic *vox populi*, 38, 183, 193, 204, 208; on poetry and people, 191, 201–2, 205; on political action, 190–91; on political power of words, 190–91; on polyvocality, 185, 197, 208; realism of, 205–7; on representational crisis, 188; scholarly debate on, 184; on self-enactment and citizenship, 37; on slavery, 185–86; on truth, 196

Whytt, Robert, 106, 108–10

Wiecek, William M., 221

Wieland (Brown): authority in, 174–75, 179–80; basis of, 171; as critique of religious enthusiasm, 167–70; divine voice in, 168, 170–72; enthusiasm in, 167–70; imagination in, 164–65, 166, 172–73, 179; influences on, 169; on popular authority and representation, 157; revelation in, 167, 171; sacrifice and murder in, 160, 171–72; on self-captivation, 164; setting and background of, 158–61, 176; voice and ventriloquism in, 37, 157–58, 163–66, 172, 175, 177, 179, 181; the will in, 165–66

Wilentz, Sean, 153

Wilkes, John, 105, 134

Will: democratic, 29–30, 32; of multitude, 49; national, 44; political, 47–48; popular, 29–30, 49, 54, 87, 88, 120, 136; reason and, 209; sense and, 165–66; sovereign, 47

Wilson, James, 12, 27, 91–92, 94, 115, 175

Wilson, Woodrow, 57

Wittgenstein, Ludwig, 61

Wolf, Friedrich, 7

Wolin, Sheldon, 19, 30–31, 32, 44, 99, 153, 157, 158, 207, 237

Women, 2

Wood, Gordon, 12, 13, 17, 26, 44, 85, 90, 133, 136, 141; on voice of people, 175

Wortman, Tunis, 144

Yates, James, 171

Young America movement, 184

Ziff, Larzer, 167, 205

JASON FRANK
is the Gary S. Davis Assistant Professor
in the History of Political Thought
at Cornell University.

Library of Congress Cataloging-in-Publication Data
Frank, Jason A.
Constituent moments : enacting the people in
postrevolutionary America / Jason Frank.
p. cm.
Includes bibliographical references and index.
ISBN 978-0-8223-4663-0 (cloth : alk. paper) —
ISBN 978-0-8223-4675-3 (pbk. : alk. paper)
1. Political culture — United States — History.
2. Political participation — United States — History.
3. Federal government — United States — History.
4. United States — Politics and government. I. Title.
JK1764.F725 2010
306.20973'09034 — dc22   2009037178